BODILY COMMUNICATION

Second Edition

Michael Argyle

'I found Michael Argyle's *Bodily Communication*, second edition, to be an extraordinary introduction to, and overview of, the entire field of non-verbal communication. Furthermore, it will be as instructive to students and researchers in the social-behavioural sciences as it will be to the general intelligent reader. Although I have been working in this area for over twenty-five years I found much to learn in its pages.'

Robert Rosenthal, Harvard University

Non-verbal communication – the eye movements, facial expressions, tone of voice, postures and gestures that we all use more or less consciously and more or less effectively – can enhance or diminish every form of social interaction. Michael Argyle's second edition of *Bodily Communication* is an invaluable up-to-date guide to a subject which in the last ten years has become recognized as an important part of social psychology and of professional training, particularly in social work, education and management.

Greatly expanded from the first edition, and significantly revised, this second edition has two completely new chapters on social skills and personality, and a new chapter on research methods. The author, a pioneer in the study of non-verbal communication, presents the second edition in the same readable style as the first, bringing to the reader both his intense interest in the subject and his authoritative knowledge of it.

Michael Argyle is Emeritus Professor of Psychology, University of Oxford, and a Fellow of Wolfson College.

BODILY COMMUNICATION

Second Edition

Michael Argyle

Routledge
Taylor & Francis Group

LONDON AND NEW YORK

First published 1975 by
Methuen & Co Ltd
Second edition 1988

Reprinted 1990, 1993, 1994, 1996
by Routledge
11 New Fetter Lane, London, EC4P 4EE

Reprinted 2001 by Routledge
27 Church Road, Hove, East Sussex, BN3 2FA
29 West 35th Street, New York NY 10001

Reprinted 2004 by Routledge
27 Church Road, Hove, East Sussex BN3 2FA
270 Madison Avenue, New York, NY 10016

Routledge is an imprint of the Taylor & Francis group

Printed and bound in Great Britain by Biddles Ltd, King's Lynn, Norfolk

This publication has been produced with paper manufactured to strict
environmental standards and with pulp derived from sustainable forests.

British Library Cataloguing in Publication Data
A catalogue record for this book is available from the British Library

   Argyle, Michael
      Bodily communication – 2nd ed.
      1. Nonverbal communication (Psychology)
      I. Title
      302.2′22   BF637.N66

ISBN 0–415–05114–2 (pbk)

Contents

Illustrations

Preface to second edition

The first edition of this book was published in 1975. Since then more work has been done on the subject than had been done before 1975, and non-verbal communication has become established as a central field of social psychology, and a topic of great scientific and practical importance.

I have tried to produce a readable acount of this literature that is both scholarly and popular – scholarly in that all the assertions are based on sound research, popular in that it is intended to be intelligible and interesting to students and the general reader alike. This book differs from other books on the subject in several ways. It deals with all the non-verbal channels separately, including appearance. It deals with the different functions of bodily communication. It deals with theory as well as empirical findings, and shows how bodily communication plays a central role in the generation of social behaviour. The analysis of social performance at this level has provided something of a new look in social psychology. The book explores the main practical applications of non-verbal communication, from treating mental patients to improving politicians' speeches.

The earliest research was into facial expression and emotion. However, in the late 1950s interest grew in a number of other areas such as gesture and paralanguage. Social psychologists and animal ethologists began to realize the similarities between human and animal communication, and anthropologists were emphasizing cultural differences. There has been considerable disagreement over methods, between behavioural, linguistic, and even psychoanalytic approaches; however, a generally agreed point of view seems to be emerging.

The first international conference on non-verbal communication was held in Oxford, and was organized by the author and Ralph Exline in 1967.

For reasons which are not entirely clear there has been a wave of popular interest in the subject, and it is constantly discussed on TV programmes and in magazines. Some of the popular writing emphasized the similarities between man and monkeys, e.g. *The Naked Ape* (Morris 1968). Some emphasized the use of NVC as a way of finding out hidden things about other people (e.g. Fast 1970). Many of the new therapies for normal people emanating from California – rolfing, encounter groups, and the rest – made use of non-verbal techniques in some way.

I am indebted to many people for the ideas and research reported in this book. Some of the early investigators have continued to develop their work, e.g. Adam Kendon, Ralph Exline, Paul Ekman, Robert Hinde, Robert Rosenthal. New stars have appeared such as Ross Buck, Judith Hall, Miles Patterson, Klaus Scherer, Howard Rosenfeld, and Miron Zuckerman, and in Britain Geoffrey Beattie, Peter Bull, and Derek Rutter. I have been greatly helped by members of the social psychology research group at Oxford, and especially Peter Collett, David Clarke, Mansur Lalljee, Catherine Peng, and Efrat Tse'elon. We have now had forty six doctorates in social psychology, many of them in the field of bodily communication and are all grateful to the ESRC for continuing to support us for so many years. In addition, I am most grateful to the staff of The Radcliffe Science Library and the libraries of the University of Kansas, USA, and the Flinders University, South Australia, for help and information. Finally, I would like to thank Ann McKendry who once again made a beautiful job of typing the manuscript.

Christmas 1986   Michael Argyle
                                          Department of Experimental Psychology,
                                          Oxford

Acknowledgements

The author and publisher are grateful to all those who have granted permission to reproduce copyright material throughout this book. All illustrations and tables other than those supplied by the author specifically for this book are given a source which refers to a detailed entry in the list of references. Copyright material is as follows:

Plates   3.1(a) Zoological Society of London; 3.1(b) William K. Redican; 3.1(c) Michael Lyster, Zoological Society of London; 3.1(d) E.P. Dutton Inc., New York; 3.1(e) Macmillan Publishing Co. Ltd, New York; 5.1 Multimedia Publications (UK) Ltd; 6.1 Kobal Collection, London; 6.2 Prentice Hall Inc., Englewood Cliffs, New Jersey; 8.1 Dr Paul Ekman, Human Interaction Laboratory, University of California, San Francisco; 10.1 Equinox (Oxford) Limited; 10.2 Globe Photos Inc., New York; 15.1 Open University, Milton Keynes; 16.1 Conservative and Unionist Party, 32 Smith Square, London.

Figures   2.1 Penguin Books Ltd, Harmondsworth; 3.1 Dr Thelma Rowell, Department of Zoology, University of California, Berkeley, California; 4.1 American Psychological Association, Washington; 4.4 Wolfe Medical Publications Ltd, London; 4.5 A.P. Watt Ltd, London; 6.4 Mouton Publishers, Walter de Gruyter & Co., Berlin; 7.2 North Holland Publishing Company, Amsterdam; 9.2 John Wiley & Sons Ltd, Chichester; 11.1, 11.2, 11.3 Plenum Press, New York; 11.4 Lawrence Erlbaum Associates Inc., New Jersey; 11.5 American Medical Association, Chicago; 11.6 Duke University Press, North Carolina; 12.1 Wolfe Medical Publications Ltd, London; 12.2 North Holland Publishing Company, Amsterdam; 13.1 American Psychological Assocation, Washington; 13.3 John Wiley & Sons Ltd, Chichester; 14.1 Mouton Publishers, Walter de Gruyter & Co., Berlin; 15.1 Lexington Books, D.C. Heath and Company, Lexington, Mass., 17.1 Duke University Press, N. Carolina.

Tables   3.1 Ballière Tindall, London; 4.1 Dr Paul Ekman, Human Interaction Laboratory, University of California, San Francisco; 4.2 *European Journal of Social Psychology*, John Wiley and Sons Ltd,

Chichester; 4.3 Mouton Publishers, Walter de Gruyter & Co., Berlin; 5.1 and 5.2 Lawrence Erlbaum Associates Inc., New York; 7.2 *European Journal of Social Psychology*, John Wiley and Sons Ltd, Chichester; 8.1 and 8.2 American Psychological Assocation, Washington; 9.1 *Journal of the Acoustical Society of America*, New York; 10.1 Springer-Verlag, New York; 11.1 Houghton Mifflin, Boston, Mass.; 12.1 Mouton Publishers, Walter de Gruyter & Co., Berlin; 13.1 *Journal of the Acoustical Society of America*, New York; 14.1 *Journal of Nonverbal Behaviour*, Human Sciences Press Inc., New York; 14.2 Speech Communication Assocation, Annandale, Virginia; 17.1 American Psychological Association, Washington; 17.3 Johns Hopkins University Press, Baltimore, Maryland; 17.4 Plenum Publishing Corporation, New York.

1

Introduction

Bodily communication, or non-verbal communication (NVC), plays a central part in human social behaviour. Recent research by social psychologists and others has shown that these signals play a more important part, and function in a more intricate manner, than had previously been realized. If we want to understand human social behaviour we shall have to disentangle this non-verbal system.

We know what these non-verbal signals are:

facial expression
gaze (and pupil dilation)
gestures, and other bodily movements
posture
bodily contact
spatial behaviour
clothes, and other aspects of appearance
non-verbal vocalizations
smell

Each of these can be subdivided into a number of further variables, for example different aspects of gaze – looking while listening, looking while talking, mutual gaze, length of glances, amount of eye-opening, pupil expansion, etc. It is a matter of sheer empirical research to find out what effects, if any, these variables have. For example, head-nods are very important, foot movements are not. We shall describe the detailed working of each kind of signal later.

In fact each of these channels functions in a distinctive way, and there is quite a different story to tell about each of them. Gaze is primarily a channel rather than a signal; facial expression is the most innate; gestures vary greatly between cultures; touch is often taboo; clothes are the most subject to changes in fashion, and so on. And these bodily signals are often quite small, subtle, and unconscious, which gives them an added interest. The correct use of NVC is an essential part of social competence, and of specific social skills; mental patients are usually deficient in this sphere.

The results of this enquiry go beyond the sphere of social psychology. There are fairly radical implications, too, for other areas of study concerned with human behaviour – linguistics, philosophy, politics, and theology, for example. The main point here is to suggest that too much importance has been attached to language in the past; we shall show that language is highly dependent on and closely intertwined with NVC, and that there is a lot which cannot be expressed adequately in words. There are also practical implications in a number of areas – the treatment of mental patients, education, design of communication systems, race relations, and international affairs, for example.

Definitions and distinctions

Non-verbal communication, or bodily communication, takes place whenever one person influences another by means of facial expression, tone of voice, or any of the other channels listed above. This may be intentional, or it may not be; in the second case we may call it non-verbal *behaviour* (NVB) or in some cases the *expression* of emotion, etc.

The basic paradigm is as follows:

There is encoding by A of his state, e.g. of emotion, into a NV signal, which may be decoded by B, not necessarily correctly.

There are a number of possibilities here:

(1) A encodes, and B decodes, using a shared code, e.g. both know that proximity signals liking.
(2) B decodes incorrectly, either because A was a poor sender or B a poor receiver, or both.
(3) A sends a deceptive message, which B may or may not be taken in by.
(4) A does not intend to communicate at all, but his behaviour contains information and B may be able to decode, e.g. perceiving that propping the head up is a sign of boredom.
(5) A does not intend to communicate, and B decodes erroneously, perhaps using widely held but incorrect beliefs about the meaning of NVC, e.g. that gaze aversion signals deception.

In addition, many NV signals are part of a rapid stream of signals, both verbal and non-verbal, and there is usually communication in both directions. Nevertheless, the encoding–decoding paradigm is a useful one, and enables us to distinguish between research on encoding and on decoding.

Verbal v. non-verbal

Verbal behaviour usually consists of speech, but also sometimes of writing, or gestures standing for letters or words. However, speech is accompanied by an intricate set of non-verbal signals, providing illustrations and feedback and helping with synchronization. Some of these are really part of the verbal message itself – the *prosodic* signals of timing, pitch, and emphasis in particular. Other non-verbal signals are independent of the speech content, including the *paralinguistic* signals, for example emotional tone of speech. However, non-verbal signals are often affected by verbal coding; symbolic acts or objects used in rituals, for example, may be named or have specific meanings, and patterns of non-verbal behaviour, e.g. styles of behaviour like 'charm', 'dignity', and 'presence' may be verbally categorized. On the other hand some non-verbal signals stand for emotions, attitudes, or experiences which are not easily expressible in words. Last, as noted above, the distinction verbal/non-verbal does not correspond to vocal/non-vocal, since there are hand movements which stand for words, and vocalizations which do not.

Communication v. unintentional signs

When a man raises his programme at an auction sale to make a bid, he consciously intends to send a message to the auctioneer; he is using a shared code, and the auctioneer perceives him correctly as a person intending to send a particular message. It is clearly different when an animal or person in a certain emotional state displays visible signs of that emotion, such as trembling or perspiring, which are then perceived by others: this is an observed sign, but there is no intention to communicate. For communication proper there are goal-directed signals, whereas signs are simply behavioural or physiological responses. In communication there is awareness of others as beings who understand the code which is being used.

Unfortunately it is very difficult to decide whether a particular non-verbal signal is intended to communicate or not: as we shall see there are communications which are motivated, without conscious awareness of intention. One criterion is whether or not the signal is modified as a function of the conditions (e.g. when telephoning instead of communicating visibly), or whether the signal is repeated if it has no effect. Another criterion is whether or not the sender varies his signal in order to elicit the correct response from the receiver (Wiener *et al.* 1972).

However in many cases non-verbal signals are a mixture of the two. Facial expressions of emotion, for example, consist partly of the spontaneous expression of emotion (i.e. NVB), partly of attempts to control it, to conform to social rules, or to conceal the true emotion (NVC). It could be argued that the spontaneous expression of emotions is part of a wider system of communication which has evolved to facilitate social life. So we will call it all non-verbal or bodily *communication*.

Conscious and unconscious

How far are people consciously aware of sending and receiving these signals? A person may succeed in dominating another by the use of such non-verbal signals as standing erect, with hands on hips, not smiling, and speaking loudly. A person may indicate that he has come to the end of a sentence by looking up, and returning his hand to rest, or indicate that he wants to go on speaking by keeping a hand in mid-gesture. In none of these cases are those involved usually aware of the signals being used or of what they mean. They are probably all cases of communication, but unconscious on both sides. We shall consider the special features of consciously controlled behaviour later.

Similar considerations apply to the perception of signs: a girl is attracted by a boy, so her pupils expand, acting as a signal which in turn attracts him, though he is not aware that this signal is doing it. Most animal communication appears to be like this. An animal responds to a situation, and this response triggers off responses in other animals. Although these signals do not appear to be goal directed in most cases, it can be argued that they are part of a goal-directed evolutionary process that has produced this signalling system.

Again this distinction between conscious and unconscious signals is a matter of degree and there can be intermediate degrees of conscious insight. For example, a person may successfully communicate his social status by the clothes he wears, but verbally categorize these clothes only as 'nice', or 'suitable'. Other cases of unconscious communication occur in primitive rituals and have a powerful emotive and possibly therapeutic effect without anyone being consciously aware of this symbolism.

We can distinguish between communications where the sender and receiver are aware or unaware of the signal, as follows:

Sender	Receiver	
aware	aware	verbal communication, some gestures, e.g. pointing
mostly unaware	mostly aware	most NVC
unaware	unaware, but has an effect	pupil dilation, gaze shifts, and other non-verbal signals
aware	unaware	sender is trained in the use of e.g. spatial behaviour
unaware	aware	receiver is trained in the interpretation of e.g. bodily posture

Some psychoanalysts have claimed that unconscious impulses can be seen in the postures and gestures of patients. Some popular books have provided advice on, for example, how to judge another person's sexual availability. We shall examine these claims later.

Five types of bodily communication

NVC has several different functions:

Expressing emotions, mainly by face, body, and voice. To understand this takes us to the heart of the psychology of emotion.

Communicating interpersonal attitudes. We establish and maintain friendships and other relationships mainly by NV signals, such as proximity, tone of voice, touch, gaze, and facial expression, much as animals do.

Accompanying and supporting speech. Speakers and listeners engage in a complex sequence of head–nods, glances, and non-verbal vocalizations which are closely synchronized with speech and play an essential part in conversation.

Self-presentation is mainly achieved by appearance and to a lesser extent by voice.

Rituals. NV signals play a prominent role in greetings and other rituals.

Different types of signal

Some NV signals are like words in being discrete, for example particular gestures, while others are continuous, like proximity or loudness of voice. Some NV signals are like words in being arbitrarily coded, but others are 'iconic', i.e. they are similar or analogous to their referents. Examples of iconic coding are showing the teeth in anger, or proximity for affection; examples of arbitrary coding are most aspects of clothes or appearance, e.g. style of hair, to show group membership. Some signals have invariant meanings, others have a probability of meaning something. Loudness of speech has a probabilistic relation to extroversion; specific gestures may have invariant meanings.

Language itself is discrete, arbitrary, and invariant in coding, and some kinds of NVC resemble language in these respects, especially gestures. I am referring here to common 'emblems' (see p.191) such as the hitch-hike sign and waving 'hello'; sign language proper is not really NVC at all, and we shall not discuss it in this book. A number of investigations have emphasized the similarity between NVC and language and have designed their methods of research accordingly (p.17f.).

However, a great deal of NVC is not like language in these ways: proximity and amount of gaze, for example, are continuous, iconic, and probabilistic. And it is not simply a case of there being two kinds of NV signals, since some are mixed on these three criteria; facial expressions are continuous, mostly arbitrary, and probabilistic, for example (Scherer and Ekman 1982).

There is physiological evidence that there are at least two levels of brain mechanisms which are responsible for NVC. The more primitive brain centres govern spontaneous emotional expressions, while higher brain centres control expressions, to conform to social rules, or to conceal immediate feelings, for example (p.124).

Human _v._ animal NVC

It was noticing the similarities between men and monkeys which gave birth to NVC research. Animal behaviour is mainly innate and its evolutionary origins can be traced, so here is part of the explanation of human NVC.

However, men are very different from monkeys. The most obvious difference is that we use language. Animal communication is nearly all about their internal states and intentions, whereas much of our conversation is about people, thing, or events outside ourselves, the past and the future. The use of language has generated a whole new set of NV signals – for accompanying and elaborating on speech, providing feedback, and managing the synchronizing of utterances (see Chapter 7). It is interesting that we have also retained the older uses of NVC – for communicating emotions and managing inter-personal relations.

The second main difference between men and animals is the extensive build-up of human cultures over the course of history. We shall discuss later the detailed ways in which NVC varies between Arabs, Japanese, Italian, Africans, and others (see Chapter 4). There may be quite new signals, for example gestures which have no meaning in other cultures; or the same signal may have a different meaning. There may be rules governing the use of, for example, facial expressions. There may be complex rituals, such as forms of greeting and religious ceremonies. The meaning of some of these signals may depend on historical events (e.g. Churchill's V for victory), or symbolize political or religious ideas.

Humans differ from animals in the complexity and degree of planning of social behaviour. Much human social behaviour consists of 'social acts', i.e. behaviour that is meaningful to the actor; it is planned, often in words, with certain goals in mind; and the performance is monitored, and follows rules. Basic NV signals are incorporated into these social acts, so that there is a hierarchical structure.

The meaning of NV signals

The meaning of a non-verbal signal to a sender can be found in his emotional or other state, or the message he intends to send. The meaning to a receiver can be found in his interpretation of the signal. The meaning of a signal to a receiver, or to a sample of receivers, can be found by asking them to fill in a series of seven-point scales.

This is fairly straightforward in the case of a particular facial expression or posture, for example. But what is the meaning of a head-nod in a conversation where this is not consciously noted but has the effect of allowing another person to carry on talking? It perhaps has a 'behavioural meaning', though a person knowledgeable about NVC might give it a cognitive meaning, of the 'you have permission to carry on talking' kind. What is the meaning of a piece of music which arouses certain emotions, images, and motor responses? Again, the meaning could be said to lie in the reactions of beholders, or perhaps in the intentions of the composer, if these can be discovered. In some cases the 'meaning' of an act can be found from the way it fits into a larger sequence of behaviour, from its antecedents

and consequences. This principle is used in the study of animal behaviour (p.15). Research on unknown languages by anthropological
linguists uses similar methods to separate out the meaningful sounds
from others (p.17). And not to shake hands when 99 per cent of
others do so has a different meaning from not shaking hands when
no one else did so. Zero reactions can be highly meaningful.

The meaning of NV signals varies with the particular social setting
within a culture. The significance of touching another person is different if that person is: (1) one's wife; (2) someone else's wife; (3) a
complete stranger; (4) a patient; (5) another person in a crowded lift;
(6) another member of an encounter group, and so on. The meaning
of an NV signal also depends on its position in time and its relation
to other signals. A slap on the back might be received as hearty congratulations or as a physical assault, depending on what has taken
place beforehand. The signals made during a meal – to ask someone
to pass something, to indicate that one would or would not like
more food, that one likes the food, that one has had enough, etc. –
would be meaningless and unintelligible without reference to the
setting.

Later in this book we shall discuss those kinds of NVC whose
meaning is more complex than the cases discussed so far. Religious
rituals are a case in point (p.303). These rituals arouse a number of
images, for example red gum is associated with menstrual blood in
one ritual (Turner 1966). However, anthropologists maintain that
rituals have a further meaning, symbolizing the unity of the tribe by
the use of symbols which represent the tribe as a whole, such as flags
and totems.

Art and music also consist of NVC; they have a primarily non-
verbal meaning and cannot be translated into words. Many experiments have been done on reactions to art and music, and they are
found to have several kinds of non-verbal meaning – arousing visual
images, arousing and representing emotions, producing bodily
movements, representing objects and events, and communicating
deeper feelings and attitudes to life (p.307).

Theory and explanation

It has sometimes been said that NVC research is 'weak on theory'.
This book will attempt to disprove that allegation. Furthermore we
shall try to give the analysis of NVC as an example of how social
behaviour in general can be explained.

It will soon be apparent that the explanation of NV phenomena
requires a number of different levels from physiology upwards.

Consider the finding that people smile when they are happy. How far is smiling due to the physiology of facial nerves and muscles, to evolution, to socialization, to personality, to social interaction processes, to strategic planning, or to culture and history? We shall see that all of these levels are involved in the generation of smiling, and other forms of bodily communication.

There are theories at the level of social psychology proper, about the nature of social interaction, all of which deal with non-verbal phenomena in some way. The affiliative balance model (p.94f.), for example, shows how different NV signals can substitute for one another under certain conditions. The social skills model of interaction (p.109) explains how NV signals combine with verbal utterances, and shows the roles of face and gaze in conversation.

There is no single overall theory of NVC any more than there is a single theory of social behaviour. A number of levels have to be considered together, and at the moment there are competing theories at some of these levels.

The practical application of NVC research

Social skills training (SST) for mental patients

There is increasing use of SST for many classes of mental patients, but especially for out-patient neurotics, disturbed adolescents, depressives, and for people who are lonely or isolated. Very often the NVC of these patients needs training, since they tend to smile, gesture, and look less than normal, and to deviate in some more specific ways (Argyle 1983, and p.264f.).

Social skills training for work

SST is increasingly being given to trainee teachers, doctors, nurses, and any others. There are special problems for air hostesses (p.78). And at a higher level, NV advice is given to American presidential candidates and other politicians (p.261f.).

Training for intercultural contact

Increasing use is being made of training for those who are going to work abroad, for example in the Peace Corps, or for business organizations. An important part of such training is directed towards the different gestures or other NV signals used in other cultures, to the 'display rules' governing when various facial and other expressions

may be shown, and to more general social skills with NV components. A great deal of racial prejudice and misunderstanding is probably based on the different styles of NVC used by other cultural
groups (Ch.4).

2

How to do research on
non-verbal communication

Some of the early research in the field of NVC was carried out very successfully with fairly simple and straightforward methods. For example, there were experiments in which distance, sex of subjects, or topic of conversation were manipulated, and amount of gaze, smiling, or speech errors measured. A wider range of techniques is now available, some of them quite sophisticated. It is possible to make more refined measurements of voice quality, hand movements, and details of facial expression for instance. New statistical procedures are available: as well as analysis of variance, regular use is made of factor analysis, multiple regression, and other methods. Most important of all, perhaps, a greatly extended variety of experimental manipulations has been devised. And in addition to experiments a number of other designs can be used, for example to study sequences of behaviour.

The period during which NVC research developed – since about 1960 – has coincided with another chapter in the history of psychological research: the 'crisis' in social psychology. This had several strands, the main one being a concern with the lack of validity of laboratory experiments. If subjects are asked, for example, to wear masks, or to meet people wearing an eye-movement recorder (looking like something from outer space), there are serious doubts over whether the resulting behaviour would occur in any other, more normal situations. In the light of this criticism some of the earlier work on NVC must be looked at sceptically, and in certain cases rejected.

It is not necessary to abandon laboratory experiments because, as we shall see in connection with encoding studies, it is possible to arouse real emotions or real feelings of liking for another person in the laboratory. There is a big question mark against posed or role-played studies, however, and an increasing preference for real or spontaneous behaviour. The same problems do not arise so much with perceptual or decoding studies, since the subjects are not in a true social situation anyway, but are asked to do their best to interpret the NV signals presented.

Another response to the crisis in social psychology was a shift to field studies. Some of these involve systematic observation rather than experiments, but here there can be problems deciding which variable was cause, which effect. Field experiments have been done in which, for example, a confederate's appearance was varied, or he did or did not touch the subject. However, this kind of procedure restricts research to brief contacts between strangers.

A wide range of methods have been used for tackling different problems, and following from different theoretical points of view. Some involve generating emotions, or other states, to see how they are encoded into NV signals; some involve presenting NV signals to subjects to see how they are interpreted, or decoded; and in others the stream of behaviour is analysed, with or without experimental manipulation, and so on.

Encoding studies

The purpose here is to find out how emotions, attitudes to other people, or other states are encoded into non-verbal signals. The earliest method was simply to ask subjects to pose the facial expressions which they would have, for example, when happy, sad, etc. Ekman (1982) used this in his important studies of facial expression, as did Mehrabian (1972) in his experiments on a wide range of NV signals. The main objection to this method is that posed expressions are not quite the same as spontaneous ones – they are stronger, less symmetrical, and they have different correlates; for example, the superiority of women over men at decoding is greater for posed signals. Allen and Atkinson (1981) videotaped posed and spontaneous expressions of understanding and not understanding on the part of ten-year-old children. Observers could easily tell which was which since, in the posed condition, the children nodded thirty times as often. It has been argued that posed expressions are useful in tests for decoding accuracy, and that they show NV expressions without the inhibiting and modifying effects of display rules.

However, we are primarily interested in naturally occurring or spontaneous behaviour, so how can it be elicited for research purposes? An improvement on posing is role-playing, which the author has used sometimes. Here subjects are asked to spend several minutes thinking about some event, thus thinking themselves into the mood to be portrayed. They then talk about it, and their NV emissions are recorded. While this is an improvement on posing, it is still not the real thing; obviously the true social situation is missing.

How can genuine emotions and attitudes be generated? There are a variety of ways, which have come to be used increasingly in NVC research:

(1) Subjects watch films, chosen to arouse disgust, sadness, excitement, or other emotions. They talk to the experimenter about each film, and while this is happening their facial expression is videotaped, and physiological measures are taken as well as subjective reports (Buck 1984).

(2) Subjects meet different confederates who behave in a very agreeable, or a rather disagreeable manner, causing subjects to like or dislike them. Their behaviour towards the confederates is then recorded (e.g. Exline and Winters 1966).

(3) Subjects bring partners into the laboratory, with whom they are in love (or not), happily married (or not), and the effect of these relationships on NVC is examined (Noller 1984).

(4) Subjects are observed in field settings in which certain real events take place. For example, they may be filmed at a bowling alley after they have hit or missed the skittles, and while facing the skittles or their friends (Kraut and Johnston 1979).

Decoding studies

Here the purpose is to study how subjects perceive, interpret, or react to NV signals. These signals can be posed or genuine, studied in a laboratory or in field settings, and the responses of subjects recorded in a number of ways.

Again the stimuli may be posed faces, voices, etc., or schematic drawings of faces or postures. Such methods are useful for studying the information conveyed, for example by posture alone. The stimuli may be role-played or they may be spontaneous. An example of spontaneous stimuli is Buck's method of videotaping subjects as they watch and talk about emotionally arousing slides or films; these videotapes are then used as stimuli, representing the portrayal of known emotions (Buck 1984). Another source is news photographs, in which the nature of the situation makes it clear what the state of the encoders is. Extracts from soap operas have also been used, though these should perhaps be regarded as 'posed' (Trimboli 1984).

In laboratory studies it is possible to vary the nature of the stimuli to be decoded. Facial expressions, bodily movements, and vocal expressions can be presented separately. Conflicting signals can be presented, for example friendly face and unfriendly voice, friendly verbal and unfriendly non-verbal; or the situation in which the encoder appears to be can be experimentally varied. In one study news photographs were used to provide the situational context, and the photographs were doctored to vary the facial expressions of certain actors (Spignesi and Shor 1981). The information available to decoders can be manipulated, for instance showing only face or body on a TV monitor, or just playing the sound track. Bull (1987) presented a large number of drawings of postures in which each component was experimentally varied, the face being left without expression (p.210f.).

Decoding studies can also be carried out in field settings, and here the posed/spontaneous issues seem to be less important. The question is, what effect does the NV signal have on the behaviour of those receiving it? For example, there are field experiments in which people are touched or not touched, to study the effect of touch on compliance.

The perceptions and other reactions of decoders can be recorded in a number of ways. It may be of interest to find out whether or not subjects noticed, or were aware of, the particular signal. It may still affect their behaviour even if they were not aware. A widely used method is to ask subjects to rate the sender or his behaviour on five- or seven-point scales, like:

friendly   —   —   —   —   —   —   —   — hostile
inferior   —   —   —   —   —   —   —   — superior
appropriate —   —   —   —   —   —   —   — inappropriate

A larger number of such scales may be used (25–30) and factor analysis carried out to find the main dimensions, which are then used in the final analysis. The behavioural responses of subjects may also be studied – whether or not they comply with requests, or their physiological reactions, e.g. whether their GSR (Galvanic Skin Response) or heart-rate goes up when they are touched or looked at. Appearance has been varied in a similar way, to find the effect on helpfulness in signing petitions and the like.

Another kind of decoding is done by psychoanalysts and some anthropologists, who make interpretations of behaviour when the performer does not know the meaning of his behaviour. Bodily communication has been claimed as a new key to unconscious desires and thoughts. Deutsch (1947) kept careful records of a female patient and reported a link between postures and free association: there were different postures for being angry with her parents and for fear of being punished for masturbation. Mahl (1968) reported that patients will fiddle with or remove their wedding ring some time before reporting dissatisfaction with their marriage. It would be possible to make these interpretations more certain by some quantification, or by studying the effect of experimental changes on topic of discussion.

Sequences of non-verbal behaviour

The main method of research here is the statistical analysis of sequences, by methods devised for animal behaviour studies. Transition probabilities are calculated, i.e. the probability that a particular kind of act will be followed by another, either in the same animal (e.g. during grooming), or in another one (e.g. during play or courtship). This can be expressed as follows:

		Following act		
		A	B	C
Previous act	A	5	80	15
	B	5	10	85
	C	90	10	0

This shows that an ABC cycle will usually repeat itself.

It is also possible to find which categories of behaviour can be grouped together. One way is to see which kind of behaviour leads to another: for example, relaxed open-mouth, hand-wrestle, gnaw, and poke all lead to each other in chimpanzees, and can be regarded as a general category of 'play' (Van Hooff 1982). Another way is to find the correlation between acts, by having the same pattern of transition probabilities with other variables, so that they are embedded in the system in similar ways, and can act as alternatives. Sequences of animal behaviour, however, have more complex structures than one act leading to the next. An act can affect the probability of another which is several moves away. This can be discovered by finding distant transition probabilities, or by finding sequences which are repeated and under the direction of a higher-order sequence in a hierarchical structure, or sequences with a structure like the phrase grammar of language (Dawkins 1976; Van Hooff 1982).

Human ethologists have adapted these methods to the study of human non-verbal sequences. For example, Heeschen, Schiefenhovel, and Eibl-Eibesfeldt (1980) studied the signals for requesting and giving food among groups of people in a remote New Guinea village. The gesture for asking for food is to stretch out the arms at chest level and then to draw them back in a self-embrace. Food, e.g.

a nut, is then offered in a special gesture, with the forearm vertical and gazing at the recipient, who then stretches out the left hand to reach for the nut. A number of other standard sequences of a similar kind were observed.

Another example is a study of how people cross the road at a zebra crossing; the detailed signals which they make, and thus avoid collisions, have been discovered (Collett and Marsh 1974). An important field in which statistical methods have been applied is in the study of the links between non-verbal behaviour and speech. There is 'self-synchrony' between the two – patterns of gaze and gesture, for example, are closely correlated with speech. The non-verbal responses of listeners are also correlated with what is said (p.106f.). There are synchronizing signals, used to manage the starting and stopping of speech (p.113f.).

More controversial is the so-called 'gestural dance', whereby the gestures and other bodily movements of interactors have been claimed to be co-ordinated down to fractions of a second. Careful statistical analysis has shown that the truth is rather different, however (p.118f.).

Sequences can also be studied experimentally. One interactor can be programmed to behave in a certain way, for example to reinforce some behaviour by the subject, to interrupt, or to gaze in a special sequence. Synchronizing cues can be examined by a decoding method in which subjects hear a recorded conversation; a certain utterance stops at a particular point and subjects press a button when they are sure the utterance has ended. This makes it possible to compare the impact of cues like pitch change and sentence completion (Slugoski 1985, and p.116). Subjects can be asked to talk while gazing continually, without being able to see each other, or under other conditions, in order to test theories about the role of visual information. Other studies have studied NVC in sequences experimentally, for example by the removal of vision, or preventing gestures.

The main weakness of sequence studies appears to be a self-imposed one: no one asks the subjects what they are thinking, or feeling, or trying to do. This is party because the research methods have been taken over from animal research, partly through a mistrust of subjective data. There are certainly areas of NVC where subjective reports have little or nothing to contribute, such as fast-moving gaze-shifts, of which interactors are scarcely aware. But there are other aspects of human social behaviour where subjective data are essential, where we need to know the intentions, strategies, rules, and ideas in people's heads in order to understand their behaviour. It is doubtful whether an observational study of cricket using sequence analysis could get very far – one would need to know the rules, and understand concepts such as 'out', 'declare', and the rest. Pike (1967) has made the point that one would not understand what was going on at a religious service, a baseball game, a fishing expedition, or a scientific experiment unless one understood the ideas and plans in the minds of the participants, together with the whole set of concepts and rules connected with the religious service, or baseball game, or whatever.

The structural method

There is an alternative method of studying sequences of NVC which has been the source of a number of important contributions. It is mainly non-quantitative, and its aim is to build up descriptive accounts of how various sequences are constructed. It follows from the structural and linguistic models to be described later (p.290f.). It is assumed that non-verbal signals, for example particular gestures, are discrete rather than continuous, have invariant rather than probabilistic relations with what they refer to, and are arbitrarily rather than iconically coded (i.e. similar), like the words in a language. It follows that research can consist of the detailed analysis of fairly small samples. The approach originated from studies of American Indian languages, which were spoken but not written, where it was not known which sounds were the words, or how they combined to make sentences. The methods which were used here were adapted for the detailed analysis of NVC.

The first step is to make a sound film of the behaviour to be analysed, preferably of a number of instances of greetings, interviews, etc. The interactions are then transcribed, as fully as possible, on to a chart so that the various NV signals are shown against time. There is then a search for recurring elements, the units of behaviour. This is actually dependent on the next stage, finding which units make a difference by their presence or absence. Finally, the larger structures are found, composed of smaller units. These may be sequences or simultaneous signals sent by an individual, or a combination of moves by two or more people. If one were studying cricket, for example, balls bowled would be repeated units, hitting the stumps would be a significant occasional event, taking pullovers off would not. Overs would be larger units, an innings a larger unit still (Kendon 1982; Scheflen and Scheflen 1972).

An example of the use of this method is the study of greetings by Kendon and Ferber (1973). Films were taken of seventy greetings, many of them at a garden party where the hostess greeted her guests as they came down the garden path. The main bodily movements were transcribed – moves down path, smiles, looks, shakes hands, talks, dips head, etc. It was concluded that greetings fell into four main phases, each consisting of several non-verbal, and sometimes some verbal signals. These are described later (p.221).

This could have been done by quantitative ethological methods; indeed, Blurton-Jones and Leach (1972) did such a study of how nursery school children greet their mothers. The grouping and the sequencing of elements of behaviour can be done by statistical analysis. It is claimed on behalf of the structural approach that it shows 'greetings as a transaction that the participants are aiming to bring off and that therefore requires steps and stages for its accomplishment' (Kendon 1982: 477). In other words, it looks at the joint intention to bring about a co-operative and culturally meaningful social event.

On the other hand no information is collected about the intentions of greeters, or about the subjective meaning of greetings to them. The only sense in which such meanings enter the analysis appears to be in the mind and experience of the investigators. Furthermore, the conclusions from the use of the structural approach tend to be based on small quantities of data, and with no statistical analysis. Sometimes these conclusions have been overturned by studies using more rigorous methods, as in the case of the 'gestural dance' hypothesis (p.118). And while some of the early discoveries about non-verbal synchronizing signals were made by the use of structural methods, later testing of alternative hypotheses has needed experimental methods.

It could be argued that if there are areas of NVC which have some of the properties of a language – discrete signals, invariant meaning, iconic coding, etc. – these methods are appropriate (Scherer and Ekman 1982). We shall discuss the fortunes of the linguistic model in Chapter 18.

Structuralists emphasize the importance of discovering what the significant variables are; however, by now we have a very good idea of the non-verbal signals which are going to be relevant. Similarly, structuralists were good at discovering or developing ideas about basic processes, but now we are more concerned with testing detailed theories and models.

The structural approach does not include any investigation of the causes or effects of social events. Other studies of greetings, for example, have found how they vary with the closeness of relationship and the social setting. This approach is important since it is possible to test theories about the functions of greetings.

Individual differences

People vary a lot in their NVC, and some of these differences are associated with familiar dimensions of personality. For example, extroverts smile and look more. All aspects of NVC are affected by persons as well as by situations. There is a certain amount of consistency, i.e. some people look more often than others in most situations, though there can be more complex interactions too. It may be important to observe people in a variety of situations before deciding that some personality trait is correlated with NVC. For example, it was found in a number of studies that schizophrenics show gaze aversion; it was then found that this happened only when they were talking to psychologists or strangers, and not when talking about impersonal topics to people whom they knew (Rutter 1976).

A variety of aspects of personality have been found to be associated with distinctive styles of NVC. These include sex, age, traits like extroversion and neuroticism, classes of mental patient, the self-image, and high and low social skills. For example, the NVC of successful and less successful doctors, teachers, salesmen, or others can be compared. The appearance of those with different self-images can be examined. Finer divisions of personality can yield stronger associations with NVC. Autistic children, for example, show almost complete aversion of gaze. And there are divisions of neurotics, and depressives, with rather different patterns of behaviour.

Important advances have been made by the use of more sophisticated measures of NVC. Equipment for voice analysis can measure the fundamental frequency (F_0) and the detailed distribution of vocal amplitude at different frequencies (Scherer 1982). Similarly, it is possible to make detailed objective measures of gestural patterns (Rosenfeld 1982). As a result we now know that schizophrenics have asymmetry between the two sides of the face (the left hand side showing much stronger expressions), and lack of co-ordination between gestures by the two hands.

In addition to studying such behavioural differences between different personalities, the accuracy of decoding can be analysed. This requires standard sets of stimuli to be decoded, and a number of tests using posed (e.g. Rosenthal *et al.* 1979) or spontaneous expressions (e.g. Buck 1984) are available. These have been used to study the accuracy at decoding of men and women, patients and others.

A related problem is individual differences in *encoding* accuracy. Subjects can be asked to try to communicate, for example, different meanings of ambiguous sentences; Noller (1984) asked spouses to say things like 'I'm feeling cold, aren't you?' to convey three different messages. Spontaneous expressions can be recorded as subjects are watching or talking about emotive films (Buck 1984); or they can give self-ratings, with items like 'I can send a seductive glance if I want to' (Friedman *et al.* 1980).

We should remember that social skill often does not involve disclosing one's actual feelings, but rather of concealing them; this last method does attempt to include the capacity to control the signals which are sent.

The evolution of NVC

Several kinds of research on human NVC have been directed to finding out how much of it is innate and unlearned. For example, there is research on infants who were born blind and deaf, and on the extent to which NVC is similar in other cultures (Chapter 4). Research on monkeys can take a step further and find out the effects of being reared in isolation – to allow growth, or maturation, but to exclude the effects of social experience. These studies have established that facial expression, for example, is mainly innate, but that gestures are not.

Tracing the evolutionary history of such innate expressions can be done by comparing the physiological equipment and the behaviour patterns of animals at different stages of evolutionary history. It is not possible to do rigorous experiments here, but a number of generally accepted conclusions have been reached, for example about the origins of smiling and laughing (p.37). Another line of research compared the development of NV signalling systems in different habitats, for example in the African plains and the South American forests.

These comparisons require detailed study of the facial, vocal, and other signals used, for example, by different kinds of monkeys and apes. This is done mainly by sequence analysis methods, to find out exactly when a certain face is made, and what effect this has on others. And here, unlike research on humans, it is not possible to ask the subjects what they are trying to do, or what they are feeling. Finally, it is possible to carry out research on animals that is not possible with humans. As well as isolation experiments, there have been physiological studies in which the facial nerves of monkeys have been cut, to find the effect on social interaction (p.35).

Cross-cultural research

Cross-cultural research is important, to find out which aspects of NVC are universal, and for practical purposes to design intercultural training courses. The earliest work was done by anthropologists who made detailed observations of gestures or ceremonies, for instance, and who later took photographs and films. The photographs of the Balinese by Bateson and Mead (1942) are a famous example. The next stage was the systematic comparison of different cultures, using standard methods of research. Ekman's work (1973) on the facial expressions of people in New Guinea is a good example (p.49f.). Another approach is to repeat experiments in other cultures, and the author has organized this on several occasions. There is a serious practical problem with this kind of study, and that is finding comparable samples of subjects. Samples of students in different cultures have been compared in a number of studies, but this is not possible with primitive cultures; also students represent different sections of the population and tend to be westernized.

Another way of comparing people from other cultures is to study foreign students. It is desirable to do this before they have been in the new country for very long, or the differences may start to disappear. However, quite clear variations have been observed, for example in studies of gaze patterns in students from different countries in America (p.57f.). Some cultural distinctions can be studied in the same country, for example class difference, or blacks, whites, and hispanics in America. In the second case it is important to hold social class constant as far as possible, or class differences may produce what look like ethnic differences.

When cultural differences have been discovered, how can they be explained? This is partly a matter of the historical origins of specific gestures. Very early history can sometimes be studied from vase paintings or other works of art, for example the gestures in Leonardo da Vinci's *Last Supper*. Literary sources can be useful: in *Romeo and Juliet* 'I do bite my thumb, Sir' describes a gesture probably derived from removing a glove prior to throwing it down as a challenge, and a forerunner of our rude thumb to nose gesture. Another useful literary source can be early etiquette books showing, for example, the growth of rules about spitting and restraining nose-blowing in Europe (Collett 1984). Geographical distribution of gestures can give a hint as to their origin: the use of the head-toss for 'no' in southern Italy matches the spread of Greek colonization in the ancient world (Morris *et al.* 1979).

Developmental studies

The interest here is in finding which aspects of NVC are innate, which are the result of maturation, and which of socialization. This is done by studying young infants and by examining changes with age, and correlations with child-rearing methods. The basic designs are similar to those for adults – encoding, decoding, and sequence analysis.

Encoding

Some emotions can be inferred from their context and similarity to adult emotions. The state of distress is clear since it occurs when the mother leaves the room, and includes crying. However, it is not always clear what is being encoded. It is not possible to bring up children in experimental isolation, as can be done with monkeys. The nearest to this, perhaps, is research on infants born blind and deaf. A group of these children were observed to display a number of facial expressions – crying, smiling, and laughing (Eibl-Eibesfeldt 1972). Observations have been made on very young infants, to examine the early development of facial expressions (p.126f.).

Decoding

This can be studied more systematically in infants. Reactions to experimental situations, such as schematic faces, can be studied at six weeks or earlier (e.g. Kaye and Fogel 1980). The infant's interpretation cannot be analysed in much detail; it is mainly a matter of looking, smiling, or crying. At six weeks infants respond positively to their mother's smile; at three months they can discriminate between friends and strangers.

Sequence analysis

A lot of infant research consists of observation of children interacting with their mothers. This requires the use of coding categories rather different from those used with adults, since the facial expressions, bodily movements, and vocalizations are different (Tronick 1982). Studies have been made of infants imitating mothers, following their gaze, playing peek-a-boo games. It is found that infants are very sensitive and responsive, and can fit into the ongoing sequence with their mothers.

Each of these methods can be repeated at different ages, and changes with age plotted. It is found, for example, that sex differences in decoding are found in infants and do not change with age; on the other hand sex differences in encoding do increase with age, and so are probably due to socialization (Hall 1984).

General research issues

Laboratory research

A great deal of NVC research is done in the laboratory. A typical lay-out is shown in Figure 2.1.

Figure 2.1 Laboratory arrangements for studying gaze

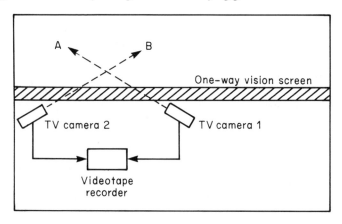

Source: Argyle 1983

It is desirable that the area for the subjects should resemble an ordinary room as much as possible, with comfortable chairs, a carpet, and so on. If a one-way screen is used it should be unobtrusive. If physiological or other obtrusive equipment is used, this does rather change the nature of the situation, and subjects become very aware of being in an experiment.

Some areas of NVC research have run into another difficulty. Experiments on the compensation versus reciprocity problem (p.95f.) have produced a lot of confusing and inconclusive results. This is probably because the effect of a series of complex experimental manipulations in the laboratory is to produce a variety of interpretations of the situation, and a variety of motivations, so that no clear pattern can be found. The solution may be to go for simpler, more robust, and more realistic designs, preferably in field situations.

There are various pieces of equipment which can be used to record

NVC mechanically. Voice-operated keys can record when each person is speaking. Research on vocalization needs equipment which will record fundamental frequency and the speech spectogram (cf. p.139f.). Research on gaze will make a great step forward when a practicable eye-movement recorder becomes available, to record exactly where a person is fixating at each moment. Videotape recorders are used to present the stimuli in decoding studies, though audiotapes and still photographs can also be used. Tachistoscopes may be used to present very brief exposures – 1/60 second in one sensitivity test (p.274f.).

Observing and filming

This can be done by observers, or with sound or videorecording, which have the advantage that the tape can be played a number of times. In either case it is necessary to count head-nods or glances, press buttons which activate pen-recorders or electronic devices, or to rate behaviour over time-intervals. Distance and appearance are the only NV signals which do not usually need observation at different points in time.

The categories which observers are to use must be decided. In most research no attempt is made to observe everything; rather, there is concentration on a particular channel and set of categories. Sometimes these are fairly straightforward, such as gazing, smiling, or nodding. Other categories are more complicated, such as bodily movements and gestures. Research is then needed to establish the types of behaviour which are most relevant for a particular study. The observers have to be trained, to achieve a high degree of inter-observer reliability.

The most important piece of equipment is the videorecorder, though film may also be used. Film or video, with sound, records a great deal of NVC, though there are a number of problems. The camera angle and distance need to be set to capture as much information as possible, in the greatest detail. If two cameras are used, pointed at different interactors, the two pictures can be presented side by side with a video-mixer. Some structural research has used film followed by frame-by-frame analysis, e.g. at twenty-four frames per second. Portable videorecorders are now widely used, and the tape can be analysed in slow motion or by stopping at set time-intervals. Sometimes subjects are filmed from a distance, or via a 45° prism, and do not realize they have been recorded. Inside laboratories it is possible to conceal cameras, or to use one-way screens. It is necessary to debrief subjects and ask permission to use the film.

Much NVC research has used straightforward experimental designs, with analysis of variance. In encoding studies, for example, different emotions can be aroused, while other variables can be included such as sex of subjects and presence of other people. In decoding studies the variables manipulated may be another's facial expression, the situation which the other is in, and the other's verbal utterances. Sequence analysis needs rather different analysis, of which the most basic is the table of transitional probabilities: how likely is it that a person will make move A after another person has made move B. More complex analyses were mentioned earlier.

Nearly all research in NVC uses statistics. A lot of good work has been carried out with quite simple statistics, but in some areas more complex methods have extended what can be done. Examples are the use of factor analysis and multi-dimensional scaling to find decoding dimensions, multiple regression to find the relative importance of different aspects of signals (e.g. verbal v. non-verbal), and sophisticated techniques of sequence analysis (e.g. Van Hooff 1982). The only NVC research which has not used statistics is research which is exploratory, or research in the structural tradition, which looks for standard repeated elements and the ways in which they combine to form larger wholes, as discussed earlier.

Sampling

All research involves the study of certain samples of the behaviour under investigation. Much of the criticism of early social psychology research was that the samples studied were unrepresentative, or unlike real life. The laboratory is obviously unlike most settings outside but, as we have seen, it is possible to arouse real emotions, and to create real spontaneous behaviour in the lab. Even in field situations some sampling is needed. We saw that schizophrenics avert gaze in some situations but not in others. Similarly the researcher has to think about his samples of subjects, if he wants to extend the generality of his findings to the population. They should not all be students, for instance, though some can be. He should include both sexes, different ages, and if possible different classes and cultures, though as we have seen the latter is a further area of research. There should be sampling of the behaviour. For example, the study of greeting described earlier was confined to a particular type of greeting occasion. For a particular study it may be desirable to reduce variation in behaviour due to sources other than the one under investigation, but it needs to be shown that the results hold up under varied conditions (Scherer and Ekman 1982).

Combining the results of different studies

The volume of research on NVC is now so great that it is sometimes possible to examine the results of a hundred or more studies of the same issue, carried out under different conditions. In what is called 'meta-analysis' a number of studies can be combined, by recalculation where necessary so that they are all expressed by the same statistic. This then gives a single result, with a greatly enlarged number of subjects and some generality of conditions. Hall (1984) carried out a meta-analysis of 125 experiments on sex differences in decoding accuracy. The overall sex difference can be expressed in several different ways, as shown on p.281.

It is possible to carry out further meta-analyses on subgroups of studies, to find the effect of different variables. In the same study, for example, the effects of a number of other variables on sex difference were investigated, such as age of subjects, sex of target, date of study, and even sex of investigators.

Proof and discovery

It is important to note the distinction between discovery and proof. Experiments are ideally suited to proof – by holding variables constant, by careful manipulation of experimental variables, and by measurement of dependent variables. However, experiments do not always lead to the discovery of new ideas; indeed they may prevent it, by restricting attention to a certain very limited set of variables or procedures – though they may produce unexpected interactions, or other interesting deviations from expectations. The value of an experiment lies partly in the theory which lies behind it, and partly in the skill of manipulating variables and holding others constant. New ideas come more often as a result of informal and less well-controlled research – clinical case studies, anthropological field studies, and intensive study of particular field situations, for example. These are 'rich' sources of data, in that they do not exclude anything in the way that experiments do. We can also learn from unusual situations, such as initiation rites in primitive societies, encounter groups, or modern drama, where certain aspects of social behaviour are exaggerated; the study of such abnormal phenomena may help us to understand familiar ones more clearly.

3

Non-verbal communication in animals

NVC research on humans has been greatly influenced by the obvious similarities between humans and non-human primates. This led to an interest in the evolutionary origins of facial expression, vocalizations, and the rest. However, an early enthusiasm for the 'naked ape' point of view has been tempered by an awareness of the gap between men and monkeys or apes – especially our far greater development of culture, longer period of socialization, larger brain, and use of language.

Nevertheless the physical equipment for sending NV signals – for example, the muscles of the face, the vocal chords – is clearly innate. And, as we shall see later, some of the NV signals, such as facial expressions for emotion, are partly unlearnt and universal to the human species. Evolutionary pressures can produce physiological structures, such as the long neck of the giraffe to eat from trees and the monkey's facial muscles to communicate. Evolution can also produce patterns of behaviour, including the special faces, vocalizations, and other signals for different occasions. Research on human and non-human primates has converged in the discovery of common signals and systems of communication. Animals conduct their entire social life by means of non-verbal communication: they make friends, find mates, rear children, co-operate in groups, establish leadership hierarchies, and get rid of their enemies entirely by the use of NV signals. This elaborate signalling system has mainly been built up in the course of evolution, as a result of its value for the survival of the species.

Signals can be studied experimentally. For example, varying different aspects of dummy birds or fish can reveal which aspect of the signal is important. Lack (1939) found that if the breast feathers of a robin were dyed brown these birds were attacked less by other robins, and experiments by Tinbergen (1951) using dummies showed that birds recognize predators from the shape of their wings. In some cases a complex and repeated set of signals is found, like the

song of an individual bird or a 'courtship' sequence. This is a more
elaborate kind of communication, which has some parallels with the
syntax of human speech.

The evolutionary origins of these signals can be studied by comparing the similarities and differences in closely related species,
which are 'older' and 'younger' in evolutionary history or which
have lived in different habitats, for example forests or grasslands,
thus creating different problems of communication.

NVC in animals has the same range of functions as for humans. In
addition, since animals have no language, it is the only way of communicating information about the physical world. But as Marler
said:

> By far the greatest part of the whole system of communication
> seems to be devoted to the organization of social behavior of the
> group, to dominance and subordination, the maintenance of peace
> and cohesion of the group, reproduction, and care of the young.
> (Marler 1965: 584)

It is usually assumed that the capacities to send and receive these
signals have evolved together, as part of the total system of communication. How far any of these signals are sent intentionally we shall
discuss later. There is evidence that the same physiological mechanisms are involved in sending and receiving in some species, so that
the same evolutionary and genetic processes lie behind both (Green
and Marler 1979).

The functions of NVC in animals

Expressing interpersonal attitudes and emotions

There are a number of basic social relationships between animals –
between mates, parents and children, friends, and so on. A complete
set of NV signals is used to manage these relationships. Animals send
information particularly about their sexual readiness, dominance,
and submission, and to keep up affiliative contacts within the group.
We will illustrate these as far as possible by reference to the non-
human primates.

Sexual. A female of most non-human primate species signals her
sexual readiness by her visible physiological condition, especially
the blue swellings in her genital area. All species engage in some kind
of courtship, to establish the bond and reduce the fear of close contact (Eibl-Eibesfeldt 1975). Birds and other species engage in much

longer sequences of courtship behaviour: the male attracts the female by his song and his appearance; there are elaborate joint rituals, in which the male may feed the female, or build her a nest. In primates, the female may present to the male, or he may try to mount her, though some learning by observation is needed to do this successfully.

Maternal–infantile signals. Mothers embrace and suckle their infants, later allowing them to cling on underneath or ride on top. Most species have a special call, and some have a special facial expression for recalling their young. Infants produce the complementary pattern of clinging, sucking, riding, and running to mother when frightened. They use special cries when they are separated from and united with their mother.

Affiliative behaviour between siblings and friends, young and old, takes several forms. A lot of time is spent in grooming – taking turns to extract small pieces of dead skin or insects from one another's coats, while lip-smacking and showing the appropriate facial expressions. Animals also spend time in bodily contact, in families, and between friends.

Young animals play a lot: the invitation to play consists of the 'playface', and the play consists of imitation, chasing, fighting, and mounting. In grooming and play there are long sequences of interaction, in which one act leads to another with a certain probability. When two animals meet they usually greet one another, by lip-smacking, touching, smelling, embracing, or mounting each other, or even by shaking hands. Mouth–mouth contact is based on mouth-to-mouth feeding, and may be the origin of human kissing (Goodall 1968).

Dominance and submission. Animals who live in groups, like monkeys and apes, establish dominance hierarchies. The dominance of an animal depends partly on its size and strength, and also on the outcome of actual fights or of threat displays. Various dominance questions, such as access to food and females, are settled by threat displays between pairs of males. Usually they do not fight, but simply make terrifying displays at one another. These threat displays consists of a number of NV signals:

facial expression: bared teeth, lowered eyebrows, staring eyes
posture: tense, head lowered, forelegs bent, swaying
movement: slow approach

bodily state: hair bristling
bodily contact: hit, bite
vocalization: barking or grunting or other loud noises

Sometimes an animal will actually attack a member of its own group, or of another group, or another species. This may take the form of charging, slapping, scratching, stamping on the back, hair-pulling, biting, lifting, and slamming down. When an animal submits to another it makes appeasement signals, which prevent further aggression. It may just turn and flee, screeching, urinating, and looking over its shoulder. It may make appeasement signals by cowering, curling up, holding out a hand, facing away and lowering the eyes, presenting for copulation, or inviting grooming. Some species, like cats and dogs, show 'defensive threat', perhaps when there is conflict between flight and attack. The hair is erected, there are self-protective responses such as eye-closing, and some aggressive signals like barking.

As well as giving submissive or threat signals which actually change a relationship, animals may make briefer gestures which merely communicate or recognize an existing relationship, and thus make social life proceed more smoothly and prevent aggression. It has been observed that monkeys may express dominance by such gestures as a brisk, striding gait, and sitting calmly; submission is expressed by grimacing and retracting the testes. Some of these signals are illustrated in Plate 3.1.

Establishing and maintaining contact. Members of a group of animals often keep in contact by means of 'contact calls'. This is common in birds, but is also found in primates, sheep, sea lions, and squirrels. Animals come to recognize the calls of their mates, parents, and children, and in some species of birds couples sing duets together. These calls are interesting in that they are spontaneous and not a response to a particular stimulus.

Interspecies signals. Many animals live in a co-operative relationship with other species, for example 'cleaner' fish eat the parasites on certain other fish. Special signals are developed to enable such co-operation to take place. More often, though, different species are in conflict with each other – one is a predator, or they are in competition for the same territory.

Threat signals are employed which are similar to those used within the species, though these are more likely to lead to an actual attack. Some birds attack predators by 'mobbing' – a special call leads to a collective attack on an enemy.

Identity signals

An important aspect of animal communication concerns identity. It is necessary to recognize the species of another animal, which group it belongs to, its sex and social status, which individual it is, and where it is.

First, it is necessary to know whether another animal belongs to the same species, to one of several different species of predators which have to be treated differently, to one of several species of prey, or to a species with which relations of co-operation or peaceful co-existence have developed. Mammals recognize another's species mainly by various crucial aspects of appearance and by vocalizations. Insects, however, recognize their own species by their distinctive pheromones (taste or smell signals), while birds recognize species both by shape and by song. The essential and universal components of a song can be established by acoustic analysis; some birds have an innate capacity to sing and to recognize their species tune.

In other species of birds, like the chaffinch, there is a basic song found in different groups but there are also detailed differences of 'dialect'. In these species there is a period of imitative learning, in the nest, or for a period each year, from the father, from both parents, or from the whole group of neighbours. These differences of dialect make it possible for birds to distinguish between members of different groups, and it is assumed that this is the biological function of imitative variations on the basic song.

When recognition is a visual matter there is usually no difficulty in perceiving the sex and age of another animal. Its social status can also be perceived from such signals as, in the case of some monkeys, an upright posture and a raised tail. Birds, too, can distinguish sex differences, and to some extent age differences, from bird-song. Some insects can signal social status by pheromones.

Particular individuals can be distinguished from others of the same species or group by their individual appearance or call. For example, a sea bird returning to a colony of two thousand can recognize and be recognized by its own family by distinctive calls. The calls vary in pitch, tone quality, loudness, combinations of these, and changes in timing, providing thousands of different versions of a basically similar call. The male and female bou-bou shrike learn to sing a duet which is in the group dialect but is also unique to that pair, so that they can recognize each other.

Bird-song contains another piece of information – where the singer is. Bird-song is used to claim territory, such as a particular tree, and has the function of attracting females and repelling males from that

Plate 3.1 Facial expressions of apes and monkeys

a A frowning adult female pigtail macaque (The Zoological Society of London 1982)

b A yawning adult male rhesus monkey just before the peak of display (William K. Redican 1982)

c A playful chimpanzee displaying the apparently evolutionary precursor to the human laugh and pleasurable smile (Michael Lyster 1982)

d Fear grimace by chimpanzee (Reynolds 1967)

e A specialized threat gesture, the baboon yawn (Jolly 1972)

a

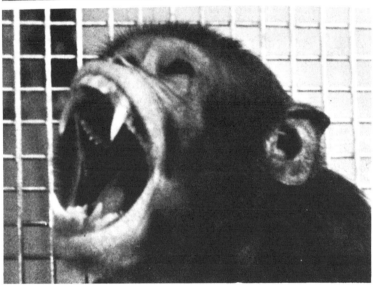

b

c

d

e

place. High-pitched song that is repeated over a long period gives
very clear information about spatial position to other birds over a
wide area.

These identity signals are included in calls which also convey
other messages. The identifying elements may be particularly clear
in the beginning of the call, while individual, group, and species
identification may be carried by different acoustic features of it.

Communicating information about the outside world

Most animal communication is of the kind already described – signalling internal emotional states, attitudes to other animals, and
identity. However, to a limited degree animals can also communicate information about the outside world. This kind of communication comes nearest to human language. We shall discuss several
examples.

Alarm calls. Both birds and non-human primates give alarm calls.
Small birds give two quite different warning calls when an owl or
other predator is sighted. If the predator is directly overhead, so that
danger is great, a bird hides and sends a constant note of a pitch
which makes it very hard to locate. If the predator is at a safe distance
the bird makes a loud, repetitive sound, over a wide frequency
range, which indicates exact location and produces a joint attack or
'mobbing' response (Thorpe 1972). We shall describe primate warning calls later.

Food calls. Birds and primates make special sounds when they find
food, sometimes for courtship, sometimes for their young. The
sounds are more intense when the food is highly attractive, such as
bananas (Green and Marler 1979).

Directing attention. In some species of birds there are particular calls
for particular kinds of predator, and these sometimes imitate the predator's call. The degree of danger may be conveyed by the loudness
of the call or its excitement. Response to such calls is innate – chickens
keep quiet inside the egg when they hear the chicken warning call.

The bees' dance. The most celebrated case of animals conveying information about the outside world is the bees' dance. Von Frisch (1967)
found that when a worker bee returned to the hive after finding a
good source of food she could tell the others where to go by means
of a dance. The angle of the route in relation to the sun was indicated

by the angle of the dance to the vertical; a greater distance was shown by a slower dance, and with a head-wind it was slower still, since more energy was needed. Experiments have shown that other bees can find the target at distances up to 1,250 metres (Eibl-Eibesfeldt 1975). This is not really a language, since the bees cannot communicate anything else, but they do send information about the outside world (Passingham 1982). Dolphins can also tell each other the position of food, by some kind of acoustic signals, but the code is not yet known. We shall discuss the powers of primates later (p.42f.).

Different non-verbal channels

Facial expression

The most primitive primates, the lemurs, can produce five facial expressions, three of them accompanied by vocalizations. Monkeys like macaques have about thirteen, and chimpanzees about twenty. Signals can be directed in several ways; in primates the commonest is to face towards and look at the animal addressed. Subordinates avoid gaze to avoid interaction. Primates learn to direct signals, such as aggressive yawning, accurately at others. When a female presents to a male, she still looks round and directs her gaze at him. Primates may communicate in more than one direction, as when a female presents to a male and threatens other females simultaneously. Facial expressions have developed most in those species of monkeys which are active during the day, live in grasslands rather than in forests, in large and complex social groups. Animals which are nocturnal and live in the trees, or in small groups, have little or much less facial expression.

Facial expression has been made possible by developments of the facial muscles. More primitive mammals could only open and close their eyes, mouth, and nose. Later mammals acquired a second layer of muscles for the facial skin. This was partly due to the need for muscles round the mouth for eating and suckling. Facial mobility was also associated with a greater dependence on vision, and less use of smell, touch, and hearing. Facial expression is very important for monkeys, as shown by Izard's experiment (unpublished) on the effects of cutting the facial nerve on subsequent social relationships.

Chimpanzees have the most extensive range of facial expressions among the primates; indeed, they have more than man, having about twenty compared with the nine main ones for man. The principal chimpanzee faces are described in Table 3.1. There are also a number of variants for some of these; three bared-teeth scream faces have been distinguished, for example.

Table 3.1   *The facial expressions and vocalizations of chimpanzees*

Face	Context	Vocalization
Food		
mouth opened at each sound, lips slightly retracted to show teeth	approaching food	loud barks, shrieks, or grunts
Sex		
glare (direct gaze)	approach for copulation	—
Aggression		
waa–bark (direct gaze) mouth open	attack	barking
Affiliation		
relaxed or alert	relaxed situation in group	soft grunt or groan
playface	playfulness, social play, being tickled	'laughter', panting
hootface	excited approach, arriving in group, hearing distant group	hoot
lip-smacking	submission, reassurance, affection	teeth clicking
Submission		
bared-teeth (grimace) (with gaze aversion)	submission, fleeing	screams
grinning	fear, submission	squeaks
mouth-open, lips pushed forward	submission	pant shrieks
Parent–child		
poutface	infant trying to reach mother (stares at goal)	'ho' call
whimperface	lost or frustrated young	whimper
Distress		
cryface	frustration, sadness	'cry'

Sources: Goodall 1968; Chevalier-Skolnikoff 1973; Marler 1976

Table 3.1 is based on extensive and careful observations, for example by Goodall, of chimpanzees in the wild. Another facial expression commonly observed in monkeys is yawning, which has been interpreted as tension-reduction at the end of an aggressive or sexual episode (Redican 1982) (Plate 3.1).

In lower primates facial expressions are fairly stereotyped and automatic. In the higher primates the effects of learning and control by cortical processes become important. Experiments in which animals have been brought up in isolation have shown that both the production of facial expressions and the capacity to recognize them in others are delayed or impaired (see p.126). It has been found that female macaques acquire the same dominance status as their mothers, apparently through learning the same dominance expressions.

The expression which an animal displays is affected by its perception of the environmental setting. Electrical stimulation of brain areas which normally elicit aggression fails to do so in the presence of friends (Delgado 1967). Macaques can produce four different kinds of threat display, depending on the dominance status of the other, and chimp faces are graded similarly (Chevalier-Skolnikoff 1973).

Can we trace human facial expressions to these primate displays?

Smile. For a long time it was thought that the silent bared-teeth face or grimace was the origin of smiling, and certainly people do sometimes give a tense smile in situations of fear and submission. It now seems more likely that the playface is the true origin; the playface is also the origin of laughing, and the smile may be a lower intensity laugh. The origin of the playface itself is that this is a relaxed face, concealing the teeth, thus signifying a non-aggressive attitude (Plate 3.1).

Fearface in humans is quite similar to the bared-teeth or tense-mouth face, used in primates to show submission and to appease.

Anger is similar to two of the chimpanzee faces, the glare and the waa-bark. The origins of these faces lie partly in showing the teeth as an intention movement, partly in the face needed to make aggressive noises (Plate 3.1).

Cryface in humans is like the similar face in chimps; the *depressed* face is similar, and also resembles the ape whimperface (Chevalier-Skolnikoff 1973; Redican 1982).

Vocalization

Vocalization is used by many species of animals, and is the main channel of communication for some birds, insects, and fish. For example, a deafened turkey will kill her young since she takes them for predators on the evidence of vision alone. Sounds are produced in several different ways, by specialized organs, as in birds and porpoises, or in non-specialized ways as by insects which rub their legs together or gorillas who beat their chests. Sounds may be transmitted through air, water, solids, or by direct contact. This channel of communication has several distinctive properties:

(1) Sounds are broadcast in all directions; they go round corners, through foliage, and reach animals whether they are listening or not. They can also travel long distances; for example, whales can communicate over distances of a hundred miles.
(2) High frequency sounds reveal clearly where they come from, while low frequency sounds conceal this.
(3) Sounds fade rapidly but can be timed accurately, and so complex sequences may be sent.
(4) Sounds are heard by the sender, who can thus monitor the signals, for example when imitating another animal. Self-feedback is impossible with visual signals.

Monkeys and apes make a lot of use of vocalization. They have a repertoire varying from seven for the lemur, ten to fifteen in most species, to thirty-six for the vervet monkey. For the lower animals vocalizations are discrete, while for the higher ones they are more continuous, representing dimensions of emotion. The main vocalizations for chimpanzees are shown in Table 3.1.

Marler (1976) compared the vocalizations of chimpanzees and gorillas. Chimps use about thirteen categories of sound, gorillas sixteen, and there are clear equivalences. Groups of chimps vocalize 10–100 times per hour, mainly when separated individuals and groups renew contact, and for keeping in touch at a distance, for example reporting meat-eating. Gorillas vocalize much less often. They keep together in small groups, the sounds are mainly made by adult males, mostly belching, during feeding, grooming, and play. Chimpanzee sounds are less discrete, more continuously graded; this is common in the higher primates, especially for vocalizations used in face-to-face situations. Sounds used for sending over longer distances tend to be discrete, categorical, and also to be purer sounds than the rather coarse grunts and belches common at closer range.

Takeda (1966) described the vocalizations of Japanese macaques. One category he describes as 'conversational' – low-pitched grunts, which are very varied, often expressing interest and joy, and used when strong emotions are absent.

Several kinds of information are conveyed by sounds for primates.

Emotions and motivation

screech: distress. The open mouth and throat constricted in fear
   produce the sound
growling: anger. The mouth is not needed and is free for fighting
soft grunt: keeping in touch while moving. Little energy is needed,
   and it is sufficient for short-range communication
clicking and chittering, by young, give precise location for parents.

Information about the environment

alarm calls: barking, gives exact location and attracts attention
information about food and water: none
attracting attention, so that further visual information can be sent

Identity. Primates who live in fairly compact groups on the ground
have not developed species signals, as have those who live in the
forests and share territory with other species. However, they do
send information about gender, and about individual identity.

As with man, primates use face and voice together, except that
voice is often used when face cannot be seen, as in thick vegetation,
with infant-lost calls, alarm calls, and keeping contact in the group.
In man the auditory (verbal) message is primary, while in primates it
is subsidiary, adding emphasis, attracting attention. As we have
seen, vocal and facial signals have evolved together, sometimes one
is primary, sometimes the other. The scream, in fear, is probably due
to the open mouth and constricted throat. Laughter is probably the
result of exhaling air while smiling.

We shall illustrate sound communication from the animals for
whom it is more important – birds. Birds have highly specialized
vocal organs which are capable of emitting complex series of
sounds. These messages fall into two distinct classes – *call notes* and
song. Call notes are short and simple; there are a number of different
call notes – warning of predators, signalling between parents and
children, aggressively defending territory – which correspond to the
main motivational states. Some of these signals can be graded to
convey information – about which predator is approaching, how
close, whether on the ground or in the air. Others can be used to
indicate the location of food and nest-building materials. And, as
described above, these calls can signal the species, the social group,
and the identity of an individual. Bird-songs are longer and more
elaborate, and are used mainly by males during the mating season.

Primate warning calls contain information about the predator, whether it is a snake, eagle, or leopard, for example, possibly by indicating slightly different emotions (Passingham 1982), whereas birds can do this by imitating the predator.

The evolutionary origin of vocalizations is difficult to discover. Andrews (1963) has suggested that they are mainly a concomitant of facial expressions, combined with exhalation of air. For example, most species of mammals have a pattern of responses designed to protect the sense organs in the face from sudden, frightening stimuli; the throat is constricted, air is expelled, making a loud noise, which later develops into an alarm call. This in turn divides for some birds and some primates into different kinds of calls. In species of monkeys which make high-pitched alarm calls, the more frightened a monkey is, the further back it pulls the corners of its mouth, producing a more high-pitched scream. Another facial expression is the snarl, with bared teeth, an intention movement for attack, which becomes a threat signal; the sounds emitted with this kind of face are quite different, and themselves become threat signals.

The gap between man and monkey in the use of vocalization is, of course, immense. This is not only because monkeys lack the cognitive capacity for language, but also the vocal tracts, even of chimpanzees, are capable of producing only a very few different sounds (Passingham 1982).

Touch

Primates make a lot of use of bodily contact, mainly using the hands, as in grooming and greeting, but also nuzzling, mounting, embracing, and huddling. The most common is grooming, which is done mainly with the hands, helped by the mouth, to clean another's head, neck, or back. It is done between those in close relationships, and by subordinates, and may be reciprocal. While grooming is partly functional – cleaning the parts of the body which the owner cannot reach himself – it can be done in subtly different ways, and is clearly a social signal. The basic message is probably reassurance, bonding, or appeasement, preventing negative reactions from the other. The main effect of grooming is relaxation, reduction of tension. There is less grooming among gorillas, where there is little problem over dominance relationships, and a lot of grooming in rhesus monkeys and baboons, where there is a great deal of dominance conflict (Marler 1965).

Greetings involve a variety of forms of bodily contact – genital and stomach nuzzling, embracing, grooming, even kissing and

touching hands. Hall (1962) found that out of twelve greeting behaviours, eleven involved touch. Again it seems that the touch
involved in greeting is able to reassure; as in humans it helps with the
ritual work of establishing greater accessibility.

Presenting and mounting are frequent in the rather active sex life
of monkeys and apes, but are also used for other social purposes, e.g.
between two males. The animal presenting for copulation is either a
female or a subordinate male. Other friendly social behaviour has a
sexual element and involves some sexual arousal, for example
embracing and touching another's genitals. Chimpanzees use a lot of
these behaviours, the peaceful gorillas do not.

Some species of monkeys huddle together a lot, with maximum
bodily contact; they cling together especially when frightened.
Chimpanzees, baboons, and others do not huddle but use the other
kinds of touch described above. And mothers and infants stay in
close bodily contact, the infant often riding on top, or clinging
underneath the mother (see Figure 3.1).

Finally there is aggressive touch, mainly between males, especially
by biting and using the feet, though this may be playful – as indicated by a playface and gentle bite. The other kinds of touch carry
the message that aggressive touch will not occur.

Gaze

This is not primarily a signal but a means of receiving signals. However, the direction and manner of gaze reflect an animal's attitudes
and hence become a social signal. Facial expressions are associated
with different types and directions of gaze. In chimpanzees aggressive faces are accompanied by direct gaze, submissive faces with
aversion of gaze (Table 3.1). Exline and Yellin (1969) found that rhesus monkeys reacted aggressively to a direct stare from the experimenter, but relaxed if he averted gaze. Clearly direct gaze can be a
threat signal, gaze aversion a sign of submission. The eyes of lions
and other mammals change in appearance or colour when threatened
or aggressive, other animals show the whites of their eyes. However, gaze is also used in greeting, play, as an invitation to copulation, and in grooming, so evidently gaze can have an affiliative
meaning too, as in man, depending on the facial expression, the
situation, and the relationship. Studying the gaze pattern in a group
of monkeys can, as with spatial position, provide a key to the social
structure. Mothers and their infants keep an eye on one another, as
do mating males and females; when two animals have a close bond
between them they look at each other and keep close together. Chance

(1967) maintains that in many species there is an 'attention structure' whereby visual attention is directed to the dominant members of the group, so that subordinates can follow leaders, get out of their way, or desist from mating in response to a rapid approach movement. This mechanism, together with special vocalizations, enables members of the group to keep together in dense vegetation. Gaze also reveals the direction of attention, or the particular animal to which other signals are directed.

Another interesting parallel with human gaze phenomena was found by Thomsen (1974), who discovered that monkeys were more likely to return a gaze at 1·8 metres than at 0·6 metres.

Gestures and bodily movements

Movements of the arms and other parts of the body are combined with facial, vocal, and tactile signals to produce an overall display. For example, threat by a chimpanzee might include the elements shown on p.29.

The gestures used by chimpanzees include the following (Goodall 1968):

threat: arm raising, hitting towards other, flapping hand, shaking a branch, slapping and stamping, throwing, waving arms, running at the other.
submission: bowing, bobbing, crouching.
flight and avoidance: flight, startle reaction (duck head, hands across face), hiding, creeping away.
frustration: scratching, masturbation, rocking, shaking branches, charging, slapping, stamping, dragging, throwing, temper tantrum (leaping into air, hurling self to ground).
reassurance, greeting: see under touch.

Gestures may acquire meaning as intention movements – that is, by being the beginning of some larger sequence of behaviour – or via other mechanisms to be described later. Sometimes such gestures are made because an animal is too busy to do more, or because there are conflicting motivations. Thus an attack on another animal may be reduced to a gesture – hitting the ground, for example – because the animal cannot be bothered to do more than this. Sometimes they are used as apparently intentional social signals, as for example when an animal reassures another by touching it.

Chimpanzees can respond to pointing, and have been seen to point themselves, though they normally make little use of this signal.

Gardner and Gardner (1978) succeeded in teaching a female

chimpanzee, Washoe, some American Sign Language – 160 signs over four years, and repeated this with other young chimps. These signs are mostly analogical, e.g. a tail-wagging sign means 'dog', though others are more arbitrary. Washoe could combine several signs together, often in the right order, such as 'gimme sweet drink', 'help key in'. In most of these cases there was one of twelve 'pivot words' like 'gimme', 'please', etc. indicating the use of a simple syntax. The Gardners suggested that the level of language use was similar to that of a child of two. Washoe could take part in simple conversations such as:

Washoe: More.
Person: More what?
Washoe: Tickle.

Hewes (1973) observed that chimpanzees in the wild can point and imitate other animals; some of Washoe's signs were based on the making or using of tools, and on bodily functions like eating and drinking.

Posture

The way an animal sits, stands, or walks reflects and communicates its emotional state and its attitude to the others present. A high-status, confident animal sprawls in a relaxed posture, and struts about with its tail in the air. A subordinate animal crouches, head drawn into shoulders, and walks cautiously with tail hanging down. A depressed animal will droop, in an apathetic way, like depressed humans. Some animals use the tail for communication; confident baboons let their tails hang loosely, anxious baboons stick their tails up vertically. Other postures are used to invite grooming: the presenting position is the prelude to copulation. A gorilla leader may signal departure by standing motionless and facing the direction to be taken (Figure 3.1).

Spatial behaviour

Most species of animals occupy territory which contains adequate supplies of food, water, and nesting places. Different primate species have ranges which vary from under a square mile for gibbons and howler monkeys, to fifteen square miles for gorillas and baboons. The ranges of different species overlap, when they eat different food, but each group has its core area, which it will defend.

Most species of primates live in groups, of about 16 for gorillas,

Figure 3.1 Posture in monkeys

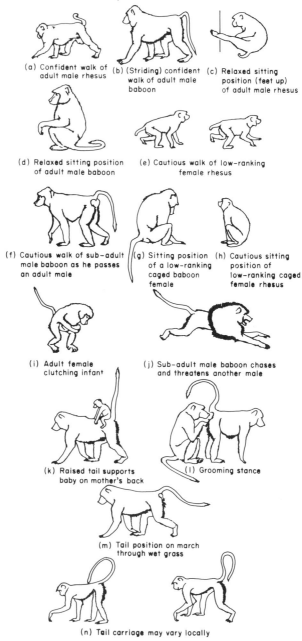

(a) Confident walk of adult male rhesus

(b) (Striding) confident walk of adult male baboon

(c) Relaxed sitting position (feet up) of adult male rhesus

(d) Relaxed sitting position of adult male baboon

(e) Cautious walk of low-ranking female rhesus

(f) Cautious walk of sub-adult male baboon as he passes an adult male

(g) Sitting position of a low-ranking caged baboon female

(h) Cautious sitting position of low-ranking caged female rhesus

(i) Adult female clutching infant

(j) Sub-adult male baboon chases and threatens another male

(k) Raised tail supports baby on mother's back

(l) Grooming stance

(m) Tail position on march through wet grass

(n) Tail carriage may vary locally

Source: Rowell 1972

and up to 185 for baboons; for chimpanzees there is no such clearly defined group. The area studied by Goodall had 60–80 in all, and they appeared in different combinations. Where a large group moves about together they adopt a characteristic spatial pattern. The dominant males, with females and their infants, are in the middle, with less dominant males around the edges, and some ahead of the group by 200–400 yards to give the alarm (Hall and DeVore 1965). When animals are separated, as is common with chimps, distant calls are used to keep contact and maintain distance. Some species, like langurs and baboons, have a 'personal space' like humans. Typical distances between two baboons vary: for example, two females sit closer than two males. Kummer (1968) interprets the spacing of baboons in terms of a balance of approach and avoidance forces – they keep to a certain degree of closeness as well as distance from one another. A more dominant male needs more space, and will only allow other animals to come to a certain distance. Approaching another animal can have different meanings depending on the other signals sent – it may be sexual, aggressive, or affiliative.

Smell and taste

Many animals have special glands which add scent to the urine or excreta, or emit liquids or gases in other ways. The same species have receptors which are often extremely sensitive and able to detect these pheromones at very low concentrations. As a signalling system the use of pheromones has certain special properties. A number of different signals can be sent in this way:

(1) Territories and trails can be marked.
(2) Repellent stimulants can lead to greater dispersal of members of the species.
(3) Other signals can lead to recruitment of more members of the group, for example among insects to co-operate over carrying a large food particle.
(4) Members of the group can be recognized, as can their sex, and sometimes their status.
(5) An alarm signal can be sent, as by some fish.
(6) Sexual availability is commonly signalled by smell, as by dogs.
(7) Information about food can be conveyed, as by bees.

These signals are nearly always discrete and stereotyped rather than continuous.

Some species of primates use chemical communication. Lemurs have special scent organs which are used to leave scent on trees, or to put scent on the tip of the tail, which is then waved in the face of another lemur. Chemical communication is used for sexual and aggressive purposes, for identification, in greetings, and for marking territory.

Appearance

An animal's bodily appearance enables others to identify its species, age, and sex, and to recognize individuals. Some species of primates have developed striking patterns of hair and skin colour, presumably to make identification easier. Changes in bodily appearance signal information about an animal's internal state. Most female primates in oestrus can be readily identified by the highly visible blue swellings in the genitalia. A female may turn the coloured area towards a male, and this acts as a releaser for sexual activity. Some fish and birds can change their colour and size under the influence of temporary emotional states. Males in a state of sexual arousal display penile erection.

Threat may be accompanied by erection of hair round the neck and shoulders, making the owner look bigger and more frightening. Some kinds of toad are able to swell themselves up to a larger size. In states of emotional arousal primates produce autonomic reactions, including raised hair, dilated nostrils, sweating, and panting. Hens increase the size of their combs, Harris's sparrows increase the size of the black bib of feathers below the beak (Krebs and Dawkins 1984).

The evolutionary origins of animal communication

Most animal signals were derived from more basic, non-communicative acts to do with eating, biting, and so on. They have been slowly shaped by natural selection to enable animals to communicate. The entire behaviour patterns of insects and other simple creatures is innate and is not dependent on environmental experience. In animals higher in the evolutionary scale learning is progressively more important, though there is still a genetic basis.

But how do certain signals come to be encoded in a particular way, and how do the recipients know what they mean? An answer can be given for the simpler forms of animal communication.

Intention movements

One way in which animal signals have meaning is when they are part of, usually the preparatory part of, a larger movement. The part comes to stand for the whole. A bird may spread its wings as a signal that it is about to depart. Bared teeth, indicating preparation to bite, become a threat display. Intention movements are perceived as standing for the whole since the rest of the pattern would be expected to follow. These signals are *iconic* or *analogical*, i.e. the signal is part of or is similar to what is referred to.

Displacement activities

Animals are often in a condition of conflict and frustration – fear of a dominant animal keeps them away from the food, or they cannot jump far enough to get it. They then often engage in behaviour which appears to be irrelevant to the main drives operating. For example, birds in an approach/avoidance conflict, motivated both to approach another bird and to fly away, fly backwards and forwards; when the conflict is high they engage in preening. Cleaning feathers or beak, drinking, or eating commonly occur in these conditions. The explanation is not agreed; it may be that when conflict inhibits the appearance of major patterns of motor behaviour, less important ones, hitherto inhibited, are allowed to appear; or it may be that a general state of arousal is produced which elicits irrelevant as well as relevant behaviour. If certain displacement activities regularly occur in some situation they can come to act as social signals. Goodall reports that chimpanzees when frustrated may scratch, yawn, groom, masturbate, rock, shake branches, slap and stamp, throw temper tantrums, or redirect their aggression elsewhere. These different acts occur in different contexts: they groom when waiting for food, scratch when worried by the presence of a high-ranking animal. If they are used as signals they are *arbitrary*, in contrast to analogical, signals, since there is no similarity between signal and referent.

Antithesis

Here a signal acquires its meaning by being the opposite of another one. For example, gaze aversion in submission is the opposite of the threatening stare. Other submissive displays, like crouching, rolling on the back, and inviting grooming can also be seen as the antithesis of threat.

Autonomic displays

Hair-erection, panting and sweating, and other bodily changes which result from heat-regulation or other autonomic activity can be perceived by other animals and thus function as social signals.

Ritualization

This is the name given to the gradual changes which take place in social signals under evolutionary pressures. It usually produces very stereotyped signals with clear meanings. A signal varying in intensity may break up into a number of discrete signals, each with a precise meaning. This is found with the different degrees of threat used by primates – intermediate intensities are rarely used, and the typical intensities vary between species.

Ritualization may make a signal more conspicuous, like the peacock's feathers used in courtship. Primates use ritualization relatively little, since they have a complex social network, and most signals do not carry constant meanings but depend on relationships. However, there are some examples of ritualized signals with precise, standard meanings. In baboons lip-smacking is derived from sucking, but has become a signal for conciliation or appeasement. The operation of selective pressure is illustrated by the shifts of warning calls among birds to conceal their presence, and on the other hand to develop mobbing calls which summon help to a particular location.

The general principles of the evolution of facial expressions were given earlier; they were derived from movements of mouth, eyes, nose, and ears. Vocalizations were originally the result of exhaling air while adopting different facial expressions.

Intentionality and deception

The clearest evidence that animals can use non-verbal displays with the intention to communicate comes from instances of deception. This has often been observed in monkeys and apes. For example, an animal pretends not to be interested in a preferred object while a dominant animal is watching, and later sneaks back for it. An animal who had been hit by the investigator kept up a limp until the latter was out of sight (Redican 1982). Lorenz (1952) gives an example of an attempt at deception:

> I had just opened the yard gate, and before I had time to shut it, the dog rushed up barking loudly. Upon recognizing me, he hesitated in a moment of acute embarrassment, then pushing past my leg raced through the open gates and across the lane where he continued to bark furiously at our neighbour's gate just as though he had been addressing an enemy in that garden from the very beginning.

4

Cultural differences in bodily communication

This is a topic of great theoretical importance. It can show which aspects of NVC are universal, and so possibly innate. Where there are cultural differences it can show to what these are due. And it can show us the range of alternative forms of NVC which different cultures have adopted. It is a topic of great practical importance, since cultural differences in NVC are a major source of friction, misunderstanding, and annoyance between cultural and national groups.

All cultures have distinctive non-verbal styles, but some are of particular interest. I shall use Japanese, Arab, and black American cultures as the main points of comparison, though Italian, African, and South American cultures will be referred to for particular topics.

Facial expression

There have been a number of carefully conducted cross-cultural studies. For example, Ekman and Friesen (1971) studied people in several cultures, including Borneo and New Guinea, who had had no contact with western culture. Stories were read illustrating six emotions, and subjects were asked to choose between three photographs of faces in each case. There was a high success rate – happiness 92 per cent, sadness 79 per cent, anger 84 per cent, disgust 81 per cent, surprise 68 per cent – but they had difficulty discriminating fear from surprise (43 per cent). The researchers also asked their subjects to pose the emotions described in the stories, and then showed photos of these poses to Americans, with the results shown in Table 4.1.

In a study of eleven cultures, Keating *et al.* (1981) found that smiling was interpreted as happiness in all of them, though the effect was weaker in Brazil (Figure 4.1). Non-smiling was seen as dominant in all cultures, except Kenya. A lowered brow was seen as dominant in most cultures, but not in the Canary Islands, Brazil, or Thailand. A raised brow was seen as happy everywhere except Thailand. It has been claimed that the rapid eyebrow flash is a universal sign

Figure 4.1   The meaning of facial expressions around the world

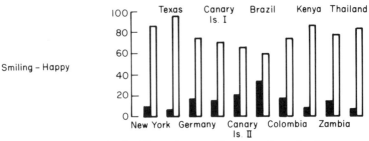

Mean proportion of models' smiling and non-smiling poses chosen by observers as happy
(Shaded bars indicate non-smiling poses; non-shaded bars indicate smiling poses)

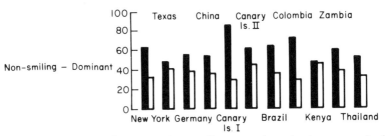

Mean proportion of models' smiling and non-smiling poses chosen by observers as dominant
(Shaded bars indicate non-smiling poses; non-shaded bars indicate smiling poses)

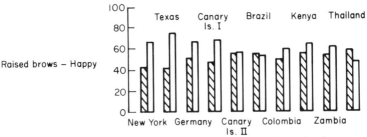

Mean proportion of models' lowered- and raised-brow poses chosen by observers as happy
(Shaded bars indicate lowered-brow poses; non-shaded bars indicate raised-brow poses

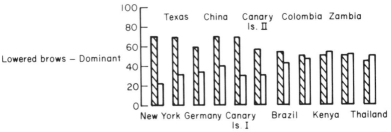

Mean proportion of models' lowered- and raised-brow poses chosen by observers as dominant
(Shaded bars indicate lowered-brow poses; non-shaded bars indicate raised-brow pos

Source: Keating *et al.* 1981

Table 4.1   *Percentage of correct judgements by US observers of New Guineans'*
intended emotions

Emotion	Percentage
happiness	73
anger	51
disgust/contempt	46
sadness	68
surprise	27
fear	18

Source: Ekman 1972

of greeting, agreeing to social contact or other friendly attention (Eibl-Eibesfeldt 1972), but it does not seem to be widely used in Britain or America.

It is evident that there are some aspects of facial expression which are universal, but that there is also variation. From the studies above it seems that there is some variation in the actual expressions used; the Keating study suggests that the brows are more variable than the mouth. Here are some examples of such variability:

Kenya: happiness by lowered brow (see above)
Thailand: unhappiness by raised brow (see above)
US blacks: anger by eye-rubbing, sucking the teeth; defiance by a limp stance (Hanna 1984)
Chinese: anger by narrowed eyes.

Seaford (1978) found an interesting regional variation within the USA, in a comparison of people who were photographed several times during an interview. He found a 'southern syndrome', of faces not observed in the north, including the pursed smile (a smile with tight lips, which may be open), tightly clamped lips, and tongue display. However, I do not believe that these are observed very often in the American south either.

More important, though, are cultural variations in 'display rules', governing when an emotional expression should be shown. A dramatic example of this was given by an experiment in which Japanese and American subjects displayed quite different expressions after watching a stressful film (p.127).

Shimoda, Argyle, and Ricci Bitti (1978) asked British, Italian, and Japanese performers to count from one to fifteen in twelve emotional styles. Judges from each culture decoded the videotapes with the success rates shown in Table 4.2:

Table 4.2   *Accuracy of decoding different expressions from different cultures*

| | Performers | | |
Judges	English	Italian	Japanese
English	63	58	38
Italian	53	62	28
Japanese	57	58	45

Source: Shimoda, Argyle, and Ricci Bitti 1978

The English and the Italians could judge their own and each other's emotions quite well, but not those of the Japanese; the latter could judge the others better than they were judged by them, but were not very good at judging Japanese emotional expression.

The Japanese have a display rule that one should not show negative emotions. The Japanese smile is used as a mask, and may express reserve or embarrassment. 'It was considered unmanly for a *samurai* to betray his emotions on his face' (Nitobe 1969, cited by Ramsey 1984). Another reason for not displaying negative emotions is that it would lead to loss of face for others.

Facial expressions may have different effects in different cultures. Alexander and Babad (1981) found that far fewer Israeli children responded by smiling to a smile from a female experimenter than did American children. Izard (1979) found that the look of contempt is dreaded most by Japanese, and induces feelings of shame.

Gesture

It is gestures which at first sight appear to vary most between different cultures. It is true that there are many gestures which are unique to particular areas, and meaningless in others. On closer inspection, however, it is found that some gestures are universal, and that others are variations within a theme.

Emblems are gestures which have a direct verbal translation, like head–nods, beckoning, and pointing. It is possible to draw up lists of highly exotic gestures of this type, such as bizarre forms of greeting found in primitive society (Figure 4.4), or the numerous hand–head or hand–face gestures used in southern Italy (Figure 4.2). Creider (in press) compared four east African cultures, Saitz and Cervenka (1972) compared the USA and Colombia. Sixty-five per cent of the

North American gestures and 73 per cent of the South American gestures were used in the four African countries as well.

The following gestures are very common, or universal:

point	halt sign
shrug	pat on back
head–nod	thumb down
clap	outline female body
beckon	tilt head with flat palm (sleep)
wave	indicate height of child with flat hand

Some of these common, or universal, gestures may be innate, such as the shrug. Others may arise as 'natural symbols', given the nature of the human body, e.g. for halting and beckoning (Kendon 1984).

Emblematic gestures may be shared within cultural areas, suggesting the effects of cultural diffusion. The six cultures above all used a head-shake for no, as in northern Europe, but this is replaced by the head-toss in Greece. Collett (in Morris *et al.* 1979) found the geographical boundary to be a small range of hills between Rome and Naples, which corresponds to the northern limit of Greek occupation in the ancient world. Darwin suggested that the origin of head-shaking was food refusal at the breast; but it is not known whether mothers hold their infants differently in different regions.

Another common gesture is flirting, by turning away, while hiding the face behind a hand, looking at the partner and giggling, often with tongue movements and eyebrow flash. This has been interpreted as a result of the conflict between approach and avoidance (Eibl-Eibesfelt 1972).

Some gestures are specific to particular regions. Morris *et al.* (1979) studied the use of twenty gestures in forty places in Europe and round the Mediterranean. Some were used only in certain areas, others had different meanings. For example, the pursed hand is rarely used in Britain, means a query in Italy, 'good' in Greece, 'slowly' in Tunisia, and 'fear' in France. The Arabs have a similar gesture: holding tips of thumb and finger of one hand pointing upwards in a pyramid and shaking the hand up and down from the wrist means that someone is beautiful, or attractive, or that something is very well done.

In some cases it can be seen how different meanings have arisen. For example the 'ring' made by thumb and finger which means 'OK' in the USA and northern Europe is perhaps based on the completion of the circle; in southern France it means worthless, based on the zero symbolism.

Sometimes the history of these gestures can be traced. For example, the V for victory sign was introduced by Winston Churchill during the Second World War. The 'horns' sign is very ancient and probably derived from bull-worship; it now means 'cuckold', or a curse, or protection against the evil eye. The 'moutza' in Greece consists of the flat hand pushed towards another person, deriving from the days when excreta would be smeared on the faces of chained prisoners in the streets (Collett 1982). Some of these local curses and obscene gestures in southern Europe have great emotional power and can invoke violence if used.

We can now see the origins of emblematic gestures. A few arise out of basic human experiences, which have become culturally standardized and ritualized – yes and no, flirting. Most are natural symbols which describe actions or people, e.g. halt and beckon. Some have ancient origins, but these are also iconic, e.g. of the bull's horns.

Gestures linked with speech, such as illustrators, also vary between cultures. In all parts of the world people use their hands and body while they speak. Efron (1941) compared the gestural styles of east European Yiddish-speaking immigrants to New York with those from southern Italy. He took films of 750 people, and observed many others, 2,810 in all. While the Italians used a lot of pictorial illustrators, the Yiddish speakers used 'ideographs', marking out the direction of thought, such as 'digging out an idea', linking one proposition to another. The gestures also have a quite different shape: the Yiddish ones involve fine hand movements, often in a vertical plane, and touching the other person; Italian gestures are from the elbow, and are more expansive (Figures 4.2 and 4.3).

Arabs use some picturesque, easy to decode illustrators: skimming the right fist with the left palm in a short horizontal motion away from the body expresses the hope for a violent end to the person under discussion. Other gestures are used for emphasis, accompanying conversation, such as moving a fist as if pounding a table.

Creider (1972) found that African languages varied in the gestural accompaniments of speech, and this was related to the languages. For the Gusii gestures mainly mark successive units of utterances, but do not add illustrations. For the Kipsigis, on the other hand, phrases are not clearly marked by vocal stress and gestures too are not closely linked to phrases.

The Italians use a lot of illustrative gestures, and they are better at conveying information in this way. Graham and the author (1975) carried out an experiment on the communication of shapes with and without hand movements. We found that hand movements improved

Figure 4.2 Some Italian gestures

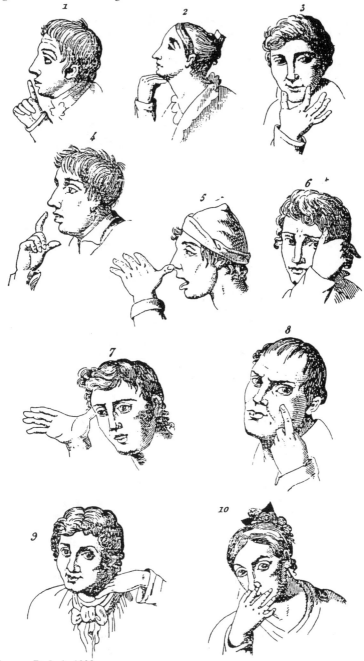

Source: De Jorio 1832

Figure 4.3 Jewish and Italian gestures in New York

JEWISH: (a) head gestures; (b) gesturing with lapel of interlocutor;
(c) gesturing with object; (d) thumb–digging movement, digging out an
idea; (e) palm on cheek or behind ear, astonishment, bewilderment,
rejection; (f) plucking beard or stroking chin in thoughtfulness,
deliberation or doubt.

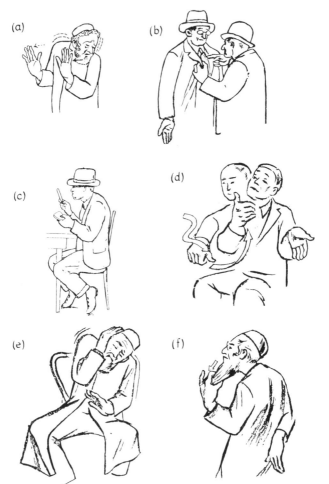

communication and that the effect was greater for Italian subjects
(see p.195f.).

Gesture languages have developed for use by the deaf, among
monks, and for other groups who cannot speak, e.g. when broadcasting. A group of aboriginals has a very elaborate gesture language
because widows are not allowed to speak for two years after the

Figure 4.3 cont.
ITALIAN: (g) 'Look out', 'You won't fool me', derisive attention;
(h) derisive attention, 'I cannot hear'; (i) good, delicious, beautiful; (j) jail,
chaingang, slave; (k) imposing silence 'I'll sew your lips together';
(l) braggadocio, arrogance; (m) bad odour, no good; (n) finished, through;
(o) jail; (p) 'You can't fool me', 'I won't swallow it', 'That man's a fool'.

Source: Efron 1941

death of their husbands (Kendon 1980). Some observers have drawn
attention to the differences between American Sign Language, British Sign Language, and others. However, it has also been observed
that there are many similarities in basic structure. Users of different
sign languages can come to understand each other fairly quickly, and
are able to establish common forms of communication (Kendon
1984).

Emotional gestures. Facial expressions for emotion are very similar in
different cultures. Is the same true of gestures? As yet little is known
about this, but it seems likely that gestures such as shaking the fist
(anger), twisting the hands together (anxiety), touching the face
(shame), showing the palm of the hand and lowering the head (submission, appeasement), yawning (boredom) may be culturally universal.

Gaze

The level of gaze varies quite a lot between cultures. Watson (1970)
studied 110 male foreign students at the University of Colorado. He

used a scoring system and obtained the results shown in Table 4.3. It can be seen that the Arabs, Latin Americans, and southern Europeans looked more than those from non-contact cultures. The numbers were small, but the differences between contact and non-contact cultural groups were significant. Other studies havé confirmed that there are higher levels of gaze for Arabs, South Americans, and Greeks. A pair of Arabs in conversation in the laboratory look at each other more than two Americans or two Englishmen. Gaze and mutual gaze are very important to Arabs, and they find it difficult to talk to someone wearing dark glasses, or when walking side by side. Not facing directly enough is regarded as impolite.

Black Americans look less than whites, both while talking and while listening, and this applies to males and females, children and adults. A meta-analysis of eleven studies found an average effect size of 0.73σ, but it was greater than this, 1.42σ, for people being interviewed (Halberstadt 1985). The low level of gaze by blacks in interviews combined with the use of very slight head-nods while listening can give the impression that they are not attending or do not understand (Erickson 1979).

The meaning of gaze can also be different. Black Americans are reluctant to look at people in authority since it is felt to communicate equality and hence disrespect (Hanna 1984). Students in south India are excited but embarrassed by a direct gaze from a member of the opposite sex; it is seen as bold but rude; there is no tradition of courtship in this region (L'Armand 1984). Since Roman times it has been believed that some people have the 'evil eye'. This is still the case in Naples, where it is ascribed to some priests, and monks, though formerly to old ladies with squints or deep-set eyes. It is believed that those who are looked at by the evil eye are cursed.

Spatial behaviour

E.T. Hall's original observation that Arabs stand closer than Americans (1959) was confirmed by Watson (1970) in his study of foreign students in the USA. Arabs also stand at a more directly facing orientation, and southern Europeans even more so. People from contact cultures stand closer, face more directly, touch and look more, and speak louder (Table 4.3).

Genuine cross-cultural studies are few, but it has been found that Indonesian students use less space than similar Australians (Noesjirwan 1978). Latin Americans on average need less space than North Americans, but there are regional variations: Costa Ricans stand closer than the Columbians or Panamanians (Shuter 1976). Within

Table 4.3   *Cultural differences in gaze, proximity, axis, touch, and voice*

	Gaze	Proximity	Axis	Touch	Voice
Contact cultures					
Arabs	1·25	3·53	2·57	6·59	3·96
Latin Americans	1·41	4·96	2·47	6·74	4·14
Southern Europeans	1·49	4·42	2·19	6·88	5·57
Non-contact cultures					
Asians	2·06	5·20	3·25	6·97	4·79
Indians–Pakistanis	2·05	3·94	3·59	6·99	4·39
Northern Europeans	2·17	5·92	3·51	7·00	4·32

Source: Watson 1970

Notes on scoring systems:

Gaze
(1) Sharp (focusing directly on the other person's eye)
(2) Clear (focusing about the other person's head and face)
(3) Peripheral (having the other person within the field of vision, but not focusing on his head or face)

Proximity
(3) Within touching distance with forearm extended
(4) Just outside this distance
(5) Within touching distance with arm extended
(6) Just outside this distance

Axis

2   3   4

Touch
(6) Accidental touching
(7) No contact

Voice
(3) Normal plus
(4) Normal
(5) Soft

the USA, hispanics stand closer than anglos. The evidence on black Americans is conflicting: most studies find that they interact at greater distances, though this may vary with the situation (Hayduk 1983). Black children stand closer than whites, but black adolescents and adults stand further away from one another; there is a strong correlation of distance with age for blacks. Blacks also adopt a less direct orientation (from meta-analyses by Halberstadt 1985). Blacks move about more when standing talking in a group, and a speaker may move away and turn his back to the group, to add emphasis.

What is the explanation of these differences in spatial behaviour? They may derive from wider aspects of the environment, such as the size of houses and the degree of crowding. Cultures develop more or less explicit rules about proper spatial behaviour. Those who stand or sit too far away are seen as cold, aloof, and withdrawn, while those who come too close are seen as embarrassingly intrusive and over-intimate.

One of the most remarkable sets of cultural rules about spatial behaviour is that governing how close the members of each Indian caste may approach one another. These rules are still kept in rural areas of southern India:

Brahmins	
Nayars	7 ft
Iravans	25 ft
Cherumans	32 ft
Nayadis	64 ft

This works additively, so that a Nayadi must not come closer to a Brahmin than 128 ft.

There are rules governing spatial behaviour for different situations in any culture. In Britain and the USA, for example, Cook (1970) found that two people sitting in a pub prefer to sit side by side, with their backs to the wall. In a restaurant or cafeteria, on the other hand, they sit opposite each other. When they are seated people adopt a considerably greater distance than when standing: 5–8 ft as opposed to 1½–3 ft.

Touch

There are great cultural differences in the amount and type of touching. Anthropologists distinguish between contact and non-contact cultures. Contact groups include the Arabs, Latin Americans, southern Europeans (Greeks, Turks), and a number of African cultures. This is illustrated by Jourard's study (1966) of the frequencies with which couples touched each other at cafes: in San Juan (Puerto Rico) they touched 180 times per hour, in Paris 110, in London 0.

Barnlund (1975) replicated an earlier study by Jourard in the USA (see p.218), and found that Japanese students reported that they had been touched on the body and legs by friends or parents far less than the American students.

It looks as if the USA is not really a non-contact culture. Goffman (1971) observed that middle-class Americans actually touched quite a lot. Nor are the Japanese non-touchers: young Japanese women touch each other often and there is a lot of touch under the influence of alcohol (Ramsey 1984). In public places in Japan there is very little bodily contact, not even hand-shaking. In crowded trains and buses, on the other hand, it is accepted and people will sleep leaning on each other. In private there is a great deal of touching, keeping warm in the winter, sleeping, and bathing together. There is less privacy than in many other cultures, but sleeping in the same room and bathing together do not have the sexual implications they have elsewhere.

The real contact areas are South America, especially Costa Rica, and the Arab countries (see Table 4.3), though it is mainly between people of the same sex, who may hold hands or have an arm around the other's shoulders. During conversation Arab males will touch each other on the upper arm with the right hand, and will slap each other's right hands at a joke. On greeting two males will hold hands loosely for some time while going through the verbal part of the greeting. Males may embrace and kiss (hands, face, or beard) after a long absence, at a wedding, or on other formal occasions. Females are not touched in public at all. There are great cultural variations in the type and extent of bodily contact during greetings (Table 4.4). American blacks also make a lot of use of touch, including some complex hand-shakes, e.g. the 'dap', 'giving skin', and the 'Black Power' hand-shake (Halberstadt 1985).

There is an important difference in the meaning of touch in some of these high-contact cultures. Bodily contact between people of the same sex is seen simply as friendly, has no sexual overtones, and there are no implications of great intimacy as in Britain or the USA. The origin of these high levels of bodily contact which has been most often suggested is frequent bodily contact between mothers and infants, but as yet there is no cross-cultural evidence to prove this.

Posture

The range of stable human postures is very large, about 1,000 according to the anthropologist Hewes (1957), who has studied the postures used in different human cultures.

Posture can be the focus of definite social rules. The Japanese recognize three levels of deference in bowing, up to 45°, and sometimes use bowing machines for instruction. Kudoh and Matsumoto (1985) asked 1,000 Japanese students to rate forty verbally described postures on sixteen scales. Three factors emerged, which were very similar to those found by Mehrabian (1972) for Americans. However, the most important factor in Japan, accounting for most variance, was a dominant–submissive factor, including postures like throwing out the chest and leaning back as opposed to shrinking the body and lowering the head. In America the friendly–hostile factor was more important, and the authors interpret this difference in terms of the concern with status and power in Japan.

Black Americans may use a limp stance and lowered head with someone in authority: this does not indicate submission, but rather that the other has been 'tuned out'.

Bodily movements

Some cultures have distinctive styles of bodily movement. For example, black Americans walk and move with energy and style, swing and swagger in a rhythmic manner, exhibiting their bodily competence and creativity. There is an ancient stereotype that blacks have rhythm, and it is generally agreed that they do indeed enjoy complex rhythms of dance, clapping, and music, though this is probably not innate (Hanna 1984).

The Japanese also enjoy rhythmic clapping, but more important is the very close synchronizing of Japanese social interaction, for example while drinking together and filling each other's cup in tea ceremonies, while pounding rice together, and in response to another's speech. These movements are very tightly codified in Noh puppet theatre (Ramsey 1984).

Lomax (1968) has compared dance and folk-song in different parts of the world, and concluded that this reflects the surrounding culture, for example in complexity and degree of social cohesion. Africa and Polynesia use synchronizing in both work and dance, while in the west there is individuality and hierarchical control in both.

Greetings vary a lot between cultures, as can be seen in Figure 4.4. Collett (1983) found a very interesting greeting among the Mossi in west Africa. In the 'poussi-poussi', used for greeting the ruler, people lie on the ground, beating their forehead in the dust, and drumming their elbows on the ground.

There are, however, a number of components which are very commonly found in human greetings:

close proximity, direct orientation
eyebrow flash
smiling
mutual gaze (twice, where a distance salutation is given, see p.222)
bodily contact (including most non-contact cultures, with the exception of India and Japan)
presenting palm of hand, either visibly or for shaking
head-toss (or head-nod, bow)

Figure 4.4 Greetings round the world

Source: Brun 1969

Vocalization

The deep voice is admired as being very masculine, perhaps as a result of western movies. It has often been observed that Americans speak in loud voices – interpreted by others as assertiveness. There is also evidence that Americans speak with a lower fundamental frequency (F_0, see p.139f.) than Germans and a lower pitch range (Scherer 1979a). Arabs speak in louder voices than in most other cultures (see Table 4.3) – seen by others as aggressive or assertive, but by themselves as 'sincere' (Adams 1957). There is less control of emotional expression generally, but especially in the voice. According to Arab tradition interactors should control their emotions, with friendly faces and moderately pitched voices. Quite often, however, they break into violent expressions of emotion, with unconcealed displays of sorrow, joy, or hostility, and men will cry and tear their clothes, or scream in public.

Ethnic groups differ in their use of pitch and stress. Gumperz (1978) found that West Indians in Britain seem rude because they do not indicate sentence endings by a rising tone, and they use sudden increases of pitch and loudness for emphasis, sounding like outbursts of bad temper. Black Americans give their utterances a rhythmic structure, and use a wide range of voice quality, sometimes quoting the speech styles of others (Akkinaso and Ajirotutu 1982).

The Japanese are restrained in this channel, as in others. They modify their vocal style according to the gender and status of the other, as in other cultures, but in a more formalized way: they distinguish eight separate tones of voice (Morsbach 1973).

Accent is a major cue to social class, especially in Britain; and the 'elaborated code' used by educated people involves clearer articulation, and more intonation. There is some evidence that it is *less* fluent and has more pauses, as would be expected from its greater complexity and need for planning (Siegman 1978). It has been said that working-class people have a more elaborated non-verbal code. In the USA, working-class teachers make more use of gesture, working-class children are more responsive to positive tones of voice (middle-class children are more responsive to verbal approval), and use different regulators (Robbins, Devoe, and Wiener 1978). It looks as if working-class children may make more use of NVC in natural situations, and are more responsive to it.

Smell

E.T. Hall (1966) maintains that Arabs make a lot of use of smell, that they deliberately breathe on each other at close quarters and smell one another's breath. However, it is not at all clear what useful information can be decoded from this source. An ingenious experiment was carried out in which subjects smelt a collection of vests, worn for seven days by themselves and others. Japanese subjects found the smells less pleasant than did German and Italian subjects (Schleidt, Hold, and Attili 1981). This could be because non-contact cultures avoid intimacy of all kinds, and the greater distance may be adopted to avoid smell (p. 250).

Appearance

In all cultures people decorate and display their bodies. Clothes are the main channel, and one of the main messages is wealth and status, shown by the quality of clothing, and the elaborate nature and expense of adornments. Status also depends on keeping up with fashion.

Clothes indicate occupational roles, and in Japan there are special uniforms for almost every occupational group, for instance students and gangsters (dark glasses), as well as for policemen. There are costumes for hiking and for striking. Company badges indicate status in the firm.

Scottish tartans, English college and club ties, T-shirts with messages are all examples of local symbolic systems of a similar kind. There are other local codes based on how clothes are worn. For example, the Ethiopian toga can be worn to indicate gaiety, sadness, pride, abasement, going to church, mourning, etc. (Messing 1960). Degrees of orthodoxy among Jews are shown by details of clothes as well as hair.

Arabs keep themselves very well covered, in contrast to the non-Arab societies of the Sudan, who go stark naked in a similar climate. Arab women in particular are subject to powerful conventions about modesty; in many areas they still stay at home most of the time, and when they appear in public are completely covered and veiled, with the face covered and only the eyes showing.

Western women adorn themselves with cosmetics and ear-rings, corsets and padding. Africans of both sexes go a lot further than this, in some tribes. Bodily decoration includes:

body-painting
tattooing
cicatrization (scarring)
nose-rings
circular plates in the lips
penis sheaths and pins

Figure 4.5   Decorating the body

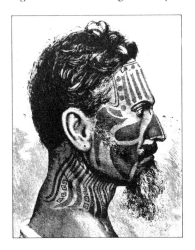

Tahitian facial tattooing

Tatooing on a native of
the Easter Islands

Source: Polhemus 1978

The extent and explanation of cultural differences

Expression of emotion

This is done in a similar way in all cultures – by face and voice. Furthermore the actual signals are very similar, especially showing pleasure by
smiling. The main difference between cultures is in the degree of
expressiveness. While Arabs, Italians, Greeks, and blacks are expressive the Japanese are not. They restrain negative emotions like sadness
and anger, while blacks show these very clearly. Presumably children
are trained to inhibit or exaggerate emotions. This in turn is due to cultural ideals, in Japan derived from samurai ideals of not showing
emotion, in Britain from the tradition of the stiff upper lip.

Interpersonal attitudes

Status and liking are communicated in generally similar ways in all cultures. The main dimension of variation is in closeness: Arabs, South Americans, and Greeks tend to stand closer, more directly facing, looking and touching more, while blacks, and to some extent the Japanese, do so less than the British or Americans. This corresponds to the distinction between contact and non-contact cultures. Contrary to the affiliative balance hypothesis, these different channels do not compensate for one another, but act as a general trait of closeness. Class differences in the USA reflect the same trait – lower-class people stand closer. Different cultures emphasize hierarchy or closeness. The Japanese signal status very clearly – by tone of voice, greeting, and by clothes. The signals for dominance are not so universal as those for emotion; most interpret a lowered brow and non-smiling as dominance, though this is not so in Africa.

Cultures emphasize different interpersonal attitudes: the Japanese and others in the east emphasize submissiveness, the Arabs assertiveness.

Supporting speech

There is considerable cultural variation in the extent of gestural accompaniment of speech. Southern Italy and South America have particularly rich vocabularies. Cultures vary in the style of gestures, for example whether they are illustrators or reflect the flow of ideas, and whether they are closely linked to verbal phases. Similarly, cultures vary in the extent of use of vocal stress, and its linkage to phrases. In each case it seems likely that the nature of the language is responsible, or perhaps we should look at the language and its non-verbal accompaniments as a single integrated system. Listening behaviour varies a lot: Japanese give very frequent head-nods, and *un's* and *ne's* (roughly, uh-huh, yes); blacks give very faint head-nods and do not look much while listening. This may explain their use of 'OK?' as an utterance ending, cueing feedback (Akkinaso and Ajirotutu 1982) like the British working-class use of 'didn't I?' (Bernstein 1959).

Self-presentation

In all cultures wealth and status are shown by clothes and bodily decoration. Group membership is displayed by local symbolic systems, e.g. ties and tartans. Bodily attractiveness is enhanced by paint and tattooing in Africa, by vigorous and skilful movement among blacks. Collett found that Arabs have a high level of self-esteem, and this is sustained by expectations of praise and affection. The inflated self-image also gives rise to boasting, exaggeration, keeping up appearances, and not telling the truth about oneself, except to close kin. Arabs are upset by signs of minor criticism or scepticism, and are at the same time suspicious of each other (Collett 1972).

Rituals

All cultures have greeting rituals, which vary widely, though with common elements. In Japan there are elaborate rules of etiquette. Gifts must be given, and returned, on a number of occasions. A typical Japanese might give and receive about twenty gifts a month, and spend a substantial part of his income on this. The gifts are not personal, but impersonal objects of known price, bought at certain shops: the whole procedure can be seen as ritualized. While this is a burdensome system, it is impossible to escape from it without being socially ostracized. It is thought to help in the maintenance of social bonds (Morsbach 1973). Much of Japanese life has a ritualistic quality, but especially formal occasions like greetings and meals. The tea ceremony expresses an ideal of social cohesion, restraint, and an aesthetic way of life (Ramsey 1984).

Meals are the occasion for ritual in most cultures. Among the Arabs there is a lot of stereotyped behaviour at meals; when offered unwanted food it is necessary to refuse three times. And of course buying and selling are conducted by an often lengthy process of bargaining.

Problems for intercultural communication

Despite the cultural similarities in NVC, the differences are sufficient to cause a great deal of misunderstanding, rejection, and even violence. Rosenthal *et al.* (1979) gave the PONS test (see p.275) to subjects from thirty cross-cultural samples. Scores varied from 173 for Canadians to 155 for New Guinea. Scores correlated with indices of modernization.

(1) *Proximity, touch, and gaze*. People from non-contact cultures find those from contact cultures disturbingly over-close, and vice versa. E.T. Hall (1966) first noticed the difficulty of establishing an agreed distance with Arabs and Latin Americans at international meetings; they appeared to chase a retreating American or European, who would back to a more suitable distance, or

rotate to establish a less directly facing position. Greeks (and probably others) are upset when coming to England because people do not stare at them in public and they feel they are being ignored.

(2) *Expressiveness*. We find the Japanese difficult because they seem to be so inscrutable, but find blacks disturbing because of their readiness to express negative emotions and attitudes.

(3) *Different meanings of gestures*. Violence may result in Greece and southern Italy from using obscene or offensive gestures, like the 'horns'.

(4) *Accompaniments of speech*. Black Americans often annoy white interviewers or supervisors by their apparent lack of response while listening.

(5) *Symbolic self-presentation*. The meaning of clothes, badges, or uniforms may be obscure, with the result that mistakes are made about another's status or occupation.

(6) *Rituals*. It is easy to cause offence through ignorance of rules or etiquette – seating guests at the wrong place at table, not bringing gifts, and so on. Pike (1967) reports the case of a missionary girl who got into difficulties with a cannibal chief because she tried to throw him on the floor (shake hands) and laughed at him (smiled). Westerners in Africa and the east often have difficulty in coming to terms with what they regard as dishonest bribery, but which is seen by locals as the customary exchange of gifts.

Awareness of these differences can certainly help intercultural contacts to go more smoothly. It is usual to make allowances for visitors from another culture, and there is often what may be described as a 'role of the visitor'. Visitors to India are not expected to wear saris or dhotis; indeed this is not approved of. Visitors to African countries, where greetings involve prostration on the floor, are not expected to do likewise. Nevertheless, small differences of NVC are a major source of annoyance and offence, can result in being regarded by other people as cold or pushy, assertive, aggressive, or simply incomprehensible and subhuman.

It is certainly possible to train people to use the NVC of another culture, and those who want to be accepted as members of that culture would do well to be trained in this way. Collett (1971) instructed a number of Englishmen in the use of some of the Arab non-verbal signals – closer proximity, more direct orientation, more looking, more smiling, and more touching. Arab subjects met a trained Englishman and a second, untrained, Englishman. The Arabs preferred the trained Englishman, would like him for a friend, and so on. The experiment was repeated with English subjects but they liked the two performers equally. An early experiment by Haines and Eachus (1965) found that subjects could be taught the non-verbal social skills of an imaginary new culture by means of role-playing with video playback. Garratt, Baxter, and Rozelle (1981) found that white American policemen shown on video interacting with blacks were liked more by black students if they stood further away, approached the other slowly, and used a low level of gaze. However, most programmes of intercultural training do rather little about NVC. Often all that people receive is some informal instruction from their expatriate colleagues abroad. The evidence in this chapter shows that NVC certainly ought to be included, and suggests the main areas where training may be needed.

5

The expression of emotion

By emotions are usually meant such states as anxiety, depression, happiness, and so on. We may also include milder states or 'moods', feelings of pleasure and displeasure, different degrees of excitement or drowsiness, and the arousal and satisfaction of hunger, sex, and other drives. In each case there are three components – a physiological state, a subjective experience, and a pattern of non-verbal signals – in face, voice, and other areas. One theory of emotion regards the subjective experience as an internal 'read-out' of the underlying state, and the expression as another read-out, for the benefit of others (Buck 1984). It is convenient to distinguish emotional states from interpersonal attitudes, though both may occur at once, for example a state of anger combined with being angry with (aggressive towards) someone. An emotional state is not in itself directed towards another person.

We saw in Chapter 3 that as apes and monkeys go about their daily affairs they emit a constant stream of signals about their inner state, mainly by facial expressions and vocalizations. Human beings do the same, though we provide much less information, as a result of controlling our expressive behaviour. Why are these non-verbal signals sent?

(1) Some are direct physiological reactions, in no sense intended to communicate. Examples are the facial expression of disgust when something nasty has been eaten, manifestations of organic states like drowsiness and excitement, and the disruption of behaviour in high degrees of arousal.

(2) Some expressive signals have been developed during evolution as social signals, which are sent spontaneously by animals and men. It is adaptive for animals to communicate, for example, a state of fear or anger. The complex evolutionary history of some of these expressions has been traced (p.46f). However, it is not clear why it should be adaptive for humans to signal emotions

like depression and anxiety – which some cultures like the Japanese try hard to inhibit.

(3) Some emotional expressions can be regarded as social signals which are sent deliberately. This is only possible because there is a repertoire of expressions with agreed meanings. However, signals in this category very often do not reflect the emotional state actually experienced. The facial expressions and tones of voice for emotions are also used for other purposes, such as accompanying speech in various ways (Chapter 7) and in rituals (Chapter 18).

The classification of emotions

The face is the most informative channel for expressing emotions, and many studies have been made of the emotions which are shown in the face. These can be classified in terms of *dimensions*: the dimensions most commonly found are pleasant–unpleasant, and level of arousal. However, facial expressions also fall into a number of discrete *types*:

happy
sad
surprise
anger
disgust/contempt
fear
interest
shame

(cf. p.121f. and Ekman 1982)

There is evidence that there are a number of other emotions which, for some reason, have been largely overlooked from the point of view of their non-verbal expression:

amusement
boredom
impatience
fatigue
pain
sexual excitement
religious feeling

However, it remains to be seen how well these states can be distinguished from the other eight.

In later chapters we will deal with the detailed ways in which face, voice, and other areas convey emotions. The main areas are these:

face: mouth, eyebrows, skin colour, facial movement
eyes: amount of opening, pupil dilation, amount of gaze
gesture: hand shape, hand movements, hands together, hands to face
posture: tense or relaxed, erectness of posture, style of bodily movements
tone of voice: pitch, speed, volume, rhythm, speech disturbances

Darwin and after

It was Darwin who started the study of emotional expression. He concluded that both in animals and men there were different expressions for different emotions, and that these had evolved from non-communicative acts, for example concerned with eating or fighting. He maintained that emotional expressions were essential to the welfare of animals living in groups, and who needed to co-operate and reproduce. He mentioned a number of ways in which emotional expression is important – enabling young infants to communicate with their mothers and obtain help from them, maintaining social interaction between mothers and infants, and others, increasing social bonds, and eliciting empathetic responses and help. Darwin also suggested that an individual's emotional expression affected his emotional state, for example regulating its level of arousal. He believed that emotional expression could be modified by experience (Darwin 1872).

All of these ideas have greatly influenced later work, and have been found to be substantially correct. However, our understanding of emotion, and the part that emotional expression plays, has been greatly extended since Darwin's time. It is now geneally agreed that there are a number of primary emotions, which are set off by different classes of external situations and which have characteristic neurochemical properties, subjective feelings, and expressions. Some psychologists think that there are eight of them as listed above. The links between stimulus and physiological response, and between the latter and expression are mainly innate. One complication is that it is the interpretation, or misinterpretation, of the stimulus which activates the emotion: Lazarus, Averill, and Opton (1970) found that an unpleasant film of circumcision among the aborigines had less effect on heart-rate and skin conductance if subjects had been told the operation was not painful.

James (1884) and Lange proposed that the experience of emotion was based on awareness of bodily states – skeletal muscle activity, including those muscles involved in facial expression, and visceral activity – heart-rate, blood pressure, and the rest. The main objection which was made to this theory was that it was believed that such bodily states were too slow and too undifferentiated to account for the variety and the speed of change of human emotions.

There is evidence in support of the visceral feedback theory: people who have had injuries to the spinal cord do not experience normal emotions. On the other hand, there is considerable evidence that facial feedback affects other aspects of emotions and it is to this theory we now turn.

One way of studying the effects of facial expression has been to ask subjects to arrange their faces muscle-by-muscle with some cover story, which does not mention 'smile' or 'frown', etc. The effect of such manipulations has been to enhance feelings of being happy, sad, angry, afraid, amused, or in pain. Another experimental method has been to ask subjects to inhibit or to exaggerate their emotional expression. Lanzetta, Cartwright-Smith, and Kleck (1976) found that subjects who were asked to inhibit their reactions to shocks reported less pain and had lower skin conductance measures than subjects who exaggerated their expression of pain. The conclusion appears to be that facial expression has some effect in regulating the intensity of emotions (Laird 1984). And it has also been found to work for anger, happiness, sadness, pain, fear, and humour. However, the effects of facial feedback are quite small, so there must be some other explanation for the link between emotional expression and experience. Furthermore some individuals do not show the effect at all – those whose emotional states are more influenced by situational cues, like placebos (Laird 1984; Leventhal and Tomarken 1986). The effect of facial feedback is to strengthen an existing emotion, not to change it into a different one (Winton 1986). However it is very interesting, and practically important, that expression can affect autonomic states.

Other kinds of bodily feedback may be relevant. It has been found that if subjects adopt a hunched and tensed posture while doing a difficult task, this produces subjective feelings of stress and of a knotted stomach (Riskind and Gotay 1982).

Schachter (1964) proposed that emotional experience depends on the combination of bodily state and perception of the situation. He found that the *same* physiological state, induced by adrenalin injections, could be experienced either as euphoria or aggression, depending on the situation. This theory has led to extensive research which has given it only partial confirmation. Drug experiments have not

consistently found heightened emotions, and often bogus physiological feedback has just as much effect. On the other hand prior
arousal, e.g. by exercise, does carry over and produces intensified
emotional response in a later situation. And it is known that distinctive physiological states underlie each emotion (Reizenstein 1983;
Leventhal and Tomarken 1986).

Waynbaum (1907), and later Zajonc (1985), proposed that facial
expressions evolved not to communicate with others, but to control
the flow of blood to different parts of the brain, and thus to affect the
temperature of those regions. However there is extensive evidence,
as we saw in Chapter 3, for the Darwinian theory that facial expression evolved for communication purposes, and we have just seen
how it serves to regulate emotions. It has also been shown that infant
facial expressions change to serve communicative needs, and serve
crucial functions for pre-verbal infants (Izard, unpub.).

We turn to the theory that emotional expression is a 'read-out' for
the benefit of other people, and subjective experience a read-out for
oneself, of the basic neurochemical activity behind the emotion
(Buck 1984). There is evidence that electrical activity in the brain can
directly influence emotional feelings, in the absence of emotional
expression. For example, electrical stimulation of the amygdala produces rage, while stimulation of the septal area produces sexual feelings (Buck 1984). However, this theory does not include the evidence
for facial feedback, nor does it do justice to the effect of the social
situation on emotional expression. Human beings do not always
display the emotional expression corresponding to their emotional
state. There are 'display rules' governing the emotions which may be
expressed, and there are often very good reasons for *not* showing
what one is feeling (p.127f.).

The physiological basis of emotional expression

The main physiological links and processes are quite clear. Consider
the face: smiling is produced by a number of facial muscles (see
p.124). Similar muscles control posture, voice pitch, and other
aspects of emotional expression. The facial muscles are operated by
the facial nerves, coming from the lower brainstem, housing programmes of emotional expression which are in turn activated by
motivational/emotional centres in the brain.

These brain centres are immediately above the midbrain and the
brainstem, but below the cerebral cortex: they are in the hypothalamus and the limbic system. We now know, from research using
electrical stimulation, that areas in the hypothalamus control general

arousal, reward and punishment systems, and more specific motivational systems such as eating and drinking. Areas in the limbic system control aggression and fear, sex and sociability, and pleasure. The limbic system is also necessary for the *expression* of emotion. The hypothalamus and the limbic system can produce dimensional variations in emotional experience, e.g. degrees of arousal, pleasant–unpleasant; they can also produce specific emotions like fear, anger, and sexual arousal (Buck 1984).

When one of these brain centres is aroused it sends neural messages via the midbrain to affect the face and other areas of emotional expression. These centres also activate the heart, blood pressure, and digestive system. This is done through the autonomic nervous system, which influences the endocrine glands, which release hormones into the bloodstream. It is these central bodily processes which are responsible for the subjective sensations of emotion, as first suggested by James and Lange.

However, emotional expression is also partly under voluntary control, and is influenced by learning. Higher centres in the cerebral cortex influence the facial and other nerves directly, making detailed facial control possible. Different parts of the body are mapped on to areas of the motor cortex for this purpose. Higher centres can also influence the midbrain to activate its emotional programmes, and to do so in connection with repeated bodily movements such as those related to walking, speaking, and breathing. This second system fails in Parkinsonism, and results in a masklike loss of facial expression (Buck 1984).

It is known that while the right hemisphere of the brain is responsible for spontaneous emotional expression, the left hemisphere, the seat of verbal processes, is more active for deliberate, posed, and learned ones. It has been found that spontaneous emotions are shown more clearly on the left side of the face (which is controlled by the right hemisphere), while posed expressions are shown better on the right side, especially for smiling (Ekman, Hager, and Friesen 1981). Generally the left side is more expressive, since many of the effects of display rules are to inhibit expression, and the right side of the face is inhibited more.

Encoding emotions

Expressing emotions is one of the main functions of bodily communication. We have just seen that there is innate anatomical and neurological equipment for doing this, though emotional expression can also be controlled voluntarily, and is affected by learning.

The evolutionary origins of facial expressions and vocalizations have been traced, and will be discussed later, as will their early development in infants, showing both the unfolding of unlearnt programmes and also the effects of socialization.

Early research on encoding used posed expressions, often with some attempt to put senders' into the moods in question. However, we know that posed expressions are slightly different from real ones – they are stronger, and facial expressions are more asymmetrical (p.125). Sometimes they are simply overacted, as when performed by children. As a result posed expressions are somewhat easier to decode than natural ones.

It is clear from decoding research, reviewed below, that the main channels for the communication of emotion are the face, body, and tone of voice, in that order. The face is the single most important area for signalling emotions, and has evolved as a social signalling area. The skin reflects physiological states directly (red for anger, white for fear); the opening of the mouth reflects aggressive intentions but also sexual ones by showing the tongue. Smiling has a more complex origin. Opening the eyes and raising the eyebrows gives better vision, while half-closing and lowering protects. Zuckerman *et al.* (1979) filmed subjects while watching an unpleasant part of *Psycho*, and other pleasant and unpleasant films, for these spontaneous displays, and also asked subjects to pose pleasant and unpleasant emotional states. Judges could distinguish the posed faces with 86 per cent success, and 76 per cent of the spontaneous ones.

Gestures, postures, and bodily movements are the second channel for emotion. Ekman and Friesen (1967) suggested that the face conveys specific emotions, the body the degree of intensity, and Graham, Ricci Bitti, and Argyle (1975) confirmed this. However, we shall later review evidence that the body can also display some more specific states (p.210f.).

Tone of voice is another important means of emotional expression. The grunts, barks, and screams of apes and monkeys are replaced in man by the tones of voice in which verbal utterances are delivered. We make far less use of emotional sounds like these grunts and screams, and do not keep up a constant signalling by this method for the benefit of those around us, but we do deliver our verbal utterances in tones of voice which indicate, among other things, our emotional state.

Are these *expressions* of emotion, or are they *communications* to others? Tone of voice scarcely applies, since people do not talk much to themselves, and babies cry less when there is no one to hear (p.127). We shall also see that people smile a lot more in the presence of others. There have been a number of studies of subjects who think they are alone in the laboratory. It is found that even if little expression is produced, facial expression when alone still has quite a good correlation with subjective emotional state. Ekman *et al.* (1980) aroused emotion by films, e.g. of animals at play, and found that activation of the zygomatic muscle correlated with feelings of happiness, and measures of negative facial muscle activation with feelings of pain and disgust.

Display rules

In the presence of others people are generally more expressive unless there are display rules to the contrary. Emotional expression is controlled by a second neural link, to the motor cortex, and by this route is influenced by social learning, and social skill strategies. People display expressions for emotions which they are not feeling. One of the main ways in which spontaneous emotional displays are modified is through the operation of *display rules*. These have been most extensively studied for facial expression, and this research is discussed on p.127f.

However, it is quite difficult to control emotional expression, and impossible to control some aspects of it, like pupil dilation and perspiration. The face is controlled best, perhaps because we look in mirrors and have a good idea what our faces look like. The voice is less well controlled, as is the body below the neck. These have been called 'leaky' areas, sinced the true emotion may leak out and be observable (Plate 5.1)

The first observation of such leakage was in a patient studied by Ekman and Friesen (1969b). Observers who saw the body part of a film of her behaviour rated her as tense, fearful, etc. whereas those who saw the head part of the film rated her as sensitive and friendly. Very brief, 'micromomentary' facial expressions are another kind of leakage: the true emotion is displayed very briefly (Haggard and Isaacs 1966). Other cases of leakage will be described in connection with the communication of attitudes to other people (Chapter 6).

There are social norms or rules about the expression of emotion for particular situations. Everyone knows the expression which they should adopt for parties, weddings, funerals, and other occasions (Argyle, Furnham, and Graham 1981). Many people in jobs where they have to deal with people have to control their expressions; this applies to nurses, doctors, and teachers, and is particularly acute for air hostesses (Hochschild 1983) and entertainers.

Plate 5.1   Trying to control emotional expression
(Argyle and Trower 1979)

Deception

Freud (1905) said, 'If his lips are silent he chatters with his fingertips; betrayal oozes out of him at every pore.' Many experiments have been carried out in which subjects are asked, for example, to answer some questions untruthfully, to describe people they like as if they did not, or to smuggle drugs through a role-played customs inspection. Zuckerman and Driver (1985) did a meta-analysis of forty-five such studies, and found that certain NV cues were significantly different overall when people were lying. They divided up studies by the level of motivation of the subjects. 'High motivation' was when subjects were promised a monetary reward for succeeding in deception, or if it was described as a test of some skill (see Table 5.1).

The NV cues which show that highly motivated people are lying are pupil dilation, raised pitch, and speech hesitations; and they have shorter utterances. They over-control other cues compared with less motivated liars – they blink, gaze, and move head and body *less*,

Table 5.1 *Behaviours associated with deception by level of motivation*

Behaviour	Low motivation N	Mean d	High motivation N	Mean d	Z of difference
Visual					
pupil dilation	2	1·65★★★	1	1·52★★	1.31
gaze	12	0·13	6	0·33	2·33★
blinking	6	0·85★★★	2	0.57★★	4·60★★★
smiling	10	0·14★	9	0·02	1.65
facial segmentation	5	0·27★	—	—	—
head movements	5	0·16	5	0·52★★	3.01★★
gestures	6	0·09	6	0·32	1·03
shrugs	3	0·14	1	1·10★	0·71
adaptors	7	0·49★★★	7	0·19	1·55
foot and leg movements	4	0·01	5	0·06	0·10
postural shifts	5	0·22	6	0·24★	2·51★
bodily segmentation	3	0·83★★	—	—	—
Paralanguage					
latency	8	0·05	7	0·00	0·20
response length	7	0·07	10	0·36★★★	2·92★★
speech rate	5	0·35	7	0·38★★★	3·03★★
speech errors	4	0·40	8	0·15	0·24
speech hesitations	6	0·55★	5	0·52★★★	0·63
pitch	2	0·08	2	1·27★★	1·99★
Verbal					
negative statements	3	0·34	2	1·88★★★	3·50★★★
irrelevant information	5	0·42	1	0·28	0·60
self-references	3	0·22	1	0·44	1·13
immediacy	2	0·77★★★	—	—	—
levelling	2	0·29	2	0·60★	1·28
General					
discrepancy	4	0·64★★★	—	—	—

Source: Zuckerman and Driver 1985

Notes: Positive values indicate that an increase in the behaviour was associated with deception.
★ *p* <0·05 ★★*p* <0·01 ★★★*p* <0·001
d is the overall ratio of the difference between means to the standard deviation.
bodily (and facial) segmentation is the number of units or segments in the stream of behaviour as identified by naïve judges.
immediacy is frequency of direct verbal statements.
levelling is frequency of overgeneralized statements, e.g. using 'all', 'everybody'.

and speak slower. There is also a certain amount of verbal leakage, for example, more use of negative statements.

Do observers use the same dues for judging that deception is taking place? An earlier meta-analysis by Zuckerman, De Paulo, and Rosenthal (1981) found that the following cues were used, in the order of size of effects:

latency
gaze aversion
more postural shifts
unfilled pauses
reduced smiling
slower speech
raised pitch
speech errors

There is quite a mismatch between the cues used for detecting deception and the cues which really accompany it. Advice to would-be detectors of deception is given in Table 5.2.

Table 5.2   *Cues for lying correctly and incorrectly used by decoders*

Correctly used	Incorrectly used	Overlooked
slower speech	latency	pupil dilation
raised pitch	gaze aversion (n.s.)	reduced blinking
speech hesitation	speech errors	fewer head movements
	postural shifts (actually a reversal here)	shorter utterances (negative statements)
	less smiling	

Ekman (1985) has observed a number of more subtle cues to deception. The face may show micromomentary expressions, under ¼ second long, which are often unnoticed but which people can learn to see with an hour's training. The face may also show 'squelched' expressions, for example when a smile is used to cover a different expression. There may be leakage in the face, such as blushing, partly controlled expressions are more asymmetrical and not well synchronized with the body, and false smiles are different from real ones in that the upper face is not affected and they end too abruptly. Ekman has also seen leakage in hand movements, for example in the use of emblems which are only partly displayed, and not in the normal presentation position.

In fact judges are not very good at detecting deception. Thus Kraut and Poe (1980), in a role-played smuggling through customs experiment, found that both real and amateur customs inspectors were quite unable to detect the smugglers. The cues which they used were lower-class and scruffy appearance, gaze aversion, nervousness, postural shifting, and hesitation before replying.

Decoding emotions

Accuracy of decoding

If photographs of faces posing the main emotions are presented, observers can correctly identify 60 per cent or more correctly. The actual percentage depends on how long the slides are exposed for – in Ekman's BART test the exposure is 1/60 second to make it more difficult (p.27f.). Posed expressions are easier to decode than spontaneous ones, and exaggerated posed expressions are easiest of all, both for face and voice (Zuckerman, De Paulo, and Rosenthal 1981). Posed expressions are less affected by inhibiting display rules. Posed facial expressions are also less symmetrical, as we shall see (p.125). Accuracy of decoding of bodily cues can be found by showing silent videotapes, with the face screened off. Accuracy for tone of voice can be found by encoders reading neutral passages in different emotional styles. Verbal contents can be removed if random splicing or a band-pass filter are used. The usual way of comparing channels is to obtain judgements for each separately, and see how each predicts to judgements of the whole message.

How accurate is decoding under normal spontaneous conditions? We saw that in Zuckerman et al.'s (1979) study, spontaneous reactions to pleasant and unpleasant films could be distinguished with 76 per cent accuracy, but this is not a very difficult discrimination. We shall describe later some experiments in which different spontaneous facial expressions were decoded with success rates which varied from 48 per cent for happiness to chance levels for surprise, sadness, and fear (p.134). On the other hand people are more expressive in social situations.

Which channel conveys the most information? Mehrabian (1972) found that facial expression carried more than tone of voice and that both carried more information about positive attitudes than verbal contents (p.91). O'Sullivan, Ekman, Friesen, and Scherer (1985) made videotapes of people when they were being interviewed about pleasant and unpleasant films. Judgements of video with sound and vision correlated with judgements of the components as follows:

	Verbal contents	Facial expression	Body	Tone of voice
felt pleasant	0·09	0·45	0·41	0·10
calm–agitated	0·18	0·29	0·54	0·02

In the research on the PONS test (p.275), Rosenthal and De Paulo (1979) found the following accuracy scores for the different channels (in ratios to standard deviations);

Facial expression	Body	Tone of voice
3·88	2·82	1·82

These studies all tell the same story: face carries most information about emotion, followed by body, followed by tone of voice.

There is another important difference between these channels, that the face is the best controlled, while voice and body are leakier (Zuckerman *et al.* 1982). There are individual differences in the weights given to these channels by decoders: in particular, women attend more than men to faces, men attend more than women to voice and body (p.281f.). However, some emotions are shown more clearly by particular channels. The face shows happiness best, followed by anger. The voice communicates sadness and fear best and happiness worst (Apple and Hecht 1982; Davitz 1964).

Bodily signals also produce bodily reactions. Lanzetta and Orr (1986) found that seeing fear faces increases skin conductance scores more than happy faces, in the absence of any threat, and can be regarded as 'prepared stimuli', as a general danger cue. Research on monkeys and infants shows that happy faces have a probably innate rewarding effect. McHugo (1985) showed eight videos of speeches by President Reagan. Different extracts produced different effects on skin resistance, facial muscles, heart–rate, and subjective emotions. Subjects smiled during happiness/reassurance displays, and frowned during anger, threat, or fear. These effects were also found for silent displays, especially for happiness/ reassurance, and were stronger for viewers with positive attitudes towards Reagan.

Emotions are recognized from a whole pattern of non-verbal signals, which are usually consistent with each other and also with the expectations created by the context, so that the task of the judge is easier than in these experiments. Bodily postures, gestures, and movements are less informative about emotions than the face. However they do provide information about intensity, about the tense *v.* relaxed dimension (Ekman and Friesen 1967). Gestures can sometimes be informative, for example clenching the fists (anger), and twisting the fingers together (anxiety).

Verbal and non-verbal information

This issue has been most extensively investigated in connection with the perception of interpersonal attitudes, and will be discussed in Chapter 6. We gave above the results of experiments by Mehrabian and by O'Sullivan *et al.*, which found by quite different methods that NV cues had far more impact than verbal ones for emotion. Walker (1977) used a similar technique to Argyle, Alkema, and Gilmour in 1972 (see p.91), and made videotapes with six degrees of confidence in both script and emotional expression. The NV cues accounted for ten times as much variance as the verbal cues. There have, however, been other findings on this topic. Whenever experimentally manipulated verbal and non-verbal cues are used the same result is found, but conflicting signals may generate an unusual style of decoding. When the separation of channels method is used, the same result is found if scales for emotion are used (as by O'Sullivan *et al.*), but not with semantic differential scales (Krauss *et al.* 1981).

However, there is also evidence that negative signals, from any channel, are weighted more than positive ones, probably because they are more likely to be genuine. What happens in the case of inconsistent signals is that one signal is discounted or reinterpreted, rather than that the two are averaged. The most common reason for such conflicting signals is a partly successful attempt to conceal an emotion. If an observer notices them he places more weight on the signals for negative emotions, which are more likely to be concealed, and perhaps on the less well-controlled signalling areas – hands, feet, skin, etc. When verbal and non-verbal signals are in conflict, more attention is paid to the non-verbal component, as is the case with interpersonal attitudes.

Decoders of emotional states in others also make use of situational cues. If another's emotional expression and the nature of the situation conflict, observers have a problem to solve. How they do it is discussed later in connection with facial expression (p.134).

6

Interpersonal attitudes

Animals find mates, rear their children, make friends, frighten off their enemies, establish dominance hierarchies, and co-operate in groups, entirely by means of bodily signals. The human race has developed language, but it is used primarily for communicating information about other persons, objects, and ideas, rather than about the feelings of one person towards his listener. Broadly speaking, NVC is used for one and language for the other. Animals developed special organs for sending and receiving bodily signals for establishing interpersonal relations, and man has inherited 'these organs. We shall describe below experiments which show that non-verbal signals have a much greater impact than equivalent verbal signals in communicating attitudes to other people. Though there is some cultural variation in the form of the bodily signals used, they are very similar in all cultures. The NV signals used here are partly innate, similar to those used by animals, and culturally universal, and partly the results of socialization experiences.

Attitudes to other people are rather similar to emotions, and may involve exactly the same signals. Being angry is an emotion, being angry with or hostile towards someone is an interpersonal attitude. Being happy or in a good mood is an emotion, liking people is an attitude, but they have very similar facial expressions. Dominant or submissive attitudes, on the other hand, involve quite different signals from the usual list of emotions: like emotions all these attitudes have three components – an underlying physiological state, subjective experience, and behaviour, especially NVC.

As with emotions, there are spontaneous and managed aspects of them. Liking and disliking are generally spontaneous, though the expression of disliking is usually restrained by social rules. Sexual attraction is spontaneous, and includes involuntary physiological arousal, though here too its expression often has to be restrained. Dominance cues, on the other hand, are very often managed, as people try to influence one another (Patterson 1983). However, in the generation of social behaviour there is a hierarchy of control, with deliberate, fully conscious plans at the top, and involuntary means of carrying them out, by smaller units of behaviour, at the bottom, with no sharp division between them (Argyle 1983).

Sometimes people are trying to establish some relationship with another person, or to change the relationship. In this case there is a motivational state – affiliation, dominance, or sexual. Making friends, for example, entails the skilled use of both verbal and non-verbal signals, though we shall see that the NV ones have more influence. Skilled use of NVC here requires the careful sending of appropriate NV signals (not too strong, for instance), and careful monitoring of their effect on the other, as described by the social skill model (Argyle 1983, and p.109). In an established relationship the only motivation involved is perhaps to maintain it. What people do is express the state of the relationship whenever they interact, by appropriate signs of closeness, submission, etc.

Factor analysis of social behaviour (verbal and non-verbal) has consistently generated two main dimensions – friendly *v*. hostile and dominant *v*. submissive (Foa 1961). The analysis of NVC alone produces a strong friendly–hostile, or affiliative factor together with dominance and other factors (Mehrabian 1972; Wish 1979). There can be combinations of these two dimensions, and the combination of friendly and dominant is particularly important for some social skills.

In addition to these broad dimensions, there are more specialized interpersonal attitudes such as sexual attraction, at different stages from courtship to marriage, and relations between parents and

Figure 6.1   The two dimensions of attitudes towards others

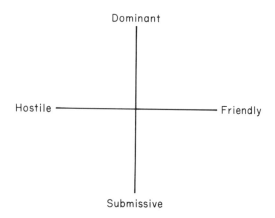

children of different ages. These attitudes can to some extent be mapped on to the two dimensions above. Sexual attraction is similar to affiliation, except that some extra signals are used – in particular pupil dilation, a higher level of mutual gaze, and touch.

In some cases the evolutionary history of a signal can be traced. We have seen how the smile developed from the playface in monkeys. Bodily contact may derive from grooming, one of the main kinds of primate affiliative behaviour. Gaze, on the other hand, is used rather differently by humans and animals: in humans gaze is used to signal interest, attention, and liking, rather than hostility or aggression. Some of these signals are found in infants, and are the same in all cultures, so are probably innate, as in the case of the eye-brow flash. Blurton-Jones and Leach (1972) and others have found that children between one and two use a number of interpersonal gestures: they wave to indicate that they want to be with their mothers, they raise their arms if they want to be carried, they suck their thumbs when separated from their mothers. Infants also cry when separated from their mothers, laugh when engaged in vigorous play with other children, smile when approaching another person, frown when attacking another child. The expression of inter-personal attitudes is affected by culture and socialization, and especially by social rules.

All social behaviour is governed by rules, specifying the behaviour which is appropriate in different relationships and situations. It is a rule of nearly all relationships that participants should be pleasant to others (otherwise they may leave the situation). In most working and professional relationship the rule is for a professional friendly attitude to be expressed, together with appropriate status relations (Argyle and Henderson 1985). There are cultural variations in these rules, particularly about the expression of intimate relationships in public – whether kissing is permitted, for example. In the Arab cultures of the Middle East such heterosexual behaviour is not allowed in public.

The methods for studying attitude communication are similar to those for emotion. Mehrabian (1972) used a role-play method with a hat-rack and Cook (1970) asked people to indicate on a series of plans how they would sit, and at what angle, in a variety of social encounters. Encoding of actual attitudes can be studied by generating them in the laboratory: subjects meet confederates who are very attractive and agreeable, or otherwise, for example (e.g. Exline and Winters 1966); or pairs of people in different established relation-ships are observed. Much of the research on this topic has used total strangers, who initially have no attitudes to one another, and as we shall see some of these experiments have obtained confusing results, which are difficult to interpret. Decoding is studied in the usual way by preparing videotapes with different NV cues or combinations of cues on them.

Affiliation, or liking

The most important dimension of attitudes to other people is how much they are liked or disliked, and how much intimacy is desired with them.

Encoding

We shall describe the use of the different bodily signals in later chapters, but the main points can be summarized here. The main signals for liking are:

proximity: closer; forward lean if seated
orientation: more direct, but side by side for some situations
gaze: more gaze and mutual gaze
facial expression: more smiling
gestures: head–nods, lively movements
posture: open with arms stretched towards other *v*. arms on hips or folded
touch: more touch in an appropriate manner
tone of voice: higher pitch, upward pitch contour, pure tone, etc.
verbal contents: more self-disclosure

These cues are all used together, to give a total impression of friendliness. Maxwell, Cook, and Burr (1985) found that when subjects liked another subject whom they met in the laboratory this was encoded as: a high level of gaze, movements synchronized with speech, an expressive face, lively tone and pitch, active bodily movement and gesture, and self-disclosure. These gave a multiple regression correlation with liking of 0·54.

When are these cues used? In a group of monkeys the degrees of closeness between all the members, and the various subgroupings, can be seen at a glance by the spatial arrangements, up to bodily contact; the animals are not deliberately sending signals or trying to manipulate one another. Human beings often act in the same way: for example, people at work choose whom to sit with during coffee or lunch. For a lot of the time work or other activities take precedence, and few social signals are sent. Husband and wife are not constantly exchanging signs of affection, though they do so some of the time.

In contacts between strangers, or during the early stages of a relationship, the first impressions of another are usually formed from their appearance, how attractive they are, and also the evidence of their personality, social class, and other properties. At such early meetings individuals often 'package' themselves carefully, paying great attention to self-presentation. If first impressions of the other are favourable, a closer relationship may be sought, by sending positive NV signals and trying to elicit similar ones in return (Argyle and Henderson 1985). Positive signals may also be sent as communications to others indicating that a couple are linked; these 'tie-signs' include gaze, orientation, distance and touch (Fine, Stitt, and Finch 1984).

The role of motivation can be studied by comparing people with contrasting strengths of motivation. McAdams, Jackson, and Kirschmit (1984) found that those strong in intimacy motivation (assessed on the TAT), smiled and laughed more, and gazed more at the other. Similar differences are found between extroverts and introverts, and we shall see that there is a general dimension of social approach, correlating with affiliative needs and extroversion: those scoring high look more, smile more, stand nearer, and use more of all the affiliative signals. Mental patients, on the other hand, produce lower levels of them (Chapter 17).

As with emotions, there are cultural rules about the display of attitudes to others. The most obvious one is that there are restraints on the expression of negative attitudes in most situations, especially in middle-class circles. At primarily social occasions, like parties, there is a generally agreed rule that only positive attitudes should be expressed (Argyle *et al.* 1979). We shall see later that negative attitudes are, as a result, quite difficult to decode. Concealing negative attitudes to other people is a common source of untruthfulness. Usually it is the words which are untruthful, but non-verbal leakage may betray the true attitude, especially in the less well-controlled channels, like voice and body. Weitz (1972) found a very interesting example of this in the expression of attitudes towards blacks by white American students (p.146).

The use of NV signals for expressing positive attitudes is an important social skill. Those people who say that they are lonely, or who are rated by others as socially unskilled, are found in laboratory encounters to look, smile, and gesture less than other people (Trower

1980). This may be interpreted as a failure to show that they like others, or more generally as a lack of rewardingness. Burgoon (1984) studied the NV behaviour of individuals who scored high on a self-report scale of 'reticence'. They looked less, smiled less, used fewer head-nods, touched themselves more, protected their bodies more, and were rated as more tense than other people. Social skills training for lonely or unskilled individuals commonly includes training in sending such positive NV signals (p.264). It should be mentioned that another cause of loneliness is insufficient self-disclosure (Argyle and Henderson 1985).

Decoding

We have seen that throughout the animal kingdom there are innate non-verbal signals for intimacy and other interpersonal attitudes. Birds respond to various call notes from birth, and infant non-human primates respond to facial expression, gaze, and touch (Chapter 3). Human infants, at a very early age, respond to faces and to female voices, and are distressed by other children crying (p.131f.). However, in monkeys the development of decoding is delayed if they are reared in isolation; evidently social learning is needed. Bugental, Kaswan, and Love (1970) presented conflicting messages to children; if a female smiled while giving a verbally or vocally negative message, this was interpreted more negatively by children than by adults. Children are wise to distrust female smiles, since women smile even more at them when delivering negative verbal messages (Bugental, Love, and Gianetto 1971).

The individual NV channels which are used to encode intimacy are decoded in the same way. Judges in the study by Maxwell, Cook, and Burr (1985) used the same cues to decode liking that had been used to encode, with one exception – relaxation was taken as a cue by decoders but had not been used by encoders. Burgoon *et al.* (1984) asked judges to rate pairs of NVC samples, and found that a person was rated more 'intimate' if he looked more, touched, smiled, came closer, and leaned forward, in that order. However this works only up to a point: there is a normal and comfortable range for each of these variables, and a person who comes too close, or gazes too much, produces increased physiological arousal and is liked less (p.94).

In the experiment by Maxwell *et al.*, tone of voice conveyed no information at all to judges, while ratings from video alone correlated 0·33 with actual liking. Touch, though more rarely used, is a powerful cue producing strong feelings of liking or disliking under different conditions (p.217f.).

Mehrabian (1972) carried out an experiment in which the relative effects of facial expression, tone of voice, and contents of speech were compared. The separate cues were initially equated for strength, as in our experiment described below: tone of voice was studied by means of a band-pass filter which makes the verbal contents unintelligible. The results were that ratings of positive attitude (liking) = 0·07 (verbal content) + 0·38 (tone of voice) + 0·55 (facial expression). In other words both of the non-verbal signals had much more effect than verbal content, and facial expression had more effect than tone of voice.

The author and colleagues (Argyle, Alkema, and Gilmour 1972) carried out a series of experiments in which verbal and non-verbal signals for friendly–hostile and dominant–submissive were compared. In the friendly–hostile experiments, three complete NV styles were constructed as follows:

friendly: warm, soft tone of voice, open smile, relaxed posture
neutral: expressionless voice, blank face
hostile: harsh voice, frown with teeth showing, tense posture

Three styles were displayed by performers seen on videotape counting from one to fifteen, to eliminate the verbal contents. These three performances were shown to a number of judges and rated on seven-point scales like:

hostile —   —   —   —   —   —   — friendly
          A   B   C

The performances were modified so that they were judged as being approximately at A, B, and C in these scales. Similar work was carried out to develop three verbal messages, with almost identical ratings, when the typed versions were judged. These messages were as follows:

Friendly. 'I enjoy meeting the subjects who take part in these experiments and find I usually get on well with them. I hope you will be able to stay on afterwards to have a chat about the experiment. In fact, the people who came as subjects in the past always seemed to be very pleasant.'

Neutral. 'I don't really mind meeting the subjects who take part in these experiments. Some of them are fairly nice. Others of course are rather tedious. You can come along afterwards and talk about the experiment if you like, but please don't stay too long. On the whole, I don't have very strong feelings about people who come as subjects in experiments.'

Hostile. 'I don't much enjoy meeting the subjects who take part in these experiments. I often find them rather boring and difficult to deal with. Please don't hang around too long afterwards and talk about the experiments. Some people who come as subjects are really rather disagreeable.'

In the experiment proper the NV and verbal signals were combined in all nine combinations, e.g. friendly (NV), neutral (V), etc. The performers spoke the verbal message in the NV styles. These performances were then rated by fresh subjects. Statistical analysis showed that the NV cues had about five times the effect of the verbal ones on the final ratings. When the two were in conflict the verbal message was largely ignored (Figure 6.2).

Figure 6.2   The effects of verbal and non-verbal signals on perceived attitudes towards others

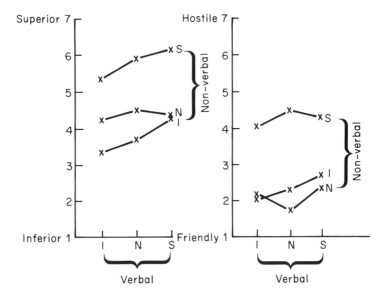

Source: Argyle 1969

These results have been confirmed using more realistic materials taken from soap opera (Trimboli 1984). However, the communication of the contents of speech certainly depends most on the verbal channel, while the communication of attitudes is mainly non-verbal (Friedman 1978).

How accurately are interpersonal attitudes perceived, and can people see through deceptive signals? Tagiuri (1958) found that members of groups could tell quite accurately who accepted them – only 4 per cent of choices were seen as rejections. However, they saw 9 per cent of rejections as acceptances. Rejection is not perceived accurately because it is often concealed and misleading signals are sent. The correct attitude can be perceived only through study of the less obvious and less well-controlled cues, as in the case of negative emotions.

Ingratiation is another interesting case. Ingratiation consists of the use of flattery, agreement, and other interpersonal rewards, verbal or non-verbal, in a misleading way, to induce another person to grant some favour. Lefebvre (1975), at Leuven, found that bodily signals like smiling and gazing are used by ingratiators, but that target persons do not realize that these signals are deceptive and strategic. Experiments by E.E. Jones (1964) have shown that rather subtle verbal forms of ingratiation are used – otherwise the strategy would not work.

Other studies have found that people do not like inconsistent messages where verbal and non-verbal signals are in conflict, and find them insincere, though also funny (Mehrabian 1972). However, it is not only a matter of one channel being weighted more than another; people make an effort to interpret the combined message. We saw how children distrust smiling female faces accompanied by a negative message; they also interpret a message as negative if either the verbal or vocal channel is negative. Bugental (1974) presented several combinations of cues, for example:

visual (+)	vocal (–)	verbal (–)	(joking)
visual (+)	vocal (–)	verbal (+)	(sarcastic)
visual (–)	vocal (–)	verbal (–)	(angry)

All these three kinds of messages were seen as equally negative. In a study with adult decoders it was found that the vocal channel dominated the verbal if a 'high credibility' voice was used (spontaneous and unpolished delivery) but not with a low credibility voice (slow and polished delivery).

Reactions to intimacy signals: equilibrium theory

Two people settle down to a level of intimacy which is expressed by their proximity, level of gaze, degree of self-disclosure, and the other cues for liking and intimacy.

Argyle and Dean (1965) found that in a given situation people seek a certain degree of proximity, lean forward or back to attain it, and feel uncomfortable if they cannot. We proposed that this is the result of a balancing of forces to approach and withdraw: people are attracted to others (as the result of past rewards) and also repelled (as the result of past punishment). Other experiments have shown that such forces fall off with distance, but that the avoidance forces decline faster, so that an equilibrium is found at the point where the lines cross (Figure 6.3).

Figure 6.3   Approach–avoidance conflicts

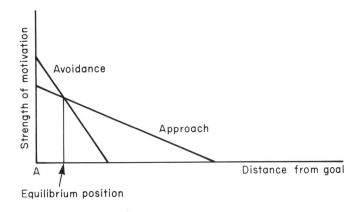

Source: Argyle 1983

If one person likes another, the approach forces will be stronger and the avoidance forces weaker, resulting in greater proximity.

It also follows from the model that if a person comes too close this will arouse stronger avoidance forces than approach, so that the other will be disturbed and back away. Support has been obtained for the existence of an approach–avoidance equilibrium in an experiment by Peery and Crane (1980). An adult experimenter sat at different distances from children aged four, and made a series of approaches and withdrawals. When E approached, the child usually withdrew, when E withdrew the child approached. However, there were more child withdrawals at a starting distance of 1 ft, more approaches at a starting distance of 3 ft.

Argyle and Dean suggested further that disturbed equilibrium can be compensated for by the use of other signals for intimacy; they found that greater distance led to more use of gaze (Figure 6.4).

Many experiments have been carried out to discover whether compensation like this occurs under different conditions. It is found that it happens in the following cases:

Behaviour by A	Reactions by B
proximity	proximity orientation lean amount of talk
gaze	proximity orientation
question intimacy	gaze self-disclosure

This means, for example, that increased proximity by A leads to reduced proximity by B, less direct orientation, leaning away, or less talk. I have included some variables relating to verbal contents, since they have been studied from this point of view (Capella 1981; Patterson 1973).

Compensation does not always take place, however. Rosenfeld (1967) found that smiles and head-nods were reciprocated by interviewees, and a number of other studies have found that under some conditions it is reciprocity rather than compensation which occurs. The clearest case of reciprocity is that verbal self-disclosure is reciprocated; this may be a special case since verbal disclosure changes the topic of conversation, and quite different principles may be involved.

Various theories have been put forward to incorporate both non-verbal compensation and reciprocity. Patterson (1976) has extended the theory to allow for this, proposing that a move towards greater intimacy leads to increased arousal in the target person: if the move is interpreted as a pleasant event (e.g. friendly) there will be reciprocity, whereas if it is interpreted as unpleasant (e.g. embarrassing) there will be withdrawal. In other words, equilibrium is being maintained.

Other versions of this theory suggest that cognitive appraisal of rule-breaking or disconfirming expectations come first and this produces arousal. However, a number of experiments which have been carefully designed to test these models have failed to produce clear support for any of them (Patterson 1984). The reason may be that they have been conducted under artificial laboratory conditions, where all manner of uncontrolled and unknown interpretations of experimental conditions are liable to be made by subjects.

Figure 6.4   Gaze and distance

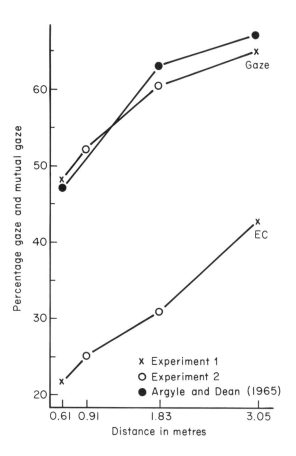

Source: Argyle and Ingham 1972

It does appear, however, that reciprocity is more common in the early stages of meetings between strangers, before a high level of intimacy has been established. If the other person gives the impression of being friendly then reciprocity will occur (as Patterson's theory suggests), but only up to a point, after which compensation will take place. The precise point at which an individual will start to compensate depends on his own preferences, e.g. for proximity, and on social norms for the situation.

A further complication is that NV signals serve other functions besides expressing intimacy. Gaze, in particular, is needed to collect information about the other: Mehrabian (1972) found that males had a high level of gaze when faced with a hostile male.

Compensation requires a choice of which intimacy variable to alter – whether to move away, look less, etc. Patterson (1983) suggests that the 'dynamic' features will be changed first, i.e. gaze, facial expression, or topic of conversation, as opposed to spatial behaviour or posture. It also makes a difference whether the interactors are sitting or standing; in the latter case they can move away or change orientation quite easily.

Dominance

Encoding

There are two different issues here. There are NV signals emitted by people who are trying to establish a position of dominance, in a group of people who are initially equal. And there are the NV cues which express dominance and submission in an established hierarchy, where there are differences of power or status. Some of the signals used in these two cases are different.

Again detailed discussion of particular channels can be found in later chapters, but here are the main signals for dominance:

spatial position: height, e.g. on a raised platform, or standing (though sitting is a sign of status on some formal occasions); facing a group; taking up more space

gaze: in an established hierarchy, less gaze, but relatively more looking while talking; when trying to establish dominance, *more* gaze and staring other down

face: non-smiling, frowning; face with mature adult features

touch: asymmetrical touching of other

voice: loud, low pitch, greater pitch range, slow (*v*. high-pitched, rising pitch contours), low resonance, more interruptions, small latency, more talk

gestures: pointing at other, or his property

posture: full height, hands on hips, expand chest; in established hierarchy – relaxation

In an established hierarchy this pattern is used all the time between individuals of different status. Leffler, Gillespie, and Conaty (1982) carried out an experiment in which subjects role-played being teacher or pupil. When playing the part of the teacher they took up more space, touched, pointed to the other, talked and interrupted more. In a similar experiment, Remland (1984) found that in a supervisor role

Plate 6.1 Dominance postures (Kobal Collection)

subjects leaned back, hands behind head, used little gaze and a loud voice; in the subordinate role they looked more, leaned forwards, and had a soft voice. Bugental, Henker, and Whalen (1976) found that adult trainee counsellors, during free interaction, were more assertive in the vocal than the verbal channel if they were high on internal control, suggesting leakage of their anticipated dominance. As the summary above shows, when people are trying to establish a dominant relationship they use some of the same signals, but also some different ones. In particular they gaze more, trying to stare the other down, and adopt a more erect and less relaxed posture. It seems to be quite normal for people who are probably going to perform well at tasks in front of a group to reflect such expectations by their expressive behaviour (Ridgeway, Berger, and Smith 1985).

Most of the cues for dominance are decoded correctly. For example, Keating *et al.* (1981) found that an unsmiling face was interpreted as dominant in all cultures studied; however, a frowning face was seen as dominant only in western cultures. Other studies have found that a high level of gaze in initial meetings is seen as dominant (e.g. Rosa and Mazur 1979; see below). Skilled forms of dominance and social influence may be misperceived: Burns (1954) found that tactfully given instructions from superiors were sometimes interpreted as information or advice by the recipient. The persuasive–democratic style, for all its advantages, can be very misleading to those who are not used to it.

There are probably rules restraining assertiveness, particularly on occasions when informality and equality are emphasized, like purely social events. It is perfectly normal for people in work settings, especially in the early meetings of newly established groups, to emit dominance signals. Rosa and Mazur (1979) found that informal status in small groups could be predicted from length of initial glance when first meeting (using the Strongman and Champness method, p.164), and from who spoke first. The foreman of a jury is often a person who has seated himself in a central position, where he can see and be seen, and who adopts an erect posture.

Women in a very general sense are thought by themselves and others to be of lower power and status (Berger, Rosenholtz, and Zelditch 1980). As we shall see, they do emit fewer dominance signals than men: they take up less space, are shorter, look more, smile more, have less loud, more high-pitched voices, and interrupt less (p.281f.). However, women in jobs which carry authority do emit some dominance cues. Steckler and Rosenthal (1985) asked male and female management students with some work experience to role-play telephone calls to different others. The women were more dominant with a superior or subordinate, less so with a peer, perhaps because they needed to assert themselves in the first two relationships. Men were most assertive with peers, perhaps because this was a competitive situation for them.

Becoming a leader of a group and influencing other people are important social skills, and the appropriate use of dominance signals is an important part of them. However, sheer dominance is not enough, the others have to be rewarded and a sufficiently close relationship maintained; a combination of warmth and dominance is required. Strangely, one of the main NV channels, the face, is not able to do this: non-smiling is dominant, but it is also unfriendly. Tone of voice, however, can convey both attitudes independently (p.145f.). Touch is ambiguous, and may be communicating either warmth or dominance (p.226f.). We shall discuss NVC in some specific social skills later (Chapter 16).

What is the origin of these dominance signals? Some are culturally universal and resemble animal threat signals – frown, touch, loud voice – while submissive signals resemble animal appeasement. Relaxation is often a sign of status in animals too, perhaps indicating lack of fear of others. The use of height as a symbol of status has been linked to the fact that parents are bigger than children, which becomes generalized.

Sexual attitudes

When two people are sexually attracted towards one another, or when they are in love, this is signalled by a particular set of bodily signals. These include those listed above for interpersonal attraction in general – a high level of proximity, gaze and smiling, and a friendly tone of voice – but in addition they use a number of special signals, as follows:

gaze: a high level of mutual gaze; pupil dilation

touch: in appropriate places and ways, depending on the situation, e.g. kiss, embrace, hold hands

posture: 'courtship readiness' is expressed by an erect posture, increased muscle tone, pulling in the stomach, arms open or stretched towards other

gesture: women preen themselves by adjustments to hair and clothes

visible arousal: in addition to pupil dilation, there may be blushing and perspiring

appearance: individuals are likely to enhance their appearance by attention to clothes, hair, and skin. Enlarging the apparent size of eyes and of the sexual organs are examples

Some of these cues do not change much with time, such as physique, or are constant over a period, like clothes. Some are autonomic reactions and can be controlled with difficulty, like pupil dilation and perspiration; some are entirely under control, are subject to social rules, and are part of heterosexual skills, such as gaze, touch, posture, and gestures. People seem to be aware of using some of these signals. Subjects reported using the following when flirting: touch, gaze, facial expression, proximity, bodily movement, tone of voice, as well as compliments, small talk, and finding common interests (Montgomery 1986). The use of these signals is controlled by situational rules: they are permitted more at parties than at work, for example. Scheflen and Scheflen (1972) have carried out careful observations of therapy groups and other situations, and presented photographs of various interpersonal attitudes being expressed. They suggest that two people of the opposite sex often go through a series of postural shifts, similar to those of courtship, as their intimacy increases, and they regard this sequence as a universal structure. The stages are:

Plate 6.2 Courtship signals (Scheflen and Scheflen 1972)

a A mild degree of courting tonus: head erect, eyes bright with lids slightly narrowed.

b High tonus shown quite visibly; accentuated by pressing upper calf against lower knee and flexing foot.

c A man's courting behaviour may resemble that used in dominance: he draws up to full height, protrudes jaw, stands close, displaying what is generally regarded as a masculine stance.

(1) Courtship readiness: high arousal, bodily alertness, grooming.
(2) Position for courtship: facing or side by side.
(3) Actions of appeal or invitation: gaze-holding, protruding breasts, rolling pelvis, hand on hips, etc.
(4) Use of qualifiers of courting behaviour to arrest the sequence: verbal disclaimers or mentions of inappropriateness of setting, incomplete or bizarre performance of postural moves.

Gergen, Gergen, and Barton (1973) carried out a very interesting experiment in which groups of seven or eight strangers spent an hour in a room 10 ft by 12 ft, some of them in pitch darkness. In the dark 90 per cent touched purposefully, 50 per cent hugged one another, and 80 per cent felt sexual excitement. There was none of this for groups who had the lights on. This suggests a high level of desire for sexual intimacy among young people which is normally kept under restraint. Often there is leakage of underlying intentions: when a girl says 'no, we mustn't', her tone of voice may suggest her real wishes.

Among young people courting, a lot of the time is spent on sexual activity, gradually increasing in intimacy. Morris (1971) suggests that in western culture couples normally go through twelve stages of intimacy, always in the same order: from (1) eye to body, via (6) arm to waist, and (7) mouth to mouth, to (12) genitals to genitals. Some go to a further stage – mouth to genitals. These steps are usually initiated by the male, but he must wait for a positive response from the female before proceeding to the next step. When couples are co-habiting or married they spend less time engaged in these activities, though they spend about eight hours a day in bed together.

The use of appropriate NV signals here can be regarded as a social skill. Comparisons of pairs of young men and young women who were more or less successful at dating have found that the successful ones looked more when talking, had a higher percentage of gaze that was mutual, were more attractive, shared the speaking time more equally, and scored higher on self-report inventories of social skill (Cherulnik et al. 1978). However, in a similar study Arkowitz et al. (1975) found that looking, smiling, or nodding did not discriminate between males who were successful or unsuccessful at dating; verbal fluency was the key factor.

The use of certain NVC has been found to discriminate reliably between happily and less happily married couples. Unhappy couples send more negative and fewer positive signals and these are reciprocated; non-verbal signals discriminate better than verbal ones (Gottman 1979). Unhappy couples communicate their feelings to one another less well than happy couples; husbands in particular are poorer senders, especially of positive feelings (Noller 1984).

What is the origin of these sexual signals? Male birds put on colourful displays of their fine feathers, male monkeys display visible signs of sexual arousal and attempt to mount females. Human sexual signals are more subtle, though they do include physiological signs of sexual arousal, and touch, which can be regarded as a sexual intention signal. Other aspects of sexual behaviour are similar to and presumably derived from early parent–child behaviour – kissing, sucking, hand–holding, and even baby-talk (Wilson and Nias 1976).

7

Non-verbal communication and speech

In the last two chapters we discussed the rather slow non-verbal signals which are used to manage social situations – to express emotions and attitudes to other people. However, while people are speaking they send another series of NV signals, which are faster and are closely connected with what is being said at the time. These signals affect the meaning of what is said, provide a simultaneous commentary by the listener, and manage the synchronizing of utterances. Some linguists now recognize that some of these signals are really part of language, not just an emotionally expressive 'paralanguage'. Abercrombie (1968) said: 'We speak with our vocal organs, but we converse with our whole body.' This is an unusual view, however; many linguists accept NV signals in the vocal–auditory channel as part of language but do not accept those in the kinesic channel, and probably none of them accept the range of functions which will be documented in this chapter.

Research methods

This topic demands finer analysis and a shorter time-scale than the types of bodily communication considered so far. It requires recording of vocal cues – pauses, interruptions, loudness, pitch contour, and speech disturbances; visual cues include gaze, head-nodding and turning, facial expressions, and gestures.

The general principles of this kind of research were discussed in Chapter 2. The alternative designs which have been used include: (1) detailed but non-quantitative study of filmed encounters; (2) statistical analysis of sequences; (3) judgement experiments, for example of when experimentally prepared utterances are thought to have ended; and (4) true experiments, for example face-to face *v.* no vision, or instructing subjects to lie, not to use their hands, etc.

There are a number of persistent problems with research in this area. Much of the early work used very small samples of behaviour – 36 seconds in one case – with the result that non-replicable findings were obtained. Some influential early studies used no statistics, and again could not be confirmed when these were applied. Very few investigations were done in field settings because of the need for detailed recording. And many of the early studies used a very short time-scale, e.g. forty-eight frames per second, whereas it turns out that little of any significance takes place below intervals of half a second.

Developmental origins

Infants interact with their mothers (or other caretakers) before they can speak, and we can see here some of the origins of the co-ordination of verbal and non-verbal signals. As Schaffer (1984) said: 'It is apparent that in a number of ways the child arrives in the world preadapted for social interaction.' Young infants can send social signals – gazes, vocalizations, and smiles – are receptive to similar signals from others, and have the capacity for interacting with this simple repertoire. The earliest interactions are during feeding, bathing, and other basic routines, and here mother and infant are very responsive to one another. Bakeman and Brown (1977) recorded interaction between three-day-olds and their mothers in five-second units; transitional probabilities showed that each influenced the other's behaviour during the following five-second unit, the mother had the greater influence, and there was some simultaneous adoption of the same behaviour. Co-ordination of mother–infant behaviour may be faster than this. Tronick, Als, and Brazelton (1980) studied three-month-olds using one-second units; mothers and infants were usually in one of six phases of activity, and when they changed phase, e.g. play to talk, this was often simultaneous. The explanation is probably that both are following familiar routines, as well as responding to one another.

By the end of the first month there is mutual gaze, and by months three and four a lot of mutual influence in terms of looking, smiling, and vocalizing. Child vocalization is often simultaneous with that of the mother, but later on infants 'respond' to maternal speech, and by the end of the first year there is definite turn-taking. This is taught by the mother, who engages in pseudo-conversations in which any noise or other act by the child is treated as a conversational turn (Snow 1977). Mother and infant engage in often-repeated games like 'give-and-take' and 'peek-a-boo', which involve turn-taking and the co-ordination of vocalization, gesture, and gaze (Bruner 1977). By the end of the second year of life there is integration of gaze and vocalization in 'conversation' (Schaffer, Collis, and Parsons 1977).

The development of verbal and non-verbal communication in

infants varies somewhat between cultures. For example, some Mexican Indian mothers do not look or smile at their babies during feeding; Japanese mothers spend much more time than western mothers in bodily contact; these mothers try to soothe and quiet infants rather than stimulating them to be expressive and responsive (Schaffer 1984). This does not, however, explain the very high rate of back-channel responses by Japanese adults (p.67).

NVC accompanying speech

While a person speaks he also emits non-verbal vocalizations, gestures, facial expressions, and gazes. These are closely integrated with his words, and may amplify or disambiguate them.

Pauses, and the temporal structure of utterances

An utterance is the string of words emitted while someone has a turn as the main speaker, though there are often brief interjections by others. It can be divided into shorter components, divided by pauses, which take up 30–40 per cent of the time. Pauses may be 'unfilled' (i.e. silent) or 'filled' (i.e. with 'ums' or 'ers').

Goldman-Eisler (1968) found that pauses were up to twice as frequent when the topic was more difficult, for example interpreting as opposed to describing cartoons. There is a lot of evidence that silent pauses represent 'thinking time', and are the occasion for planning the words and clauses to come. This has been found at the level of individual words; Goldman-Eisler found that pauses were longer before words which were less predictable from those before, i.e. carrying more information. Boomer (1978) found that nearly half hesitation pauses came after the first word in 'phonemic clauses', i.e. chunks of up to eight syllables spoken with a single stress, and he concluded that these pauses are used to plan the clauses. However there is evidence that planning covers longer strings of words than phonemic clauses. Several investigators have found that spontaneous speech usually has a rhythm, alternating between fluent and hesitant phases, and it seems likely that the fluent phases are planned during the hesitant ones. Butterworth and Beattie (1978) found a cycle of average length 8·8 clauses, lasting 22 seconds, for Cambridge supervisions. These pauses seem to be necessary: Beattie and Bradbury (1979) 'punished' subjects for pausing by means of a light signal; there were fewer pauses but instead there were many more repetitions.

How are these pauses decoded? Lalljee (1971) found that users of many filled pauses were interpreted as anxious or bored, users of silent pauses as anxious, angry, or contemptuous. Of course there is another side of decoding: listeners are receiving information about grammatical structure.

Speakers make use of other non-verbal vocalizations. Pitch patterns can indicate a question, and frame or comment on an utterance in a number of ways. Stress is used to emphasize certain words and can thus disambiguate utterances (p.110). A falling pitch in mid-utterance makes a listener response more likely (Dittman and Llewellyn 1968).

Gestures

While people speak they make a number of bodily movements, especially with their hands. Many of these are 'batons', i.e. movements giving emphasis. Bull and Connelly (1985) studied conversation between pairs of strangers and found that most points of vocal stress are accompanied at exactly the same time by movements of the head, hands, or other parts of the body; indeed, a great variety of movements are used in this way. In a study of the behaviour of TV news-readers, Bull (1987) found that gestures were used to indicate new topics; each newsreader had a characteristic gesture, and it occurred ½–1 second after the verbal start of the new topic.

Many gestures are 'illustrators' of the verbal contents: they copy shapes, objects or movements, or have metaphorical meaning (p.194). Dittman (1972) found that they occur at the beginning of phonemic clauses, arguing that they reflect the planning or encoding of these phrases. Butterworth and Beattie (1978) found that gestures preceded the words to which they were related by an average of 800 milliseconds. They also found that speech–related gestures occurred most often during pauses in otherwise fluent phrases of speech. They suggest that gestures are produced first because there are far fewer gestures than words to select from, so the decision is made more quickly. However, McNeill and Levy (1982) did not find that illustrative gestures preceded phrases, or even the verbs in phrases, but were just as likely to fall afterwards as before.

A possible way in which gestures precede words, according to psychoanalysts, is in the case of gestures representing thoughts which are not yet conscious, but may become so a few minutes later (p.14f.).

There is quite good, though not perfect, synchrony between words and gestures. Lindenfeld (1971) did a careful examination of conversation during psychotherapy, and found that 30 per cent of kinesic units did not fit syntax units. However, most of the 'violations' were minor – most kinesic units fell within sentences, though they crossed phrase boundaries; he also found that kinesic patterns fitted the surface structure of speech better than the deep structure.

Scheflen (1964) and Kendon (1972), from intensive though non-quantitative study of short film segments, concluded that body movements have a hierarchical structure, corresponding to different sizes of verbal units.

Emphasis can be provided by hand or head movements just as by changes of pitch or loudness. Mehrabian (1972) found that speakers who were trying to be persuasive looked more at their listeners, used more gestures and head-nods, more facial activity, and spoke faster, louder, and with less hesitation (p.259f.).

How far do these bodily accompaniments of speech communicate anything to listeners? We shall show later that shapes are communicated much better when the hands can be used and seen (p.195). On the other hand, comparison of telephone and face-to-face communication shows that for many purposes vision makes little difference – communicating most kinds of information, solving problems, and persuasion (p.119f.).

McNeill (1985) argued that gestures and speech are part of the same psychological structure, that gestures are direct manifestations of the speaker's inner speech, his thinking process. Iconic, illustrative gestures are synchronized with the clauses which they illustrate; gesture and language develop together in childhood, and are affected in a similar way by brain injuries; if speakers are prevented from using gestures, their speech is affected. Graham and Heywood (1976) asked subjects to keep their arms folded, and found that there were more pauses, and more use of demonstratives and words describing spatial relations. In a similar study Rimé *et al.* (1984) placed subjects in a chair which restricted movements of head, arms, and legs. The result was reduced richness of verbal production suggesting less imagery, and more non-verbal activity in the organs which were free to move – eyebrows, eyes, mouth, and fingers.

Gaze

Speakers look intermittently at their listener(s). The amount they look varies: we found about 40 per cent for pairs of strangers 2 metres apart talking on innocuous topics. Beattie (1983) found 67 per cent for couples who were not strangers and who were seated further apart. We shall see that there is more gaze at greater distances, between people who like one another, and more looking while talking for dominant individuals (Chapter 10).

Speaker gaze is intermittent, in glances of about three seconds. Speakers look more at the ends of utterances, and look away at the beginning of them, especially if they have been asked a question, as Kendon (1967) and others have found. Speakers also look at grammatical pauses, especially at the ends of long clauses (Beattie 1983). Goodwin (1981) analysed fifty hours of conversation in natural settings, e.g. parties, shopping, meals. He concluded that a speaker wants others to show they are listening and attending, and looks up to elicit responsive gazes. Duncan and Fiske (1977) regard clause completion and head-turn towards listener as the 'speaker within turn signal', designed to elicit back-channel responses.

Gaze is also used to send information. The 'eyeflash', lasting about 0·75 seconds, is used at points of emphasis, and with adjectives, by some speakers (Walker and Trimboli 1983). Ordinary glances are used to emphasize particular words or phrases, or simply to add to expressiveness. The direction of gaze may be used to point to particular persons or objects, for example to suggest who should speak next.

However, the main reason that speakers look at listeners is to obtain information, especially to obtain reactions to what has just been said, in the form of head-nods, gazes, and facial expressions – showing interest, agreement, surprise, etc. The motor skill model proposed that interactors are like performers of a motor skill, making skilled moves, observing reactions to them, and taking corrective action, in order to pursue a goal (Figure 7.1).

Figure 7.1   The motor skill model

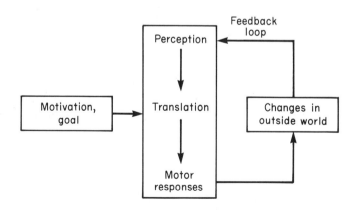

Source: Argyle 1983

Glances by speakers are made at the precise points at which feedback is needed – at the ends of utterances and at grammatical breaks within them. Gaze is averted at the beginning of utterances, since no information is needed at this point, and because such information would interfere with the cognitive planning of the utterance. People also look less at hesitant phases of speech, especially in the early parts of clauses when planning is going on (Beattie 1983).

The reason speakers do not look all the time may be because of cognitive overload, or perhaps because the arousal generated by gaze at the other would interfere with cognitive planning. Beattie (1983) asked subjects to gaze continuously while answering questions, and found that they produced far more false starts and more filled pauses – both signs of overload. A series of other investigations has compared gaze while speaking about easy or difficult topics, or topics on which speakers have different degrees of expertise. In all cases speaker gaze level was reduced for the difficult topics (e.g. Ellyson, Dovidio, and Corson 1981); and, of course, looking while talking is usually much less than looking while listening (p.159), presumably because speakers have to do more planning than listeners.

NV modification of the verbal message

Bodily signals can add to or modify the meaning of words in other ways. Fonagy (1971) has drawn attention to the way that utterances are 'double-coded' – by the words and by the non-verbal accompaniments. Similar effects can be produced by either medium: for example, emotions can be aroused by emotive words or emotive expressions, tension can be created by leaving crucial words to the end or by the manner of delivery. Extra messages can be added by using accents or special intonations, using question intonation for statements, and in other ways.

Rosenthal's research (1966) on non-verbal experimenter effects is an example. He found that experimenters can drop small, unintentional hints to subjects by the way in which they give the experimental instructions. In one experiment subjects who heard voice only were influenced 53 per cent as much as those who had access to the visual channel too; those who received only visual cues showed 75 per cent as much influence.

Another example is the series of experiments by Noller (1984) on NVC in marriage. Spouses were asked to deliver verbally ambiguous utterances in three non-verbal styles, e.g. 'I'm feeling cold, aren't you?' to mean 'Please shut the door', 'Are you also, as a matter of fact, feeling cold?', and 'Please come and warm me with your body'. Husbands in unhappy marriages were poor decoders, especially of positive feelings.

Non-verbal signals are also used to 'frame' the words, that is indicate how they are to be taken. A question is indicated by a rising pitch (apart from why, and other wh- questions). The speaker can indicate by other cues whether or not he expects an answer, whether it was supposed to be funny, or whether the listener is in deep trouble. Crystal (1969) found that quite different vocal patterns were used when speakers were asked to speak the same sentence in different styles – haughty, puzzled, amused, matter of fact, precise, excited, or angry. From common observation, facial cues are involved as well.

Back-channel (feedback) signals

Back-channel signals have a powerful effect on speakers. Small reinforcements such as head-nods and smiles will rapidly increase the rate of production of whatever was reinforced, e.g. talking, topic of conversation, giving opinions (Krasner 1958). The absence of back-channel signals is taken as a negative reaction, and will result in the speaker repeating his utterance more loudly or shutting up (Wiener *et al.* 1972).

While one person is speaking, others may be listening; if so they send signals too, whether they realize it or not, and whether the speaker attends to these or not. The main back-channel signals are head-nods, short vocalizations, glances, and facial expressions, often in combination (Rosenfeld 1978). Back-channel signals may be: (1) 'listening behaviour', indicating attention and understanding; (2) feedback, for example agreement and approval; (3) imitation, matching the speaker's behaviour (Kendon 1970).

Duncan and Fiske (1977) studied the different 'back-channel' signals which may be made by listeners, while the other is speaking; they found that these usually followed the speaker's 'within-turn signal', i.e. pausing and turning head towards listener.

Gestures

Two of the most common back-channel gestures are head-nodding and shaking. It has been found that head-nods usually mean 'yes', especially if they are of large amplitude and with repeated cycles of nodding, and they usually follow speaker elicitation. Smaller, one-way nods are used as attention signals or synchronizing, following a speaker disfluency (Rosenfeld and Hancks 1980). Head-shakes are less common and may signify 'no', a query, or accompany laughter (Hadar, Steiner, and Rose 1985).

Posture

Bull (1987) found that agreement was accompanied by sideways lean, presumably due to relaxation, while in disagreement subjects were more likely to fold their arms, cross their legs tightly above the knee, and support their head on one hand. Disagreement postures seem to be a vigilant and defensive, body-closing response to threat, together with the head-propping boredom posture (p.210f.).

Facial

Brunner (1979) found that after a speaker had paused and looked, listener smiles were very common; they were used in exactly the same way as head-nods. Purvis, Dabbs, and Hopper (1984) found that individuals who reported being able to get others to talk and open up used more brief simultaneous speech, and also a more attentive facial expression, showing interest in the other.

The face can show pleasure by smiling, displeasure by frowning. The eyebrows are very useful for sending feedback, different degrees of raising and lowering indicating disbelief, surprise, neutral, puzzled, angry.

Forsyth, Kushner, and Forsyth (1981) asked judges to sort 280 photographs of faces of people engaged in conversation, posed as if listening. Four factors were found:

annoyance–pleasure
interest
puzzled–understand
spontaneity

Gaze

Listeners typically look 70–75 per cent of the time, in quite long glances – 7·8 seconds for Duncan and Fiske (1977). They are looking to pick up the NV accompaniments of speech, together with some lip-reading if they are deaf. The reason it is less than 100 per cent is presumably, as in the case of speakers, to reduce either cognitive overload or arousal.

Vocalizations

These include uh-huh's and similar grunts as listening signals. There are also feedback signals such as 'good', 'really?', and sometimes listeners help out by finishing the sentence for the speaker.

How feedback is elicited and perceived

We showed above that, according to the social skill model, speakers look up at the points at which they need feedback from listeners. They need to know whether the listener is still attending, or is willing to hear more, understands what was said, likes it, agrees with it, and so on. Listeners, who are looking at speakers 70–75 per cent of the time, will see most of these glances.

Synchronizing utterances

When two or more people are conversing they take it in turns to speak, and usually manage to achieve a fairly smooth 'synchronized' sequence of utterances, without too many interruptions or silences. How good is this synchrony in fact? One index is the length of switching pauses. These are on average 500 milliseconds, i.e. half a second, though many are much less than this. When the pause is 200 milliseconds or less, a length which is noticed by about 50 per cent of observers, it is known as a 'smooth transition'. Many switching pauses are less than the normal reaction time of 150–200 milliseconds (Walker 1982). Another index of synchrony is the number of interruptions. The proportion of switches where there is overlapping speech varies between different kinds of conversation – 10·6 per cent in Cambridge tutorials, 34 per cent in seminars, 37 per cent in political TV interviews (Beattie 1983). However, not all of these involve one person talking another down. The most common kind are 'overlaps' (where the second speaker simply started too soon), followed by 'simple interruptions' (not intended to stop the other speaking, e.g. 'good'), 'butting in', and 'silent interruptions' (first speaker failed to complete sentence, no simultaneous talk) (Ferguson 1977). In the community described in the Dead Sea Scrolls, interruptions at a meeting led to ten days on reduced rations (Vermes 1962). (I am indebted to G. Ginsburg and M.G. Lalljee for drawing my attention to this.) At Oxford interruptions in the middle of phrases are definitely disapproved of, those at ends of clauses less so, while those at ends of sentences are acceptable (Argyle and McCallin, unpub.).

Human beings have been conversing successfully (in most cases) for thousands of years, but not one of them has known, until very recently, how this synchrony is achieved. We will consider the evidence for the possible cues.

There are several sets of signals to consider when:

speaker ending, wants to yield the floor
speaker wants to keep the floor, within-turn signals
listener wants to take the floor
listener wants to decline offer of the floor

However, most research has been directed to finding out how listeners know when the speaker is yielding the floor.

Terminal gaze

Kendon (1967) found that interactors often (62 per cent) give a prolonged gaze at another, starting just before the ending of long utterances, and that when such terminal gazes are not given there is a longer pause before the other replies (Figure 7.2). The subjects were pairs of Oxford students, initially strangers, who were asked to get to know one another. Others have also found that terminal gazes commonly occur, though gazes are also used at grammatical breaks within utterances. Rutter *et al.* (1978) found that terminal gaze was effective between strangers, not between friends, and Beattie (1983) found that it did not work in Cambridge supervisions. He argued that terminal gaze operates as an effective signal only if the general level of gaze is low, e.g. between strangers.

Harrigan and Steffen (1983) found that in a group conversation a speaker usually looks at a listener as he starts to speak, especially when interrupting.

Falling pitch contour

This was first suggested by Duncan (1972) as one full-stop signal among others. The most spectacular demonstration of its power was in Beattie's (1983) study of TV interviews with Mrs Thatcher. It had been observed that she was interrupted a great deal, more than Mr Callaghan for example, so it seemed that she was giving misleading full-stop signals in mid-utterance. A comparison was made of ten of her utterances followed by a smooth switch, ten which were interrupted, and ten sentence ends in mid-utterance. Judges who listened to the audiotapes thought that the utterance had ended nearly as often in the disputed cases (56 per cent) as in those followed by smooth utterances (62 per cent), though there was a greater difference

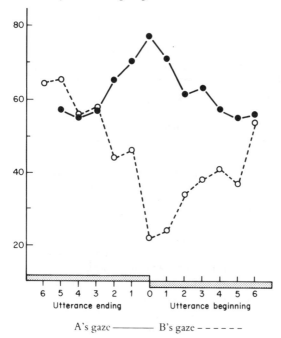

Figure 7.2   The synchronizing of glances and utterances

A's gaze ———— B's gaze ------

Source: Kendon 1967

for those who saw vision only (see Table 7.1). It looked as if the misleading cue was an auditory one.

Table 7.1   *Cues for interruption in Mrs Thatcher's TV interviews*

| | Judged to be completed | | Pitch levels | |
	vision only	sound only	previous peak	fell to
smooth switch	76·4	62·2	238	141
interruption	38·6	55·9	263	167
mid–utterance	18·6	32·4	275	171

Data compiled from Beattie 1983

Analysis of the audiotapes showed that, in the disputed utterances, there was a fall in pitch as great as in the others, though it did not fall so low. There was a similar fall in mid-utterance (where there was no interruption), so clearly visual cues were involved as well.

Gestures

At the end of an utterance people usually return any gesturing hands to
the resting position. Keeping a hand in mid-gesture becomes a sign
that a speaker intends to continue speaking. Duncan (1972) described it as an 'attempt suppressing signal', and found that it was
nearly always successful. Bull (1987) found that when a person
makes a statement, which often involves claiming the floor, he raises
a hand, raises a foot, or draws his legs back, which people do not do
when responding to such initiatives. Before asking a question people
raise their head to the other; when replying they turn their head away.

Grammatical structures

These can indicate the end of an utterance in several ways – end of sentence, especially when a question, and tag-endings like 'you know'.
There is evidence that this is not a very successful cue, since there can be
shorter switching pauses after incomplete utterances (0·39 seconds)
than after complete ones (0·64 seconds) (Beattie 1983). However, Slugoski (1985) carried out an ingeniously controlled experiment in
which conversations of four utterances were recorded, ending on an
utterance which varied in whether or not there was falling pitch, and
whether or not the sentence was completed. Subjects pressed a button
when they thought the last utterance had ended. Sentence completion
led to faster button-pressing than did falling pitch.

   Sacks, Schegloff, and Jefferson (1974) argued that there are certain
points in utterances, certain clause-endings, which are 'possible
completion points', and which can be anticipated by listeners. They
also found that speakers 'selected' the next speaker by a terminal
gaze directed towards him.

Combinations of several cues

Duncan and Fiske (1977) proposed that turn-yielding is achieved by
a combination of several out of six cues, two verbal (clause completion, ending tags), three vocal (rising or falling pitch, drawl on final
syllables, drop in loudness), one visual (end of gesture). Their study
provided some evidence for such additivity. However, Beattie
(1983) was not able to replicate it, and found the most frequently
used cues were clause completion, fall in pitch, and final drawl,
usually in combination. The Thatcher study suggests that fall in
pitch combined with some visual cues (end of gesture, terminal gaze,
perhaps) were operating together.

What is the difference between a speaker's within-turn and end-of-turn signals? According to Duncan and Fiske the within-turn signal is a clause-ending and head-turn (i.e. gaze), while ending involves several further cues, such as end of gesture.

If a listener wants to take the floor, what can he do? Duncan and Niederehe (1974) found four cues, of which at least one was used in 95 per cent of switches:

> turn head away from listener
> start gesticulation
> loud speech
> sharp inhaling of breath

Normally someone who wants to speak will anticipate a clause-ending pause by the speaker, and move in at this point. If the speaker does not yield the floor the interrupter can win if he increases his loudness or, if that fails, speaks louder than the other (Meltzer, Morris, and Hayes 1971).

Synchrony over the telephone

If visual cues like gaze and head-nods are important in synchrony, there should be more interruptions and longer pauses when these are unavailable, e.g. over the telephone. A number of experiments have been carried out to test this hypothesis. Some typical findings are given from a study by Rutter and Stephenson (1977), who allocated pairs of subjects either to the telephone or face to face in fifteen-minute discussions of issues in industrial relations (Table 7.2). They found *fewer* interruptions over the telephone.

Table 7.2   *Synchrony over the telephone and face to face*

	Telephone	Face to face	
number of interruptions	9·0	14·0	(p $<$ 0·005)
length of simultaneous speech (seconds)	9·4	18·7	(p $<$ 0·001)
length of mutual silence (seconds)	14·4	18·9	n.s.
length of utterances	34·3	25·7	(p $<$ 0·05)
speech disturbances (per 100 words)	8·2	6·3	(p $<$ 0·05)

Source: Rutter and Stephenson 1977.

Cook and Lalljee (1972) also found fewer interruptions in no vision, and several investigators have found more pauses (Argyle and Cook 1976). Beattie and Barnard (1979), in a comparison of real telephone calls and rather different face-to-face conversations, obtained similar results but with more filled pauses over the telephone, perhaps used to keep the floor.

The main point is that synchrony over the telephone is slightly *better* than face to face. This shows that we can certainly do without visual cues for meshing though, as we have seen, they are in fact used. Why are there so many interruptions face to face? As Rutter and Stephenson say: 'Face to face, interruptions can occur freely because the visual channel allows the communication of non-verbal signals which maintain the interaction and prevent the breakdown which interruptions might otherwise produce' (1977: 35). The telephone is a more formal channel (Rutter, in press), with longer, more complete utterances, and fewer short interjections. It is a different communication skill, which has to be learnt.

The gestural dance

We have seen that there is a considerable degree of synchrony between speakers and listeners at the level of the phonemic clause, and of longer units, up to complete utterances. For example, a speaker starts gesticulating and looks away as he starts to speak, and reverses this when he stops. There is an intricate co-ordination of pausing and looking within turns, followed by head-nods, smiles, and gazes.

Interactional synchrony has been called a 'gestural dance', and likened to a waltz. In dancing there is very close co-ordination and near-simultaneous movement, but this is assisted by the music and by the learnt, often-repeated programme. Boxing is perhaps a closer analogy, and here too each responds to the other, apparently at speeds greater than the normal reaction time (Stern 1977).

Gaze and mutual gaze appear to be very finely co-ordinated, though Rutter and Stephenson (1977) showed that the percentage of mutual gaze was no more than would be expected by chance, i.e. by multiplying the percentages of A's and B's individual gaze. However, because of the alternation of looking more while listening than while talking, the expected level is really much less than the observed level and the observed level is a little higher than this (Argyle and Ingham 1972). The study by Goodwin (1981) showed how speakers try to elicit back-channel gazes, i.e. mutual gazes from listeners. There are several other sources of synchrony – imitation of posture and other movements, compensation for too much intimacy, and the effects of head-nods and other kinds of reinforcement.

It was claimed by Condon and Ogston (1966), and others, that there is interactional synchrony on a much finer time-scale. They analysed film of adult subjects and of mothers and infants at forty-eight frames per second, and report that the bodily movements of both speakers and listeners are co-ordinated to the boundaries of phonemes at 1/24 second or less, and hence are synchronized with one another. A high percentage of changes in direction of speed or direction of hands, arms, etc. are synchronized with phonemes in this way. Kendon (1970) reported similar observations, as did Bird-whistell (1970) for encounters not involving speech.

However, no statistical evidence was provided to show that this was more than a chance phenomenon. McDowall (1978) filmed a group of 6, 3 of them friends, at 8 frames per second, recording 18 parts of the body for 1,000 frames. He studied synchrony in any of 18 parts of the body for each dyad; only one out of 57 such comparisons showed above chance synchrony, and this was based on joint timing of the right leg of one and the left hand of the other. There was no more synchrony between friends than strangers, but there was more synchrony at smooth speaker switches (under half a second latency). It is possible that the interaction in this discussion was not sufficiently intense for synchrony to develop, but this study has caused doubts over whether the gestural dance exists, at least at the split-second level of timing. It is quite possible that Condon and Ogston's results were due to lack of independence in coding the boundaries of phonemes and bodily movements (Rosenfeld 1978).

Other aspects of no-vision conversation

In a series of experiments Rutter (in press) found that no-vision encounters were marked by greater formality, they were more task-oriented, depersonalized, and less spontaneous. They were experienced as more socially distant, with less social presence. His explanation is that they are relatively 'cueless'; since there are fewer personal cues, interactors focus on the communication task in hand. Morley and Stephenson (1969) had found that if bargaining or negotiation is done without vision, the person with the stronger case always wins, whereas under face-to-face conditions interpersonal processes, e.g. of liking and wanting to be liked, interfere. This confirms the importance of gaze for forming an interpersonal relationship. Other studies have found that people like more those they have met face to face compared with those they have only spoken to on the telephone (Short, Williams, and Christie 1976).

However, there are several puzzling findings about no-vision interaction. It is found that the telephone is just as good as face to face for conveying information, and for simple problem-solving (Short, Williams, and Christie 1976). Perhaps we have simply become accustomed to the telephone as a medium for business-type conversations, and are able to use it efficiently, while suppressing interpersonal considerations.

It might be expected that blind people would find interaction very difficult. Indeed this has often been reported, though not on the basis of any systematic research. Kemp (1981) carried out careful experimental comparisons of interactions between blind–blind, blind–sighted, and sighted–sighted people. Contrary to expectations, it was found that the blind–blind pairs were *more* spontaneous (shorter utterances, interrupted more), were no more impersonal, and formed more positive impressions of one another. These were blind people who were supporting themselves in the community, and they had clearly adapted and developed skills of coping with interaction.

8

Facial expression

The face is the most important non-verbal channel. It is particularly important for expressing emotions, and attitudes to other people. Facial expressions change rapidly and play an important role in social interaction; they are closely monitored by gaze directed to faces. Finally, the shapes of faces as well as the expressions on them are decoded in terms of personality properties.

How many facial expressions are there?

People can make a lot of different faces, if asked, but decoders can discriminate only between broader groupings of them. Osgood (1966) asked fifty performers to pose forty different faces in all, but found that judges could discriminate only eight emotions. There is very good agreement between different studies here, and the following six emotional expressions have been found by all who have investigated the problem (Ekman 1982).

happiness
surprise
fear
sadness
anger
disgust/contempt

There are a number of other facial expressions which are not quite emotions:

interest
shame (Izard 1977)
pain (similar to pain, fear, and sadness, i.e. strongly negative (see p.131)
startle (Ekman 1985)

religious excitement (perhaps extreme arousal; Sargant 1957)
puzzled, amazed, questioning, and other back-channel signals

Some of these are quite similar to each other, and difficult to discriminate, especially fear and surprise. On the other hand some can
be subdivided further.

Ekman and Friesen (1982) suggest that smiles can be divided into
felt, false, and miserable. A false smile is due to self-presentation; it
differs from felt smiles in that certain facial muscles are not activated,
so that eyes and cheeks are not involved. These smiles are also more
sudden in onset (Bugental 1986). An ironic smile is due to conflict
between two sets of muscles (Rinn 1984).

However, the classifications described so far are mainly about
faces linked to emotions. Facial expressions are also linked to speech,
and the eyebrows in particular are an important source of conversational signals, like 'do not understand', and disbelief (Ekman
1979).

Another way of classifying facial expressions is by factor analysis.
Judges are asked to rate each of a series of faces on a number of scales
and the dimensions are extracted (e.g. Frijda 1969). The argument
here between different investigators is not so great as it was with
categories, and the following three dimensions have commonly been
found, among others, for posed emotions (Ekman 1982):

pleasant–unpleasant
intensity–control
interest

How many expressive elements are there?

Birdwhistell (1970) concluded that there were thirty-two 'kinemes',
or basic elements of expression in the face. More systematic work by
Ekman, Friesen, and Tomkins (1971) led to the development of the
Facial Affect Scoring Technique (FAST), in which three areas of the
face are scored separately, by matching against photographs. There
are eight positions of the brows and forehead, seventeen for eyes and
lids, and forty-five for the lower face. Slowed-down film or videotape is scored for the duration of each facial element in each of the
three regions, by independent judges. The method takes a lot of
work – three hours for each minute of videotape, but was used
successfully in cross-cultural research.

There is an advantage in scoring facial expressions in terms of the muscles which are responsible. FAST detects the action of the nervous system, and permits analysis of the effects of opposing muscles and of different sources of 'eye-openness', for example (Rinn 1984). The most elaborate muscle-based scheme is FACS (Facial Affect Coding Scheme) developed by Ekman and Friesen (1978; 1982). It is based on small facial movements or Action Units (AUs), mostly due to single facial muscles, but which are also visible to observers, and discriminable from one another. The FACS Manual gives descriptions, still photographs, and filmed examples of the thirty-three AUs, forty-four combinations of them, and information about many other combinations.

Ekman (1979) used FACS to analyse eyebrow movements. There are three action units for the eyebrow:

inner brow raised
outer brow raised
brow lowered

These three, and a number of combinations of them, are used for different emotions, and for different signals used by speakers and listeners. Surprise, for example, is action units 1 plus 2.

FACS was used by Wiggers (1982) who found that eight judged emotions could be predicted successfully from FACS units, and that it was possible to isolate the action units used by decoders. For shame these were: lip bite, lips part, head lower.

It is important to study facial expression over time, preferably by slowed-down videotape. Some emotions involve more movement, as opposed to static expressions, than others. Bassili (1979) placed fifty white spots on faces, and took three-second films of emotional response; these would be recognized from movement alone, with no information about expression, especially for happy and surprise, and in the lower face. During social interaction the face is in constant motion. Izard and Dougherty (1981) developed an 'affectogram' for scoring the duration of each of nine emotions, second by second. The duration of some expressions may be very short, and when under 1/5 second these 'micromomentary expressions' are invisible unless the film or tape is slowed down (Haggard and Isaacs 1966).

Some muscular activity fails to produce any visible changes in the face. However, recording of electrical potentials in facial muscles by electromyograph (EMG) can detect them. It was found that induction of positive moods by drugs in depressed patients produced positive facial expressions at this level only (Schwartz et al. 1976).

The physiological and evolutionary origins of facial expression

Physiology of facial expression

Why do people smile and frown? In the first place because they have facial muscles which can move the facial skin and produce facial expressions. One of these muscles is the *zygomatic* which produces an upward curve of the mouth; frowning is done by the *corrugator* muscle, which pulls the brows together. These muscles are controlled by the facial nerve which has five main branches, corresponding to the main areas of the face. The facial muscles emanate from the facial nerve nucleus, which is in the *pons* in the brainstem, containing 7–10,000 nerve cells, mapping the different parts of the face.

The facial nerve nucleus can be activated in two ways:

(1) When the organism is emotionally aroused there is activity in the *hypothalamus* and the *limbic system* in the lower brain, which influences this facial nerve nucleus via the extrapyramidal tract.
(2) When someone poses a facial expression a different route is involved. Impulses now start in the *motor cortex*, which also maps the parts of the face, going directly to the brainstem, and the facial nerve nucleus, via the pyramidal tract. The face is given a lot of space in the motor cortex, especially the lower face, compared with other parts of the body; this is why we can make fine facial movements there, such as those used in speech.

In normal social interaction facial expression is partly spontaneous, partly posed. It is a combination of the operation of routes (1) and (2), sometimes of a battle between them. We discussed the resulting leakage on p.78.

Why do we have facial muscles, nerves, and the rest? They are there as the result of evolutionary processes. We discussed the evolution of facial expression up to the higher primates in Chapter 3. One of the residues of this evolutionary history is the great visibility of facial expressions, which can be decoded correctly at 45 metres (Hager and Ekman 1979).

It is the view of both Ekman (1982) and Izard (1977) that there are a number of innate (and culturally universal) neurophysiological programmes (six and eight respectively) for the production of emotional expression and emotional experience. While these are the result of evolution, there have been several further developments between apes and men. Humans have a further reduction in muscles devoted to ears and scalp, and there are muscles for the mid-face, the lips, and the cheeks. We have one extra muscle, the *risorius*, which pulls the corners of the mouth.

However there is another, more important difference. In animals emotional behaviour is fairly stereotyped, and does not vary much with the situation. The main source of emotional expression is route (1) described above. Decorticated cats and dogs can eat, fight, develop rage, and engage in sexual activity; this is not the case with humans. For us, the second route has become extremely important, and emotional expression is greatly affected by learning and voluntary control (Buck 1984; Rinn 1984).

The asymmetry of facial expression

It has often been found that emotional expressions are stronger on the left-hand side of the face (i.e. left hand from the owner's point of view). This has been studied by a variety of methods, including the use of FACS and EMG recording. However, asymmetry is only found for posed emotions, not for spontaneous ones, while simulated moods are intermediate (Ekman, Hager, and Friesen 1981); and the effect is greater for negative emotions. Stringer and May (1981) found that the left side of faces is seen as happy and receptive, while the right side is seen as active, outgoing, and thinking.

It would not be expected that route (1) expressions would be asymmetrical at all, since the brainstem mechanisms are not lateralized. However, route (2) expressions could very easily be lateralized. One possible explanation is that in posed emotions the cortex acts mainly to inhibit facial expressions, and such inhibitions would originate from the cognitively specialized *left* side of the cortex, thus inhibiting the *right* side of the face. As we have seen, asymmetry is greater for negative emotions but smiles are also more vigorous on the left side (Ekman, Hager, and Friesen 1981), and we should not expect much inhibition of positive expressions. A second explanation is that although most volitionally induced movements are due more to the left cortex, the right cortical hemisphere is specialized for faces because of the visual–spatial features of voluntary movement here (Rinn 1984).

Expression of emotion in the face

The development of facial expression in children

We should expect route (1) to be innate, and hence either present shortly after birth or appearing when maturation has taken place. Route (2) would be expected to depend on socialization.

Studies of rhesus monkeys reared in visual isolation find that they show the same emotional expressions as those reared in view of other monkeys, except that these appeared a little later, and were less likely to be made to a particular stimulus (Mason 1985). These experiments, which cannot of course be done with human infants, show that some at least of the monkey repertoire of emotional expressions are innate. The first to appear are screeching (distress) at one month, lip-smacking (affiliation) and grimacing (appeasement and greeting) by two months. Each of these expressions has a distinctive gradient of appearance against time, suggesting that an innate programme is unfolding.

The first expression to appear in human infants is crying, in response to physiological disturbance, e.g. pain and hunger. Crying is able to elicit the help of caretakers in controlling the infant's bodily state. Later on crying becomes differentiated into more specific negative expressions – hunger, pain, and anger. The startle reaction occurs in the newborn, to sudden stimulation, as do faces like adult disgust, to nasty tastes. Smiling appears early, not from wind but during REM sleep; infants smile at faces by two and a half months. Next to appear are laughter and cooing, followed by interest, sadness, surprise, and anger by four months and fear by six months (Izard 1978).

Different emotions are at first elicited by certain physical stimuli. For example, smiling is elicited by groups of dots, some kinds of touch, and certain sounds. Other noises produce fear, loud noises produce startle, physical restraint anger. These are all physical stimuli. Later it is mainly psychological stimuli which elicit emotions. By the age of six months infants display the full range of emotional expressions, mainly as a result of the maturation of innate systems. The next stage is due to learning, the assimilation of cultural display rules, and the acquisition of voluntary control of emotional expression (Malatesta 1985).

Infants show contagion to the crying of other infants, and as early as one to two months are able to imitate the facial expression of another person, including tongue, lip, and brow movements, and can imitate whole facial expressions for emotion (Meltzoff and Moore

1977). It is likely that imitation plays a role in the fine-tuning of emotional expression. Mothers react differentially to emotional expression: between three and six months mothers often match infant expressions, and usually make positive responses. However, they manage to make boys more stoic by responding less to crying, and they give a greater range of responses to girls (Malatesta 1985). Another way in which infants are influenced by others is by looking at their mother to see how she is reacting, and then expressing the same state. This happens when the infant is uncertain how to react, and is found from six months onwards (Feinman 1985).

The expression of emotion is at first very similar to an automatic reflex response – startle is an example. Gradually it comes under voluntary control, and is used in the service of more complex social plans. This is first shown in the instrumental use of crying and smiling, by withholding such expressions when there is no one to see or hear, and equally to exaggerating them when there is, as is found at twelve months. Thus the use of emotional expressions to communicate with other people seems to be a very basic feature. As we shall see, adults use facial expressions far more in the presence of others (Cole 1985).

The clearest demonstration of route (2) is in the operation of *display rules*. Members of different cultural groups are taught how facial (and other) expressions should be controlled. Expressions may be intensified, deintensified, neutralized, or masked with the behaviour associated with another emotion. Most of the differences in emotional expressions between cultures are caused by such display rules. Friesen (1972) carried out an experiment in which twenty-five Americans and twenty-five Japanese watched a very unpleasant film of sinus surgery, while seated alone; their facial expressions were videotaped, unknown to the subjects, and very similar expressions of disgust, etc. were shown by both groups. However, in a subsequent interview about the film the Japanese subjects produced happy faces while the Americans continued to show negative expressions.

Saarni (1979) suggested that display rules can also include personal display rules, direct deception, and pretending, in the service of expression management and entertainment, for example. She set up an experiment in which children were disappointed by receiving undesirable gifts (a baby's toy) for helping in the experiment. Displays of negative affect fell off with age between six and ten, the older girls controlling them most, the younger boys least. In another experiment she asked children to choose the right facial expression for the last frame of a series of pictured episodes. With increasing age there was an increasing tendency not to choose the face corresponding to the emotion experienced. The reasons they gave for concealment of true state were avoiding trouble (44 per cent), maintaining self-esteem (30 per cent), not hurting others' feelings (19 per cent), and politeness (8 per cent).

This gives the explanation of keeping to display rules – avoiding negative social consequences. People are aware that if they show inappropriate emotions, for example at funerals or occasions for celebration, there will be negative reactions; women are especially aware of these effects (Argyle, Furnham, and Graham 1981). There are considerable social pressures on air hostesses, nurses, teachers, and others to express appropriate, positive emotions and interpersonal attitudes (Hochschild 1979).

Harris, Olthof, and Terwogt (1981) asked six-, eleven-, and fifteen-year-old children how they would 'pretend not to be angry', and so on. The most common method was simply changing facial expression, or other aspects of display. However, the older children were also able to alter the emotion itself, by changing the situation, or by internal changes such as not thinking of something sad.

One of the main sources of display rules is the surrounding culture. Cultural variations in emotional expression include: (1) variations in the degree to which all such expression is restrained; (2) cultural conventions, especially about laughing and crying in public; (3) cultural variations in the events which elicit emotional reactions (if the birth of twins will result in the twins and their mother being put to death, as was the case at one time in the Niger delta, the birth of twins is not an occasion for rejoicing); (4) variations due to the fact that language and ideas may affect the way emotions are categorized (the Japanese make a clearer distinction than other cultures between 'sad' (e.g. because of a tragedy) and 'depressed' (an irrational mood)).

Cultural rules, and parental styles, are passed on through socialization in the family. Individual differences and gender differences in expressiveness can be partly explained in this way.

Expression of emotion in the face

Encoding

The generally accepted evolutionary theory of facial and other expressions is that these are 'read-outs' for other members of the species, which have evolved because they make social co-operation easier. However, we have just seen that infants begin to inhibit their emotional expressions, at about twelve months, if they see that there is no one to receive these messages. Or perhaps there is maturation of additional circuits, which require the presence of others, in addition to an emotional state, before the read-out is provided.

To what extent are emotional expressions produced in adults in the *absence* of others? There are few studies of this. Ekman, Friesen, and Ancoli (1980) showed happy and unpleasant films to subjects who were tested individually in a closed room. The happy films showed, for example, a gorilla playing at the zoo; the unpleasant films showed, for example, the tip of a man's finger being cut off by a saw. Facial activity of subjects was recorded by a concealed videocamera, and analysed by FACS. The happy films produced more Action Unit 12 activity (zygomatic major, lip corners pulled), while the unpleasant films produced more Action Units corresponding to disgust, pain, anger, fear, sadness, and contempt. In each case the stronger the subjective report of emotion, the greater the Action Units score.

Friesen (1972) discovered that subjects shown disgusting films, thinking that they were alone, showed disgust expressions. However, there is no doubt that stronger facial expressions are shown when people are in the presence of others – showing the importance of route (2). For example, in a study in a bowling alley it was found that people were much more likely to smile or frown at their friends, when they had hit or missed, than at the skittles (Table 8.1).

Table 8.1 *Smiling at the bowling alley (%)*

	Hit	Missed
at people	42	28
at skittles	4	3

Similarly, people in the street smile more on a sunny day, but especially if they are with other people (Table 8.2).

Table 8.2 *Smiling in the street (%)*

	Good weather	Bad weather
with others	61	57
alone	12	5

Source: Kraut and Johnston 1979

How are emotions shown in the face?

The main research method has been to ask a number of subjects to pose emotions. Ekman, Friesen, and Tomkins (1971) used eighty photographs from twenty-eight persons, taking examples from the stimuli of earlier investigators, and covering the six main emotions. The photographs were judged by eighty-two observers. Fifty-one of the photographs were retained and analysed by FAST for expressions in each part of the face.

Plate 8.1   Facial expressions for emotion (Ekman and Friesen 1976)

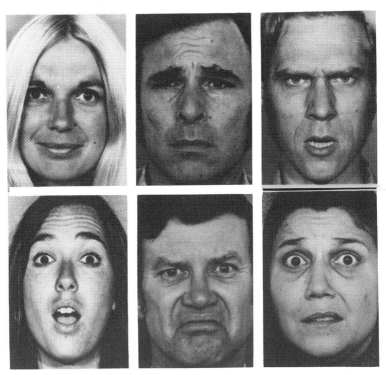

Happy, for example, consists of (1) the corners of the mouth are drawn back and slightly up, the lips may be together or slightly parted; (2) there are wrinkle lines from the nose to the corners of the mouth, and the cheeks are raised; (3) crow's feet wrinkles go outward from the outer corners of the eyes; lower eyelids show wrinkles below them (Ekman and Friesen 1975). All three areas of the face are involved in each emotion. However, some emotions are shown predominantly in certain parts of the face, as follows:

Fear and sadness, decoded from eyes/eyelids.
Happiness, from cheeks/mouth, eyes/eyelids with cheeks/mouth.
Surprise, from brows/forehead, eyes/eyelids, and cheeks/mouth.
Anger could not be decoded from any one area, but needed a view
of all three.

(Boucher and Ekman 1975)

FACS was used in recent studies of the facial expression of pain.
Craig and Patrick (1985) induced pain by cold in females, and found
6 AUs or combinations of AUs were affected. However, Patrick,
Craig, and Prkachin (1986) induced pain by electric shock and found
that only 4 AUs were affected: 4 (lower brow), 6 (raise cheeks), 10
(raise upper lip), 45 (blink).

The same emotion can be expressed in different ways, often corresponding to different degrees of intensity. In a more intense smile,
for example, the mouth is opened and the teeth show. Anger with
violence has a closed mouth, but of course with verbal abuse the
mouth is open. Several kinds of surprise have been distinguished –
questioning, amazed, dazed, and full (Ekman and Friesen 1975).

Sometimes the face shows more than one emotion at the same time
– this has been called a 'blend' – usually expressing different emotions in different parts of the face. A pleasant surprise, for example,
may produce a blend of happiness and surprise – an open smile plus
raised eyebrows. Receipt of bad and frightening news could produce
a combination of sadness and fear (Ekman and Friesen 1975).
Another kind of blend appears when an attempt is made to conceal
the emotion which is actually being experienced, and to mask it with
a different one – a conflict between routes (1) and (2). We discussed
these cases of deception and leakage on p.78.

The development of decoding in children

Infant monkeys reared in isolation start to discriminate between
friendly and threatening faces at the age of two months. Evidently
the ability to decode emotions in monkeys is at least partly innate,
but needs a period of maturation (Sackett 1966). Human infants are
able to respond to voices during the first days of life – they are
aroused by loud noises, and orient away from sudden noises, they
prefer female voices, can discriminate their mother's voice, prefer
her to use a lower-pitched sound, and they are distressed by the crying of other children (Dolgin and Azmitia 1985).

The visual responsiveness of infants is less well developed. In the
early days of life infants can discriminate between shapes at 50 cm,

and they are attracted by oval shapes which have some contrast and symmetry and which move; the mother's face fits all these requirements. They scan the perimeter of faces at first, but make eyecontact at about three-and-a-half weeks. Between three and five months infants come to discriminate first joy, then surprise, fear, and sadness. Happiness or joy is both the first to be recognized and the easiest to recognize, fear the most difficult (Ekman 1982). Between five and seven months infants can make similar responses to the same expression on the faces of different target persons and of different sexes (Dolgin and Azmitia 1985).

The capacity to decode further emotions from faces develops with age – by the age of two years children can recognize the six main facial expressions for emotion. Older children are aware that another's inner emotion may be different from what they are expressing, especially in the case of negative feelings. They take account of the situation as well as the observed behaviour and expression (Harris, Olthof, and Terwogt 1981).

No doubt learning plays a part in the acquisition of these and further, finer discriminations. In the case of monkeys, those raised with others, or even with dogs are more responsive to the details of faces shown on slides than monkeys reared in isolation, and recognize friendly and threatening faces earlier (Mason 1985). Human infants evidently learn to discriminate their mother's voice even *before* birth, and learn to recognize her face by three months. However, if the expression of emotions is mainly unlearnt, and since encoding and decoding must have evolved together as part of a total communication system, it is to be expected that decoding is largely unlearnt as well.

We saw earlier that there is evidence of an innate emotional response to positive and negative faces. Stammers, Byrd, and Gabriel (1985) found that the speed of response to faces is greatest for pleasant female faces, 0·72 seconds, as opposed to 0·81 for unpleasant male ones, for example. This could, however, be due to the effects of early socialization.

The accuracy of decoding

How accurately can people judge another person's emotional state from his or her face? We argued that the evolution of facial expression took place because the availability of this read-out was so useful for social life and co-operation in groups. However, the development of route (2) in humans has made faces very much more difficult to decode.

Some early studies used candid photographs of faces taken from newspapers and magazines. Judges did quite well here – 70 per cent or more were correct in judging them. However, these were probably extreme and unrepresentative expressions, perhaps hammed up for the camera, and it is not known with certainty what emotions were being experienced (Ekman 1982).

Most experimental work on decoding accuracy has used carefully posed facial expressions, i.e. emphasizing the operation of route (2), with an element of route (1) if something like 'method acting' is involved, where performers try to put themselves into the mood in question. Ekman (1982) reviewed nine such studies, and I have averaged the accuracy scores:

happy	79%
surprise	65%
fear	62%
anger	55%
sad	57%
disgust/contempt	54%

The precise degree of accuracy depends on a number of factors. Exaggerated posed expressions are easiest, followed by posed, followed by spontaneous (Zuckerman *et al.* 1981). It also depends how long a slide is exposed: in the BART test for decoding ability this is reduced to 1/60 second to make it harder (see p.274f.). McLeod and Rosenthal (1983) found that accuracy increased if sequences of three segments of 1/8 second were shown in the usual order. If the 'best' photographs are used, accuracy may go up to 80 per cent, and higher than this for happiness, fear, and determination. Woodworth (1938) found which facial expressions can be distinguished most easily: anger may be confused with disgust and fear, but not with love or surprise.

There are individual differences in ability to send and to receive. Sending ability can be assessed by using a sample of decoders, receiving ability by a sample of senders. Both kinds of individual difference are discussed in Chapter 17.

Interest has shifted to the study of spontaneous expression, i.e. generated mainly by route (1). Buck *et al.* (1972) devised the following technique: subjects sat alone in a cubicle, were shown twenty-five slides for ten seconds each – scenic, sexual, maternal, unpleasant, or unusual – and then described them to the experimenter; the subjects were filmed by a concealed TV camera and seen over CCTV by decoders who rated their facial expressions for pleasantness. Decoders did better than the chance level of 20 per cent – 32·5 per cent in this experiment, 31·8 per cent in a later one (Buck, Miller, and Caul 1974).

A number of other studies produced stronger negative states by electric shocks. It was found that judgements of pleasant–unpleasant could be made with a fairly high degree of success (Ekman 1982). But can individual spontaneous emotions be decoded? Wagner, MacDonald, and Manstead (1986) selected ten slides which reliably created certain emotions, and showed them to senders, who were asked to try to match their emotions to the moods, and who were alone. Judges were shown 10-second segments of video of the senders and were asked to give verbal labels to their expressions. The percentages correct are given below. Catherine Peng (unpub.) in a recent experiment at Oxford obtained rather higher accuracy scores. Emotions were aroused by film, and she asked subjects to match 10-second segments to comparison displays – no words were involved. It is possible that stronger emotions were aroused.

	Wagner et al. (1986)	*Peng*
Happy	48·4%	85%
Disgust	22·7%	53%
Fear	chance	52%
Surprise	chance	42%
Anger	12·7%	40%
Sad	chance	33%

The use of contextual information

It was assumed for a long time that information about situational context would add to non-verbal cues and lead to more accurate judgements of emotion. This information may consist of a verbal description of the situation, or of the rest of a photograph, which shows what is happening as in news photos, or a piece of film indicating what has just taken place. However, a careful analysis by Ekman (1982) found contextual information often does not add to accuracy of judging emotions from faces. For example, a reanalysis of Munn (1940) found that sometimes the addition of contextual cues added to accuracy, but that sometimes it reduced it.

Another early view was that the context provides more information than the face. In a number of studies it was found that sometimes one is more informative, sometimes the other. This depends on the clarity of each source, such as how unambiguous they are, and how intense.

Judges also use their knowledge of psychology: if a sad story is combined with a happy face they assume that the face is not genuine; if a sad face is combined with a happy situation they assume that it is (Frijda 1969). Sometimes they think that the emotion has some cause other than the current situation, sometimes they reinterpret the situation (Lalljee, unpub.).

Spignesi and Shor (1981) found the same, in a study in which either the face or the surrounds were masked in news photos, and judgements of pleasant–unpleasant made. Judgements of emotion were closest to face for five combinations, closest to the situation for one, and between the two in three. Subjects tried to make sense of the information in front of them, and used their experience of the world to do so.

Facial expressions and interpersonal attitudes

Some interpersonal attitudes are almost identical with emotions – anger, fear, contempt. The most important interpersonal attitude – liking or attraction – is expressed in exactly the same way as happiness. Sexual attraction is a little different. The other important pair of attitudes – dominance and submission – are different from emotions in the way they are expressed.

Encoding studies show, if this needs to be shown at all, that attraction is signalled primarily by smiling, and the whole facial configuration that goes with it (Mehrabian 1972). Rosenfeld (1966) found that subjects who were seeking another's approval smiled more. On the other hand Beekman (1975) found that although sociable and friendly males smiled more in an interview, females who felt uncomfortable smiled most. Smiling is decoded in terms of warmth and liking and, in the case of therapists, as empathy. In one study smiling was the behaviour most highly correlated with judgements of warmth, 0·67 (Bayes 1972).

Dominance is also communicated by faces – when they are not smiling, and if the brow is lowered (in western cultures, see p.49f.) (Keating et al. 1981). Mehrabian and Williams (1969) asked subjects to enact three levels of persuasiveness. There was greater facial activity when more persuasiveness was attempted. Lefebvre (1975) found that subjects who were trying to ingratiate smiled more.

During social interaction the face is very active, both for speakers and listeners. Smiling is one of the main reinforcers, a powerful source of interpersonal rewards; as well as indicating positive feelings towards the other smiles can be used to reinforce particular acts, such as talking, or talking about particular topics. Frowning does the opposite. The face provides other kinds of back-channel signals, such as surprise and not understanding, mainly achieved by eyebrow movements. Some of these are conventional signs, and are sent deliberately in a form which displays only part of a normal emotion, e.g. eyebrows raised (question) while the rest of the face is static, a wink, a nose wrinkle (disgust) – which Ekman and Friesen (1975) called 'facial emblems'.

These are all cases of co-ordination of facial expression with speech. Facial interaction can also occur in the absence of speech. Izard *et al.* (unpub.) found that relationships between monkeys are destroyed if the facial nerve is severed. Kendon (1977) analysed the sequence of events in a 'kissing round' and found that facial expression played a central part in the sequence. For example, while a closed-lips smile from the girl led to a kiss, an open-mouth smile did not.

An important sequence may be simultaneous smiling with mutual gaze. This happens in greeting (p.22). Americans normally reciprocate smiles, and this correlates with social competence; Israeli children, however, do not do this (p.52).

Facial expression affects attributions and associated reactions by others. Forgas, O'Connor, and Morris (1983) showed varied photographs of a supposed offender. Smiling targets were evaluated more favourably and thought to be less responsible for the crime, especially if it was a minor one. Facial expression works in a very similar way here to physical attractiveness (p.252f.).

However, as we saw in Chapter 6, while the face is the most important channel for expressing emotions, for interpersonal attitudes, signals like proximity, gaze, posture, and touch also carry a lot of weight.

Face and personality

There is only a limited sense in which personality can be said to be encoded in the face. Thin people have thin faces, and physique has some correlation with temperament (p.245f.). Facial expression is often taken as a cue to permanent emotional state, and can be deliberately managed to create a certain impression. The appearance of the face can be changed by means of cosmetics, spectacles, and attention to hair (p.247f.). However, even the aspects of the face which cannot be altered in these ways may be decoded in terms of personality traits.

Many experiments have been carried out using experimentally varied identikit displays. The main finding has been that 'babyfaces' are seen as less mature. Faces with a small, rounded chin, large and rounded eyes, high eyebrows, a large forehead, and smooth skin are perceived as belonging to people who are more warm, submissive, dependent, weak, naïve, honest, less threatening, and less mature. They are also seen as younger, but if perceived age is held constant they are still seen as possessing these age-associated properties (Berry and McArthur 1986). The explanation of the maturity effect is presumably a generalization from the properties of children.

These immature facial features in a woman are seen as attractive, in a man as unattractive (Keating 1985). We shall discuss the facial features of attractiveness later (p.250). Part of the explanation of those results is that biologically healthy people are thought to be good mates; perhaps the same applies to youthful females and mature males.

More complex aspects of faces had been studied earlier by Secord, Dukes, and Bevan (1959) who used twenty-four news photos of men, which were rated for twenty-three physiognomic features by one set of judges and on thirty-five personality traits by others. The faces which were grouped together as similar in shape were also thought to be similar in personality. Clusters of physiognomic features were correlated with clusters of traits, as follows:

Features	*Judged as*
shallow-set eyes light eyebrows bright eyes	carefree, easy-going, cheerful, with a sense of humour, honest, warm-hearted
younger face few horizontal wrinkes	energetic, conscientious, patient, honest, warm-hearted, friendly, intelligent, responsible, kind, trustful, easy-going
older face averagely thick lips	meek, studious
older face thin lips	distinguished, intelligent, refined
dark complexion oily, coarse skin	hostile, boorish, sly, quick-tempered, conceited
younger face low eyebrows narrowed eyes	carefree, excitable sly, conceited

Secord and Muthard (1955) did a similar study on twenty-four photographs of the faces of young women, who had been asked not to smile, though some of them did. Four clusters of personality features were found, and they correlated with physiognomic features as follows:

Features	Traits
bright eyes, widened eyes	moral character (sincere, conscientious)
eyelids not visible, smooth skin, well-groomed, smiling	social acceptability (likeable, good mixer)
high eyebrows, tilted head, narrowed eyes	golddigger syndrome (likes men's attention, conceited, demanding)
narrowed eyes, relaxed mouth, beautiful, thick lips, smooth skin, well-groomed, much lipstick	sexuality

It is unfortunate, however, that nearly all this research is based on judgements of photographs, or very brief exposure of the target persons, in view of the finding that the effect of wearing spectacles on judgements of intelligence wears off after a few minutes' observation of the target person (p.249).

What is the explanation of these inferences from faces? Some of them are clearly based on ethnic and other stereotypes, for example photographs of people with curly hair, dark skin, and thick lips are seen as black, or partly so, and associated stereotypes are applied.

Facial features can lead to impressions of personality in several other ways, as Secord has pointed out. A person's face is similar to that of other people one has known, and creates the anticipation that he will be similar in personality too. If he smiles or looks anxious one may assume that this is his normal condition, and not in this situation alone. There may be inference from the function of parts of the face – high foreheads are thought to contain large brains, thick lips to be good at kissing, spectacles are used for reading and intellectual work. And there may be metaphorical associations, for example, people with coarse skins and dishevelled hair are thought to be coarse and aggressive. Empathy may also be involved; by imagining what we would feel like if we adopted that facial expression, we imagine what it would feel like to be the other person.

To the extent that facial features can be manipulated, communication is involved, but the code used depends on the kinds of judgement commonly made, as described above. Probably the main way in which people manipulate their facial features is by adopting certain expressions – suggesting that they are happy, keen, thoughtful, or superior.

9

Non-verbal vocalizations

Vocalizations consist of sounds, of different frequencies and intensities, put together in different sequences. Some of these are encoded and decoded as meaningful speech, while others express emotions or interpersonal attitudes, or convey information about the sender.

The most objective way of describing sounds is in terms of their acoustic properties, which are:

(1) Duration, rate of speech.
(2) Amplitude (perceived as loudness).
(3) F_0, fundamental frequency (perceived as pitch) and pitch range.
(4) Spectrum of frequency × amplitude (perceived as voice quality, e.g. robust, hollow, shrill).
(5) Pitch contour, i.e. change of frequency with time (Scherer 1982).

Another way of describing sounds is by verbal labels which can be used by listeners, such as breathy, nasal, throaty, resonant, clipped, harsh, warm, etc.

It is useful to distinguish between the sounds which are part of language and those which are independent of it.

Emotional cries

These include moans and groans, shrieks and screams, crying and laughing, oohs and ahs, even roaring and grunting, and are of interest since they are the most similar to animal vocalizations. They have nothing to do with language.

Language

In terms of evolution, language is a later system which has been incorporated in the vocal channel, superimposed on more primitive vocal messages.

Vocalizations linked to speech

Prosodic signals are really part of language – e.g. rising pitch to ask a question, pauses and other aspects of timing to show syntax, loudness to give emphasis. Although prosodic signals appear to be part of language, they also convey emotional information.

Synchronizing signals. The synchronizing of utterances is partly achieved by vocal signals, such as a falling pitch at the end of an utterance (p.114).

Filled pauses, ers and ahs, are not emotional sounds, but one of a number of kinds of speech disturbance; others are repetitions, stutters, incoherent sounds, omissions, sentence changes, and incompleteness.

Paralinguistic aspects of vocalization

These express emotions and attitudes to other people by the way in which words are spoken; the non-verbal message is given simultaneously with the verbal one. This information is conveyed by speech qualities like pitch, loudness, and speed. Other aspects of paralinguistics overlap with prosodic signals. 'Pitch contour' can be a prosodic signal indicating end of utterance; it can also be a paralinguistic cue for emotion.

Information about the speaker

The way a person speaks can convey information about his or her personality, age, sex, social class, regional origins and, above all, who they are. We can classify these different signals as shown in Figure 9.1.

The production of sound

Sounds are made by exhaling air from the lungs, setting it into vibration, as in an organ pipe, modified by the settings of the pharynx, palate, tongue, teeth, and lips.

The perceived pitch of a sound is determined by its fundamental frequency (F_0), and the quality of the sound by the pattern of harmonies or resonance based on that frequency, which make up the speech spectrum.

Sound properties are generated in three main ways:

Figure 9.1   Non-verbal vocalizations

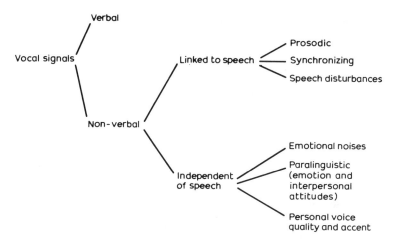

(1) The setting of the larynx, the vocal chords in the throat, largely determines pitch. Air vibration is produced by rhythmic opening and closing of the glottis.

(2) The vibrating column of air passes through the upper vocal tract, which has many folds; the setting of these alters the strength of different harmonies, and thus changes the quality of the sound. Muscular tension, resulting in constriction and shortening of various parts of the larynx and pharynx, has the effect of raising F_0, and increasing the strength of its resonating 'formants', F1 at about 500 Hz, F2 at 1500, and F3 at 2500.

(3) Voiced consonants and vowels are generated by lips, tongue, and mouth. It is in this region that evolution has given man a greater repertoire of sounds than monkeys (Scherer 1982).

The processes of encoding are not fully understood. Part of the story is that unpleasant feelings produce constriction of nose and mouth (as in disgust) and hence a nasal tone, while pleasant feelings produce a different sound quality via a relaxed throat and smiling face. Arousal leads to greater larynx and pharynx tension, as described above (Scherer 1986).

The evolutionary origins of vocalization

Many have noted the similarity between the screams, groans, and other emotional sounds made by man, and the sounds emitted on similar occasions not only by apes and monkeys, but also by lions and bears. This is one reason for thinking that human vocalizations for emotion are mainly innate. And, as we shall see, infants produce a standard repertoire of calls. The origins of vocalization are in breathing in and out, to prepare for exertion, to expel disgusting smells, or while closing the throat protectively. These sounds became ritualized for communication purposes, appearing as distress calls and the rest (p.37f.).

We have seen that apes and monkeys have repertoires of about thirteen calls, corresponding to the main emotions. These are an advance upon the vocalization of lower animals in that use is made of continuous dimensions of sound, and of several dimensions at once. For example, the spectral composition of the cries of rhesus monkeys varies with dominance.

However, while primates can only make about thirteen different calls, the human vocal system has evolved so that we can make a much larger number of sounds. And birds have the capacity to learn to recognize the voices of their near-relatives from those of thousands of others, just as we can.

While animals emit calls mainly in conditions of intense emotion, man uses sounds of disgust or satisfaction as controlled 'social emblems', where it would be less satisfactory simply to use words (Scherer 1981).

Vocalizations of human infants

The main vocalizations of infants consist of crying, which they do from birth onwards, in response to a variety of forms of distress or annoyance. Several different kinds of crying soon appear: (1) hunger cries, which are rhythmic, lasting about 0·65 seconds; (2) anger cries, lasting about the same time, but with a much coarser quality; (3) pain cries, typically 4 seconds at first, followed by 7 seconds of silence (Wolff 1969). There can also be lower pitched moaning from week three, to get attention, and fear cries by the seventh month, when strangers appear. Bowlby's (1958) explanation of crying is that it is a survival mechanism, a means of eliciting maternal care.

Human infants also make some positive vocalizations. Smiling starts very early in life, and is accompanied by cooing from early in the second month. Laughter appears a little later in response to tickling, at about three months, as it does in primates (Malatesta 1981).

Infants respond to vocalizations at an early age. Even when in the womb loud noises produce increased heart-rate several weeks before birth; by three days babies can distinguish between their mother's voice and that of a stranger. Infants are receptive to and prefer higher-pitched voices with smooth pitch contours. Mothers exaggerate both features in 'motherese'. To soothe babies they use a lower pitch and falling contours (Aslin, Pisoni, and Jusczyk 1983).

The communication of emotion

Much research has used posed vocal expressions, where performers have been asked to read something as if they were in some emotional state. Other studies have used role-played scenarios, while some have used mood-induction procedures to produce the required emotions. Here, as elsewhere in bodily communication, posed expressions are not quite the same as the real thing. Posed fearful voices increase raised maximum pitch correctly, for example, but do not raise the minimum pitch (Williams and Stevens 1972).

Several different methods have been employed to remove the effects of the verbal contents of speech – reading neutral passages or counting, using a band-pass filter which cuts out sounds over 400 or 500 Hz, random splicing of tapes in 2-in. segments, and playing tapes backwards.

Davitz and his colleagues (1964) carried out an important series of studies in which senders posed up to fourteen expressions while reading neutral passages, like 'I'm going out now, if anyone calls say I'll be back shortly'. They found the range of accuracy of senders and receivers, and which emotions were communicated most accurately.

In these and similar studies, with between four and ten emotions, the average accuracy level is 56 per cent versus about 12 per cent by chance, which is about the same as the recognition of facial expressions. Some emotions are more easily recognized: negative ones are decoded more easily than positive ones – anger, followed by sadness, indifference, and unhappiness (Scherer 1981). Joy and hate have been found easier to recognize than shame or love. Some emotions are often confused with each other, because their acoustic properties are similar. Emotions with a high level of activation are confused, e.g. anger, elation, and fear, as are those with a low level, e.g. sadness and indifference.

One problem is that some senders are easier to decode than others; Davitz (1964) found a range of 23–50 per cent for different senders. They are easier to decode if they exaggerate, followed by posed performances, with natural ones the most difficult. Receivers also vary in sensitivity – from 20 to 50 per cent in the Davitz studies.

In order to separate encoding from decoding, acoustic measurements are needed. An example of encoding research is an experiment by Williams and Stevens (1972) using three male actors as senders, and two acoustic measures of voice quality (Table 9.1).

Table 9.1   *Speed and pitch for posed emotions*

	Neutral	Anger	Fear	Sorrow
speed (syllables/sec)	4·31	4·15	3·80	1·91
pitch (F_0)	110	158	139	101

In a rare study of real and intense fear, it was found that the pitch range of the pilot of a crashing plane shifted from 168–272 Hz to 288–492; both upper and lower limits of pitch were raised (Williams and Stevens 1972).

An example of decoding research is a study by Scherer and Oshinsky (1977) who incorporated a wide range of acoustic variables in sounds from a Moog synthesizer, and asked judges to rate the emotions.

Many such studies have now been done on how emotions are encoded. Scherer (1986) reviewed thirty-nine of them. Some of the main findings are as follows:

Joy, elation: raised pitch, pitch range in an utterance, pitch variability, intensity, speech rate, gentle contours.

Depression: lowered pitch, pitch range, intonation, intensity, speech rate, less energy at high pitches.

Anxiety: raised pitch, faster speech, more speech disturbances (except for ah-errors), silent pauses, breathy voice quality, but there is wide individual variation, e.g. some people speak slower when anxious. Nervous public speakers have more and longer silent pauses. Raised pitch speed, and hesitations in speech indicate deception (p.80).

Fear: raised pitch, pitch range, variability, high energy at higher pitches, speech rate, special voice quality as in crying.

Anger: raised pitch in rage, lowered in cold anger, raised intensity, harsh voice quality, higher speech rate, sudden increases of pitch and loudness on single syllables (Scherer 1986).

To what extent are these cues used to encode emotions? The main dimension for both senders and receivers is clearly arousal – communicated by loudness, pitch, and speed, which correlate together. Joy, confidence, anger, and fear all score high. To discriminate between these emotions we have to look at more subtle acoustic parameters. In fact, variables which communicate each emotion are quite similar to those shown above.

The importance of sequential information was shown in an experiment in which tapes were played backwards; this reduced decoding accuracy from 89 per cent to 43 per cent (Knower 1941), showing that contour is important. Synthesizing sounds with all components except spectral structure reduced accuracy from 85 per cent to 47 per cent (Lieberman and Michaels 1962), so the frequency distribution is important too.

Pitch contour produces some finer differences (Frick 1985).

happy: gentle contours
angry: sudden increases
surprise: rising pitch
sarcasm: fall on stressed syllable
contempt: fall at end of phrase
coquetry: upward glide on last syllable
question: rise at end of non-ah utterance

As we saw earlier (p.78), the voice is a 'leakier' channel than the face, i.e. it is not so well controlled and is more likely to reveal true feelings. Men attend more than women to this leaky channel (p.286).

Interpersonal attitudes

There is some overlap here with emotion, since no distinction is made in the voice between anger as an emotional state, and as an attitude directed towards particular individuals. The Davitz studies, for example, did not distinguish between the two and included admiration, affection, amusement, anger, boredom, despair, disgust, dislike, fear, and impatience – all of which can be directed towards others. In a series of studies by the author and colleagues (1970) a number of interpersonal styles were created, using tones of voice (while counting numbers), facial expressions, and head orientations. We had no difficulty in creating tones of voice, corresponding to friendliness, hostility, superiority, and inferiority (p.91f.). Mehrabian (1972) found that tone of voice contributed slightly less than facial expression but much more than the contents of speech to impressions of interpersonal attitudes.

Everyone knows what friendly voices are like: they are like happy ones which, as we have seen, are high pitched, with a lot of gentle upward pitch variation, pure tones, and regular rhythm. Infants porduce such sounds very early in life – cooing while smiling. Hostile voices are like the angry ones described before – loud, fast, harsh, sharply rising pitch contours, often lowered pitch – babies make these sounds too (Scherer and Oshinsky 1977).

Dominant and submissive are communicated a little differently. Dominant is expressed by a loud voice, low pitch, broad spectrum, often slow. Submissive, like animal appeasement, is higher pitched, sometimes very high, with less resonance, final rising pitch contours, similar to friendly but more tense, anxious, and higher (Frick 1985).

As with the expression of emotion, the voice is often more truthful, more 'leaky' than words. Weitz (1972) rated the voices of eighty supposedly 'liberal' white students as they rehearsed the instructions they were to give to another subject, known to be black or white. It was found that tone of voice (rated for *friendly* and *admiring*) predicted friendly behaviour towards black subjects, e.g. physical proximity and choice of intimate task. On the other hand verbally expressed attitudes to blacks were *negatively* correlated both with tone of voice and friendly behaviour. Those expressing very positive attitudes in fact showed covert rejection of blacks. Tone of voice is leakier than the face, as was shown in connection with the expression of emotion.

Tone of voice is important in social skills and in maintaining relationships. Noller (1984) found that one NV variable which discriminated between happily and unhappily married couples was that the happy couples made more use of the vocal channel for wifehusband communication.

Vocal style has been found to affect persuasiveness. Mehrabian and Williams (1969) found that speakers who spoke faster, louder, and with more intonation were perceived as more persuasive. Later experiments studied the amount of persuasion achieved, and found that the above style is indeed more successful (e.g. Miller *et al.* 1976). In one experiment tapes were speeded up, slowed down, or altered in pitch. Slower tapes were judged to be less truthful and persuasive, more passive; higher pitched tapes were judged similarly (Apple, Streeter, and Krauss 1979).

The credibility of a speaker depends on other aspects of vocal style. Pearce and Conklin (1971) found that an actor was judged as more credible when using a serious, scholarly voice (low pitch and volume, small variation in both) than when using a more emotional delivery. Addington (1968) found that throaty, nasal, breathy, or tense deliveries were found low in credibility and competence.

Other research on social skills has found that social influence needs a combination of assertiveness and rewardingness (Argyle 1983). It is interesting that it is impossible to achieve this combination with the face, since they require opposed expressions. It is possible to signal this combination with the voice, however.

Accent affects persuasiveness and credibility. In Britain an educated 'r.p.' (received pronunciation) accent is regarded as more expert and trustworthy, produces more co-operation, and is more likely to be given a job (Giles and Powesland 1975).

Voice and personality

If judges are asked to rate the personalities associated with different voices, there is quite a high level of agreement between them. However, there is much less agreement between these judgements and objective measures of personality. We should expect some connection between voice and personality, since people do have some consistency in the emotions and attitudes which they express.

Extroversion is one of the best-established dimensions of personality, and it does correlate with voice – higher pitch (for males), greater vocal affect, faster speech, and fewer pauses (for females). Scherer (1978) produced a 'lens' model showing how extroversion, for American males, is encoded as pitch and vocal affect, which are perceived as loudness and (lack of) gloom, and interpreted as extroversion (Figure 9.2).

Figure 9.2   The 'lens' model for extroversion

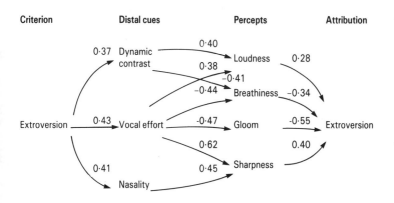

Source: Scherer 1978

A number of experiments have varied the speech style of the same speaker to see how judgements of personality are affected. Rate of speech is one of the most influential variables; faster speech is perceived as potency, extroversion, and competence. Pitch has two effects: raised pitch is judged as extroversion, assertiveness, confidence, and competence, but also as tense and nervous, perhaps because raised pitch is a cue for emotional arousal, which is generalized by perceivers to be a personality trait (Scherer 1979a).

Anxious people do not have quite the same speech qualities as those produced by anxious situations. They speak fast, but with silent pauses, especially long pauses (over 1 ½ seconds); perhaps they need more planning time, and succeed in controlling other kinds of speech disfluency (Siegman 1985).

Another group who have been found to have a particular kind of voice are 'type A' personalities – those who are competitive, aggressive, impatient, and with a strong drive to succeed. They may succeed, but they are also susceptible to coronary heart disease. Their voices are loud, fast, with explosive emphasis, a lot of variation in speed, and little pause before speaking (Jacobs and Schucker 1981).

We shall discuss the vocal characteristics of neurotics and other patients in Chapter 17. They differ in very interesting ways on the speech spectogram.

Research on judgements of voices have found three main dimensions – socioeconomic status, pleasing $v.$ displeasing, and active-passive (Mulec 1976). There is extensive evidence on the stereotypes associated with different voices. Addington (1968) asked male and female performers to speak in nine different ways, and these were then rated by judges on forty scales. There was most agreement on the scales for old–young, masculine–feminine, enthusiastic–apathetic, energetic–lazy, and good-looking–ugly, with interjudge reliabilities of 0·80 or more. Some of the main perceived links with personality were as follows:

breathy: younger, more artistic
flat: more masculine, sluggish, colder, withdrawn
nasal: socially undesirable in various ways
tense: older, unyielding, cantankerous
throaty: older, realistic, mature, sophisticated, well-adjusted
orotund: energetic, healthy, artistic, sophisticated, proud, interesting, enthusiastic
fast: animated, extroverted
varied in pitch: dynamic, feminine, aesthetically inclined.

It is not fully understood what the origins of these stereotypes are.

They may be based partly on true associations with personality, partly on the voices of those for different ages, sexes, and cultural groups, partly on analogy – loud, pleasant, shaky, for example.

However, accuracy of judging personality from voice alone is not very great. Judgements from voice have been found to correlate with overall judgements based on voice, face, and contents of speech less well than judgements based on face or verbal contents (O'Sullivan *et al.* 1985).

Voice and social class

Voice is one of the basic cues to social class. This is because in Britain and many other countries there are class differences in accent as a result of historical processes such as the Victorian public schools' propagation of a particular accent and the BBC's of another. A number of experiments in England and the USA have shown that class can be inferred from accent alone. Sissons (1971), at Oxford, found that accent and clothes were the two best single cues to class. Many people try to modify their accent towards that of a higher class, but this is difficult to do. Ellis (1967) found that speakers' real class could still be judged, with a correlation of 0·65, when they were imitating upper-class accents. Harms (1961) found that American students could judge class after the first 10–15 seconds of taped conversation.

Accent varies greatly between situations. Labov (1966) found that with increasingly careful speech, for example when reading lists of words, lower-class Americans shifted not only towards upper-middle-class speech, but on some indices they 'hyper-corrected', i.e. they went beyond upper-class speech. In England it has been found that there is a hierarchy of accents of different status. There is some evidence about the vocal characteristics of these accents. Middle-class and educated accents are more clearly articulated, use more intonation, and are less blurred. Consonants are sounded more clearly and there is less stumbling over words. This is not the whole story, though, since there are additional features of accents which are quite arbitrary, and serve solely as indicators of social class.

Regional accents

Having categorized the speaker by social class, listeners then apply whatever stereotyped beliefs they have about different social classes to the owner of a voice. Giles and Powesland (1975) used the 'matched guise' method to study this process. Speakers were used who could simulate the accents of different social groups in Britain, and tape-recordings were then assessed by judges. The most prestigeful voices in Britain, with 'received pronunciation' (r.p.), were judged to be most ambitious, self-confident, intelligent, determined, and industrious. In a study which used thirteen different accents, a single dimension of prestige was obtained: r.p., American and French, north of England, Cockney, and Birmingham. Furthermore, people with less prestigeful accents and from the regions where these are spoken, to a large extent shared these stereotypes. However, Scots judging Scottish accents and Yorkshiremen judging Yorkshire accents judged the speakers to have greater personal integrity and to be more good-natured and good-humoured than r.p. speakers.

Lambert *et al.* (1960), working in Montreal with English- and French-speaking Canadians, found evidence for similar shared ethnic stereotypes. Anisfield and colleagues (1962) in America found that a speaker using a Jewish accent was rated as shorter, less good-looking, and lower in leadership – by Jews as well as by Gentiles. They were also rated as higher in humour, entertainingness, and kindness by Jews but not by Gentiles.

Gender

This can be recognized with almost complete success from voice alone. The main difference between males and females is that women's voices are higher pitched, though there is some overlap in the distributions. Women's voices also have greater variation in pitch, especially upward contours (surprise, appeasement), while men use more falling pitch contours. Men talk louder. In addition they try to control conversations and interrupt more. The overall conversational style of men has been characterized as more assertive and less polite (Lakoff 1973). However, both men and women use more assertive voices when talking to men, despite a common belief that women are more submissive with men than with women (Hall and Braunwald 1981). (See also p.281f.)

Use is made of gender stereotypes in deciding whether a voice is male or female, and the stereotypes do not entirely correspond to the actual differences between the sexes. For example, the use of tag-questions is regarded as female, whereas in fact there is no difference. But it is widely believed that male speech is loud and aggressive, women's speech friendly, gentle, and trivial (Smith 1979).

On the decoding side, women attend less than men to the vocal channel, and more to facial expression (p.286f.). This may be because the vocal channel is leakier, revealing what people want to conceal, or because the vocal channel is more concerned with power and dominance, the face with friendship and attraction.

Vocalizations related to speech

The 'prosodic' signals of pitch, stress, and timing are able to convey information about emotions and other aspects of the speaker. They are also able to modify the meaning of the message. This is shown by the method used by Noller (1984) in which spouses were asked to send verbally ambiguous messages to give different meanings (p.110f.). Similar effects can be produced by words or NV vocalizations, for example emotions can be aroused by emotive words or emotive expressions, tension can be created by leaving crucial words to the end, or by the manner of delivery. Extra messages can be added by using accents or special intonations, using question intonation for statements, and in other ways.

Pitch

We have discussed pitch changes as a cue for emotions and attitudes. Perhaps the most basic meaning of a raised pitch is emphasis, interest, and excitement, and it is often accompanied by upward movements of mouth, eyebrows, hands, and shoulders. In addition there are standard pitch patterns in every language for different kinds of sentence. In English, for example, questions beginning with 'How', 'What', etc., are spoken with a falling pitch; but questions with an inversion of subject and verb are spoken with a rising tone. Pitch patterns can be varied to 'frame' or provide further meaning for an utterance. 'Where are you going?' with a rising pitch on the last word is a friendly enquiry, whereas with a falling pitch it is suspicious and hostile. This expresses more than a paralinguistic attitude to the recipient of the question; it indicates additional thoughts on the part of the speaker, and indicates what sort of answer is needed. Pitch pattern can negate the words spoken, sarcastically, or when the word 'yes' is spoken to indicate such unwillingness that it really means 'no'. Changes of pitch can also be used to accent particular words, though this is usually done by loudness.

Stress

The prosodic system of any language includes rules about the patterns of loudness of words in different kinds of sentences. In English the main nouns and verbs are usually stressed. The same sentence may be given different meanings by stressing different words, as in 'they are hunting *dogs*', and 'they are *hunting* dogs'; or a sentence may retain the same basic meaning but attention can be directed to quite different parts of the message, as in '*Professor Brown's daughter* is *fond* of *modern music*' – each of the italicized words could be stressed, and this could change the significance of the utterance. In stressing *daughter* there is some implicit reference to a *son* – a case where a NV signal refers or helps refer to an absent object. Speakers can also make soft contrast by speaking some words very quietly.

Duncan and Rosenthal (1968) found that the amount of stress placed on words in the instructions given to experimental subjects had a marked effect on their responses. Subjects were asked to rate the 'success' or 'failure' of people shown in photographs. There was a correlation of 0·74 between their ratings and the amount of emphasis placed by the experimenter on the words *success* and *failure* when describing the scale to be used.

Pauses

Utterances vary in speed, for example a subordinate clause is spoken faster, and a slower speed is used to give emphasis. Pauses are frequent in speech. Pauses of under 1/5 second are used to give emphasis. Longer ones are used to signal grammatical junctures, for example the ends of sentences and clauses. Other pauses occur in the middle of clauses and may coincide with disfluencies, such as repetitions and changes of sentence. About half of speech is taken up by pauses. Unfilled pauses are longer if a speaker has a more difficult task (p.106). Most unfilled pauses come at grammatical breaks, before phonemic clauses, often before fluent or complex strings of words, suggesting that the pauses are providing time for planning. However, not all pauses are like this and some may be due to anxiety (Siegman and Feldstein 1979)

10
Gaze

Gaze, or looking, is of central importance in social behaviour. It is partly a non-verbal signal but more a means of perceiving the expressions of others, especially their faces. However, the act and manner of looking also have meaning as signals, showing for example the amount of interest in another person, and are partly intended as signals. So gaze is both signal and channel, a signal for the recipient, a channel for the gazer.

Gaze, like distance, can be measured in a fairly straightforward way. However, this 'measurement' involves observations by human judges and is therefore open to error. There are several different aspects of gaze, which have different causes and consequences.

Amount of gaze at other

The usual measure is percentage of time spent looking at another in the area of the face. People do not usually fixate steadily on a single point but make a series of glances of about $\frac{1}{3}$ second fixated on different points, especially the eyes and mouth (Yarbus 1967) (Figure 10.1).

Mutual gaze is the percentage of time that two interactors look at each other in the region of the face. 'Eye-contact' has been abandoned as a useful variable, since it is impossible to record with the equipment normally available.

Looking while talking (L_T) and while listening (L_L). These can be measured separately; the ratio between them, L_T/L_L, reflects status.

Glances

Gaze consists of glances, typically of two to three seconds. The average length of glances is another dimension of gaze. A special kind of glance is the 'eyeflash', used to give emphasis.

Mutual glances. Similarly the average length of periods of mutual gaze can be recorded; they are typically about one second.

Pattern of fixation. It is possible to record the precise pattern of fixations, e.g. from left eye to right eye or eye to mouth, or to different parts of another's anatomy; this requires special equipment.

Pupil dilation

The amount of dilation of the pupil is another aspect of gaze, one which has effects on the behaviour of others, though they may not be aware of it.

Eye expression

The eyes are expressive in other ways, by how far they are opened, and the amount of white showing above and below the pupil. This may be seen as 'staring', looking 'intently', 'looking daggers', or 'looking through' the other person, i.e. fixating beyond them, etc. (Fehr and Exline, in press).

Direction of gaze-breaking

When not looking at others, depressed people look downwards; and interactors may break gaze by shifting to the left or right.

Blink-rate

This can be counted, and varies for example with anxiety and concentration.

Research methods

Encoding research

This has studied the amount and type of gaze, not only under the influence of interpersonal attitudes, emotions, and personality, but as affected by such factors as distance between interactors and topic of conversation. Most of this research has been conducted in laboratories, in view of the difficulties of recording gaze accurately elsewhere. Sometimes the subject meets a confederate who gazes a controlled proportion of the time; this has the disadvantage that he or she may feel uncomfortable so doing, and emit unwanted signals.

Plate 10.1   The pattern of visual fixations (after Yarbus, Morris 1977)

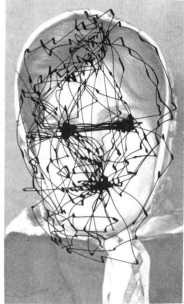

Sometimes pairs, or triads, of genuine subjects are used. Gaze may be assessed as it occurs by observers who operate recording equipment, or it can be videotaped using two cameras and split-screen recording and analysed later at leisure, making it possible to slow down the tape and use multiple observers.

Even if subjects are told that they will be observed, it is desirable that observers and equipment should be unobtrusive. A common procedure is the use of a one-way screen, as shown in Figure 2.1.

Some gaze research has been done under very artificial laboratory conditions. It is better to create settings which have some resemblance to real life, and whose rules and conventions are familiar. A few studies have observed gaze in field settings: LaFrance and Mayo (1976) used stopwatches to record gaze in waiting-rooms and cafeterias, others have filmed from a distance.

Several kinds of recording equipment have been used. To record the total amount of gaze and the number of glances a cumulative stopwatch is sufficient. To record mutual gaze it is necessary to have two observers operating electronic counters, or four-channel event recorders which produce a record on moving paper. The latter makes it possible to analyse in detail sequences of glances in relation to speech. For detailed analysis of where interactors are fixating, an eye-movement recorder is needed. The equipment so far available, however, requires subjects to wear it on their heads, making normal interaction impossible.

Nearly all studies of reliability have found high inter-observer agreement on whether or not a subject was looking at another during different time-intervals – typically 91–94 per cent for one-second units (Fehr and Exline, in press). Validity has been assessed by instructing a confederate to carry out a sequence of gazes which are unknown to the observers. It is found that observers can detect face-directed gaze with some accuracy, but that at two or three metres a proportion of glances to the side of the face are wrongly included (Von Cranach and Ellgring 1973). However, it is doubtful whether in real life people do look just beyond the ears. Observers are less accurate at detecting 'eye-contact'; they can only detect face-directed gaze. But, as we have seen, interactors do not gaze fixedly at eyes; they scan round others' faces, especially the eyes and mouth.

Gaze recording is accurate only under certain conditions: it declines with the distance between sender and receiver, as the sender's head is turned away from head-on, and when eyes are concealed by spectacles or long hair (Kruger and Huckstedt 1969).

Decoding research

This involves the use of trained confederates who are able to control their amount or type of gaze. It may be carried out in the laboratory, where the subjects meet confederates thinking that they are other subjects. It can also be done in field settings, where confederates stare or do not stare at people in libraries, or at motorists at traffic lights, or adopt different levels of gaze when making requests for help. The decoding of gaze can be studied at different points. Receivers may be asked whether or not they noticed the particular gaze pattern. They can be asked about the subjective or phenomenal meaning of being gazed at, mutual gaze, etc. They may be asked to fill in seven-point scales to describe the sender. Or the receiver's behaviour can be recorded, e.g. offering help, leaving the situation.

Interaction sequence analysis

This requires a sample of interaction which is recorded, so that sequences of glances and their relation to speech can be studied, e.g. by Markov analysis. It is possible to introduce experimental variables, such as task difficulty (Argyle and Cook 1976; Fehr and Exline, in press).

The evolutionary, physiological, developmental, and cultural origins of gaze

Gaze is widely used by animals, as a threat signal and as a means of collecting visual information in social situations. Moths and fish have fake 'eye-spots', birds have 'eye-rings', which have evidently developed as social signals to repel predators. It has been found that if the eye-spots are removed from butterflies, birds will eat them, whereas when the eye-spots are present birds will retreat. While it has been suggested that eye-spots are the product of evolutionary 'mimicry' of the eyes of predators, Scaife (1974) argues that this is not so: often they are quite different from, for example, the eyes of owls and their power may simply be due to their being strong stimuli with good black and white contrast.

Gaze is used by primates as a threat signal, and it evokes aggression or sumission; cut-off or gaze aversion signals appeasement. However, gaze is also used as an affiliative signal, for example in grooming and play, and animals in a group direct their visual attention upwards in the status hierarchy, forming an 'attention structure', though it is not known whether this is a cause or effect of the hierarchy. Some animals can change the colour of their eyes under emotion, e.g. red for anger (p.41f.).

Exline and Yellin (1969) carried out a study in which the experimenter approached a rhesus monkey (in a strong cage); if he stared at the monkey the latter tried to attack him in 47 per cent of trials, if he averted his gaze attacks were made on only 28 per cent of trials. Gaze version is an appeasement signal, while gaze is a threat signal.

Eye movements are controlled by four neural systems: one controls saccadic sweep between fixations, another directs pursuit of moving objects, another corrects for head-turning, and the last coordinates the two eyes, between them affecting the six muscles which move each eyeball (Robinson 1968). Pupil dilation is produced by low levels of light, emotionally arousing stimuli, and thinking (Hess 1972).

Human infants, in the first hour of life, will follow a moving object with their eyes; by three or four weeks they respond particularly to a pair of eyes, or to masks including this design. It is not known whether this early interest in eyes is innate or, as Fantz (1961) suggests, there is an innate preference for stimuli of a certain degree of complexity, brightness, and rate of movement. The mother's eyes would be the most arresting object in sight, and there may be early learning of and attachment to the mother's eyes and face. Schaffer (1971) concludes that there is an innate template to respond to stimuli with certain properties, that the mother's eyes have these properties and are at the right distance during feeding. Wolff (1963) found that infants seemed to focus on an observer's eyes and make real eye-contact by 25–28 days. There may be a critical period during which this interest in eyes is established. Later, in the first two months, a mask with two dots will produce a smile, while a real face with eyes hidden will not (Spitz and Wolf 1946). Papousek and Papousek (1977) found that five-month-old babies looked two or three times as long at films of themselves if these allowed eye-contact. Infants have surprising powers of perception: Scaife and Bruner (1975) found that many infants of eleven to fourteen months could follow the experimenter's line of regard, to see what he was looking at – the beginning of seeing another's point of view.

Infants and their mothers play games like peek-a-boo, involving sequences of looking, breaking gaze, smiling, and vocalizing, which can be regarded as the beginnings of conversation, including turn-taking and feedback (Bruner 1977). Gaze produces physiological arousal, and breaking gaze may be a way of controlling level of arousal (Stern 1974). Early mutual gaze may play a part in the establishment of bonding between mothers and infants. It is experienced as very rewarding by mothers, and probably strengthens their maternal responses (Robson 1967).

Gaze levels increase from four to five years, decline during adolescence, and increase again in adults (Levine and Sutton-Smith 1973). Some gaze phenomena are found in children, such as the preference for higher levels of gaze by females; others do not appear until later, such as decoding gaze as liking, the use of terminal gaze in conversation, and learning to avert gaze (Kleinke 1986).

Levels of gaze vary between cultures, though the main phenomena are the same. Latin Americans and southern Europeans look more than the British or white Americans, while black Americans look less (p.57f.). There are rules about gaze, which vary between cultures, and children are instructed to 'look at me', not to stare at strangers, and not to look at certain parts of the body. These norms greatly constrain gaze behaviour; people have to look in order to be polite, but not to look at the wrong people or in the wrong place, e.g. at deformed people.

Gaze during conversation

During conversation two people look at one another quite a lot of the time. Here are the basic statistics for two people in conversation, on an emotionally neutral topic, at a distance of 6 ft:

individual gaze	60 per cent
while listening	75 per cent
while talking	40 per cent
length of glance	3 seconds
eye-contact (mutual glance)	30 per cent
length of mutual glance	1½ seconds

These figures are averages, and there is wide variation according to the personalities of those involved, their attitudes towards each other, and the topic of conversation, as will be described below. In groups of three, for example, each person divides his gaze between the other two, and each person spends only about 5 per cent of his time in mutual gaze with each of the others. The detailed co-ordination of looking with speaking was described in Chapter 7. Here we are concerned only with overall gaze levels.

There is much more gaze, and mutual gaze, when interactors are further apart, as Argyle and Dean (1965) found and many others have confirmed (see Figure 6.4, p.96). This finding provides support for the affiliative balance theory. However Aiello (1972) found that, while this pattern was true for males, there was a curvilinear pattern for females, with reduced gaze at 10 ft, possibly because this distance for women is beyond the boundary for social interaction. In general, gaze acts as one sign of intimacy, which can substitute for others, and hence is likely to vary inversely with them. As well as there being less gaze at closer distances, there is less during deeper self-disclosures.

Those who look more during interaction are seen as attentive, those who gaze little are seen as passive and inattentive (Kleinke 1986). There is much less gaze when there are other things to look at, especially when there is an object of legitimate mutual attention. Argyle and Graham (1977) found that the gaze level in dyads fell from 76·3 per cent, when there was nothing much else to look at, to 6·4 per cent when they were discussing a holiday and there was a relevant map between them. Similarly Argyle, Alkema, and Gilmour (1972) found a very low level of gaze in department stores between sales staff and customers.

Jellison and Ickes (1974) gave subjects the choice of opening or closing a panel between them. If they were going to interview the other they wanted it open; if they were going to be interviewed they wanted it shut; if they expected a co-operative encounter, most wanted it open. These studies clearly demonstrate the use of gaze for monitoring the other's facial expression. Argyle, Lalljee, and Cook (1968) varied the amount one interactor could see another. They became increasingly uncomfortable as visibility was reduced, from normal vision to dark glasses, mask with only eyes showing, and one-way screen (other invisible). However, they were quite happy to be invisible themselves.

Other studies, which were reviewed in Chapter 7, show that glances are timed to collect information when it is needed, and that people look away when it is not needed. Experiments in which subjects are asked to gaze continuously find that this creates distracting cognitive overload. Exline and Winters (1966) found that gaze was reduced when difficult topics were discussed.

Information-seeking may be the reason that people look at others who are crippled or pregnant (especially if they can look unobserved) (Kleck 1968), and at non-reinforcing confederates and people who have given negative evaluations – to find out why (Kleinke 1986). This all points to one of the main functions of gaze – collecting information from the expressions on others' faces. It also shows that too much of this information is distracting. We shall see that there are other functions of gaze – starting and stopping encounters, expressing attitudes to others, acting as a social reinforcer, and helping to synchronize speech.

The effects of gaze on others

Do people notice the gaze behaviour of others? Some do not, probably as a result of not looking very much themselves. However, most subjects notice the difference between 15 per cent and 80 per cent gaze levels. The general impression formed of a high level of gaze is that the other is interested, or wishing to initiate interaction. Being looked at by another can be a source of discomfort – self-consciousness, a feeling of 'being observed', or being an object for another (Argyle and Williams 1969). Mutual gaze gives a feeling of intimacy, mutual attraction, and openness (Simmel 1921). More specific interpretations, in terms of interpersonal attitudes, emotions, and personality are discussed below.

A number of experiments have found increased levels of physiological arousal during periods of mutual gaze, in terms of GSR and heart-rate (Gale *et al.* 1978). These effects are rather inconsistent, but appear to be stronger when the gaze is likely to be interpreted as threat, competition, or close intimacy (Kleinke 1986). However, these studies have used very artificial situations, with no conversation.

Does gaze affect another person's behaviour? We have argued that gaze is a source of information, especially giving feedback, i.e. reactions to one's own behaviour. It follows that those who do not look enough are likely to be incompetent interactors. This is found to be the case: socially inadequate mental patients often have low levels of gaze (Trower 1980, and p.255f.). Burgoon *et al.* (1985) found that confederate candidates with low levels of gaze were less likely to be given jobs by interviewers, even though their qualifications were no different from those of other candidates.

A series of experiments has used confederates to ask other people for help, varying their gaze levels: when they looked more, more help was given (Snyder, Grether, and Keller 1974). The amount of help given is greater when the confederate is of the opposite sex, and when the request is legitimate (Kleinke 1980). Gaze, like touch and physical attractiveness, is a powerful reinforcer and has the power to strengthen any kind of social influence. However, while people are aware of touch, they are not aware of gaze (Brockner *et al.* 1982). People who are trying to be persuasive gaze more, and are indeed more persuasive (p.259). Teachers who look more at their pupils in school or college generate more work and more learning (Kleinke 1986). Those with higher levels of gaze are seen as credible and trustworthy, though in fact gaze aversion is not a very reliable cue for deception (p.80). Evidently gaze is a common feature of a wide range of social skills.

Interpersonal attitudes

Gaze plays an important role in negotiating when social encounters will start and when they end. In public places people signal their awareness of others and usually their lack of interest in and lack of threat to them, by short glances when at a distance – what Goffman (1963) called 'civil inattention'. Interaction between strangers is more likely to take place when inside a room, especially following an episode of mutual gaze (Cary 1978). To initiate interaction with another requires manipulation of proximity, facial expression, and gaze, but especially gaze. Greetings proper, and partings, involve complex sequences of NVC, in which the making and breaking of mutual gaze plays a central part (p.221).

Liking and loving

Patterns of gaze play an important role in establishing relations between people. Gaze functions as an efficient signal here in that there is a match between encoding and decoding – people interpret gaze patterns correctly.

People look more at those they like. Exline and Winters (1966) arranged for subjects to talk with two confederates. As expected, each subject preferred one stooge to the other; they were asked to say which one they preferred, thus making their preferences more salient. It was found that subjects looked 2·7 times as much at one stooge as at the other. Similar results have been obtained using role-playing, though Mehrabian (1969) found that subjects gazed most in the intermediate liking condition.

Married couples who report marital discord look at each other less (Beier and Sternberg 1977); younger couples who are most in love have a higher proportion of gaze that is mutual (Rubin 1970), suggesting that their mutual gaze is sought, not a matter of chance. Females decorate their eyes to enhance size and contrast, and at one time used drops of belladonna to dilate their pupils. The exchange of gaze is important in courtship, especially in Bali, it is reported (Mead 1928).

People gaze more if they anticipate positive reactions from another. Efran (1968) found that subjects looked more at a smiling and nodding member of a triad. Modigliani (1971) found that subjects looked less at a critical confederate after failing at a task. Male subjects look more at females when attractiveness has been experimentally enhanced (Kleck and Rubenstein 1975). This suggests that people look partly to perceive rewarding facial signals, and avert gaze to avoid negative ones.

Other people, and their faces, have been associated in the past with both rewards and punishments. It follows that the approach–avoidance conflict model can be applied (p.94), and that an intermediate level of gaze will be adopted, reflecting the strength of the two forces. If the level of gaze is higher than the equilibrium level, avoidance forces are stronger and the experience is aversive, as with too much proximity or touch. We have seen that gaze acts as one of a number of signals for intimacy and that it can substitute for proximity, and others.

Individuals look more when co-operating than when competing (Foddy 1978). This supports a different theory of the looking–liking effect, that interactors are 'willing to share affective involvement' (Exline and Winters 1966).

A number of studies have found that a high level of gaze is interpreted as liking, using both natural variations and experimentally varied gaze levels. For example, Mehrabian (1969) arranged for an interviewer to look much more at one subject than another. Both thought that she liked the gazed-on subject more. On the other hand in some experiments it has been found that females like males or females who looked at them a lot, but males preferred males or females with a lower level of gaze (Kleinke *et al.* 1973). Other experiments have found that people like those who look at them more – up to a point, since 100 per cent gaze is found uncomfortable (Argyle, Lefebvre, and Cook 1974).

Pupil dilation is another sign of sexual interest: Hess and Polt (1960) found that male pupils dilated to photographs of female nudes, while female pupils dilated to partly clothed muscular men and to babies, and homosexual males to male nudes.

In a classic experiment Hess (1972) found that young men preferred the photo of a girl whose pupils had been touched up to show dilation, and that their own pupils dilated, though they had no conscious awareness of the cue to which they were responding (Plate 10.2). But do people react to pupils under normal conditions of social interaction? Stass and Willis (1967) experimentally manipulated both the amount of gaze and the size of pupils (using a drug), and found that subjects chose as a partner the person who looked more, but that pupil dilation also had some effect. Pupil dilation is a difficult cue to use – it can only be seen at close quarters and in good light, and pupils respond in any case to changes in the illumination, by enlarging when it gets darker.

Plate 10.2 Pupil dilation (Globe Photos, Inc.)

Dominance and status

We have seen that gaze in primates mainly signals dominance and threat. In threat displays during battles for dominance between males gaze is used as part of the display, and the defeated animal looks away. If he does not do so he is likely to be attacked. But in an established hierarchy gaze is directed upwards in what Chance (1967) has called an 'attention structure', whereby subordinates monitor the behaviour of their leaders. Both of these effects are found in humans. Strongman and Champness (1968) found a pecking order in groups in terms of who could stare whom down. But in dyads where the members were of different ranks in the Reserve Officers Training Corps the lower status person looked 25 per cent *more* (Exline 1971). And in groups people look more at the leader – amount of gaze received correlated 0·69 with leadership ratings in one study (Burroughs, Schulz, and Aubrey 1973). However McAndrew and Warner (1986) found that the person higher in Arousal Seeking won staring-down contacts in 90 per cent of trials.

As we saw above, interactors normally look more while listening than while speaking (p.159). However, for people who are high in motivation to control, or of higher academic status, or more expert on the topic under discussion – three different experimental manipulations of dominance or status – there was no difference (Ellyson *et al.* 1981). Status or dominance is reflected in the relative amount of looking while listening, higher status people looking relatively less while listening, more when talking.

Amount of gaze is decoded in terms of power and dominance. Argyle, Lefebvre, and Cook (1974) found a linear increase with gaze level in ratings forming a potency factor. Relative amount of looking while talking is interpreted in the same way, as Ellyson *et al.* found (Table 10.1):

Table 10.1 *Power ratings and percentages of looking while talking (average of four studies)*

	High L_T (55%)	Moderate L_T (40%)	Low L_T (25%)
power rating	3·93	3·24	2·40

Source: Ellyson, Dovidio, Corson, and Fehr 1981.

The explanation of the looking while talking effect is fairly obvious. A high-power person wants to make sure that others are listening, and taking note while he is talking; a low-power person wants to make sure he understands what the other says.

Other uses of gaze in public places

Sometimes people stare at strangers in a hostile or threatening way. The 'hate stare' once used by whites towards blacks in the southern states is an example. Such stares are found very aversive. Prolonged staring in public places, between strangers, is found threatening. Ellsworth, Carlsmith, and Henson (1972) found that staring confederates on motorcycles caused motorists to move off more rapidly from traffic lights; similar results were obtained using pedestrians. Thayer (1969) found that people stared at in a library showed signs of uneasiness, sometimes protested, and in a few cases got up and left the room. There are two interpretations of these results. The authors think that they show the operation of gaze as a threat signal. Another explanation is in terms of deviance from norms; staring on the part of strangers constitutes a bizarre piece of rule-breaking whose meaning is unclear, and from which the person stared at might well want to escape. Marsh at Oxford has been studying violence at football grounds, and has found that a glance at a member of the opposing group of supporters can be the occasion for violence, with cries of 'He looked at me!' (Marsh, Rosser, and Harré 1978). Staring can be quite useful – it is used successfully to defend territory, e.g. library tables or areas of lifts, and fewer shocks are given to a staring confederate (Kleinke 1986).

However, gaze at strangers can be interpreted in other ways too, depending on facial expression and situation. For example, it can lead to help, after a confederate has 'collapsed', and to motorists stopping for hitchhikers. This is a striking example of the effect of different interpretations or attributions of another person's gaze. This came up in Chapter 6 in connection with Patterson's model to explain why high levels of gaze can lead to reciprocity or compensation (p.95).

Emotions

Does gaze vary with emotional state, and if so does it communicate anything to other people? Several investigators have found that gaze varies with the intensity of emotion rather than with different emotions. Others, however, have found higher levels of gaze with feelings of warmth and elation, lower levels with anxiety, submission, and depression, i.e. more gaze in positive moods (Kleinke 1986).

Lalljee (1978) asked subjects to role-play emotions and found that gaze level was highest for surprise, followed by excitement, joy, and scorn, and was lowest for despair, annoyance, rage, and anxiety. Lalljee concluded that gaze was greatest where the object of emotion was outside the self, lowest when the self was the object of emotion. The most consistent finding is that people look less, and look downwards, when sad (Exline *et al.* 1968). There is also a reduced level of gaze when people are embarrassed: Edelman and Hampson (1979) found reduced levels during periods of an interview when subjects later agreed that they had felt embarrassed. There is aversion of gaze with a variety of negative feelings, such as when giving another person shocks (Milgram 1974).

Emotion also affects the expression shown by the eyes and their immediate surrounds. Tomkins and McCarter (1964) conclude from observations by themselves and others that the main emotions involve the eyes as follows:

> *interest–excitement*: eyebrows down, eyes track and look
> *enjoyment – joy*: smiling eyes, circular wrinkles
> *distress–anguish*: cry, arched eyebrows
> *fear–terror*: eyes frozen open
> *shame–humiliation*: eyes down
> *anger–rage*: eyes narrowed

Pupil dilation occurs not only in response to sexual stimuli but also to other arousing stimuli – the pupils dilate to works of art and silverware patterns – not always in accordance with the verbally expressed views of subjects; for example, not all who claim to like modern art produce pupil reactions to it. Pupil dilation can act as a cue for changes in emotional arousal, but it is affected by other variables too, such as light intensity. Blink rate varies with arousal; it is increased during states of anxiety or tension, but decreased during concentrated thinking or visual attention (Harris, Thackray, and Schoenberger 1966).

The main research on decoding emotion from the eyes has been on expression. Nummenmaa (1964) showed photographs of different parts of the face taken from posed expressions by one male sender, and found that certain mixed emotions could only be decoded from the eyes, e.g. pleasure and anger, pleasure and surprise.

Personality

There are a number of clear correlations of gaze with personality, and these will be reported in Chapter 17. The main findings are that gaze is *less* in males, introverts, autistic children, and most kinds of mental patients. Gaze levels are higher in those who are extroverted, dominant or assertive, and socially skilled. And gaze is decoded in terms of the same personality variables. People who look more tend to be perceived more favourably, other things being equal, and in particular as competent, friendly, credible, assertive, and socially skilled (Kleinke 1986).

Kleck and Nuessle (1968) made films in which interactors looked either 15 per cent of 80 per cent of the time; judges who saw the films rated them as follows:

15 per cent	*80 per cent*
cold	friendly
pessimistic	self-confident
cautious	natural
defensive	mature
immature	sincere
evasive	
submissive	
indifferent	
sensitive	

But are the same results obtained in real interaction situations? In a study in which subjects met programmed confederates, Cook and Smith (1975) found very little effect on ratings, but for subjects who noticed the target persons' gaze patterns, free descriptions revealed that the low gaze target persons were seen as nervous and lacking in confidence. Those who looked more were seen as more self-confident.

11

Spatial behaviour

Spatial behaviour consists of proximity, orientation, territorial behaviour, and movement in a physical setting. As we have seen already, there are physical limitations on proximity and orientation due to the characteristics of our organs for sending and receiving signals. However, there is a range within which variation is possible, and this variation is one of the main ways of expressing friendly–hostile attitudes to other people. Spatial behaviour also expresses certain properties of personality, and it is used as an interaction signal, for example to begin and to end encounters.

In some ways spatial behaviour is the most straightforward nonverbal signal, since it can be easily measured in terms of distance or orientation. So liking is encoded into closer proximity, and usually this is correctly decoded.

As well as dealing with positions in space we shall discuss the creation and invasion of territories, and the design of social spaces, for example by furniture and decoration.

Research methods

Proximity

This is the distance between two people. It can be regarded as a case of NVC by one of them, or it can be taken as joint behaviour by both – for purposes of cross–cultural comparisons, for example. A variety of research methods have been used of differing degrees of realism.

Observation in real-life settings. Hall (1966) took many photographs in different countries to collect proximity data. While this is a highly valid source of data, it is difficult to carry out controlled studies of the effects of different variables.

Unobtrusive laboratory methods. Here two subjects are asked to have a conversation in the laboratory, either sitting or standing. For example, a subject can be left in a waiting-room with someone who appears to be another subject but is actually a confederate who does not move, though he replies to conversation. After a few minutes the distance between them is measured. Alternatively the subject is offered the choice of a number of chairs in different positions. This is probably the most valid laboratory procedure.

Move and stop. In this method one subject or a confederate is asked to move towards a second subject, until the latter just begins to feel uncomfortable about being too close. Alternatively the stooge moves up to the subject in a series of small steps. This technique has been widely used and has high reliability, but it does not correlate very closely with naturalistic, unobtrusive methods. It is possible with this technique to augment subjective reports of discomfort with physiological measures such as GSR, and observations of other NV signals such as gaze aversion and postural shifts.

Projective methods. Subjects can be asked to place dolls or cut-out felt figures in the positions they think they would adopt. Mehrabian (1972) asked subjects to go up to a hat-rack as if the hat-rack was a person of given age, sex, or social status. Although the doll and cut-out method have been widely used, it is now known that the correlation between the projective and the move-and-stop measure of proximity is very low – an average of 0·39 over a number of studies – and in addition the empirical findings are sometimes different with these measures (Hayduk 1983). Another version, which has been used to study perception of crowding, is to ask subjects to place as many figures as they can, without overcrowding, in a box 2 ft by 2 ft.

Invasion of territory. This is often done quite realistically in field settings, for example by sitting very close to people in libraries and observing how they react.

While physical proximity can be regarded simply as a physical variable, it takes on qualitatively different properties at different ranges. Hall (1966) suggested that there are four main zones:

(1) *Intimate,* from contact to 6–18 in., for people in intimate relationships; they can touch, smell, and feel heat, can talk in a whisper, but cannot see very well.
(2) *Personal* distances, from 1½–4 ft; this corresponds to 'personal space', closer than which discomfort is commonly experienced;

it is possible to touch the other by reaching, and they can now be seen clearly, but not smelt.

(3) *Social* distances are from 4–12 ft, and are used for formal business purposes, e.g. across a desk. Interactors use a higher level of gaze, and need to speak louder; body movements are visible.

(4) *Public* distance is over 12 ft and up to 25 ft or more, and is the distance kept from important public figures. Facial expression is more difficult to see, a louder voice is needed, and bodily movements need to be exaggerated.

Altman and Vinsel (1977) analysed eighty studies from this point of view. They found that there was a major difference between sitting and standing; dyads were much closer when standing – the far range of zone 1, than when sitting – the near range of zone 3. However, close friends chose, when standing, the far edge of zone 1, or zone 2, those who did not like each other chose zone 3, and the more formal the setting the greater the distance.

Orientation

This is the angle at which one person faces another, usually the angle between a line joining him to another and a line perpendicular to the plane of his shoulders, so that facing directly is 0 degrees. (This refers to the orientation of the body, not the head or eyes.) Again, orientation can be regarded as a piece of NVC if there is individual choice. The waiting-room, and other techniques described for proximity, can all be used for orientation. Another method is to offer a choice of chairs, either in reality, or in a diagram. For example, a subject is invited to go and talk to X who is sitting at the table shown in Figure 11.1.

Figure 11.1   Orientation preferences (a)

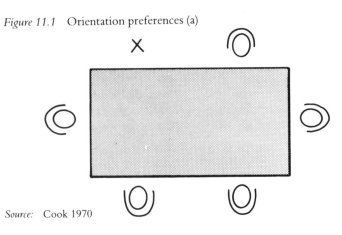

Source: Cook 1970

His choice of seat indicates preference for orientation; the same information can be obtained by observations in real-life situations, in pubs and restaurants, as was done by Cook (1970). It has been found in a number of experiments that there is an inverse relation between orientation and proximity, i.e. a head-on orientation goes with greater distance. Proximity and orientation are alternative cues for intimacy, and different combinations of the two are chosen on different occasions.

Position in a physical setting

The significance of spatial positions and movements depends on the physical setting, in several ways:

(1) Certain areas have the significance of being the territory of some person or group, e.g. behind a counter or desk. Moving into another person's territory is a special kind of social act. Leaving one's own territory, for example to welcome somebody to it, is another.

(2) Certain areas have the significance of having high or low status, for example the dais, high table, and front seats in a lecture or concert hall are of high status. To move into or away from such areas is a definite social act.

(3) Certain areas or seats are associated with particular social roles – in a law court, for example, the judge's seat, the dock, the jury benches; at an interview, the candidate's seat, the chairman's seat, and the other interviewers' seats.

(4) The parts of a house have distinctive symbolic significance – upstairs *versus* downstairs, sitting room *versus* bedroom, 'front' *versus* 'back' regions. There are rules and taboos about who may enter different rooms.

(5) The size and shape of a room, and the arrangement of furniture may act as constraints on how close and at what angle people sit. They may have to sit closer or at a different angle from the one they would prefer.

(6) The existence of physical barriers may make it possible for people to sit much closer than they would otherwise – for example, across a narrow table.

Origins of spatial behaviour

In many animals, those in close relationships huddle together, animals have a personal space shown, for example, by the constant distances between birds on a rail, more space is given to higher status animals, and groups of animals will defend territory containing the food, water, and nesting places that they need. When there is overcrowding, biological mechanisms to prevent further breeding are activated (Calhoun 1962).

Human infants start life in close proximity to their mothers, and cry to demand further bodily contact. A little later infants are satisfied if their mother is sufficiently near, can be seen and heard, though they stay very close to their mothers when in strange environments. Studies of personal space show that this increases from about 0·2 metres nose to nose, indoors, at 2½ years to 0·5 metres at twenty (Hayduk 1983). This is not simply due to increasing body size; Aiello and Aiello (1974) found increases from ages six to seventeen using a measure based on bodily dimensions, e.g. one arm's length scored as fifty. On the other hand, using the more naturalistic method of observing a large number of children in the centre of a city, Burgess (1983) found *no* age change between six and sixteen in distance from nearest companion, but an increase in distance from second and third companions, and from strangers.

The extent of personal space probably reflects features of the body and the sense organs. Within personal space it is possible to be touched by, and perhaps hurt by another, though close distances also make grooming or other rewarding bodily contact possible. The rather greater distance corresponding to Hall's personal distance is the best for seeing and hearing the main signals for social interaction. Territoriality raises quite different issues of the need for various biological facilities in the environment.

However, we have seen that there are quite substantial cultural differences in use of space (p.58f.). While Arabs stand just outside touching distance with elbow by the side, Europeans and Asians stand outside touching distance with whole arm extended. Arabs also stand more directly facing. Black Americans stand further away, and they also take up more space than white Americans by bouncing about a lot.

Within any one culture there are definite norms for proximity and for other aspects of spatial behaviour. However the norms do allow a range of latitude, within which variation is permitted. Beyond these limits people are regarded as deviating, breaking the rules.

Interpersonal attitudes

People stand closer to others whom they like. This has been found consistently using a variety of methods. For example Rosenfeld (1966) found that female subjects when seeking approval stood at 57 in. as opposed to 94 in. when trying to avoid it. Mehrabian (1968a) found that sitting distance varied from 68½ in. for a liked person to 110 in. for a disliked one. Willis (1966) found that subjects stood at different distances in real-life settings, in order of closeness as follows:

parents
close friends
friends
acquaintances
strangers

Individuals sit or stand closer to each other if they are of similar rather than different status, or age (Lott and Sommer 1967), or if they are similar in other ways, such as race. Thayer and Alban (1972) found that people in New York backed away further from an interviewer wearing a peace (anti-Vietnam) badge, compared to an interviewer wearing an American flag badge.

People stand further away from others who are stigmatized. Kleck (1969) found that they sat further away, and placed figures further apart when the other person had, or appeared to have, an amputated leg; 'epileptics' and 'mental patients' were kept at even greater distances.

Orientation is also affected by liking: people generally sit side by side with close friends, while with those they do not like they choose a directly facing position. The main exception to this is that people like to eat facing friends (Cook 1970). The same applies to co-operation and competition (Figure 11.2).

Figure 11.2 Orientation preferences (b)

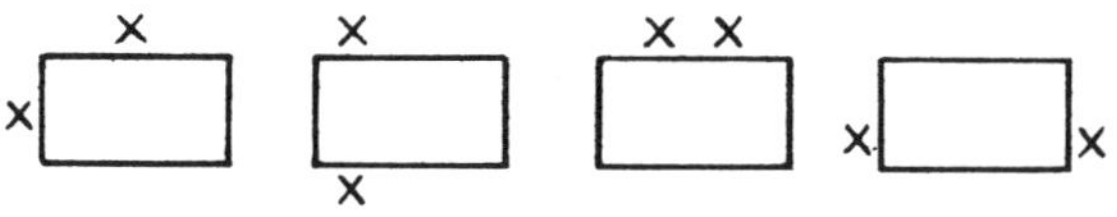

Co-operation	22	16	44	6
Competition	6	41 (U.S.A.)	7	18 (U.S.A.)
		11.5 (G.B.)		51.5 (G.B.)
Conversation	44	38	11.5	4.5

Mehrabian (1972) found that in a hostile situation with another male, male subjects adopted a directly facing orientation, together with a high level of gaze, suggesting vigilance in relation to physical threat. Animals, when frightened of other animals, keep at a distance from them, but keep them under surveillance.

Proximity is decoded in terms of liking and disliking. Patterson

Figure 11.3   Approach and avoidance

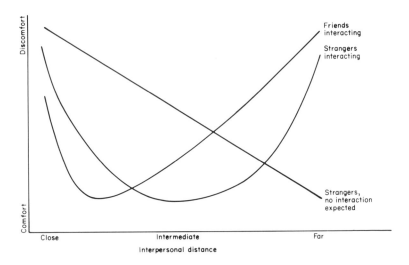

Source: Sundstrom and Altman 1976

(1968a) found that confederates who stood closer to subjects were rated as warmer and liking the subjects more.

Argyle and Dean (1965) put forward a theoretical model to account for some of these findings. They found that people seek a certain degree of proximity, lean forward or back to attain it, and feel uncomfortable if they cannot.

It follows from the model that if a person comes too close this will arouse stronger avoidance forces than approach, so that the other will both be disturbed and back away. Particular discomfort is produced if the other is too close, and for people who like one another a different kind of discomfort is produced by being too far apart. In either case attempts are made to restore equilibrium. This can be done by changes in spatial position, for example by moving further away, leaning backwards, or adopting a less direct orientation (Patterson 1973). Other ways of restoring equilibrium are discussed on p.95.

Support has been obtained for the existence of an approach–avoidance equilibrium in an experiment by Peery and Crane (1980 p.94).

Sundstrom and Altman (1976) expanded the approach–avoidance conflict model: with strangers the equilibrium position is further away; with strangers there is (usually) no approach motivation, only an avoidance one. This is summarized in Figure 11.3.

If there is an approach–avoidance conflict, it follows that there will be a V-shaped pattern of discomfort with distance, discomfort increasing as people move closer or further from the equilibrium point, and this has been found. The avoidance gradient as people move too close is particularly clear, though it may not be linear, and may have an increasing slope. Evidence for the approach gradient, for those who are too distant, is less clear (Knowles 1980) (Figure 11.4).

Figure 11.4   Discomfort as a function of distance

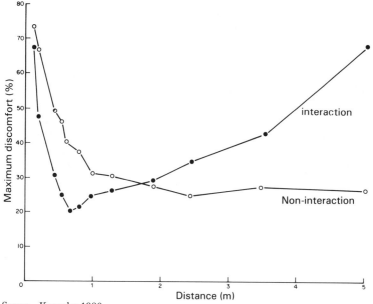

Source: Knowles 1980

Dominance is expressed through spatial behaviour. Hall's 'public distance' of 12 ft or more referred to the distance kept from public figures. We saw that greater distances are chosen between people of unequal status. The greater the public figure the greater the distance kept, until he invites others to come closer. Dominant monkeys, in groups of baboons for example, are given a lot of space in a similar way.

There is probably some connection between status and height: it is very common for leaders or people of higher status to be placed physically at a higher level, as on a rostrum. This may be because height is a kind of natural symbol for status, or it may be so that as many people as possible can see the leader.

However, the most important way in which dominance is signalled is by the use of spaces which have symbolic value. A person communicates dominance or high status by occupying one of the most important seats, e.g. in the front row or at the high table, or by occupying positions associated with high status roles, e.g. the head of the table, the pulpit, or sitting behind his desk rather than coming round the front of it to meet someone, or by having a larger territory, a large desk, etc. Lott and Sommer (1967) asked people where they would sit for various kinds of encounter. The higher status person was usually placed at the head of the table with a lower status person at 90 degrees. When there was a status difference people were not placed side by side and were placed a greater distance apart. These spatial positions are decoded in terms of status. The person seated at the head of the table is usually elected foreman of a jury (Strodtbeck and Hook 1961), or becomes the informal leader of a committee. Again this may be because a leader places himself where he can see and be seen by everyone, or by the symbolic meaning of such a position.

Dominance is expressed by freedom of movement. A high status person is able to start and stop encounters, and to choose degrees of proximity with greater freedom than low status people can. This has been described by Mehrabian as 'non-reciprocity', since the initiative is one-sided.

Spatial position is affected by the situation and task. It is a traditional army problem that soldiers tend to 'bunch up' under fire. We have seen that infants seek bodily contact with their mothers in strange situations. It is probably a general principle that external threat results in closer proximity among those under threat. On the other hand, expectations of embarrassment within the group can lead to greater distance. For example, after seeing erotic slides those who did not like them sat further apart in heterosexual encounters (Griffit, May, and Veitch 1974). Students anticipating criticism sat further away from the experimenter than those expecting praise (Leipold 1963). At friendly and relaxed social occasions like drinks parties, proximity becomes very close, probably helped by the influence of alcohol, which weakens avoidance motivation.

Side-by-side orientation is informal, head-on is formal. Russell, Firestone, and Baron (1980) found that social influence was greater if it was in a form congruent with orientation. Operant conditioning of the labelling of neutral facial expressions was greater if 'personally pleased' rewards were combined with side-by-side orientation, and 'correct' rewards with head-on, at least for internally controlled subjects.

Distance and orientation at work depend on the nature of the work. People may be literally working together and need to sit side by side, in order to look at the same materials. If they are on 'opposite sides', as in the case of interviews, sales, or other negotiations, then that is where they tend to sit. Cook (1970) and Sommer (1969) asked people where they would sit, with the results shown in Figure 11.2. The main Anglo–US difference is that the competing Britons would sit further apart.

Personality

The clearest finding is that mentally disturbed people of all kinds adopt greater distances, and this is most marked for schizophrenics. Maps of the personal spaces of schizophrenics and others are shown in Figure 11.5.

Figure 11.5   Personal space of schizophrenics and non-schizophrenics

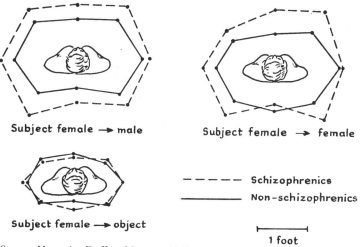

Subject female → male   Subject female → female

Subject female → object

– – – – –   Schizophrenics
————   Non-schizophrenics

⊢——————⊣
1 foot

Source: Horowitz, Duff, and Stratton 1969

Violent prisoners have also been found to have larger body-buffer zones. Kinzel (1970) found that violent prisoners had zones of 22·3 square ft, compared with 7·0 for non-violent prisoners. Their zones were larger behind than in front, and there was evidence that they feared physical or homosexual attack from the rear. Disruptive and aggressive adolescents needed 32·4 square ft, controls needed 20·5, using the stop method in another study (Newman and Pollack 1973).

We shall show later that individuals who come closer also tend to look more, smile more, talk more, and in general have a trait of social approach. This trait correlates with extroversion, and a number of investigators have found that extroverts come closer, but others have found no difference (e.g. Porter, Argyle, and Salter 1970). Perhaps the effects of extroversion affect only greater toleration of close interaction distance, as J.L. Williams (1971) found. Other studies have found that anxious people are more distant (as mental patients are), while individuals high in confidence, self-esteem, or assertiveness come closer (Altman and Vinsel 1977). Strube and Werner (1984) found that type A personalities claimed more personal space (83·5 cm. radius *v*. 66·7 for type Bs) in a role-played sales encounter; this appeared to be related to need for control. Hartnett, Bailey, and Gibson (1970) found that male subjects high in heterosexual motivation came closer to female subjects.

Proximity is decoded in terms of personality qualities. Patterson and Sechrest (1970) asked subjects to interview a number of people, who had been instructed to approach to different distances. They sat on one of a series of chairs placed side by side at 2 ft, 4 ft, 6 ft, and 8 ft. The impressions formed of these people varied with the distance they chose, as shown in Figure 11.6. Those who came closest were rated as friendly, extroverted, aggressive, and dominant.

A great deal of research has been carried out on sex differences. The main findings are that women approach closer than men, and are approached closer, especially by other women (p.283f.).

Spatial behaviour as an interaction signal

Movements in space are used as moves in social interaction. They differ from NV signals of other kinds in that they mainly indicate the beginning and end of sequences of interaction, for example, the beginning and end of an encounter. Spatial movements do not normally occur within periods of interaction. In order to interact with someone it is necessary to come near enough for speech to be heard and the face to be seen. Movement towards a person becomes a signal, indicating the desire to interact. This intention is made clear by the gaze, facial expression, and speech that accompanies the spatial move. It may be necessary to obtain the other's approval in order to approach beyond a certain point, such as the door to his room or house.

Entering someone's room is achieved by knocking and waiting, knocking and entering without waiting, or just walking in without knocking – depending on the relative status and the intimacy of those concerned. Joining a group of people standing at a social occasion is performed by moving up, and waiting to be invited; if two people are joined they usually move to make a gap. Someone sitting at a dinner table can terminate a boring conversation with the

Figure 11.6   Proximity and impression formation

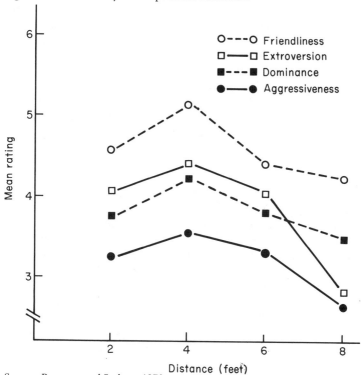

Source: Patterson and Sechrest 1970

person on his left and start one with the person on his right simply by reorienting the upper part of his body. This is better than putting his desires into words: 'Please stop talking to me, I want to talk to X.' Similarly, encounters are terminated by moving or turning away – accompanied by appropriate NV and verbal signals. Spatial moves alone are a very powerful means of starting and ending encounters, though they need to be accompanied by other NV signals, such as looking and smiling at the person approached.

Special phases of an encounter are usually initiated by spatial moves. If someone is going to make a speech he stands up, and others move to positions where they can hear and see him. If a ceremony is going to take place, the priest (or equivalent) takes up a prominent, perhaps raised, position; the initiates stand in front of him, with their assistants at their side or behind them, others looking on from a distance. If two or more people are going to play a game, they take up opposing spatial positions accordingly.

Spatial behaviour may also signal a particular definition of the situation. Just as orientation communicates co-operative and competitive relationships, so a greater distance indicates the desire for greater formality. This is usually accompanied by other cues like posture and facial expression.

The sequence of conversation in a group is affected by spatial position. When a person has stopped speaking, the next person to speak is much more likely to be opposite rather than alongside, probably because the last speaker looks at someone, and this 'nominates' the next speaker (Steinzor 1950).

Territorial behaviour

Some of the most important aspects of spatial behaviour are connected with 'territory' – establishing it, invading it, and defending it. This does not quite fit the categories of communication we have been using in this book; perhaps it comes nearest to self-presentation. Many species of animals engage in territorial behaviour; a group of animals may regard a certain area as its exclusive preserve, and defend it fiercely against rivals. While there may be an innate basis for this kind of behaviour it has the biological purpose of controlling access to food, water, and shelter. Human beings appear to display a similar pattern of behaviour, in relation to different kinds of areas and resources. One can distinguish three kinds of territory of different sizes.

Personal space

This is the area individuals maintain around themselves, into which others cannot intrude without arousing discomfort. It can be measured by the move and stop method. Personal spaces are roughly circular, but with rather more space in front than behind, though violent offenders have more space behind, as well as having larger spaces as a whole (Hayduk 1983). Plans of the personal space of schizophrenics are shown in Figure 11.5. One theory of why people need personal space is that it is for protection (Dosey and Meisels 1969). This can be translated into affiliative balance theory terms – there is a stronger avoidance slope for some individuals (hostile ones), and for some relationships (unfriendly ones). However, people seem to be able to tolerate loss of personal space in crowded trains, lifts, etc. Vine (1973) suggests that under crowded conditions people regard each other as physical objects rather than persons, and the usual non-verbal means for sustaining encounters are reduced to a minimum. This would also explain the high level of anti-social behaviour in cities. In prisons and other overcrowded places people withdraw from social interaction, do not move about much, and avoid quarrels with one another.

Personal territory

This is the rather larger area which an individual owns, has exclusive use of, or controls. This space often provides him with privacy, or social intimacy. His house, garden, car, or office are one kind of personal territory. More temporary territories include rooms in hotels, tables and seats at restaurants, seats in cinemas, a tennis court, a table in a library. A territory may be established simply by repeated occupation of a particular seat or table. In most homes each member of the family has a bed, a chair, and an area which is regarded as his or her own domain. Altman and Haythorn (1967) studies the establishment of territories when pairs of sailors occupied an experimental room in isolation for a number of days. Each man came to use a certain bed, chair, and area of the room. This was most marked when the pair were incompatible, as that led to social withdrawal from one another. Groups where there was little territoriality in the early part of the isolation period were more likely to fail to complete the twenty days of the experiment – suggesting that territoriality was adaptive in this situation. Studies in mental hospital wards have found that secluded territories are sought by schizophrenics and patients low in the pecking order. Territories can be established by moving the furniture or the pattern of social behaviour.

Home territories

These are areas of otherwise public space which are normally used by the members of a particular group. Examples are the cafes and other places frequented by juvenile gangs. 'This place is ours,' said one of the motorcycle gang. 'This and the Aloha. This is our territory, you're a surfer, come in here and you're dead' (Sommer 1969: 39). Other examples are corners of pubs, clubs, and hotels used by certain groups of regulars. In the case of gangs, at least, home territories are defended with violence. This kind of territoriality is similar to that of animals.

Two or three people can establish a temporary home territory by sitting or standing talking to each other. Knowles (1973) found that while 75 per cent of people walking down a corridor walked between two waste-barrels, when two people talking stood in the same position only 30 per cent walked between them. I have carried out a similar experiment on a broad pavement in Leuven, Belgium. Pairs of people stood 4 ft 6 in. apart, without attending to one another; then they started a conversation without moving; the number of people passing between them per minute was counted in the two conditions – conversation reduced the number to one-tenth. It was found that the effect is greatest if the people talking are less than 4 ft apart, are of opposite sex, of high status, and if there are four of them rather than two. Two or more people in a larger gathering, or in a public place, may indicate that they are for the time being a closed group, by their spatial positions, and also by their arm positions, low tone of voice, and so on. If they are more open to new members they will stand side by side, with a greater distance between them, and look around at others present. When a person passes through a group, especially a closed group, he does so quickly, with lowered head, avoiding eye-contact, and with some embarrassment.

Kendon (1977) observed the spatial behaviour of free-standing conversational groups. He showed that such groups sustain an identity, a boundary, and common focus of attention, which he called an F- (facing-)formation. Group members co-operate to do this, for example compensating for movements by the others, and making way for new members. The precise shape of the F-formation varies with the relationships in the group, and the physical setting.

Invasion of territory

One can invade another's territory in several ways – by moving physically close, looking or listening, making a noise, using the facilities, or by contaminating or disturbing parts of the territory. The method of sitting very close in libraries, or sitting directly opposite and staring, is a way which has been used experimentally (Russo, in Sommer 1969).

Invasion leads to discomfort or annoyance on the part of the individual invaded – he or she has a rise in GSR, averts gaze, sometimes by making a barrier with the arms or with piles of books, turning or leaning away, giving hostile gestures and glances, and finally going further away or leaving the scene (Sommer 1969). Discomfort increases with the degree of invasion. Typically people start to feel a little uncomfortable at 28 in, moderately so at 20 in., and very uncomfortable at just over 12 in. There are individual differences in the 'permeability' of personal space, and those with large personal spaces allow a smaller proportion to be invaded before feeling uncomfortable (Hayduk 1981). It depends who does the invading. It is far less disturbing, indeed can be very rewarding, by a close friend or a very attractive person, but more disturbing when done by a high status stranger (Barash 1973), and probably by a lower status one too.

Reactions to invasion depend on attributions about the reason for it. Cross-sex invasions are more likely to be attributed to sexual intention, and are often not objected to by females (Skolnick, Frasier, and Hadar 1977). However, females are more disturbed by invasions from the side, e.g. at library tables, males by invasions from the front. This may be because women see a lateral invasion as a demand for affiliation, while men see a head-on invasion as threatening (Fisher and Byrne 1975). The way an invasion is interpreted depends also on evidence from facial expression, and of course on what is said by the invading person.

There are a number of ways of defending personal space. Animals often mark their space by depositing urine or other scent round the edge; humans mark their territories by leaving coats on chairs, books on library tables, or putting their names on the doors of rooms. Sommer asked students to show how they would sit at a table to defend it against other users; they chose a position in the centre of a long side, facing towards the door of the room; they thought it was easier to defend a small table, against the wall, at the back of the room. Sommer and Becker (1969) found that places at library tables were most effectively defended by leaving a coat and open notebooks. These techniques are also used by people who want to keep compartments in railway carriages, or tables at restaurants to themselves.

Crowding and isolation

People feel crowded if there is little space available per person, but a better predictor is the average distance of the nearest other (Hayduk 1983). In other words the feeling of being crowded is dependent on the amount of encroachment of personal space.

Many studies have shown the negative effects of overcrowding. Laboratory experiments have found increased GSR, subjective discomfort, lower levels of work, and disliking strangers met under these conditions. In field settings similar results have been obtained, e.g. more physical illness and complaints among overcrowded prisoners (Cox, Paulus, and McCairn 1984). However the effects of overcrowding are less, or non-existent under certain conditions (Harper, Wiens, and Matarazzo 1978):

parties *v*. work
co-operation *v*. competition

internal controllers
individuals with small personal space
individuals high in need for affiliation
women *v.* men

Three main processes have been held to be responsible for the negative effects of overcrowding (Altman 1975):

(1) Inability to control events – internal controllers perhaps still feel they can control things.
(2) Interference with pursuit of goals – the goals are different at parties, and not upset by crowding.
(3) Too much social stimulation – females and others with smaller personal space can cope with such stimulation. Extroverts and those high in affiliative needs, when asked to put as many figures in a box, without overcrowding them, put in more (Miller and Nardini 1977).

The need for sufficient privacy is reflected in a widely agreed social rule that in all relationships one should 'respect the other's privacy' (Argyle, Henderson, and Furnham 1985).

However, too much isolation is also a cause of discomfort, producing feelings of loneliness and other forms of distress. So people need both privacy and company – further evidence for the approach-avoidance conflict which we postulated is behind choice of proximity (Altman 1975). Individuals seek privacy in various ways, but especially in their personal territory and in public places (Taylor and Ferguson 1980).

Effects of the physical environment

All social behaviour takes place in a physical setting. Sometimes settings have been deliberately arranged by one of the participants, for example, by positioning desks or chairs. Sometimes they have been arranged by architects or interior decorators, with some idea of how to produce certain forms of interaction. And sometimes the physical arrangements are a residue of previous encounters, where the interactors have altered things to suit a particular kind of social event. The design of social spaces can be looked at as an extension of spatial behaviour, and indeed as a kind of social skill.

Furniture

We have seen how seating position at a rectangular table affects leadership (p. 176) and whether the situation is perceived as co-operative or competitive (p.173). It is possible to encourage degrees of co-operation by the angle between chairs.

The placing of office desks affects the relation between the occupant and his visitors. Joiner (1976) found that senior officials in the British government and in management placed themselves behind their desks between them and a visitor, thus dominating the room, as opposed to putting their desks against the wall or window. In the USA professors who did the latter were rated as more willing to give individual attention to students, and to encourage the development of different viewpoints by students (Zweigenhaft 1976).

Outdoor social behaviour is also affected by the furniture. Ciolek (1977) observed a large number of outdoor gatherings in the centre of Canberra. Most consisted of two or three people talking; they stood close to the main lines of pedestrian traffic but also close to tables, chairs, barriers, etc. rather than in open spaces, especially in the case of males. Usually they were not using the 'furniture' in any way. Ciolek suggested that the reason is that objects help to define territory. Sommer (1966) was able to increase the amount of social interaction in an old people's home by moving the chairs; instead of the chairs lining the walls of rooms in long rows they were placed in groups round tables. Ittelson, Proshansky, and Rivlin (1970) similarly increased social interaction between psychiatric patients by adding a sun-lounge, with comfortable chairs carefully arranged. A great deal of subsequent research has been carried out to find the most therapeutic environmental designs for different kinds of patients (Baum and Singer 1982).

Domestic furniture can be arranged to encourage friendly interaction. Two easy chairs facing the fire are a preferred position (Canter 1977). Sofas can be of degrees of friendliness, up to the Victorian 'love seat' with high back and ends.

School desks can be arranged in a number of different ways:

(1) Traditional rows of desks, for teacher-centred sessions with little discussion, or for taking exams.
(2) Groups of four desks facing each other, or a library table.
(3) A number of pupils in a row behind the teacher's desk, the others facing in a semi-circle, for reading a play.
(4) A hollow square, for committee work.
(5) Rows of desks, facing on two sides of the room, teacher in middle with slides, taperecorder, etc., e.g. for a language lesson.
(6) A semi-circle of desks, for discussion (Richardson 1967).

Decor

The decor of spaces also affects social interaction. Maslow and Mintz (1956) constructed a beautiful room, an average room, and an ugly one (like an untidy janitor's storeroom). Subjects rated faces seen in the beautiful room most favourably. The general style of a room can suggest very clearly whether it is intended for, for example, high-powered committee work, romantic meetings, or police interrogation (Bennett and Bennett 1970). This is partly done by choice of furnishings, and colour is an important feature. Colours are associated with certain moods, and can to some extent produce them. Some of the main associations are shown in Table 11.1.

Table 11.1   *The moods created by colour*

Colour	Moods
red	hot, affectionate, angry, defiant, contrary, hostile, full of vitality, excitement, love
blue	cool, pleasant, leisurely, distant, infinite, secure, transcendent, calm, tender
yellow	unpleasant, exciting, hostile, cheerful, joyful, jovial
orange	unpleasant, exciting, disturbed, distressed, upset, defiant, contrary, hostile, stimulating
purple	depressed, sad, dignified, stately
green	cool, pleasant, leisurely, in control
black	sad, intense, anxiety, fear, despondent, dejected, melancholy, unhappy
brown	sad, not tender, despondent, dejected, melancholy, unhappy, neutral
white	joy, lightness, neutral, cold

Source: Burgoon and Saine 1978

Children who were tested in blue, yellow, yellow-green, and orange rooms scored twelve points of IQ more than those tested in white, black, or brown rooms. They were more friendly and smiled most in the orange room (*Time* 1973). Lighting is important. Bright lights are arousing, dim ones more intimate.

Architectural arrangements

These can have complex effects on social interaction. Barriers are one way of creating spaces in open-plan offices, and directing large bodies of people in public places. Visibility is another: the height of garden walls affects whether neighbours can talk to each other over them; lace curtains act as one-way vision screens to the advantage of whoever is on the darker side; apartment blocks are now designed to avoid dark corners where juveniles can cause trouble outside the surveillance of adults (Central Policy Review Staff 1978). Height is used to create both visibility and authority for lecturers and judges. The architecture can create circuitous routes into the boss's office, past various secretaries, ending up on the wrong side of his desk.

12

Gestures and other bodily movements

There is a great deal of bodily movement during social interaction, though movements of the hands are the most informative. By 'gestures' are usually meant voluntary bodily actions, by hands, head, or other parts of the body, which are intended to communicate. Emotional expressions, e.g. gripping the hands together with anxiety, are something different (Kendon 1983).

It has been found useful to distinguish between three main kinds of bodily movement:

(1) *Emblems* are those non-verbal acts, usually hand-movements, which have a direct verbal translation, usually into between one and three words, for which this meaning is known by all or most members of a group or subculture, and which are sent deliberately (e.g. the hitchhike sign) (Ekman and Friesen 1969a).
(2) *Illustrators* are 'movements which are directly tied to speech, serving to illustrate what is being said verbally' (e.g. drawing a spiral staircase) (Ekman and Friesen 1969a).
(3) *Self-touching*, or 'body-focused movement' (Freedman and Hoffman 1967).

We shall also consider bodily movements as part of personality, and look at the inferences made by observers. There are further types of bodily movement connected with speech, to control synchronizing, and to provide feedback; these are described in Chapter 7.

Research methods

For encoding research some method is needed to generate gestures or other movements. For emblems one way is simply to ask people to enact expressions like 'be quiet', or 'I don't know'. For illustrators people can be asked to describe shapes or objects, and their bodily movements observed. For self-touching and emotional movements it is necessary to create the emotion as usual. For encoding research it is also necessary to describe or classify bodily movements. We saw how this can be achieved in terms of physical variables in the cases of spatial and vocal behaviour. There are a number of elaborate and sophisticated ways of doing the same for bodily movement, methods which have been devised for sports psychology, for example (Rosenfeld 1982). However, such methods have not as yet been found useful in the study of bodily communication. It has been more usual to codify movements using the perceptions of trained observers, using categories which have been established by research workers.

An early approach was that of Birdwhistell (1970), who developed a large and detailed vocabulary of bodily movements with the idea that these would function like the words in a language. However, no evidence has been collected that these elements are used consistently, in different contexts, or that they are linked by a grammar, and the scheme has not been used by others. Laban (1975) devised a method for describing movements in dance, which is used for recording ballet. There are a lot of elements for the feet, and for broad bodily movements, and great skill is needed to use the system. This too has seen little use in NVC research (but see Davis 1979).

Much more successful have been category schemes devised by ethologists. McGrew (1972), for example, listed over a hundred bodily acts used by children, and this has been the basis of successful research. The list includes twenty-nine hand gestures. There are other ways of analysing hand movements, too, and McNeill and Levy (1982) used thirty-eight features in their study.

Another approach is simply to use the main categories of gesture used in a culture. We shall see later that in our own culture there are about eighty common emblems for example.

In decoding research the problem is to create the bodily movements to be decoded. In practice the ones used have been those which have consistently appeared in the encoding studies, to check that they have the same meaning to receivers as to senders. A related research design is to compare the information received by decoders with and without visual information.

Origins of gesture

Animals make very little use of gesture. Biologically the hands have evolved for grasping and manipulating objects, including other animals. The hands can also communicate, however, particularly by illustrating objects and movements. In higher mammals and men a large area of the brain is associated with them. We have seen that primates use gestures: (1) to express attitudes to others, for instance, by banging and stamping (truncated intention movements); (2) as 'displacement activities' such as scratching, in states of conflict or frustration; (3) for pointing, indicating direction of attention. Primates can also be taught gesture languages, but apparently do not use them spontaneously.

Human infants use gesture to communicate at an early age. By nine months they can use several kinds of gesture:

(1) Reaching, later partly reaching, combined with gaze at an adult.
(2) Giving, showing, and pointing to objects out of reach.
(3) Social routines like bye-bye, saluting, peek-a-boo, etc.
(4) Imitation of eating, drinking, sleeping, etc. out of context.

At first children's gestures are close imitations of the objects or movements which they represent. For example, running is shown by movements of the legs, not the fingers. Even by thirteen months these gestures start to become stripped down, more abstract versions of objects. Older children of five or six use even more abstract and metaphorical gestures, e.g. of cupped hands for a container, representing meaning, or with a why question; they start to use batons to show grammatical groupings. They make much less use of simple pantomime gestures, more use of gestures which modify the meaning of words (Jancovic, Devoe, and Wiener 1975). There is good evidence that language and gesture develop at very much the same time, for example in their degree of abstractness, though children of thirteen to twenty months find gestures easier (Bates *et al.* 1983; McNeill 1985). Older children make less use of simple hand movements, but increase the use of complex ones; and adults use gestures a lot when trying to put difficult materials into words, and when excited.

Something is known about the neurological basis of gestures. To begin with, gestures are mainly done by the right hand, in right-handed people, whereas left-handed people use both hands. This may be because speech is mainly controlled by the left hemisphere in right-handed, but is less lateralized for left-handed people (Kimura 1976). However, this only applies to representational gestures, not to batons, which are given more by the left hand (McNeill and Levy 1982).

The two main kinds of aphasic patient show different kinds of gestural deficit. In Broca's aphasia there are lesions in the left anterior area; words are kept but not grammar. In these patients there are iconic gestures but no batons. In patients suffering from Wernicke's aphasia the lesions are in the left posterior region; the meanings of words are lost but syntax of a rambling kind remains. These people can produce few representational gestures, but they do give batons. There appears to be a close link between the verbal and gestural deficits (Bates *et al.* 1983; McNeill 1985).

As we saw in Chapter 4 there are extensive cultural variations in the use of gesture, showing that it is the non-verbal signal that is most affected by socialization and by cultural history. We also saw that there are a number of gestures of universal meaning – pointing, beckoning, halting, etc. It is not very likely that these gestures are innate, more likely that they are natural symbols, the most obvious way of using the human body for certain messages. Cultural diffusion can explain the use of similar gestures over wide geographical areas, where these are not shared by peoples in more remote regions, such as the signs for 'no'. A number of gestures can be seen as variations on a theme, for example those used in greeting (p.63). Where there are gestures which are unique to a culture, or to an area, it has sometimes been possible to trace their history.

Emblems and interpersonal signals

Gestures are not used much to show interpersonal attitudes, such as friendly and hostile. They are used a great deal for other interpersonal messages, in the form of 'emblems', as defined above. They are often used at the same time as speech is being used, but are not closely related to it in the way that illustrators and synchronizing signals are. Emblems can be used for private comments on the side, for avoiding embarrassing speech, or for more emphasis (Kendon 1983).

A number of methods have been used for listing the emblems used in a culture. Johnson, Ekman, and Friesen (1975) compiled a list of 220 verbal messages, then asked informants if they could encode each of them and found the percentage who did so in a similar way. The emblems were then performed for other informants who were asked if they could decode them, and who also rated how far they thought each emblem was commonly used. Charade-type gestures were excluded. Emblems were accepted if at least 70 per cent of decoders gave the intended meaning, and at least 70 per cent thought the emblem was used normally (see Table 12.1). Other methods of sampling have been used but this method seems to produce the most extensive lists of emblems – 76 for the USA, 98 in Iran (Sparhawk 1978).

There are several ways of describing emblems. Physical description is less important than classifying the gestures which have an agreed meaning. Sparkhawk used the method originally used to classify ASL, American Sign Language. There are three components:

(1) *Place*: the area to which the hand directs attention, e.g. stomach, temple.
(2) *Shape* of hand, e.g. fist, pointing, flat.
(3) *Movement*, e.g. up, down, towards self.

Persian emblems have fifteen places, twenty-one shapes, and twenty-eight movements.

In the American research by Johnson, Ekman, and Friesen (1975) eight main areas of emblems were found; examples are given in Table 12.1.

Table 12.1   *American emblems*

Message type	Meaning, for example	% decoded correctly	% considered natural usage
Commands (n = 20)			
	sit down beside me	100	100
	come here	100	100
Own physical state (11)			
	I'm full of food	93	93
	how could I be so dumb?	100	95
Insults (5)			
	fuck you (finger)	100	100
Replies (10)			
	OK	100	100
	I don't know	100	100
Own affect (5)			
	I'm angry	100	94
Greetings and departures (2)			
	good-bye	94	100
	hello	80	100
Physical appearance of person (1)			
	women, nice figure	100	100
Unclassified (12)			
	you	100	100
	hitchhiking	100	94

Source: Johnson, Ekman, and Friesen 1975

A number of these signs are so rude and insulting that they have been made illegal, especially in Mediterranean countries (p.53f.). Kendon (1981) reviewed similar studies from different parts of the world and concluded that emblems fall into three broad areas – interpersonal control, announcement of own current state, and evaluative response to a third person – which account for about 80 per cent of emblems on average. Gestures for commands were always the most frequent; very few stand for objects (nouns) or actions (verbs).

Emblems acquire their meanings by their relation to different kinds of 'base':

intention movements, e.g. biting, kissing, head-toss, halt
action patterns of others, e.g. flat hand flick for sudden departure
concrete objects, e.g. fig hand for female genitals (closed with protruding thumb)
symbolic objects, e.g. V-sign, cross
abstract entities, e.g. hand purse for money.

What are the origins of emblems? Some are culturally universal, or very widely spread, but it seems unlikely that they are innate. Many could be natural iconic symbols since they are so similar to their referents, e.g. stop, come here, attractive woman. There is no clear connection between emblems and language, since they cross many language barriers. This may be the result of cultural diffusion. However, a gesture may fail to diffuse to another area perhaps because there is a gesture for the same meaning there already, or there may be religious or political reasons for not using it; the finger cross, for example, did not spread to non-Christian countries. The history of a number of gestures has been traced, either to recent history, or to more ancient history, such as the 'horns' from bull-worship, and the head-toss for 'no', dating in southern Italy from the Greek colonization of that region in 690 BC (Morris *et al.* 1979).

There are a number of reasons why these emblems are used – they may be faster than speech, they are silent (and can therefore be used for private comments), they have more impact than words, and they can be received at a greater distance (Kendon 1981). When any of these factors become very important elaborate gesture systems may develop. For communication at a distance there are the tic-tac gestures used by bookmakers, and signs used by umpires. Gesture systems develop in noisy factories like sawmills, and by flight mechanics, underwater swimmers, and broadcasters (Figure 12.1). It is a further step to the emergence of gesture languages proper, which are not tied to a limited range of messages. Gesture languages proper have grown up among the deaf, Trappist monks, and in a certain tribe of Australian aboriginals (p.57). This takes us beyond non-verbal communication, however.

A comparison between Persian emblems and ASL found that the Persian emblems were more iconic, less arbitrary; there were fewer

Figure 12.1   Non-verbal signals in broadcasting

Source: Brun 1969

emblems, and their meaning was based on contrasted bodily movements, making less use of detailed finger movements, and with no
syntax (Sparhawk 1978).

Illustrators

These are movements, mainly of the hands, which are directly related
to speech, e.g. pointing to oneself, making a shape with the hands.
Illustrators are more closely linked to speech than emblems, and
serve to clarify or repeat what is being said.

In Chapter 7 we showed how these gestures are closely co-
ordinated with speech, and in Chapter 16 we show that they play an
important part in the effective performance of social skills. Here we
shall describe the different kinds of illustrators and the information
which they can convey.

There are several kinds of illustrator:

batons, showing tempo or rhythm
pointing, to people or objects
spatial movements or *relationships*, e.g. under, round
pictographs, showing shapes, e.g. a spiral staircase
ideographs, tracing a line of thought
showing *bodily actions* (Efron 1941).

Although most people make some bodily movements while speaking, there are very wide variations in how they do it, and it appears that the rules which may exist here are very flexible. One of the most standardized illustrations in English is perhaps the indication of 'I' and 'you', which is done by movements of the hand towards self and others: 'we' and 'you' are shown by short sweeps of the hand. Other common signals are those for 'yes' and 'no', 'up' and 'down', and so on. In some countries there is a more elaborate gesture language, and in ordinary conversation some of the words are replaced by symbolic hand signals.

People still use these gesticulations when speaking on the telephone, but use fewer of them (Cohen and Harrison 1973). And people who are not allowed to use gestures put more spatial terms and demonstratives into words (Graham and Heywood 1976).

Illustrators add considerably to the amount of information conveyed by speech, especially about shapes, physical objects, and spatial relations. Graham and Argyle (1975) carried out an experiment in which subjects had one minute to describe each of a number of shapes to a decoder with or without hand movements. The decoders drew what they thought the shapes were, and these drawings were then rated by judges for their similarity to the originals. It was found that the drawings were more accurate when the hands could be used. This effect was greater for more complex shapes which it is very hard to describe in words (Figure 12.2).

In a similar study Riseborough (1981) gave senders the task of indicating one of three objects to a receiver. The time taken was on average less (23·0 seconds) if the whole body could be used, compared with 34·5 seconds for face only, and 36·6 seconds for sound only. However, gestures were useful only for certain rather difficult choices, where words were inadequate to do the job easily.

Iconic gestures are used for verbs as well as objects. McNeill and Levy (1982) observed forty-four aspects of gestures used for thirty-eight verbs, by six people telling stories. Many verbs, especially those describing movements in space, were often accompanied by iconically similar hand movements; for example, a downward motion was shown by a downward gesture, horizontal motion by

Figure 12.2   The effects of gesture on the communication of shapes

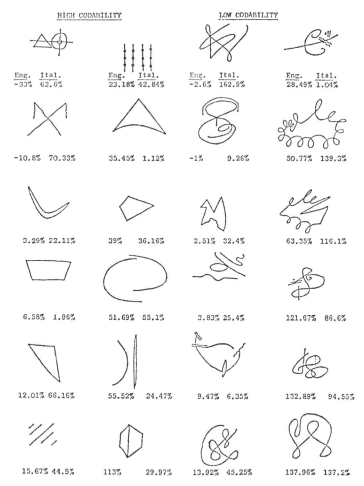

Source: Graham and Argyle 1975

left–right gestures, achievement of an end-state like catching or connecting by a two-handed gestures. The same investigators also found the use of metaphoric illustrators. Examples are treating an idea as a physical object shown by a gesture, holding on to an idea, weighing alternatives, opening a hand as the container for the answer to a question, and various metaphors for mathematical ideas such as limits and loops (McNeill 1985).

The Graham and Argyle experiment was repeated in Italy, and the benefits of gestures for communicating shapes, especially complex ones, were greater for these Italian subjects. Walker and Nazmi (1979) found a similar difference between housewives of Italian and British origin living in Sydney, for memory of geometrical figures. Efron (1941) showed that Italian emigrants to New York used far more illustrators of objects and movements than Jewish immigrants, who used more ideographs (p.54f.).

It is not entirely clear why or when people use gestural illustrations. They are probably used when the gesture is easier to produce than the words, as in describing shapes, or in a shop in a foreign country. On the other hand it has been found by Baxter, Winter, and Hammer (1968) that people with greater verbal facility used *more* gestures, suggesting that gestures are supplements rather than substitutes. Illustrations are a straightforward example of analogical coding, and the hands are very well adapted to this kind of signal.

Self-touching, and other emotional signs

Emotions are expressed primarily in the face. However, emotions are also shown by movements of the hands and feet, including emotions which are being concealed by the face. Ekman and Friesen (1969b) showed judges some film of a depressed woman who was pretending to be cheerful and friendly because she wanted to be discharged from hospital. Observers who saw films of head only thought that she was cheerful and friendly, but those who saw body only thought that she was tense, nervous, and disturbed. Another of their patients showed repeated foot sliding when first admitted, but replaced this with more varied foot movements when he recovered (1968).

Other studies of patients have found that emotions seem to be expressed by hand movements. Wolff (1945) observed the following ones:

(1) *Extreme inhibition*: withdrawal movements, stereotyped movements, hair gesture, general motor unrest, unnecessary movements.
(2) *Depression*: movements are slow, few, hesitating, non-emphatic, use of hiding gestures.
(3) *Elation*: movements are fast, expansive, rhythmical, spontaneous, emphatic, self-assertive, affected.
(4) *Anxiety*: gestures involving the hair, hiding the face, wringing and interlocking of hands, opening and closing of fists, plucking eyebrows, scratching face, pulling hair, aimless fidgeting.

Freedman and Hoffman (1967) made a valuable distinction between gestures which are linked with speech and oriented towards objects, and those which are directed towards the self. They suggest that the first are intended to communicate while the second merely release tension. Animals produce 'displacement activities' such as scratching themselves when in states of conflict or frustration, and as we have seen these acts can become ritualized and act as social signals. Sousa-Poza and Rohrberg (1977) found that subjects used more object-focused gestures when asked impersonal questions, and more body-focused gestures when asked personal questions ('How well do you get along with people, particulary the person closest to you?'). Is self-touching produced by anxiety or by cognitive difficulty? Freedman *et al.* (1972) later found that after a 'cold' interview subjects touched themselves more. The interview was intended to generate some hostility, which was analysed from the speech of subjects. Those who expressed aggression overtly used more object-focused movements, while those who produced only covert aggression had more body-focused ones (Freedman *et al.* 1973).

A number of studies have found that patients touch themselves more than others, and that self-touching correlates with ratings of how upset patients are (Harper, Wiens, and Matarazzo 1978). In particular, self-touching is associated with hostility and suspicion. Touching the face goes with shame or other negative attitudes toward the self. On the other hand, Barroso and Feld (1986) found most self-touching when doing a shadowing task (repeating the words of the speaker who spoke first, with binaural hearing), and Barroso *et al.* (1978) that distraction (the Stroop test) produced more self-touching than water-jar problems; it is argued that self-touching is generated by focusing attention during distraction.

Self-touching occurs more under certain conditions: informal *v.* formal interviews (showing that it can be restrained), when in lower status roles (like being interviewed), and when with the opposite sex (Goldberg and Rosenthal 1986).

Clearly emotions are expressed by bodily movements in ways which are not intended to communicate, and indeed do not do so at all clearly. These have sometimes been called 'autistic' gestures. They have also been called 'self-adaptors' on the theory that they were originally to satisfy some bodily need, such as a skin irritation. And most gestures of this kind are body-focused, touching the self.

Fidgeting is another activity which often involves self-touching. Mehrabian and Friedman (1986) established a forty-item scale of different kinds of fidgeting. It correlated with frequency of smoking, eating and drinking, listening to music, watching TV, and daydreaming. This is similar to extroversion as conceived by Eysenck (1976), corresponding to a high need for stimulation.

Self-touching can also be a minor courtship display. Scheflen and Scheflen (1972) described hair-stroking and similar preening as a 'quasi-courtship display'. Goldberg and Rosenthal (1986) found that in role-played job interviews, female 'candidates', and male 'interviewers' touched their hair more during cross-sex encounters.

Krout (1954) carried out an experiment in which emotions were aroused, by questions of the following kind:

Experiment 8

(1) People consider strong feelings of one person for another of the *same* sex strange. Don't they? (Pause for answer).
(2) But, don't *you* sometimes have more than friendly feelings for your best (boy, girl) friend? (Bend forward, point finger) – I mean *more* than friendly feelings. Think it over.

The subjects were asked to delay their reply to the second question, in each case until the experimenter gave a signal, which was given after a gesture had appeared. They were later asked to decide which statement represented their feelings most closely. A number of gestures were regularly connected with emotions, and nearly all involved touching the self. Examples are hand to nose (fear), finger to lips (shame), and making a fist (anger – males).

Other self-touching gestures are covering the eyes, ears, or mouth, movements connected with eating and excretion, auto-erotic movements, grooming, and picking the nose, ears, or teeth. These gestures are mainly used in private or in intimate relationships and are inhibited in public; other people present usually ignore them.

There are probably a number of quite different reasons for touching the self, including keeping warm, grooming, cleansing and preening, reducing or increasing pain, displaying or concealing emotional states (e.g. covering face), helping mental activities by clutching the head, and as part of gestures, postures, or rituals (Poyatos 1983). Some of these are done more in private, some more in public, some in preparation for public appearance.

Daly *et al.* (1983) observed seventy-five young people in the restrooms of bars and restaurants and measured the time that they spent grooming. Women spent longer (47·1 seconds) than men (14·6 seconds); and the time spent depended on how well they knew their companions:

	Seconds
married, close friend	9·8
established dating	27·9
early dating	57·8
pick-up	46·8

Self-grooming gestures are not intended to communicate in them-selves – though the results of the grooming are. These are rather different since they take place in specific social situations – greetings, courtship, and when about to appear or perform in public. The reason is presumably that attention is focused on the self-image being presented, including the body–image, on these occasions.

Gesture and personality

Do individuals have characteristic gestures or gestural styles? It is a common experience that we can recognize people from a distance or from behind by their bodily movements, just as we can recognize them from their faces and voices.

To begin with, are individuals consistent in their style of gestures and bodily movements? An extensive study carried out by Allport and Vernon (1933) of twenty-five young men measured movements of different parts of the body in thirty different situations. They did not study specific emotional expressions, but styles of bodily move-ments such as shaking hands, drawing circles, and walking out of doors. It was found that the subjects were very consistent in the same situation from one occasion to another. There was also a con-siderable degree of generality between different parts of the body. The similarity between movements due to different groups of muscles was as great as the similarity between different actions by the same group of muscles. People who had large strides also drew large circles and made larger movements when idle – making up a factor of 'expansiveness'. There was also a factor of 'emphasis', based on voice loudness, writing pressure, and so on.

But how far are these gestural styles correlated with, and in prin-ciple diagnostic of, personality dimensions? As yet there is very little evidence on this point. Allport and Vernon did find some congruence. One subject, for example, had bodily movements which were 'pre-dominantly firm, strong, forceful, emphatic, expansive, well-spaced', and in personality was 'assured, incisive, expansive, with capacity for prudent delay and caution'. It seems likely that extro-verts would be more expansive, for example; and it has been found that mental patients use rather few hand movements.

Several aspects of gestural style are related to rewardingness and other aspects of social effectiveness. Trower (1980) found that socially inadequate mental patients use fewer gestures, and others have found that mental patients touch themselves more than others do. Rosenfeld (1966), in an encoding study, asked subjects to seek another's approval: they did this by using more smiles and gesticulations. Other studies have found that expressiveness is decoded as warmth and likeability. The important gestures here are head-nods and object-directed gestures (D'Auguelli 1974). Head-nods are one of the main forms of social reinforcement, together with smiles and glances, in the operant conditioning of verbal behaviour (Matarazzo *et al.* 1964). Use of gestures adds to the effectiveness of some kinds of communication, and it has been found that people with greater verbal facility use gestures *more* than other people (Baxter, Winter, and Hammer 1968).

The relation between gestures and other aspects of personality depends on several different processes. First, some gestures reflect a prevailing emotional state, such as anxiety, or a general style of behaviour, such as aggression. The gestures are correctly seen as part of the whole. Second, people control and manipulate their behaviour and may even produce the opposite gesture to their true state, as when a nervous person has a loud voice or a firm handshake. Third, a person's gestural style is partly a product of his cultural and occupational background, age and sex, health, fatigue, and so on.

Since there are some links between gestural style and personality, it follows that some use could be made of gestures in assessing personality. However, decoding does not seem to be based on the established links between gesture and personality. Gittin (1970) found four factors from ratings of thirty-six photographs of gestures:

(1) Activation, e.g. gripping.
(2) Evaluation, e.g. not drooping.
(3) Weak and submissive.
(4) Control and push.

It is not yet known whether such styles truly reflect personality traits.

Psychoanalysts think that they can decode the unconscious meaning of gestures, which may be unknown to the sender. Mahl (1968) offers the following examples:

Gestures	Interpretations
very frequent patting and stroking of hair; even gets up and preens hair in front of mirror on wall at one point	narcissistic, complains that people do not pay enough attention to her

a great deal of ring play	marital conflict; frustrated by life at home
spasmodic clutching of bodice	fears of bodily mutilation, illness and death
frequently takes off glasses	use of denial as a defence

The sort of evidence presented is that a patient may remove her wedding ring during therapy, and several minutes later complain about her husband. However from a scientific point of view this must be regarded as inadequate evidence.

The same applies to schemes of personnel selection based on analysis of gestures (rather than the contents of conversation) during selection interviews. There is simply no evidence that valid selection can be done in this way.

We have seen that there are extensive cultural variations in the use of gestures (p.54f.). There are also some quite interesting sex differences. In fact one of the greatest differences between the sexes in the use of NVC is the greater expansiveness of male gestures (p.284). Mahl (1968) observed some characteristically male and female gestures among his patients. While females clasped their hands together, or patted their hair, males used more pointing outwards.

13

Posture

Dogs, horses, monkeys, and other animals each have a number of characteristic postures. Rhesus monkeys, for example, have five sitting positions – upright, relaxed, hunched, cat-like, and crouching. They have other postures for threat, sex, grooming, defecation, sleeping, and so on. And, as we have seen, posture plays an important role for many animals in signalling dominance, threat, submission, and other interpersonal attitudes. We shall see that very similar signals are used by man.

There are three main human postures:

standing
sitting, squatting, and kneeling
lying

Some research has used sitting postures, some standing positions, while psychoanalysts have used lying (e.g. Mahl 1968). Each of these has further variations corresponding to different positions of the arms and legs, and different angles of the body. Some are used only in particular cultures (see p.61).

In primitive societies there are about a hundred common postures, most of them not used at all in more advanced societies – such as standing on one leg, squatting, sitting with legs crossed, kneeling on one knee, and leaning on a spear. The postures which are used in a particular community depend on such factors as the nature of the ground, whether it is cold or wet, and the clothes worn. In western countries we have found sitting or lying on the floor unsatisfactory and are accustomed to using furniture.

The ways in which particular attitudes or emotions are expressed vary from culture to culture, but there are common features. For example 'humility' may be expressed in the following ways:

Behaviour pattern	Culture group
Throwing oneself on the back, rolling from side to side, slapping outside of thighs (meaning; you need not subdue me; I'm subdued already)	Batokas
Bowing, extending right arm, moving arm down from horizontal position, raising it to the level of one's head, and lowering it again (meaning: I lift the earth off the ground, and place it on my head as a sign of submission to you)	Turks and Persians
Walking about with hands bound and rope around one's neck	Ancient Peruvians
Joining hands over head and bowing (ancient sign of obedience signifying: I submit with tired hands)	Chinese
Dropping arms; sighing	Europeans
Stretching hands towards person and striking them together	Congo natives
Extension of arms; genuflection	Preliterates
Prostration	European peasants
Crouching	New Caledonians Fijians, Tahitians
Crawling and shuffling forward; walking on all fours	Dahomeans
Bending body downwards	Samoans
Permitting someone to place his foot on one's head	Fundah and Tonga Tabu people
Prostration, face down	Polynesians
Putting palms together for the other person to clasp gently	Unyanyembans
Bowing while putting joined hands between those of other person and lifting them to one's forehead	Sumatrans

Source: Krout 1942

Nearly all these postures involve bowing, crouching or lowering the body.

For every situation in a culture there are approved postures. There are correct postures for eating, giving a lecture, being interviewed, sunbathing, and riding a horse. A person who fails to adopt the

Figure 13.1 The meaning of some postures

(a) curious; (b) puzzled; (c) indifferent; (d) rejecting; (e) watching; (f) self-satisfied; (g) welcoming; (h) determined; (i) stealthy; (j) searching; (k) watching; (l) attentive; (m) violent anger; (n) excited; (o) stretching; (p) surprised, dominating, suspicious; (q) sneaking; (r) shy; (s) thinking; (t) affected

Source: Rosenberg and Langer 1965

correct posture may be the object of savage disapproval – he is
regarded as slack, immoral, uncivilized, or eccentric.

There are special postures for rituals. At religious services the
participants have to adopt a series of postures. Often the priest at a
ceremony adopts a standing posture, and may raise one or both
arms; those being processed kneel or stand with heads bowed.
Monks and nuns lie face downwards on the floor when taking their
final vows.

Research methods

A number of elaborate methods have been devised for describing
and categorizing bodily positions and movements, as described
earlier. However, in every culture there is a limited repertoire of
postures, and most investigators have worked with these. It is
necessary in encoding studies to describe the postures which are
adopted. A number of elements are commonly used, such as:

lean,	forwards
	backwards
	sideways
arms,	open
	closed
	on hips
head,	lowered
	raised
	tilted sideways
legs,	stretched
	open
	crossed

In addition it is possible to use broad dimensions of posture, such as
tense–relaxed, and these in turn are found to correlate with the elements above.

In decoding studies several methods have been used to isolate the
effect of postures. Sarbin and Hardyck (1953) used stick figures, as
shown in Figure 13.1. Some postures are seen as interpersonal attitudes, some as emotions, some as activities.

A similar method is the use of schematic drawings which are
experimentally varied to study the effect of different components of
postures. Examples from Spiegel and Machotka (1974) are shown in
Figure 13.1 and from Bull (1983) in Figure 13.3.

Mehrabian asked encoders to adopt varied postures, and used
photographs of these as stimuli (1968a).

Figure 13.2   Postures in male–female encounters

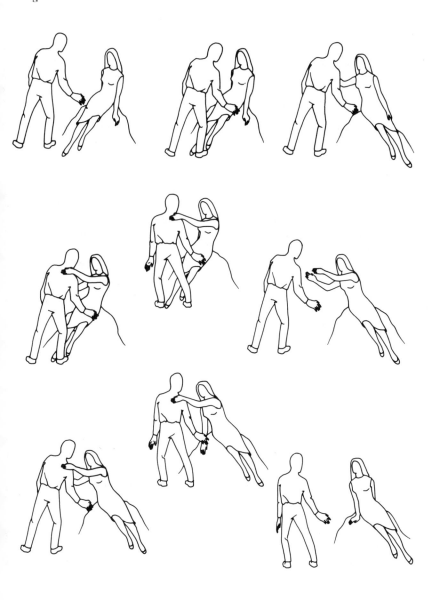

Source: Spiegel and Machotka 1974

Interpersonal attitudes

Animals convey dominance by size, strength, strutting, and expanding
the chest, and by signs of relaxation and lack of fear; submission is
shown by the opposite. Animals give appeasement signals to submit in
fights, lowering the body towards the ground; primary school children
have been observed to do the same – bowing the head, slumping shoulders, kneeling, tying shoe laces (Ginsburg, Pollmen, and Wauson 1977).

In adult humans, dominance and status are shown by drawing up to
full height, expanding the chest, hands on hips, expansive gestures –
all ways of increasing apparent size – while submission is shown by
lowering the head, shrinking, and bowing. These are especially used
in Japan where this is a very salient dimension of posture.

Some of the main experiments with humans were done by
Mehrabian (1969). He used encoding methods, in which subjects
were asked to imagine they were meeting a person standing in the
position of a hat-rack, whom they liked, disliked etc.; then several
aspects of their posture were coded by observers. In decoding experiments photographs were prepared of target persons seated or standing in varied postural positions, and the photographs were then
rated by judges as friendly–hostile, etc. Mehrabian found that one of
the ways in which posture communicates dominance is through
relaxation, which consists of:

asymmetrical arm positions
sideways lean
asymmetrical leg positions
hand relaxation
backwards lean

The relaxed postural style is used towards others of lower status,
more to females than males, to a person of the opposite sex more
than to a person of the same sex. Females adopt a more open-arm
position with a low status other, when seated, but the reverse when
standing, probably because these are the relaxed ways of sitting and
standing (Mehrabian 1969). The head is raised more when talking to
a person of higher status. A less relaxed posture is adopted by males
towards other males who are disliked. A number of these results
were obtained by Mehrabian in his highly controlled but rather
unrealistic experimental situations, but similar results were obtained
by other workers in real-life situations. Goffman (1961), for
example, noticed that the most important people at meetings in a
mental hospital sat in the most relaxed postures – as well as
occupying the best seats, at the front of the room.

Liking, interpersonal attraction, or openness are also clearly communicated by posture. Mehrabian (1972) found a dimension of *immediacy* with the following components. *Immediacy* consisted of:

leaning forwards   gaze
touching   direct orientation
proximity

This style of behaviour is used towards people who are liked, and by females more than by males. The different components of immediacy all have the effect of reducing distance or improving the visibility between two people. Leaning forward acts in a similar way to moving closer, and looking more as one of a number of non-verbal signs for intimacy (p.94f.).

Spiegel and Machotka (1974) asked subjects to rate the attitudes of couples shown in line drawings, as in Figure 13.2. Arms folded across the body were seen as rejecting and unyielding, open arms as accepting, especially when stretched towards the other. However, Mehrabian (1969) found that openness of arms signalled a positive attitude only when used by females, in both encoding and decoding experiments. Arms akimbo, i.e. on hips, were also found to communicate a negative attitude, both for senders and receivers.

While relaxation primarily communicated dominance, it also signalled disliking. People are moderately relaxed with those whom they like, and very relaxed with those who are not liked or respected. However, males are very unrelaxed with those seen as threatening (Mehrabian 1972).

It has been observed that interactors often adopt postures which are mirror-images of each other, and suggested that this might be a sign of good rapport (Kendon 1970). A number of careful quantitative studies have confirmed this, for example between therapists and patients, between teachers and pupils. LaFrance (1979) measured mirroring by the degree of coincidence of torso (nine positions) and arms (fifteen positions) for university teachers and pupils in classes of about fifteen, with ten measures per session. Rapport was assessed on fifteen seven-point scales completed by the subjects. Mirroring and rapport correlated 0·44 and 0·63 at different times. In a later study sixty pairs of strangers were observed in a 'waiting-room' for five minutes; here there was a *negative* correlation. When there was good rapport they talked more; where there was poor rapport they engaged in more mirroring, perhaps as an attempt to improve it, a strategy adopted more by women and by androgenous men (La France and Ickes 1981). LaFrance (1985) compared the effects on posture of co-operation and competition between two pairs of subjects.

In competition there was more within-dyad congruence, in co-operation there was more between-dyad congruence. Postural congruence is decoded by observers of interaction as a sign of rapport, as an experiment by Trout and Rosenfeld (1980) showed using staged psychotherapy interviews.

Dabbs (1969) carried out an experiment in which a confederate did or did not copy the postures and gestures of subjects. When they did so, subjects evaluated the confederate more favourably, believed that he thought like they did, and said that they identified with him. Maxwell and Cook (1985) found that not only were congruent postures seen as signs of liking, but that subjects who were asked to sit in chairs which produced congruent postures liked one another more.

Emotions

Ekman and Friesen (1967) suggested that while the face is the most effective channel for expressing specific emotions, the body communicates more general dimensions such as *tense–relaxed*, or degree of arousal. Graham, Ricci Bitti, and Argyle (1975) found that video-tapes of the body could be decoded more accurately than those of the face for five levels of arousal, but less accurately for most of a range of specific emotions, though for English performers anger was communicated better by the body. We have just seen the components of relaxation, as found by Mehrabian (p.208). A tense person sits or stands rigidly, upright or leaning forwards, often with hands clasped together, legs together, muscles tense.

Extreme emotions can be seen in the postures of certain mental patients. Depressives have a drooping, listless posture, and sit brooding, looking at the floor. Manics are alert and erect, their body in a high degree of arousal. This is partly a difference along the tense–relaxed dimension, but it includes other components as well. Patients in anxiety states are highly aroused too, but here the specific emotion is anxiety rather than euphoria, and this is shown in their muscular tension.

Can posture also communicate specific emotions? Bull (1987) videotaped subjects while they were listening to videorecorded talks and rated them for emotions. They adopted certain postures during items rated for certain emotions:

interested – forward lean, draws back legs
bored – lowered head, supports head on hand, leans back, stretches legs, turns head away (suggesting reduced arousal and attentiveness)

Figure 13.3   Posture and emotion: (1) and (2) boredom; (3) interest

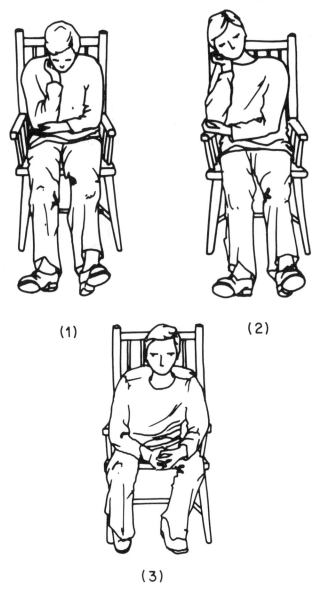

(1)

(2)

(3)

Source: Bull 1983

In a decoding study, using drawings, it was found that subjects decoded these postures correctly (Figure 13.3). In the Sarbin and Hardyck study (Figure 13.1), a number of stick figures were commonly thought to indicate emotions: indifferent, shy, self-satisfied, excited, affected, violent, angry.

Personality

There has not been much experimental research on the relation between posture and personality. However, there is little doubt that some people do create impressions of their personality through posture – the stiff, military bearing or the affected, superior posture, for example.

A number of psychoanalysts have offered interpretations of the postures adopted by patients during therapy, either lying on a couch or sitting on a chair. These interpretations are based on the personalities of particular patients. Another method used is to adopt the posture in question and then introspect. Some of the postures in the list in Table 13.1 have been interpreted in the same way by several analysts, and there appears to be a tradition of interpretation. However, there is no clear scientific evidence for the validity of these interpretations.

Table 13.1 *Psychoanalytic interpretations of postures*

	Posture	Interpretation
Arms	(1) folded arms, self-wrapping	self-protection, especially of breasts, withdrawal
	(2) bodice of dress clutched	fears of bodily damage
	(3) shoulders shrugged, palms out	passive helplessness
Legs	(1) high crossing (females)	self-protection, withdrawal
	(2) uncrossing	flirtation
	(3) exhibitionistic leg crossing (females)	flirtation
	(4) no movement in pelvis	sexual inhibition
Trunk	(1) stiff, military bearing (males), prim and upright (females)	imprisoning anxiety
	(2) vain, affected bearing	conflict between flirtation and shyness
	(3) dropping, listless, immobile	helplessness, request for help
	(4) nestling into chair, languid, erotic manner	expresses sexual impulses

Source: papers by Mahl 1968, Scheflen and Scheflen 1972, and others.

Posture may also play a part in more intentional self-presentation. A man may adopt a stiff military posture to show that he is a soldier rather than to imprison his anxiety. He may adopt a quiet and humble manner because he is a monk, an eccentric and relaxed posture to show he is an intellectual, and so on. Posture is probably affected by the body-image. Adolescent girls who are proud of, or ashamed of, their breasts will adopt quite different postures. People may display or conceal their height, their legs, or other features of their bodies. As the psychoanalytic interpretations suggest, people may also try to protect various parts of their body, and they may try to appear more relaxed than they really are.

Men and women adopt very different postures, and these are described on p.284f.

Posture and speech

Postural changes can be regarded as a kind of extension of gesture, consisting of larger and slower bodily movements. Scheflen (1973) reports that a patient will adopt from two to four postural positions during a therapeutic session. A person often repeats his postures when the same emotion or topic comes up; the code is an individual one, and cannot be decoded without experience of that individual.

Posture is intermediate between gestures and spatial behaviour in its scale and functions. Posture frames and defines a period of interaction longer than that of a gesture, shorter than that of a spatial position. This is not so much communication as the adoption of a suitable posture for the period of encounter in terms of relationships with others; however, certain postures have come to be associated with particular relationships.

Gestures accompany and support speech in a number of other ways, and may on occasions turn into postural changes – in providing illustration, in synchronizing, in giving comments on utterances and feedback on those of others, especially agreement and disagreement. These are described in more detail in Chapter 7.

14

Touch and bodily contact

Bodily contact is the most primitive form of social communication; it is found in very simple organisms, and in young children. Other forms of NVC are a later development both of evolution and growth. Primates use a number of different forms of bodily contact – infants cling to their mothers, and engage in rough-and-tumble play with each other; adults groom each other; presenting, mounting, and embracing take place between sexual partners; in dominance hierarchies rival males may bite, strike, and pull fur; greetings consist of genital and stomach nuzzling, kissing, embracing, and grooming. Bodily contact is involved in some of the most basic types of social contact – sex, feeding, fighting – as well as in sheer affiliative behaviour, such as grooming and play in primates.

In humans a large area of the brain is used to receive messages from the body surface, and these guide bodily movements. Bodily contact stimulates several different kinds of receptor – responsive to touch, pressure, warmth or cold, and pain. The skin sends various kinds of signals about its condition – by its colour, taste, smell (e.g. of perspiration), and temperature. Infant monkeys when anxious prefer to make bodily contact with a surrogate 'cloth mother' who provides comfort because its skin feels right, than with a 'mother' which provides milk (Harlow and Harlow 1965).

Touch is the most important channel of communication at first for infants. A number of studies have shown that infants who do not have enough bodily contact become anxious and disturbed. It seems likely that they have an innate need for the right kind of touch, as monkeys do, and that contact with the mother is one origin of the maternal bond. Most children seek attention by crying, and stop when picked up. However, Schaffer and Emerson (1964) found that some infants ('non-cuddlers') actively resist physical contact and obtain comfort from being able to see their mother, or to hold her skirt. Mothers respond to infants by cradling, caressing, cuddling, carrying, rocking, and tickling, and most infants are in turn responsive to this. To a lesser extent fathers and siblings treat infants in a similar way. During the first year of life games of tickling and other forms of bodily contact are the main means of relating to infants. It has been found in different studies that parents touch their children most between the ages of one and two, when they are first walking, but that touch declines after this age.

When children are six months old mothers touch girls much more than boys, and at thirteen months, perhaps as a result, girls seek bodily contact with mothers more than boys do, in an open space situation (Goldberg and Lewis 1969). Doctors and other medical staff make a lot of bodily contact with children – on 89 per cent of occasions they touched, 49 per cent held hands, 45 per cent hugged, and 22 per cent had children on their laps. There is more bodily contact with younger children and girls (Cowen, Weisberg, and Lotyczewski 1983).

Bodily contact among children declines until age twelve but is still well above adult levels; boys of six to eight engage in a lot of rough and tumble play, like monkeys. Most touching is between same-sex children (Willis and Hoffman 1975). After a low period at about twelve, bodily contact with the opposite sex becomes important.

We reviewed the extent of cultural differences in touch in Chapter 4, and showed the considerable differences between so-called contact and non-contact cultures. Figure 14.1 gives an example of cultural differences here. Some of these cultural differences are in male–male interaction, which is liable to be interpreted as homosexual in non-contact cultures. But the same behaviour has different meanings, because the rules are different. Indeed, touch is a tightly rule-bound matter, and infringement of these rules is heavily sanctioned.

How much bodily contact occurs among adults in Britain and the USA?

(1) With children, up to adolescence. After about twelve there is almost no contact with them.
(2) Among adolescents and students, heterosexual (and homosexual) activity, from holding hands to sexual intercourse, is an important part of life.
(3) With a spouse, both during sexual intercourse and more casually as part of everyday domestic life, touch is permitted, and occurs much more often than with other people.
(4) With other relations and friends various kinds of greeting and farewell are allowed, including hand-shakes, embraces, and kisses on the cheek with members of the other sex, especially after a long absence; congratulations take the form of hand-shakes and

pats on the back; a certain amount of mild touching occurs in flirtation with non-spouses; dancing is an occasion for close bodily contact between non-spouses.

(5) Between relative strangers, and in public places, bodily contact is rare. There is a lot of contact in crowds and on public transport, but this is not socially defined as touching. A number of professionals touch people in the course of their work – doctors, tailors, nurses, gynaecologists, dentists, masseurs, gymnastics instructors, barbers, beauticians, and shoe salespersons. However, this kind of touch is neutralized and defined as non-social, though it may well be enjoyed socially by some of those who give or receive it. A number of games involved touching, e.g. rugby football and wrestling. Certain ceremonies and rituals involve special kinds of touching, as at christenings, weddings, and graduations.

(6) Encounter groups are partly designed to fulfil the need for more bodily contact, and include a number of exercises involving touch.

Research methods

A number of research designs have been used to study touch.

Experiments on the effects of touch

A number of field experiments have been carried out, with touch as the experimental variable. The dependent variable has been behaviour, such as compliance with a request, attitudes towards the toucher (e.g. liking him or her), amount of self-disclosure, and therapeutic consequences, for example in hospital. Sometimes there has been some effect on behaviour but no effect on evaluation. These experiments have been restricted to brief touches between relative strangers, rather than to more extended touch, or repeated touch over a longer period in longer-term relationships.

Experiments on the meaning of different kinds of touch (i.e. decoding)

One procedure is to ask subjects to rate pictures of touching. Major and Heslin (1982) showed slides of touch v. no touch on the shoulder, reciprocated or not, for all combinations of males and females. The dependent variable was ratings of perceived dominance, masculinity, warmth, and sexual desire.

Surveys of the occurrence of touch

There have as yet been no experiments where touch is the dependent variable. However, there have been a number of surveys of the extent of touch as a function of situation, relationship, sex of those involved, and so on. For example, Heslin and Boss (1980) observed a sample of greetings at airports. Jourard (1966) introduced a self-report method, described below, in which subjects could report which parts of their body had been touched by whom.

The most extensive attempt at classification was by Jones and Yarborough (1985) who analysed 1,500 touches recorded by thirty-nine observers. They found eighteen types of touch, in the following main groups:

(1) *Positive affect*, from reassurance to sexual
(2) *Playful*
(3) *Control*, e.g. directing behaviour, getting attention
(4) *Rituals*, especially greetings and partings
(5) *Mixed*, e.g. greeting and affection
(6) *Task-related*
(7) *Accidental*

A type of touch which is missing from this list is aggression – important because the possibility of aggression is a source of anxiety connected with touch.

Heslin (in Heslin and Alper 1983) suggested a five-category scheme of degrees of intimacy, which are mainly subdivisions of group (1) above together with group (6):

(1) *Functional/professional*, e.g. by doctors, shoe salespersons, and others
(2) *Social/polite*, e.g. shaking hands, and other greetings
(3) *Friendship/warmth*, touch which goes beyond (2) but not as far as (4), and which can easily be misinterpreted
(4) *Love/intimacy*, e.g. holding the other's hand
(5) *Sexual arousal*, further degrees of bodily contact.

Jourard (1966) used a map of the body on which subjects reported *where* they had been touched by different others. In Figure 14.1 the results of a more recent American study are shown, together with comparable results in Japan.

Touch as the expression of interpersonal attitudes

Most touch can be regarded, as far as the toucher is concerned, as

Figure 14.1 Where the body has been touched in the USA and Japan

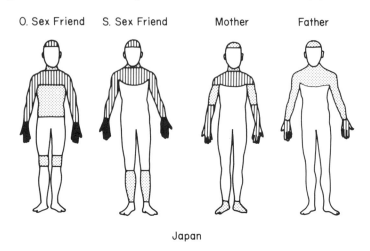

O. Sex Friend   S. Sex Friend   Mother   Father

Japan

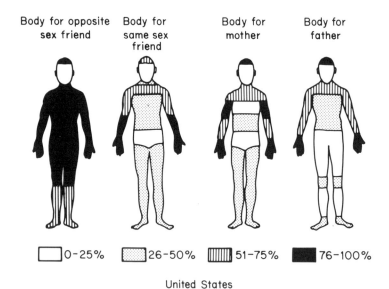

Body for opposite   Body for   Body for   Body for
sex friend   same sex   mother   father
                     friend

☐ 0-25%   ▨ 26-50%   ▥ 51-75%   ■ 76-100%

United States

Source: Barnlund 1975

expressing attitudes towards another person. We will consider later how the person touched decodes it.

Sex

The ultimate goal of sexual motivation is intercourse and the pro-creation of children. The forms of bodily contact involved are highly arousing and highly rewarding, and they lead to very strong attach-ment to the partner, which has the biological advantage of providing a stable home for the children produced. The bodily contacts related to sex are similar in all cultures and have a biological basis. There are also variations, and there are cultural rules about what people may do when they are unmarried, engaged, and married. There are a number of different kinds of bodily contact of progressive intimacy. Pisano, Wall, and Foster (1986) asked subjects to rate the meanings of thirty-one kinds of touch between romantic couples:

16 were seen by most people as warmth or love, e.g. stroking partner's arm
7 were seen as playfulness, e.g. punching partner's arm
6 were seen as sexual desire, e.g. stroking partner's leg
none were seen by a majority as dominance or control, though 14 per cent saw kicking the other's behind, and 10 per cent saw slapping the other's behind in this way.

Henley (1973), in an observational field study, found that men touched women much more often than women touched men – and much more than people touched others of the same sex. However, a number of other studies of this issue have failed to confirm that men touch women more than vice versa. In fact most studies have found that females touch males more, especially among children, and when indoors rather than outdoors (Hall 1984). But we shall see later that touch is often interpreted both as warmth, including sex, *and* as dominance. Women like being touched more than men do, and when men touch women it may be because they know this. Both sexes often avoid touch, and while men avoid same-sex contact, women more often avoid opposite-sex touch (Stier and Hall 1984).

Affiliation

A lot of animal and human behaviour can be classified as affiliative, that is, directed towards establishing friendly relations with peers. There is a rather fine distinction between affiliation and sex, though affiliation stops short of the later stages of sexual intimacy. The biological purpose of this form of motivation is probably to restrain aggression and bring about co-operative behaviour in groups. In apes and monkeys affiliative behaviour has its origins in bodily contact with the mother and siblings, develops into rough-and-tumble play with other young animals, and is expressed in adults by long periods of grooming, as well as by co-operation and mutual help. In humans the origins are similar, but much less bodily contact occurs in adults: the content of affiliation appears to be conversation, and co-operative work and play rather than grooming. There is a limited amount and intensity of these signals. Many studies have shown that people touch more those whom they like, those in closer relationships. Jourard (1966) found that students had been touched on more parts of their bodies by best friends of the opposite sex. Hibbard (cited by Heslin and Alper 1983) found that couples who were most in love engaged in most touching, both sexual and non-sexual.

Aggression

As in the case of sex, aggression is expressed primarily by bodily contact. Aggression is the innate response to attack, frustration, and competition for resources. Animals use horns, teeth, or other parts of their anatomy designed for aggressive purposes. However, threat displays are more common than actual fighting: there is a built-in appeasement mechanism which prevents members of a group from damaging each other unduly. Human infants scream, kick, and beat with their fists; aggressive tendencies may become strengthened during childhood, but restraints on aggression are acquired as well. Boys up to about ten spend a lot of time in friendly wrestling. Girls fight less, though they may pull one another's hair, and they make more use of verbal aggression. Parents spank their children, young adults engage in rough games like boxing, judo, or rugger, and there is institutionalized aggression in war, though this does not involve much bodily contact nowadays. In some cultural groups there is aggression between adult males – in some criminal groups, and at one time in the Wild West, for example. In each of these cases the form of aggression, and how far it is permitted to go, are controlled by cultural rules.

Bodily contact is the basic way biologically of expressing interpersonal attitudes. In animals and children there is a great deal of these forms of bodily contact. In adults they become replaced, to a very large extent, by other forms of communication of a more symbolic kind, using the distance receptors of vision and hearing, and also language. However, these signals derive their emotive power from their origins and links with bodily contact, and symbolize bodily contact – as clenching the fists stands for punching, and extending the arms stands for embracing. Football fans fight a lot, but most of the fighting between rival groups is symbolic, consisting mainly of threatening expressions and insults (Marsh, Rosser, and Harré 1978).

Dominance

Henley (1973) argued that men touched women more than vice versa as an expression of dominance (we have just seen they do not). Is it the case that touch reflects or signals dominance? It is true that doctors touch patients more than vice versa, but the same applies to shoe salesmen and their clients. Observational and self-report studies in a variety of settings, however, confirm that higher status or older people usually initiate touch (Heslin and Alper 1983).

Touch as an interaction signal

Greetings and farewell

These include bodily contact in most cultures. This is also the case with apes and monkeys: they smack their lips and touch each other; one may present for copulation and the other mount, regardless of their sex; a chimpanzee may hold out a hand and touch the other's head, shoulder, or genitals; a pair of apes may embrace each other enthusiastically. This indicates a biological basis for bodily contact in greeting; Lorenz (1952) suggests that ritualized greeting ceremonies have the purpose of preventing aggression; lip-smacking, for example, invites grooming and acts as an appeasement signal. There are great variations between different human cultures in how greetings are performed (p.63) but they have a common structure and common elements – including some form of bodily contact. In India and Japan, however, the commonest form of greeting does not include touch, and in Britain daily greetings do not.

Greetings can be regarded as a ritual, a series of symbolic acts, a rite of passage which has the function of beginning an encounter, starting a period of mutual accessibility, perhaps as affirming a social bond. Such ceremonies are able to perform the 'ritual work' of bringing about such changes of state (Goffman 1971; Schiffrin 1974).

Greenbaum and Rosenfeld (1980) observed 103 greetings at American airports. The numbers who used each kind of touch were as follows:

no touch: 41
kiss on mouth: 41
touch on head, arm, or back: 38
kiss on cheek: 30
light hug: 23
solid hug: 19
arm round waist or back: 15
holding hands: 12
hand-shake: 10
extended embrace: 10
extended kiss: 3

While men shook hands with one another, any greetings involving females were likely to include a kiss and an embrace, ending with a hand touch to the upper body.

Kendon and Ferber (1973) carried out an observational study on greetings at a garden party, using the linguistic–structural method (p.17f.). They found that the greetings had the following sequence of components:

(1) *Distant salutation* (non-verbal only): two people sight each other, a distant salutation like a wave or smile may be made, one or both approach.

(2) *Approach and preparation* (non-verbal only): gaze is averted, they groom themselves, and an arm may be brought across the front of the body; in the final approach there is mutual gaze, smiling, the head is set in a special position, and the palm of the hand is presented.

(3) *Close phase* (verbal and non-verbal): stereotyped utterances are exchanged ('Hello', 'How nice to see you'), usually with bodily contact – hand-shake, embrace, or kiss.

(4) *Attachment phase* (mainly verbal): there is less stereotyped conversation, establishing the identity and status of the other if necessary, enquiring after his recent activities, enquiring purpose of visit, looking after his immediate needs, for example providing him with a seat or a drink.

In other studies it has been found that greetings between strangers are much shorter than this: mutual glance, head gesture, verbal salute, personal enquiry (but no touch).

Partings are the reverse of greetings, a rite of passage which closes an encounter, and prepares those involved for a period of separation. Knapp *et al.* (1973) observed partings after role-played interviews in the laboratory, and found that the main NV signals used were:

breaking gaze
orients body towards exit
leans forward
nods head

Smiles were less frequent. Partings, too, are truncated for those who do not know each other well, but are much more elaborate, with extensive bodily contact, for those in close relationships preparing for a long separation. The ritual sequence with bodily contact achieves a synchronized separation. Collett (personal communication) found that there were many 'failed partings' between people talking in the street, through lack of agreement on when the parting should occur: one would try to leave but be kept in play by the other.

Congratulations

Congratulations often include bodily contact – when someone has achieved some success in sport, or career. The signals used are exactly the same as for greetings. An interesting form of congratulations is the embracing of footballers after a goal has been scored, and similar episodes in other games. This is curious, since men do not normally embrace, and this is associated in Britain with homosexuality. Smith, Willis, and Gier (1980) observed white and black Americans in a bowling alley. There was quite a high rate of touching – 31·2 times per hour for blacks, 6·5 for whites. And the blacks did touch each other after a success, mainly hand to hand.

Ceremonies

These usually include bodily contact. As we describe in Chapter 18, ceremonies have three stages: separation–transition–incorporation. At the height of the ceremony, usually during the transitional period, a symbolic act of bodily contact is performed by the priest, or whoever is empowered by the community to carry out these ritual functions. It is accepted that this person, by performing these symbolic acts, has the power to bring about certain changes of state in the initiates. The commonest form of touch is laying a hand or hands on the initiate's head. It is not clear why this is done: it may be to symbolize the continuous chain from St Peter, or some other spiritual source. In healing and ordination a number of priests or elders lay their hands on at once, perhaps to increase the spiritual forces being activated. Here are some examples:

Ceremony	Bodily contact	Symbolic meaning
graduation confirmation ordination	places hands on initiate's head	passes on continuous chain of authority
healing ceremonies	anoints with oil or other substance	application of medicine
wedding	places ring on bride's finger	ring stands for marriage bonds
monk taking vows	puts his new clothes on him	clothes represent his new status
prize-giving	presents cup or other prize, shakes hands	prize is mark of groups' recognition for success
adolescent initiation	inflicts physical damage	test of manhood

We shall discuss the symbolism involved in these ceremonies in Chapter 18.

There is further bodily contact by friends and relations before and after such ceremonies. There may be hand-shakes or embraces beforehand; these would be regarded by anthropologists as 'separation', i.e. farewell signals, but may be regarded by those involved as preparations or good wishes for the ceremony. Afterwards there are greetings – for the person in his new status as an adult, graduate, married person, etc. These are more than greetings; they are used to establish a somewhat different relationship with the person in his new social position.

It is interesting that fans of pop stars or other heroes want to touch the body or even the clothes of their hero. (It happened to Jesus too.) This suggests that bodily contact is believed to convey spiritual power in some way, and this may be the real reason that touch is used in ceremonies.

Rules about touching

Touch is theoretically rather puzzling. It involves invasion of personal space, but it is sometimes very well received. From the affiliative balance point of view it should be accompanied by otherwise cold behaviour, yet we know this is not always so. Certainly there are many situations when touch would be quite inappropriate and many types of touch which would provoke a negative reaction. There appear to be definite rules which permit certain kinds of touch, between certain people, on certain occasions only. Bodily contact outside these narrow limits is unacceptable.

Sussman and Rosenfeld (1978) carried out an experiment in which subjects were touched on the shoulder for the three minutes of the experiment by a confederate; for half the subjects a justification for this was provided – touch was to be used as a time-signal. For males, touch was regarded as intrusion, though less so when justified; touch led to reduced task performance. For females touch led to greater liking for the experimenter, and was not seen as intrusive.

Nguyen, Heslin, and Nguyen (1975) asked people to rate the amount of invasion of privacy, and other reactions, from being touched on different parts of the body, and by different people. Invasion was seen as playful, but not pleasant, friendly, or loving. Stroking, for example, was seen as linked with love and sex, and was regarded as less invasive from a close, opposite-sex person.

In which public situations is bodily contact permitted? Common observation suggests the following: sport, dancing, games, crowds, medical and other professional attention, encounter groups, greetings, and partings. In all of these situations different rules apply – a specialized kind of touch is used, with no implication of great intimacy. Shaking hands in greeting does not have the same significance as holding hands by courting couples; nor does embracing of football players who have scored goals. Professional attention by tailors, shoe salespersons, nurses, and others has to be done with care, especially when intimate parts of the body are involved, or where gentle massage is used. In addition there are intimate situations between people in close relationships. And finally there are dominant relations of a variety of kinds – doctor–patient, supervisor–worker, etc. Henley (1977) found that touch is more likely on the part of someone who is giving an order, information or advice, asking a favour, or trying to persuade.

Bodily contact is encouraged between people in certain relationships, discouraged in others. Argyle, Henderson, and Furnham (1985) found a number of rules for different relationship. Touching was prescribed for certain close relationships – spouses, dating couples, close family, and in-laws – but was not permitted (in general) for less close relationships, e.g. at work, between neighbours, or in professional relationships. Heslin *et al.* (in Heslin and Alper 1983) found that in the USA touch by a person of the same sex is disliked, especially if he or she is a stranger, and if this touch is in an intimate area. While men particularly dislike being touched by men, women dislike being touched by strangers. There must be congruence between relationships and touch, except that men accept touch from female strangers, perhaps reflecting the basic promiscuity of males (Heslin and Alper 1983).

Finally, touch is allowed on certain parts of the body, e.g. hands, arms, and back, but not in more intimate areas, as shown in Figure 14.1.

The meaning of touch

Perhaps the most basic meaning of touch is that an interpersonal bond is being offered or established, rather like a direct glance or a shift to greater proximity. And, like gaze, it seems to function to strengthen other messages, for example of persuasion. However, touch also carries the implication of invasion of privacy, and exposure to aggression or sex.

Touch has two main dimensions of meaning – warmth and dominance. Major and Heslin (1982) asked subjects to rate couples seen in silhouette, where one touched, or did not touch the other. The ratings are shown in Table 14.1.

Table 14.1   *The perception of toucher and touched*

	Toucher	Touched	No-touch
status/dominance	9·36	7·61	8·58
warmth/expressiveness	10·01	8·25	8·93
instrumentality/assertiveness	10·34	7·20	8·76

Source: Major and Heslin 1982

It can be seen that the person who touches is seen as having enhanced status, assertiveness, and warmth, while the person who is touched is seen as having less. Florez and Goldman (1982) conducted an experiment with blind subjects; their self-reports were similar to those above. In addition the touched subjects evaluated their partner (who had touched them) more than the task, while the touching subjects evaluated their partners less favourably than the task. It seems that a person who touches acquires higher status, a person who is touched has less.

Within the warmth component there is further ambiguity about how warm, i.e. how far up Heslin's five-point scale, a particular touch is. There is usually little doubt about professional touch at one end, or sexual touch at the other. It has been suggested that it is the middle of the scale – friendship/warmth – which is most difficult to decode; it is often unclear how far there is a sexual element.

Can we put together a vocabulary of different kinds of touch? From published research and from common observation Table 14.2 gives some suggestions (cf. Jones and Yarborough 1985):

Table 14.2   *A vocabulary of touch*

Touch	Meaning
stroke, caress, lick: body, face, hair	sex, affection
pat: hand, arm, back	friendship, reassurance, support
shake hands, formal kiss	greeting, parting
hug, embrace	intense greeting, parting, congratulations
sustained embrace, hand-holding	enjoy close relationships
touch hand, arm, or shoulder while speaking	enhancing social influence
brief touch	getting attention
pull, push, guide	direct movements
professional touches, e.g. medical	attending to body, but non-social
tickle	play
hit, scratch, slap, kick	aggression

However, it should be emphasized again that touch is not a very clear channel of communication.

The list is different in some other cultures. For example, in parts of Africa it is common to twine the legs together during conversation. It is interesting that the list of touches with familiar meanings is so short. The possible combination of types of touch and area touched is far greater than this, and touch would be a very useful channel of information, especially to the blind.

The effects of touch

Liking for the toucher

We have seen that touchers are rated as warm both by observers and by the person touched. We have seen that people find being touched pleasant if by a close friend of the opposite sex and, in the case of males, by a stranger of the opposite sex. Does touch lead to liking? Boderman, Freed, and Kinnucan (1972) did an 'ESP experiment', which provided an excuse for a female subject to explore the face of a female confederate and vice versa; subjects found the confederate more responsive and evaluated her more favourably when this was done. Breed and Ricci (1973) thought that this could be because a touching confederate became warmer, and found that touch had no effect with warmth held constant; perhaps touching works *because* it generates warmth of other kinds in the toucher.

Other studies with strangers have found that touching under less artificial conditions leads to liking strangers. Fisher, Rytting, and Heslin (1975) arranged for librarians to touch borrowers for half a second when returning their library cards. Female, but not male, borrowers who were touched liked both the librarian and the library more, and were in a more positive mood afterwards; the sex of the librarian had no effect. In several studies in a counselling setting, a counsellor who touched the client was evaluated more favourably. In all these cases there was some justification for touching, which would remove the invasion element of touch.

Social influence

A number of field studies have shown that touching a stranger when making a request results in more social influence. If a coin is left in a telephone box, asking the next person if they have found it results in surrender of the coin more often if they are touched. If people are asked to give money, for a telephone call, numbers complying are lower, but touch makes a big difference (Kleinke 1977); and more people will sign a harmless petition, or agree to give a brief interview (Willis and Hamm 1980):

Table 14.3   *Effect of touch on compliance*

	Touch	No touch	
	(percentage complying)		
return 10c found in telephone box	96	63	
give 10c	51	29	(Kleinke 1977)
sign petition	81	55	
give short interview	70	40	(Willis and Hamm 1980)
pick up forms	45 (upper arm)	28	(Paulsell and Goldman 1984)

Willis and Hamm stopped people in the street. More subjects complied with a female interviewer both to sign a petition (88 per cent v. 59 per cent) and to give an interview (66 per cent v. 44 per cent).

In a further study in this tradition people were stopped by an interviewer in a shopping centre and some were touched. The interviewer then dropped ten interview forms. Some subjects helped to pick them up. The percentages helping were as follows (Paulsell and Goldman 1984):

male interviewer		shoulder	28
male subject	14	upper arm	45
female subject	18	lower arm	35
female interviewer		hand	28
male subject	60	no touch	28
female subject	38		

Females touching males had the greatest effect. The upper arm was the best place to touch. Females who touched males here were helped in 90 per cent of cases.

Another study analysed the size of tips left for waitresses who touched (Crusco and Wetzel 1984). Tips as a percentage of the bills were:

touch on shoulder	14·4%
touch on hand	16·7%
no touch	12·2%

It is clear that touch can add considerably to social influence, in a variety of settings, between strangers, and in situations where there is a defined relationship.

What is the explanation for this effect of touching? Patterson, Powell, and Lenihan (1986) found that compliance did not correlate with liking the person who made a request in the touch condition, though there was a correlation of 0·30 in the no-touch condition. Perhaps touch simply strengthens the message, or perhaps the assertive component of touch adds influence.

Touch sequences

Finally, touch may lead to more touch. Jones and Yarborough (1985) observed a number of repetitive sequences, for example where an affectionate touch is reciprocated, greetings are reciprocated, or repeated greetings or partings take place between three or more people. They also observed 'strategic sequences', for example an affectionate greeting leads to prolonged bodily contact, an affectionate touch is followed by a request, a touch is rejected but followed by a mollifying touch on the part of the rejector, an assertive or mildly aggressive touch is responded to by a similar one, in order to equalize power.

Therapy

Jourard and Friedman (1970) studied the effect of touch on self-disclosure in an experimental situation. They found that touch combined with self-disclosure on the part of a confederate resulted in more self-disclosure by subjects. Aguilera (1967) found that if psychiatric nurses touched patients more, the patients talked more.

Touch can have more profound medical consequences. Whitcher and Fisher (1979) varied the amount of handling of patients by nurses prior to operations. Female patients who were handled more were less anxious and had lower blood pressure after their operations. For male patients these effects were reversed. It was suggested that this was because women are more used to being handled medically, and that men dislike the reduced status implied by such handling.

Some therapies, especially those emanating from California, make a lot of use of bodily contact. Examples are Rolfing, which involves painful deep massage, and the body awareness therapy of Feldenkrais, which is much gentler (Schutzenberger and Geffroy 1979). Of most interest to us are encounter groups, where clients are encouraged to touch one another in various symbolic ways. These groups were first conducted at the Esalen Institute at Big Sur in California, and have subsequently spread to other parts of the world. A number of different versions have been devised. The main purpose of the groups is therapy or training, by means of various individual and interpersonal exercises, many of them involving bodily contact and intimate relationships with other members of the group. For some people the groups are an end in themselves, since they enjoy the bodily contact and intimacy, and they feel that ordinary life is too inhibited and restraining in these respects.

An example of an encounter group exercise is 'break in'. Some of the group form a tight circle with interlocking arms. The person left out tries to break through the circle in any way he can. This is intended to help people who have difficulty in making contact with others (Schutz 1967).

What is the effect of encounter group exercises? A careful follow-up study was carried out of 206 Stanford students who attended encounter groups, T-groups, etc., and 69 control subjects. Success was estimated by a combination of criteria – self-ratings, ratings by friends, and so on. About a third of the group members and 17 per cent of the controls improved, while 8 per cent of the group members were harmed by the experience (for example, needing psychiatric help afterwards), in addition to the drop-outs and those who showed negative changes. There were no consistent differences between encounter groups and non-touching groups; differences between individual group leaders were more important (Lieberman, Yalom, and Miles 1973). From the popularity of the movement, these experiences are clearly enjoyed by a lot of people – though whether they have any therapeutic effect is another matter. Quite a number of people drop out because they find the exercises too disturbing.

Individual variations

We discussed sex differences above and showed that in male–female pairs most studies have found that females initiate touch more. Female–female pairs touch each other more than do male–male pairs – more solid hugs, and touches on hand, arm, and back (Heslin and Alper 1983). In some studies women have reacted positively, men negatively to touch by strangers, for example by nurses (Whitcher and Fisher 1979), librarians (Fisher, Rytting, and Heslin 1975), or experimental confederates (Sussman and Rosenfeld 1978). On the other hand several studies have found that males and females react quite similarly to being touched. It has been found that touching by women has most effect, when stopping people in the street (Willis and Hamm 1980; Paulsell and Goldman 1984), though sometimes cross-sex touching has most effect, as when asking for coins left in telephone boxes (Kleinke 1977).

Nguyen, Heslin, and Nguyen (1975, 1976) asked subjects to report their reactions to being touched by friends and strangers of both sexes. Males liked being touched by females, whether friends or strangers, but women did not like being touched by strange men, perhaps because they regard their bodies as more vulnerable. Neither sex liked being touched by their own sex. The most pleasant touches were of sexual areas by a close, opposite-sex friend. Women liked next best stroking of non-sexual areas by a close male friend; men, however, rated next best a female stranger stroking their sexual areas. Other research suggests that men can fall into a romantic relationship more rapidly than do women (Argyle and Henderson 1985).

There are systematic individual differences in touching behaviour. Heslin (in Heslin and Alper 1983) found three dimensions of attitudes towards touch:

(1) Touching non-intimates, liking to touch and be touched by strangers, new acquaintances, friends, and relatives.
(2) Non-sexual touching with spouse, lover, or most intimate friend.
(3) Sexual touching with spouse, lover, or most intimate friend.

It is not yet known how these dimensions correlate with other aspects of personality.

15

Clothes, physique, and other aspects of appearance

It is only shallow people who do not judge by appearances. The
true mystery of the world is the visible, not the invisible.

Oscar Wilde

Can appearance be looked at as a mode of communication? Some
aspects of physique can be altered very little, but even so other
people are likely to decode it, in terms of personality properties for
example. It *is* possible to modify physique by clothes, diet, and
exercise. Clothes are most under our control – though our choice is
affected by considerations other than communication, e.g. keeping
warm and conforming to conventions. Some people go to a lot of
trouble to arrange their appearance, think a lot about their clothes,
hair, and skin, and change between different social engagements. We
may conclude that most people, some of the time, use their appearance to send information to others.

Do clothes or other aspects of appearance have an agreed meaning? In a study of adolescent girls in the north of England, Gibbins
(1969) found a high degree of agreement on the kinds of girls who
might wear various items. There is very good agreement on which
people are judged to be attractive. On the other hand, many people
wear badges or ties which mean nothing to most observers, unless
they belong to the same college or club. It is common for one individual to think that another 'looks awful': in this case there is clearly
disagreement on the significance of appearance. And the meaning of
an item of appearance may vary with the situation, e.g. wearing a tie
at an interview or at a tutorial (Rees, Williams, and Giles 1974).

The most important theory here is Goffman's doctrine of 'self-
presentation' (1956). He postulated that people manipulate the
impressions formed of them by others, by deliberate self-presentation, in the form of quasi-theatrical performances, appearance being
an important part of the performance. There are various motivations
to manipulate impressions in this way – it may be in the other's

interest, as in the case of the activities of doctors and undertakers; it may be for immediate material gain, e.g. getting a job at an interview; to make friends; or to persuade others of one's desirable qualities in order to strengthen the self-image. Verbal self-presentation is often unsuccessful, especially in claims to status, since it may be disbelieved and ridiculed unless done very subtly and indirectly. However, non-verbal methods, especially appearance, tend to be taken at face value, as with other spheres of NVC. This line of thinking suggests the occasions on which self-presentation will take place – interviews, public performances, formal occasions, or whenever reputation is at stake, or the goodwill of others is sought (Argyle 1983).

The theory also leads us to see which aspects of self need to be communicated. These include:

> displaying positive features of the person, which he may or may not possess, or features which will be approved by others
> enhancing physical attractiveness
> displaying parts of the self-image, e.g. colourful, masculine, radical
> conforming to norms of situations, or deliberately deviating, e.g. not wearing a dinner jacket
> showing membership of a group, e.g. punks, undergraduates
> membership of a social class, e.g. upper
> occupational roles, e.g. nurse, judge, king

Appearance is used by animals as a means of communication. Male birds, such as peacocks, are endowed with the capacity for spectacular displays which they use for impressing females. Some birds have markings like the black bibs of some sparrows, which elevate the owner's social status if experimentally enlarged (Rohwer 1977). The bottoms of female monkeys turn blue at times of sexual availability.

Wearing clothes that send the right messages has to be learnt during socialization. Stone (1970) suggests that children go through three stages here:

> *pre-play*, wearing clothes chosen by mother
> *play*, dressing up in fantasy costumes
> *game*, wearing peer-group-approved uniforms, indicating the identity as a group member and as an individual

Adolescents and others who are uncertain of their self-image are often very concerned about their appearance, and very keen to look exactly like other members of the peer group.

We shall see later that while there are astonishing cultural variations in bodily decoration, the same general principles apply to all. Each culture develops fashions of appearance, and sets of symbols of agreed meaning. Where appearance differs from all other areas of NVC is that fashion keeps changing, and the same elements of appearance have very different significance at different dates.

The research methods used to study appearance are similar to those for other kinds of NVC.

Encoding

There is a real gap in our knowledge, since very little work has been carried out on how self-image, personality, etc. are encoded into appearance. The main exception has been group membership, together with work on the amount of effort put into grooming, and the use of cosmetics.

Decoding

Most research on appearance has been on decoding. For example Hoult (1954) asked subjects to rate photographs in which the clothes and the faces had been recombined independently.

Effects on behaviour of others

Many field experiments have been carried out in which the appearance of an 'interviewer' has been varied, to suggest different social classes, tidy *v*. scruffy, etc. to study the effect on helpfulness or willingness to be interviewed.

Clothes

The 'measurement' or classification of clothes has never been attempted systematically. Could it be done in terms of objective variables, as with spatial behaviour and tone of voice? These could include colour, length, amount of body exposed, clean *v*. dirty, material (e.g. cotton, leather), new *v*. old. However, the social meaning of all these variables keeps changing with fashion, as is most familiar in the case of skirt lengths: the same skirt which was seen as outrageously provocative one year is seen as dull and old-maidish at a later date.

Clothes do seem to communicate some particular dimensions of social meaning, however. These are: (1) formal–informal, appropriateness for different social situations, as well as for other situations like different kinds of sport; (2) group membership, including uniforms, social class, and membership of groups like punks and Sloanes;

(3) attractiveness and fashionability, especially for women, 'dressing-up' and attracting attention *v.* dressing down and avoiding it; (4) colourfulness, and other ways of expressing personality or mood.

Impression management

There is a lot of evidence that people choose their clothes in order to manipulate the impressions formed by others. Von Beyer *et al.* (1981) found that women attending a job interview wore clothes and accessories that were more feminine if they had been told that the interviewer held traditional views about women. We shall describe a number of studies below showing that clothes, cosmetics, and other aspects of appearance are carefully planned, especially when people are worried about their appearance, or the reactions of particular audiences, or if they are self-conscious or socially anxious.

Conformity to situation norms

There are very strong pressures to conform to group norms in matters of clothes, perhaps more than in any other area, and perhaps because they reflect on the image or respectability of the group. Snyder (1979) distinguished between high self-monitors who try to fit in with the demands of each occasion, and low self-monitors who prefer to 'be themselves'. Davis and Lennon (1985) found that people with high scores on self-monitoring thought that conforming in clothes was important, and that the use of clothes in presenting individuality was also important; they also reported exhibiting more fashion leadership. Solomon and Schopler (1982) had found similar effects for a measure of public self-consciousness; and the effects were stronger for men than for women. People usually wear different clothes for sport, sleep, and work. Some people make much finer distinctions, and Tse'elon at Oxford carried out depth interviews and found that women dressed differently for about six separate situations (unpublished). Gibbins (1969) found that his subjects agreed well on whether the clothes being judged were suitable for church, shopping, a formal dance, or a party. Many people engage in leisure activities which require special outfits – Scottish and other kinds of dancing, tennis, skiing, etc., even walking and jogging. This is one of the areas of life in which there are often strong pressures to conform, though of course there are deviates who do not. It is often said that there has been a shift towards greater informality among young people, but they too can be seen dressing appropriately for sport, discos, and the like.

Uniforms

These provide a formalized model of clothes operating very clearly to display group membership and status. In hospitals it is quite clear who are the doctors, sisters, nurses, cleaners, patients (pyjamas), and visitors (no uniform). Medical uniforms seem to be necessary to impress patients with the medical expertise of the wearers, though white coats also create more social distance. The formal suits of bankers and administrators proclaim their status and trustworthiness, the white habits of religious orders show commitment and separation from the world (Kaiser 1985).

A person may indicate his role in a particular situation by his appearance – a barrister puts on a wig, an academic puts on a gown – to indicate the role he is about to play. On ceremonial occasions it is common for the king, priest, vice-chancellor, or whoever is in charge to put on a special costume. This indicates that he is not acting on his own behalf but is using the authority vested in him and symbolized by his ceremonial gear. Priests usually wear robes which are both impressive and in strong contrast to those of the laity. The other participants may feel that the role performer has special status, powers, or holiness when he is dressed up (E. Crawley, in Roach and Eicher 1965). Members of working organizations indicate by their appearance how they define their job: for example, a foreman may look more like a manager or more like a shop-floor worker. Others express 'role distance', indicating that they differ from others in the same role – as with a scientific doctor or a radical psychologist (Goffman 1961).

Social groups and subcultures

The main division in modern society is between different social classes, and this is signalled in Britain most clearly by clothes and accent. At one time there were clear differences in the clothes worn, e.g. top hats *v.* cloth caps; there was something of a fashion lag, upper-class people wearing the new styles earlier. This is much less true now (see p.244), when the main difference is evidence of expense and distinctiveness; rich people buy their clothes at different shops, and they may have exclusive labels in them. Upper-class people, however, do not bother much with fashion, and stick to well-made 'classics'. Veblen (1899) in his *Theory of the Leisure Class* described how rich people engaged in conspicuous consumption, with expensive clothes and jewellery which were obviously quite unsuitable for manual work.

Different social groups often define themselves by aspects of their appearance. Punks, hippies, skinheads, rockers, Sloane rangers, and the rest, have all developed elaborate and distinctive styles of appearance. Sociologists have tried to interpret the symbolic meaning of these styles.

> The Teddy Boy sub-culture can be 'read' as the theft of an upper-class style to celebrate heavy working–class masculinity; . . . skinhead' rolled-up jeans, cropped-hair, industrial boots . . . can be understood as an attempt to recover and assert the virtues of the traditional working–class community.
>
> (Roberts 1983: 121)

A common way of indicating group membership among the young is by T-shirts with writing on them. Cialdini and Richardson (1980) found that more students wore the university T-shirt after the team had won at football.

It is not only rebellious youth who develop special styles. The same is true of other groups. Policemen, postmen, monks, and others wear distinctive uniforms. Orthodox Jews have a status hierarchy which is based on frequency of religious observance and intensity of religious emotion, not on wealth or occupation. There are six distinct levels in this hierarchy, which are recognizable by appearance – by the state of the beard and side locks, the kind of hat and the kind of coat worn (S. Poll in Roach and Eicher 1965).

Personality

Several aspects of personality are communicated by clothes. A number of correlations have been found between personality traits and choice of clothes. Erickson and Sirgy (1985) found that for 390 women from the faculty and staff of an American university, those higher in achievement motivation were more likely to wear businesslike clothes. Compton (1962) found that sociable young women chose strong, saturated colours, and Rosenfeld and Plax (1977) found that confident and aggressive students were more exhibitionist in their choice of clothes, while those high on a clothing-consciousness scale were more compliant and anxious, less independent and aggressive. American research has found that radical and conservative political attitudes are expressed in clothes (Thomas 1973).

Emotional states and interpersonal attitudes

It is widely believed that clothes have a sexual role, both in concealing the sexual organs and in drawing attention to them, and generally making the wearer sexually more attractive. The conflict between modesty and decoration leads to all kinds of ingenious compromises in female dress, particularly in the area of the breasts. Male pop stars have been reported to pad the fronts of their trousers to exaggerate the size of their vital parts. Sexual attractiveness depends partly on clothes, partly on hair, grooming, skin, and physique.

Animals often put on threat displays, for frightening and inducing submission in other animals. This is normally done by males towards other males. In primitive societies it is common for men to dress up in impressive and terrifying war costumes, painting themselves from head to foot with paint or mud and wearing head-dresses or masks. Until recent times men went to war in handsome uniforms, and the sword and spurs were worn on other occasions too. To dress in a threatening way is now rare in civilized countries, though members of motorcycle gangs wearing black leather clothes with studs, swastikas, and knives are an example.

In Ethiopia togas can be worn to express a number of moods and attitudes, for example:

thrown back over shoulders – debonair assurance
hanging full length – sadness
covering mouth – pride
upper body bare – self-abasement

In addition there are several non-symbolic arrangements of the toga, for example to keep the arms free while working, or to prevent sunstroke (Messing 1960).

Decoding clothes

Sissons (1971) found that a person's social class could be judged quite accurately, either from a still photograph of his clothes, or a recording of his voice, or from a photograph of his face. In her 'Paddington Station experiment' she arranged for an actor to stop eighty people in Paddington Station and ask them the way to Hyde Park. For half of them he was dressed and behaved as if upper middle class, for half he appeared to be working class. The interviews were filmed and tape-recorded, and the social class of the respondents was obtained by subsequent interview. It was found that the middle-class/middle-class encounters went most smoothly compared with

Plate 15.1   Clothes and social class (Sissons 1971)

the other three combinations of social class; there was instant rapport, the encounters lasted longer, respondents smiled more, and
there was a definite ending (Plate 15.1).

Social class is symbolized in ways that keep changing, and the
clothes that convey status change quite rapidly – a case of the 'circu-
lation of symbols'.

Appearance is manipulated with a more or less clear idea of what
information is being sent, or with deliberate self-presentation. Gibbins (1969) studied fifteen- and sixteen-year-old grammar school
girls in the North of England. They were asked to judge photographs of six outfits of clothes, taken from magazines, on seven-
point scales. There was a high degree of agreement on the kind of
person who would wear the clothes in terms of the following
variables:

snobbish
fun–loving
rebellious
shy

and behaviour patterns such as

> number of boy-friends
> sexual morals
> whether she smoked
> whether she drank
> hobbies (sporting *v.* artistic)

Clothes may be decoded in terms of a number of different dimensions of meaning, but the most common are probably: evaluation of attractiveness, expense, neatness, and fashionability (Kaiser 1985).

Hamid (1968) showed coloured photographs of girls wearing different clothes to decoders. There was a high level of agreement in the way in which they were judged, but little agreement on the faces alone. Girls with short skirts, bright dresses, and make-up were seen as sophisticated, immoral, and attractive. Sweat and Zentner (1985) presented four styles of women's clothes (Figure 15.1) and asked 370 subjects to rate them on a number of scales. This produced four factors, and the images of the clothes were as follows:

> *dramatic*: very unconventional, approachable, somewhat sophisticated and dominant
> *natural*: very conventional, somewhat approachable and unsophisticated, slightly dominant
> *romantic*: very approachable, unconventional, sophisticated, and somewhat submissive
> *classic*: very sophisticated and dominant, conventional, somewhat unapproachable

Effect of clothes on the behaviour of others

Many studies have been carried out in which an experimental confederate, dressed to look tidy or untidy, respectable or disreputable, stopped people in the street to request an interview or other help. Nearly all of these studies found that a conventionally or tidily dressed person elicited more help or co-operation. When a smartly dressed person violated a 'do not cross' sign, more others followed him than if he were sloppily dressed (Lefkowitz, Blake, and Mouton 1955). The exception is studies where those approached were untidily dressed peace demonstrators (Suedfeld, Bochner, and Matas 1971).

A second principle, then, is that people are responsive to those with similar appearance to themselves, probably indicating a similar outlook or group membership. Further, the effect of appearance in this setting is greater for older respondents, and quite weak for

Figure 15.1 Four styles of female dress

Dramatic

Natural

Romantic

Classic

Source: Sweat and Zentner 1985

younger ones. The behaviour requested was fairly trivial in all cases, and it is not known whether appearance has a similar effect in other settings, though research on simulated counselling interviewers found that appearance had little effect (Noesjirwan 1981). Wasserman and Kassinove (1976) found that parents were not affected by the informality of a psychologist's clothes when giving advice on children's reading skills, though the 'informal' clothes worn were quite respectable. Uniforms may have special power: someone wearing a vague uniform produced more compliance to requests to pick up a bag, put a coin in a meter, or stand on the other side of a bus stop than someone dressed as a milkman or a civilian (Bickman 1974).

Molloy (1975; 1977) recommended that ambitious people should 'dress for success', e.g. wear a suit and tie for men, and restrained dark costumes for women. There is some evidence that this works. In a market research survey Green and Giles (1973) found that wearing a tie produced more compliance, though not with working-class people. Forsythe, Drake, and Hogan (1985) showed videotapes of a woman 'job applicant' for a middle management position wearing four different outfits which varied in masculinity. Personnel administrators gave much higher ratings on forceful, self-reliant, dynamic, aggressive, and decisive to the second most masculine outfit. Harp, Stretch, and Harp (1985) found that newscasters were thought more credible and the news was remembered better when they wore conservative rather than trendy or casual clothes, especially for viewers who wore conservative clothes themselves.

Another kind of effect on others is where clothes enhance physical attractiveness. As we will show below, clothes are an important factor in attractiveness, and the latter has far-reaching effects, not only on heterosexual attraction, but in many other spheres.

Clothes also affect the wearer. Even when a person is constrained to wear certain clothes, e.g. a uniform, this affects the way he or she is labelled, not only by others but by himself. Tharin (1981) found that at roller-skating rinks, on nights when respectable clothes were required, there were fewer accidents and confrontations, and less noise.

As everyone knows there are constant changes in fashion for clothes – making them different from other NV signals. A study of the length of skirts, diameter of waists, and depth of necklines found that there was a basic 100-year cycle, with lesser cycles every 20–25 years, and much smaller annual changes in these measurements. The authors concluded that leaders of fashion try to out-do last year's length until a limit is reached, whereupon they reverse this process (Richardson and Kroeber 1940). It was Simmel (1904) who first proposed the 'trickle down' theory of fashion – that changes in fashion were started by the upper classes; other people imitate them to gain status and attractiveness themselves; the élite then change their appearance to distinguish themselves from imitators. This doctrine received strong support in 1928 from a survey by Hurlock (1929). She surveyed 1,500 people and found, among other things, that 25 per cent said that they changed their style of clothes because of fear of disapproval, 100 per cent of men would wait for a new style to be accepted while 19 per cent of women would adopt it at once, 40 per cent of women and 20 per cent of men said they would follow a fashion in order to appear equal to those of higher social status, and about half said they changed their styles when their social inferiors adopted it.

However, the fashion scene has now changed. First, the initiators of fashion are not so much the upper class as pop singers, film stars, and others in the public eye. Fashions even trickle upwards when the styles of youth, even of rebellious and radical youth, become popular. Second, the clothing industry now reproduces new styles at all levels simultaneously, so that the fashion lag is much less marked. Indeed, fashion is really trickling horizontally here; people are trying to keep up with current mass fashions as opposed to imitating anyone in particular (Kaiser 1985).

Adopting new fashions is not just a matter of imitating the upper classes or pop stars. Adopting a very new fashion will attract attention, and convey a definite message. We saw that high self-monitors tend to be early adopters of new fashions (p.271f.). Innovators and opinion leaders are also likely to be young, well-educated, of high social status, and venturesome and non-conformist in other ways. Followers of fashion are people who are socially anxious, conformist, and other-directed (Millenson 1985; Kaiser 1985).

Early adopters of fashion are seen as more romantic, frivolous naughty, bold, etc. And girls who wear more fashionable clothes have self-images which are nearer to this image than wearers of less fashionable clothes. When the fashion is well established, however, not adopting it is to invite scorn and rejection (Gibbins and Gwynn 1975).

As well as conforming to fashions, many people try to individuate themselves by creating a distinctive appearance, but within the fashion. Snyder and Fromkin (1980) found a dimension of need for uniqueness which affects clothing as well as other behaviour. We saw one example earlier in the expression of role distance (p.237), and another in the expression of personality characteristics (p.238).

Each item has meaning by itself. This may be arbitrary and digital, as in the case of badges. It may be arbitrary and a matter of degree, as in meanings derived from similarity with a person imitated. It may be analogical, as beards stand for achieving manhood, and low necklines for sex. There can be more elaborate symbolism, as in the masks worn in primitive rituals. Information is conveyed by the way items are combined: for example, a dark suit may be combined with a red tie. Information is also conveyed by the manner of wearing: for example, a uniform may be very smart or very scruffy. In all these ways people can send quite involved messages about themselves and their attitudes to other people, including identity conflicts and other complexities.

Bodily physique

The second aspect of appearance that we shall consider is bodily size and shape. Three aspects of physique have been found to be important – height, weight (i.e. fatness), and shape. Three shapes have often been used in research:

endomorphs: fat, round, and soft
ectomorphs: tall, thin, and fragile
mesomorphs: muscular, bony, and athletic

The physique of an individual can be described by his relative scores on these three dimensions (Sheldon, Dupertuis, and McDermott 1954).

Since physique is often interpreted in terms of personality characteristics, we should ask whether there is any connection between physique and personality. In fact there is some link between the two, but the relationships are weak. Mesomorphs tend to be more aggressive and delinquent, though also athletic; ectomorphs tend to be intelligent and anxious; and endomorphs relaxed, happy, and lazy. Depressive patients are often fat, schizophrenics thin (partly because they are younger) (Parnell 1958). However, it must be emphasized that most of these relationships are very weak, rarely amounting to a correlation as high as 0·30.

Can physique be regarded as communication? Physique is inherited to quite a large extent, but can be modified by diet and exercise; and apparent physique can be modified quite a lot. For example, apparent height can be increased by high-heeled shoes, hair coaxed to stand high, a tall hat, and by standing up straight.

Physique can be manipulated within limits. In some primitive societies bodies are extensively deformed by binding the feet to make them smaller, as in the past among Chinese women, and binding the head to make it more oval, as in parts of Africa. While there has been a trend towards less bodily deformation in modern societies, there is still quite a lot of binding of waists, mainly female, by corsets, and a great deal of supporting and padding of bosoms. Fatness is controlled by slimming, muscularity increased by exercise, and the general appearance of the body manipulated by the stance adopted – with shoulders back, and so forth. Whether people manipulate their appearance or not, others decode it and react to it in terms of personality traits, as we shall see. Thus physique does function as communication to some extent.

Interpreting and reacting to physique

We will not speak of 'decoding' here, since most of physique was not encoded in the first place.

Height has a considerable effect on others' reactions, especially the height of men. Taller men are more likely to be given jobs in American firms, and get higher starting salaries; those over 6 ft 2 in. received 12 per cent more than those under 6 ft in one study. On the other hand, the actual performance of tall people, as salesmen for example, is no greater than that of shorter men. Tall people are more likely to succeed in politics – the taller candidate has usually become president of the USA, and bishops are taller than other clergy in the Church of England. It was found by Wilson (1968) that the estimated height of an English visitor to Australia, who was presented briefly to groups of students, varied from 5 ft 8½ in. when he was described as a student to 6 ft 3 in. when he was said to be a professor. However, there is no evidence that these effects work for women (Hatfield and Sprecher 1986).

The great majority of marriages are between a man who is taller than his wife, and women prefer a mate who is 6 in. taller, though men prefer a woman who is 4½ in. shorter (Gillis and Avis 1980). On the other hand, very tall people sometimes become self-conscious, and some jobs are open only to short people.

Weight. There is considerable rejection and discrimination against fat people, especially women. Children and adults, shown drawings or photographs, prefer people with facial disfigurement, a hand missing, one leg, blind, or paraplegic to those who are fat. Fat people are less likely to be accepted by American colleges than others of the same IQ, less likely to get jobs, especially jobs dealing with people, and much less likely to earn high salaries. What is the reason for this prejudice against fat people? It is mainly because they are thought to be irresponsible through laziness, greed, or lack of self-control. It has been found that fat people who are said to have a thyroid problem, or to have recently lost weight, are rejected less, though they are still rejected (DeJong 1980).

Shape. Wells and Siegel (1961) showed silhouettes of endomorphic, mesomorphic, and ectomorphic physiques, and asked subjects to rate them on twenty-four scales. The fat person was rated as, among other things, more warm-hearted, sympathetic, good-natured, agreeable, and dependent on others; the muscular person was seen as stronger and more adventurous; the thin person was seen as more tense and nervous, pessimistic, and quieter. In this and other studies muscular men were seen as most masculine, thin females as most feminine, while the other body types for each sex were regarded as 'androgenous' (Guy, Rankin, and Norwell 1980). Jourard and Secord (1955) found that males were more satisfied with their bodies when they were large, and that females were more satisfied when they were smaller than average.

Hair, cosmetics, and spectacles

In this section we will consider the impact of a number of minor aspects of appearance – hair, cosmetics, teeth, spectacles, badges, and other decorations. Hair can be long, or short, from hippy to skinhead, and of different colours. It can include beards and moustaches. In modern societies men may have different kinds of facial hair, while women use cosmetics for their lips, eyes, and cheeks, and wear ear-rings. In primitive societies, like some Australian tribes, the face is often decorated by 'cicatrization' – deep scars. Duelling scars were fashionable among German students until quite recently. The face can also be decorated by tattooing and painting. It can be mutilated by making holes for ear-rings or nose-rings, by flattening the nose, or putting circular plates in the lips. The body can be decorated by scars, tattooing, paint, or mud. In the USA about 10 per cent of males are tattooed, mostly on the hands, and usually by themselves. Burma (in Roach and Eicher 1965) found that a large proportion of delinquents were tattooed, and that most of them wanted it removed. Teeth can be good or bad, depending how much care and dentistry has been applied to them. Spectacles can be replaced by contact lenses in those who prefer them. Badges include ties, blazers, jewellery, and ornaments of all kinds.

First we will look at when and why people adopt these forms of decoration. Hair is rarely left to grow wild, but is cut and dressed. It is possible to dress the hair in a great variety of ways, and only some of these are acceptable in each cultural group. Some young men find that to acquire girl-friends they need long hair, while to acquire a job they need short hair. One anthropologist, Hallpike (1969), has suggested that long hair has a widespread symbolic meaning in many societies: it indicates being outside society, beyond social control, and is worn by outcasts, wild animals, intellectuals, hippies, and ascetics. Cutting the hair represents re-entering society or living under a disciplined regime (like monks, or soldiers). On the other hand shaving the head, or wearing the hair extremely short has been used by skinheads and other rebellious groups. It has been suggested that lack of control over hair symbolizes and communicates a state of society where there is a lack of control over the members. But there is still the problem of why such intense feelings are attached to length of hair. A Freudian interpretation is that cutting the hair symbolized castration, and long hair sexuality. Hair length depends a lot on the norms of different groups – short for monks and soldiers, and long for 'Latin lovers, free thinkers, way-out professors, social rebels and hippies' (Knapp 1978).

Cosmetics are used far more by women than men, and more time is spent applying them in early dating than in more established relationships (p.199). Cash and Cash (1982) asked women to imagine themselves in various situations with and without make-up. These women thought that they would feel more self-confident and sociable with it, and have less social anxiety; they were more likely to use cosmetics if they were dissatisfied with their weight or some parts of their body, and if they were high in public self-consciousness. Rook (1985) measured 'cathexis', i.e. emotional involvement, with different parts of the body and found that both males and females used more grooming products on the areas in which they were most involved. The highest rated areas, for both sexes together, were hair, eyes, sex organs, ears, face, chin, height, and teeth.

Good teeth are the product of money spent on orthodontics and other aspects of dentistry. Spectacles can be avoided by contact lenses, good luck, or being prepared not to see very much. Badges like ties, blazer pockets, trade union pins, small crosses, and engagement and wedding rings all convey their messages. Women in western society, and both sexes in more primitive societies, wear beads, head-dresses, or other decorations, whose aim is mainly to increase the beauty of the wearer. They may also signal her wealth or sexual desirability and availability. In primitive societies the scalp, teeth, bones, or horns of victims may be worn as trophies.

Perceiving and reacting to hair, cosmetics, and spectacles

Length of (male) hair was an important issue in the 1960s and 1970s. Long hair definitely indicated rebellious youth. Beards and moustaches have been studied experimentally, for example by using varied identikit pictures as stimuli. Pellegrini (1973) took photographs of men at different stages of beard-removal. They were regarded as most masculine, mature, good-looking, etc. with a full beard; moustaches and goatees had an intermediate effect. In 1969 in the USA women reported feeling more feminine with bearded men, but other bearded men felt more tense with them (Freedman 1969). And gentlemen do prefer blondes. Subcultural groups have often picked hair styles as one of their main badges of membership. The punk hair-style with its mohican spikes is the most notorious example in the 1980s.

Shaw (1986) found that 10–13-year-old children were teased for a wide range of physical deficiencies, but teasing over teeth caused the most distress.

Spectacles make people look less attractive, if photographs are judged, or if the wearer is seen briefly (Hamid 1972). It has often been said that 'men seldom make passes at girls who wear glasses', and this turns out to be correct. The author and McHenry (1970) found that target persons were judged to be more intelligent by fourteen points of IQ when wearing spectacles, if they were seen doing nothing for fifteen seconds. However, if they were seen in conversation for five minutes the effect of the spectacles vanished.

After the application of cosmetics and hair care girls are rated as more attractive, and as more pleasant, sociable, sincere, etc. (Graham and Jouhar 1980; Hamid 1972). Frizzy wig *v.* nice hair-do have been used to vary physical attractiveness in a number of experiments. McKeachie (1952) found that lipstick affected impressions formed of girls after a ten-minute interview. With lipstick they were judged to be more frivolous, more conscientious, and *less* interested in men. Women at work are seen as more suitable for management if they do not have elaborate facial cosmetics, long curly hair, or a lot of jewellery (Cash 1985). Graham and Furnham (1981) asked males and females aged fourteen to eighteen to rate how attractive they thought various cosmetics made girls of their own age. Highest ratings were given to perfume, followed by mascara, eyeshadow, eyeliner, nail varnish, and lipstick. All cosmetics were considered to have more effect at night than in the daytime.

This shows that we must consider smell. In our own culture we go to a lot of trouble either to avoid emitting bodily smells, and to avoid breathing on each other, or to improve on these smells with perfume. For Arabs things are quite different:

> Arabs consistently breathe on people when they talk. However, this habit is more than a matter of different manners. To the Arab good smells are pleasing and a way of being involved with each other. To smell one's friend is not only nice but desirable, for to deny him your breath is to act ashamed.
>
> (Knapp 1978: 171)

A number of experiments have been carried out on the recognition and evaluation of odours from skin and breath, for example by collecting underclothes after they have been worn for a week. It is found that subjects can distinguish male and female odours from sweat or breath, well above chance, and women are better at making this discrimination. Male smells are found to be stronger and less pleasant by both sexes. Individuals can recognize their own smell and that of their sexual partner, and find the latter more pleasant than the smells of others. Vaginal smells during menstrual periods have been found to be a source of sexual attraction for monkeys but not for men (Doty 1985; Schleidt, Hold, and Attili 1981).

Little is known about the effects of badges and jewellery. Many badges are meaningful only to members of the same school, college, or club, and so all they communicate is that the wearer is pleased about belonging to something. Subcultural groups like punks and skinheads proclaim their group membership by their total appearance, leading to recognition and acceptance by other members, and rejection by others. Goffman (1956) has observed that there are great temptations for people to misrepresent their social class, but that this is prevented by the use of symbols which it is difficult to fake – wearing very expensive clothes or jewellery, or objects which are very scarce, and keeping hands or body in a condition which requires time, money, and avoidance of work

Physical attractiveness

One of the most important dimensions of appearance is good looks, beauty, or physical attractiveness (p.a.) in the eyes of others. Good looks are especially important for women, but they make a difference for men, too. The measurement of p.a. in practice is easy: a five- or seven-point scale from 'not at all attractive' to 'extremely attractive' is used, and two or more raters assess the persons in question and the ratings averaged. There is a surprisingly high level of agreement on anyone's p.a.: Iliffe (1960) persuaded 4,355 readers of a paper to rank twelve photographs of women in the middle range of p.a. There was a very high level of agreement, and all sections of the population agreed with each other.

On the other hand, people are seen as more attractive when they smile (Mueser *et al.* 1984). There is a rather weak correlation between self- and other ratings of p.a.: 0·33 for males, 0·24 for females (Murstein 1972). And there are great cultural differences in what is regarded as attractive – Arabs and others like fat women, some African tribes like drooping breasts.

What makes a person attractive to others? Men are attracted by female shape, weight, face, hair, cosmetics, and clothes. A recent study (Cunningham 1986) obtained ratings of the attractiveness of fifty faces, and separated the physical features which contributed most to p.a. These were:

wide cheek bones
narrow cheeks
high eyebrows
wide pupils
large smile

Other studies suggest that attractive faces are those which are regular, smooth, with a nose that is neither too long nor too short, and eyes which are not too close or too far apart. Women with 'babyface' features like a high forehead, or large and rounded eyes, are seen as immature but also as attractive by men (Berry and McArthur 1986). Winners of the Miss World competition are usually aged 21, 5 ft 8 in. tall, blonde with brown eyes, and measuring 35–24–35. Girls who appear in *Playboy* and *Penthouse* measure 37–24–35 (Wilson and Nias 1976). We have seen that being obese is a major source of social rejection. Men prefer women with an average sort of shape, but with large breasts, and medium to small buttocks. There are some interesting individual differences in what men like. For example, extroverts like pictures of nude and well-developed females; depressed and submissive men prefer clothes and smaller bosoms (Mathews, Bancroft, and Slater 1972; Wiggins, Wiggins, and Conger 1969).

What kind of men do women find attractive? They like men to have small buttocks, to be tall, slim with a flat stomach, thin legs, medium-thin lower trunks, and medium–wide upper trunks (Wilson and Nias 1976). Women are sexually attracted by non-physical aspects of men too – manners, sense of humour, and intelligence (Morse, Gruzen, and Reis 1976). Men with babyface features are seen as immature and as unattractive by women (Berry and McArthur 1986).

Why should these particular sizes and shapes be so attractive? Sociobiological ideas would lead us to expect that health, energy, and capacity for child-rearing would be found attractive in women, and health and strength in men. However, blonde hair, delicate skin, high eyebrows, and thin waists do not seem to fit this theory (M. Cook, personal communication).

Impressions formed of attractive and unattractive people

The standard procedure here is to ask subjects to rate a number of photographs for attractiveness and on a number of personality scales. The first such study was carried out by Dion, Berscheid, and Walster (1972), who found that attractive men and women were thought to have more desirable personalities, better jobs, greater marital competence, be more likely to get married, and to be happier. The only negative feature was that it was thought they would be less competent parents. The difference between average and unattractive people was greater than that between attractive and average, on most scales. This 'physical attractiveness stereotype' has been confirmed in many other studies. However, Dermer and Thiel (1975) added further scales and found further negative components of the stereotype: attractive women were judged to be unfaithful in marriage, unsympathetic to oppressed people, materialistic, vain, and egotistical. In another study women with large breasts were thought to be less intelligent, competent, moral, and modest than other women (Kleinke and Staneski 1980).

Physical attractiveness stereotypes affect many different groups and relationships. Children aged four to six think that attractive children will be nicer, less aggressive or anti-social; teachers think that attractive children will be more intelligent, academically successful, and popular; among low IQ children teachers think the unattractive ones should be put in a class for the mentally retarded; therapists think that attractive female patients are less disturbed (Hatfield and Sprecher 1986).

Among students, the attractive ones enjoy a rather different pattern of social life. Attractive males are more assertive, interact more with women, and their encounters are more intimate and disclosing. Attractive females, on the other hand, are *less* assertive; their heterosexual encounters are initiated by men, though they find them satisfying and intimate; they enjoy these contacts despite their lack of assertiveness or other social skills to bring them about (Reis *et al.* 1982).

Every kind of stigma is unattractive, and results in negative reactions – bad teeth, obesity, facial scars and blotches, hare lips, etc. Bull (1979) found that people with apparent facial scars were judged to be dishonest, and less warm, affectionate, sincere, to have fewer friends and less sense of humour. Rumsey, Bull, and Gahagan (1982) placed a confederate on a busy pavement where people had to wait to cross the road. When she had a strawberry 'birthmark' people stood 100 cm away, with a facial 'bruise' 78 cm, and with neither 56 cm.

Are attractive people really any better than others? This might be expected simply because they do have rather different social experiences, in that others react more positively towards them. A number of differences have been found: attractive people have been found to be somewhat happier, more self-confident, assertive, socially skilled, and in better psychological health, especially in the case of women (Mathes and Kahn 1975). However, these differences are small and there are many exceptions (Hatfield and Sprecher 1986). The relationship between p.a. and self-esteem is quite small; this may be because attractive people discount positive reactions from others as only due to their p.a. and not to more important qualities. Major, Carrington, and Carnevale (1984) found that attractive people discounted praise for their work more when they had been visible to the praiser.

Attractive people generate different responses from others, and here there are some quite strong effects.

Dating

Frequency is greater both for attractive women (r = 0·61) and men (r = 0·25) (Berscheid *et al.* 1971). A 'computer dance' was arranged by Walster *et al.* (1966) who invited 752 students to a freshman dance, and 'randomly assigned each to a partner; attractiveness was assessed on a seven-point scale by a group of young experimenters. It was found that physical attractiveness was the most important predictor of how much each person was liked by their partner, and how much they wanted to date them again – for males as well as females – with correlations of about 0·40. Attractive people are found to be sexually warmer, have more premarital intercourse, do everything at an earlier age, and attractive girls find richer husbands (Udry and Eckland, cited by Hatfield and Sprecher 1986).

Attractive individuals of both sexes are more likely to get jobs, and when they get them to be paid more: Quinn, Tabor, and Gordon (1968) found that handsome men were paid on average 18·5 per cent more ($1,809) than 'plain and homely' men; good-looking women earned 21 per cent more than the plain and homely ones. Attractive people are less likely to be reported for blatant shop-lifting, less likely to be found guilty in law courts (unless they used their looks in the crime or in very serious crimes), and if found guilty are given lighter sentences (e.g. Efran 1974).

Singer (1964) found that attractive female students, especially if they were first-born, were given higher grades in classes in an American college. This was not due to greater intelligence but to using their charms by sitting in the front of classes and speaking to instructors more often. Mental patients, especially the most disturbed ones, are unattractive – they were the least attractive at school, and became worse later (Napoleon, Chassin, and Young 1980). In a follow-up study of discharged mental patients, among the women the most attractive ones coped better outside and had fewest days in hospital (Farina *et al.* 1986).

The main negative aspect of life for very attractive women is that other women are often jealous and hostile, so that they have difficulty making friends. Attractive people of both sexes can have too many approaches from the opposite sex, and platonic relationships are difficult to sustain.

It is quite possible to increase p.a. – by better clothes, hair, teeth, cosmetics, diet, and exercise, or even by plastic surgery. There is clear evidence that it is worthwhile removing serious defects. A before-and-after study of the effects of surgery on the mouth or lower face found that those treated were rated as more attractive and intelligent afterwards (Elliot *et al.* 1986). Experiments have recently been done in giving plastic surgery to criminals with disfigured faces; it has been found that removing scars, tattoos, or other disfigurements had a considerable effect on the recidivism rate (Kurtzberg, Safar, and Cavior 1968). Cosmetic therapy for women undergoing chemotherapy for cancer improved their appearance, and they felt less ill-at-ease and self-conscious, and had more positive expectancies for social behaviour (Mulready and Lamb 1985). On the other hand, some people who have experienced sudden changes in their appearance, via cosmetic surgery or rapid weight loss, found this unsettling, and that it made them less happy and confident than before (Hatfield and Sprecher 1986). Perhaps the conclusion is that slow or moderate improvements and the removal of stigma are worth doing, but that it is not worth making more dramatic improvements in appearance.

16

Social skills, persuasion, and politics

The general non-verbal expressiveness factor

We shall see in the next chapter that different aspects of NVC make up a general social approach factor, consisting of moderately high levels of smiling, gaze, proximity, and loudness and pitch of voice. Socially unskilled and mentally disturbed people differ from others in talking, smiling, looking, and gesturing less, but touching themselves more (p.276f.).

The pattern of affiliative and expressive non-verbal behaviour has many positive effects on others. One of the main effects is to reinforce their behaviour. Many experiments have shown the powerful effects of head-nods, smiles, gazes, and leaning forward on conversation and on learning (Krasner 1958). Counsellors and therapists who smile more, look more, and are generally more expressive are judged to be warmer and more competent by their clients (Leathers 1986; Patterson 1983). Pupils get on with their work more when teachers smile a lot, and this is stronger than the effects of verbal rewards (Keith, Tornatzky, and Pettigrew 1974). Other studies have found higher levels of attention when pupils are looked at more, more learning when teachers gesture more, higher IQ scores when testers lean, gaze, smile, and nod more (Saigh 1981).

This provides an explanation for the 'Pygmalion in the classroom' effect (Rosenthal and Jacobson 1968). If teachers are told that certain pupils are 'bright', they smile, gaze, and lean more towards them, and this produces better work from them (Ho and Mitchell 1982).

Some interesting research has been carried out into the non-verbal behaviour of candidates who are interviewed for jobs. Although what candidates *say* is the best predictor of whether they get the job, success is also more likely if they have a higher level of gaze, smiling, head movements, gestures, and produce more fluent and expressive speech (e.g. Forbes and Jackson 1980).

We do not know what the reason is for the power of this general factor. It may be because it signals liking, indicates enthusiasm, or acts as a reinforcer. In addition to this general factor, however, NVC affects social competence in a number of more specific ways, to which we now turn.

NVC and the social skills model

The behaviour of individuals is said to be socially skilled if the goals of interaction are attained. These goals may be interpersonal (e.g. making friends), or professional (e.g. teaching, persuading, etc.). And socially skilled behaviour requires correct use of NVC at a number of points.

The nature of socially skilled behaviour can be explained by means of the social skills model (see p.109). This model was proposed as a general conceptual scheme for the analysis of social interaction. It proposes an analogy between social and motor skills: in each case the performer is trying to attain certain goals, by affecting the behaviour of machines or of other people; he is responsive to feedback, and takes corrective action so that the goal is attained. The link between receiving feedback and taking appropriate corrective action can involve complex cognitive processes and strategic planning. The model sees social behaviour as hierarchical, where the smaller, lower level elements are automatic and habitual, while the higher level social acts are under more direct cognitive control, though there can be goals and feedback at all levels.

Interaction between two or more people also takes place at different levels. It consists partly of the exchange of meaningful utterances, and partly of carefully planned reciprocity of behaviour. At a less reflective level one person may influence another by reinforcing his behaviour with small smiles and head-nods, of which both parties are normally completely unaware. Speech is synchronized by a series of small nods, gaze-shifts, and grunts, which often function outside the region of conscious control (see p.113f.).

What is the origin, basis, or explanation of the social skills model itself? It is a particular example of a fundamental psychological process, of attaining goals via corrective action (Miller, Galanter, and Pribram 1960). The social side of it is probably acquired in early childhood, when mothers teach infants how to take turns, respond to prosodic signals, and make use of gaze during interaction (McTear 1985). Social competence consists of mastery of the skilled sequences needed for the goals being pursued.

One limitation of the model is that it says nothing about the rules of behaviour – skilled acts and corrective action must fall within the rules of a situation. The model fits simple one-way interaction best, such as teaching or interviewing; it needs some extension to deal with two or more interactors with independent goals and initiative (Argyle 1983).

Non-verbal communication plays several important roles in this model.

Perception of the other(s)

The social skills model emphasizes the role of feedback from the other, which is the basis for corrective action. For teachers it is important that they know whether the pupils understand what has been said. We shall see below that the accuracy of such judgements can be measured, and if necessary trained (p.274f.). Sensitivity scores on the PONS test (p.275f.) have been found to correlate with ratings of competence on the part of teachers and doctors (Rosenthal *et al.* 1979).

In a number of jobs, perceiving or assessing others is an important goal, as in the case of selection interviewers and clinical psychologists. We shall see that non-verbal behaviour can be diagnostic of different mental disorders (p.277f.), and it is possible to classify patients on the basis of NVC alone (Waxer 1978). It is also possible that greater attention to NVC might speed up or improve the accuracy of clinical diagnosis. Doctors are often helped in their diagnosis by facial expressions, indicating amount of pain (sometimes different from what is reported verbally), and gestures illustrating the nature of internal bodily sensations. In order to make maximum use of non-verbal signals emitted by others it is necessary to look at them a lot, at the body and hands as well as the face, and to listen carefully to the tone of voice.

The NV behaviour of the performer

The general expressiveness factor has been found to be important for professional roles, including teachers and doctors. In addition to these rewarding behaviours some degree of assertiveness is needed on the part of teachers and others in leadership positions and professional roles. This may be signalled by loudness of voice, raised elevation, facial expression and posture, as well as by verbal directions.

Many people in occupations dealing with people have to be able to control their own facial and other expressions. We mentioned this in connection with air hostesses (p.78), but it applies to a wide range of professions. Teachers, social workers, and others cannot usually express negative attitudes to others, or states of boredom, anger and other negative emotions.

Many professional roles involve bodily behaviour, and the manner of performing it is another aspect of NVC. Doctors and nurses have to touch patients, in a way which is reassuring and not sexual; we have seen that touch can have positive medical effects, on female patients at least (p.230). This is probably an important part of the 'bedside manner', though the doctor's voice has also been found to be important (Milmoe *et al.* 1967). Harrigan, Oxman, and Rosenthal (1985) found that there was greater rapport when doctors used more 'immediacy' behaviours (faced more directly, did not cross legs), and were not too relaxed, which suggests dominance. Salespeople can communicate the value of goods by the 'reverence' with which they are handled. Friedman *et al.* (1980) found that people in the 'social' professions had higher scores on self-rated expressiveness than those in manual jobs.

NV accompaniments of speech

All social skills involve conversation. Most unskilled people and mental patients are poor conversationalists, and this is partly because of a failure to manage the NV accompaniments of speech.

It is important, for example, to control the amount of talk by others. If the other is not talking enough, one can ask more open-ended questions, or use more (non-verbal) reinforcement, such as head-nods, gazes, and encouraging noises. If he is talking too much the opposite strategy is needed. Similarly, it is possible to control the topic of conversation, not only by what is said, but also by differential NV responsiveness to what the other says.

Social skills involve either an alternation of utterances, or more complex cycles of them. Teaching, for example, often consists of a three-step cycle:

    teacher: expounds something
    teacher: asks question
    pupil: replies

There can be more complex cycles than this, and these can be established and sustained by non-verbal as well as verbal cues (Flanders 1970).

Woodall and Burgoon (1981) varied experimentally the extent to which face, voice, and gestures synchronized with speech. If these were out of synchrony, the verbal messages were recalled less well than with minimal NV cues, were accepted and believed less, and the NV part was distracting. There were smaller advantages of a highly synchronized signal in these respects.

Self-presentation

We have seen that people who are respectably dressed and physically attractive elicit more favourable reactions from others, including miscellaneous helpfulness, more dates, and better jobs. We shall see that persuasiveness is partly mediated by the perceived credibility of the persuader. This depends on such signals as a high level of gaze, emphatic gestures, an assertive posture, and a confident, expressive voice (Leathers 1986).

For most social skills it is necessary to present an image of one-self as a competent and socially acceptable person. We have seen that appearance can do a lot here. Other non-verbal cues include the arrangement of offices, with large desks, signed photographs from impressive bearded figures, thick and learned books, and the rest.

Persuasiveness

The study of NV cues for persuasiveness started with three experiments by Mehrabian and Williams (1969). In the first experiment subjects were asked to deliver a message with zero, subtle, or strong persuasiveness. The latter was encoded as more gaze, (51 per cent v. 40 per cent), more vocal and facial activity, and in other ways. In the second encoding experiment subjects were asked to deliver messages in an informative or a persuasive manner. The third experiment was on decoding, and varied gaze, distance, shoulder orientation, and relaxation. Together these three experiments provide an impressive body of data about the NV cues for persuasion.

In the first place there was a good correlation between intended and perceived persuasiveness, and the same cues were used for encoding and decoding. Several of these cues are the same as those used for liking, or reinforcement – gaze (weak effect), proximity, less direct orientation (for males). A second group of variables was interpreted as responsiveness to the recipient – faster speech, greater volume, more vocal activity (frequency and intensity range), and more facial activity. A third group of variables related to persuasiveness formed the relaxation factor – sideways lean, leg and arm asymmetry, and arm openness. Slightly relaxed was most persuasive for males, slightly relaxed or tense for females. A dominance factor emerged from factor analysis of the NVC in these experiments, but was independent of persuasion. And smiling and head-nodding were associated both with persuasiveness and with submission. It is also worth nothing that there was some evidence that adoption of higher status behaviour results in less persuasion.

Later research has extended these findings in a number of ways. *Liking* or *involvement* have been confirmed as important features of NV cues leading to persuasion. If the would-be persuader stands closer, looks more, smiles, and touches, several experiments have found that he is more successful, at least for simple requests. In police interrogation the interrogators may sit very close, with a knee between the suspect's knees (Patterson 1983). We reported a number of experiments on the effects of touch earlier (p.227f.). However, outside police stations too much intimacy may lead to withdrawal and loss of persuasion. Albert and Dabbs (1970) found that recipients were influenced more at less close distances.

Vocal cues are very important in persuasion. Mehrabian and Williams found that louder, faster, and more expressive voices were seen as more persuasive, and this has generally been confirmed. Hall (1980), in a telephone survey study, found that there were more volunteers if interviewers were more expressive, natural, warm, calm, and pleasant. The fluency of speech is important. Too many speech errors reduce the perceived credibility of the speaker, though Sereno and Hawkins (1967) found no effect on attitude change. Pearce and Conklin (1971) found that a 'scholarly, dispassionate yet very involved . . . yet serious' style was judged as more trustworthy and likeable than a passionate and emotional style.

Members of simulated juries who were perceived as more influential had voices which were louder and with a greater pitch range – in America, but not in Germany (Scherer 1979b).

Other research on persuasion has found that credibility and perceived trustworthiness are important factors. The perceived expertise and trustworthiness of therapists is increased by visible diplomas and certificates, but only if the therapist also has a high enough level of gaze, smiling, leaning, and gestures (e.g. Siegel 1980). We shall see later that politicians are judged more favourably if they have a sufficiently assertive non-verbal style.

Mehrabian and Williams found that submissive rather than dominant cues were more persuasive, when used by equals (smiling, nodding, self-touching). On the other hand, in established hierarchies, the use of normal dominance behaviour is effective.

The bodily communication of politicians

In previous historical periods influence was exerted by leaders, politicians, and prophets by word of mouth at public meetings. A number of studies have shown that emotive messages have more effect than rational ones; 'emotive' messages involve a combination of verbal and non-verbal signals. The leader's performance on these occasions is very important in building up the right image. He must look right, and he must sound right – Labour Party leaders often cultivate regional accents. Religious leaders frequently develop a very intense and dramatic manner, with the result that they are seen as especially holy, 'charismatic' characters. This probably explains why a number of severely disturbed persons have become successful religious leaders for a time.

Roosevelt made much use of the radio, and later political leaders have used TV. The Kennedy–Nixon debates influenced many of those who saw them to vote for Kennedy, partly because of his evident persuasiveness and charm, partly because of the less favourable impression created by Nixon's face. The percentage of voters who said they would vote for Kennedy increased from 44 per cent to 50 per cent – though there was little change of attitude on political issues (Comstock *et al.* 1978). In these debates what a candidate looked like was more important to voters than what he said (Kraus 1985).

Leathers (1986) describes how he trained Carter for his debates with Ford. Despite his reputation for not being able to walk and chew gum at the same time, Ford emitted a much more credible image at the first debate:

a high level of gaze
powerful gestures, like a karate chop
arms and feet spread wide in an assertive posture
loud volume of speech

Carter, on the other hand, displayed a great deal of downward and apparently shifty gaze, a high blink-rate, weak and self-touching gestures, a narrower and rather passive posture, and he spoke very quickly, dropping his voice at the end of sentences, with a lot of disfluencies. Leathers recommended that Carter should change these NV behaviours; Carter was judged to have won the second debate by most people, and his media advisors thought that this was partly due to his changed pattern of NVC (Leathers 1986). Exline (1985) also analysed those debates and found that subjects who were shown segments of video-tape in which one candidate was non-verbally superior (i.e. fewer blinks, disfluencies, less body sway, and lip-licking) judged him as more competent.

At a later date the Reagan image was so positive that viewers were happy to overlook major factual errors or lack of knowledge; it was said that the President was 'coated with Teflon', since nothing negative seemed to stick to him (Kraus 1985).

Heritage and Greatbatch (1986) analysed British political speeches, and found that whether or not rhetorical points led to applause depended on the use of non-verbal emphasis, especially terminal gaze at the audience, increase in loudness, increased pitch or loudness variation, and a change of rhythm or gestures. When two or more of these were used there was more than a 50 per cent likelihood of applause, with one 25 per cent and with none 5 per cent. Atkinson (1984) recorded a number of British political speeches and observed that 'spontaneous' applause was often produced by certain rhetorical devices such as lists of three, and 'contrastive pairs', in both cases with appropriate emphasis and pauses. He discusses the 'charismatic' quality of speakers like Tony Benn, and suggests that it may be due to the use of intense gaze, extensive use of gesture, and the rhetorical devices already mentioned. Bull (1987) analysed a speech by Arthur Scargill in which there were twenty-five rhetorical points, of which twenty-two received prolonged applause. The most successful rhetorical devices were contrasts, three-part lists, and 'headline-punching' (the speaker proposes to make a declaration or promise, and then makes it). In the sections which produced most applause he used strong hand movements, for example '*they* say . . . ' (left-hand gesture), but '*we* say . . . ' (right-hand gesture).

Eugene Burdick (1964) describes in a novel *The 480* how real and bogus events affect a politician's public image. The hero of this novel takes part in various real events. One is highly symbolic: he prevents a war between India and Pakistan by hanging perilously from a crane on a girder between the ends of an unfinished bridge between the two countries, and by making a speech reminding the two sides of when they had suffered together, with the result that the bridge was completed and the war averted. There was also a series of completely managed events – a man is paid to throw a tomato at the hero's part-Filipino wife, and a crowd of students create what appears to be a spontaneous riot on behalf of the candidate outside the convention hall.

It is also possible to change the images of political parties. The first use of advertising by a British political party was in the 1959 election. It had been found that 27 per cent saw the Conservative party as the party of the privileged minority. Posters were then designed

Plate 16.1 'You are looking at a Conservative' (Butler 1960)

with the verbal message 'The Conservatives are the party of the whole country'; others carried a primarily non-verbal message, with photographs of a cloth-capped worker peering through a hole in a boiler, saying: 'You are looking at a Conservative' (Butler 1960) (Plate 16.1). In this campaign the person shown in the posters was skilfully varied between different newspapers: the cloth-capped worker was shown in the *News of the World*, a clerical worker in the *Sunday Express*, a young scientist in the *Observer*, and a working woman in the *Sunday Pictorial*. By the end of the campaign only 17 per cent of the population associated the Conservative party with privilege.

Attempts to change the social position of a group

Racial and other minority groups, members of lower social classes, and young people occupy underprivileged positions in society. In addition to their material frustrations there are also those of being treated as social inferiors in everyday social contacts: the style of non-verbal behaviour of members of superior groups constitutes the main source of frustration. For a long time it was common for low-status people to accept their position, to behave in a humble manner towards their superiors and to adopt their fashions. In recent years the blacks, some of the young, and others, have abandoned this strategy in favour of an aggressive assertiveness. From 1964 onwards American blacks changed their appearance, adopting the Afro-Asian hair-cut and treating whites with hostility and contempt. Many students in 1960s gave up behaving nicely and trying to be approved of by their elders: by their clothes, hair, and manner of behaviour they communicated the message that they were totally rejecting the way of life of polite, middle-class society, and that they constituted a new social group with ideas of its own about how life should be lived.

Training in NVC

Can people be trained to improve their bodily communication? In fact, such training plays a central part in several kinds of social skills training (SST).

Perception of others

Accuracy of recognition of facial expression can be assessed by BART or other tests (p.274f.). If training is needed it can consist of discussing the features of different expressions, and showing different slides of them, such as the photographs provided by Ekman and Friesen (1975). Training on recognition of tones of voice can follow a similar procedure. Research with the PONS test (p.275) found that people did better the second time they took the test, an average gain of 1·79 s.d.s, or if given a ninety-minute training session beforehand (0·58 s.d.s), and that such gains correlated with reported better relationships with people of the opposite sex (Rosenthal et al. 1979).

   Using one-minute films of children being taught, Jecker, Maccoby, and Breitrose (1965) found that experienced teachers were little better than beginners at perceiving whether or not children had understood. However, both Davitz (1964) and Jecker and his colleagues found that increased sensitivity could be taught quite quickly by running through a series of stimuli and studying the essential cues. DePaulo and Pfeifer (1986) found that customs officers and others with extensive on-the-job experience of detecting deception were no better than students, and they suggest that this may be because there is little feedback on success, and hence little learning. However, Zuckerman, Koestner, and Colella (1985) found that lie detection improved rapidly with experience, regardless of whether or not feedback was given.

Training for doctors has emphasized history-taking skills, especially signs of emotional distress, and symptoms which patients are reluctant to reveal (Maguire 1981).

Expression and control of expression

Most training has focused on improving expression, since unskilled people are not usually good at expressing themselves. Facial expression can be trained by modelling photographs, in front of a mirror, and later trying to keep up an expression over a period, then playing back a videotape of the performance. Vocal expression can be trained by modelling home-made tapes, like those used for training in decoding.

A common problem for SST clients is difficulty in making friends, with the same or opposite sex, due in part to being low on the general expressiveness factor. Part of the training has been to increase the level of smiling, gaze, and the rest (Argyle 1983).

SST with children can include a non-verbal component. Straub and Roberts (1983) trained children with learning disabilities in both sending and receiving non-verbal signals for emotion. After the training they received higher ratings from their peers on acceptability and scales such as 'plays nice' *v.* 'plays mean'.

In marital therapy there has been an emphasis on increasing rewardingness, both verbal and non-verbal. It is particularly important to avoid reciprocity of negative signals (p.102f.); and it is important to train husbands in the expression of affection.

Professional skills training is usually done by modelling, followed by role-playing with videotape playback. Using this method, trainees become aware of their facial and bodily behaviour rather than their voices. To get them to concentrate on verbal and non-verbal aspects of speech it is possible to use an audiotape recording alone. Elizabeth Sidney and the author (1969) developed techniques in this way for training interviewers, which include the use of stooge candidates who present a variety of typical problems, and the use of an ear microphone for instructions from the trainer during role-playing. Follow-up studies have shown that modelling plus role-playing plus feedback is the most effective way. The most widely used application of this is 'microteaching', in which trainee teachers role-play short lessons with small classes.

In cross-cultural training it is possible to train people to use the NV expressions of another culture. Collett (1971) trained a number of Englishmen in Arab non-verbal signals with successful results (p.69f.). An early experiment by Haines and Eachus (1965) found that subjects could be taught the non-verbal social skills of an imaginary new culture by means of role-playing with videotape playback.

NVC and speech

The most common problem is training people in conversation, for example in the cases of mental patients and other socially inadequate individuals. Of course the contents of speech are important too – making positive and relevant contributions, asking questions, and so on. In the non-verbal sphere there are a variety of forms of failure – not being attentive to feedback, not giving feedback signals, not giving the necessary NV accompaniments of speech. Sometimes there are synchronizing problems, through not giving end of utterance signals.

Professional skills often involve special sequences of utterances which have to be managed together with their NV accompaniments. Part of the sequence of selling, for example, is to produce, demonstrate, or wrap up the goods.

In cross-cultural training it may be necessary to prepare people for the low back-channel signalling rate of black Americans, or the high rate of the Japanese (p.67).

We showed above how politicians can be trained to give more convincing TV performances, and can elicit more applause at political meetings if they accompany their rhetorical points with vocal and gestural emphasis.

Self-presentation

This is a less common sphere of NVC training, but one where training can be very successful and very quick. Some mental patients have a very odd and socially unacceptable appearance. Changing their appearance or voice can make them more acceptable to other people and make life much easier for them. Plastic surgery for criminals to remove tattoos and scars has been found successful (p.254).

We have seen that physically attractive people are at an advantage in many ways, and that physical attractiveness can be manipulated. We concluded that it was particularly beneficial to remove obvious blemishes, especially for women. Depressed female patients have been helped by designing and modelling attractive clothes.

Personality and NVC

There is a great deal of variation in NVC between different social situations, as we have seen in other chapters. For example people smile and look more, and stand closer to those they like. However, there are consistent person effects in that if A smiles more than B in one situation he will probably do so in others. Kendon and Cook (1969) studied the gaze behaviour of fifteen subjects, each interacting with between four and eleven others. There was a high degree of consistency for the looking behaviour of individuals, though the identity of the partner also made a difference.

However, there can be *interaction* between persons and situations, i.e. individuals may respond in different ways to situations. Exline (1963) found that women looked more in co-operative situations if they were high in need for affiliation, but looked *less* if low in this need (Figure 17.1).

Table 17.1 *Percentages of variance accounted for by different sources of variance in behaviour categories*

| Category | Source | | | |
	Persons	Settings	$P \times S$	Within
hand and arm movement	16·8	11·9	31·9	39·4
foot and leg movement	27·4	10·0	26·7	35·9
scratch, pick, rub	30·7	13·1	24·5	31·6
general movement and shifting	17·3	1·4	47·1	34·1
nod yes	4·2	42·9	33·5	19·4
smile	35·3	3·6	35·4	25·6
talk	10·5	68·3	13·9	7·4
smoke	41·9	7·1	20·7	30·2

Source: Moos 1969

Figure 17.1   Individual differences in gaze

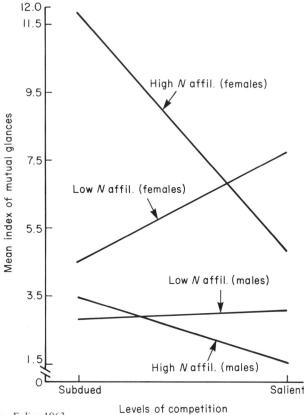

Source: Exline 1963

Another way of tackling this question is to analyse variance due to persons, situations, and P × S interaction. Moos (1969) did this for various aspects of the NVC of a number of mental patients, who were observed in several different hospital settings (see Table 17.1). This shows that 35·3 per cent of the variance for smiling was due to persons (a fairly high degree of consistency), only 3·6 per cent to situations, a lot (36·1 per cent) to interaction, and the remainder (25·6 per cent) to further unexplained variation.

Each channel can only communicate certain aspects of personality. Facial shape indicates mainly attractiveness and the positively evaluated stereotypes associated with it. Facial expression mainly indicates positive and negative emotions and attitudes to others. Voice can do this too, but in addition can communicate dominance. Spatial behaviour could show affiliation, but in fact the correlations with extroversion and related traits are very weak; the main personality correlate of proximity is emotional disturbance (see p.177f.). Posture mainly displays the tense or anxious *v.* relaxed dimension, associated with both dominance and anxiety. Gestures and other bodily movements vary along dimensions, some of which are similar to personality dimensions. The main link to have been established with personality is that mental patients, and anxious and socially inadequate individuals, touch themselves more and use fewer outward-directed gestures. Touch does not seem to reflect any aspect of personality. Appearance works in a quite distinctive way, since deliberate encoding is involved far more than for the other channels, and this is one of the main channels for self-presentation.

Personality dimensions and bodily communication

Every non-verbal channel is correlated to some extent with aspects of personality, and this has been documented in earlier chapters. Some of the main effects are summarized in Table 17.2.

Table 17.2   *The main personality correlates of NVC*

Facial expression	smile – affiliative, extroverted
	non-smile – dominance
Voice	
amount of speech	extroversion
pitch	extroversion, assertiveness
loudness	dominance, type A
speech errors	anxiety
silent pauses	introversion, anxiety
rate of speech	extroversion, anxiety
interruptions	dominance
Spatial proximity	mental disturbance (–), extroversion, self-confidence, dominance (–)
Gaze percentage	extroversion, neuroticism (–)
looking while talking	dominance
Bodily movements	
self-touching	anxiety
relaxation	dominance, anxiety (–)
Judgement accuracy	self-monitoring, physiological reactivity (–), experience of acting and social occupations
Expressiveness	extroversion, neuroticism (–), self-esteem, dominance, social skills

Can these NV variables be reduced to a smaller number of broader dimensions? Several factor analyses have been carried out on this topic (Campbell and Rushton 1978; Mehrabian 1972; Riggio and Friedman 1986). All investigators have found a social approach dimension, and several have found dimensions of anxiety and dominance. Individuals also vary in the extent to which they monitor their expressive behaviour, in encoding skill, and in accuracy of judging the expressions of others.

Social approach

All of the factor analyses of NVC found a dimension in this area, typically consisting of more gaze, proximity, smiling, speech, louder voice, higher pitch. This is not a tight unitary factor, however, and some factor analyses have obtained a separate factor for smiling (Campbell and Rushton 1978), or fluency of speech (Riggio and Friedman 1986; Mehrabian 1972).

This factor, and all of its components, correlates quite strongly with extroversion and need for affiliation. The explanation of this connection is very straightforward – these NV signals are the ones which are likely to lead to closer interpersonal contacts. However the link with the most obvious way of doing this – proximity – is very weak (Hayduk 1983).

Anxiety and inhibition v. *relaxation and expansiveness*

The agreement between different factorial studies is not so clear in this case, and there may turn out to be more than one dimension here. We will suppose that there is a single, rather broad dimension. It consists of low proximity, low gaze, non-ah speech disturbances, and self-touching *v.* other-directed gestures, relaxed posture, facial expressiveness, and expansive bodily movements (see individual chapters for details). This dimension, and its components, correlates with another of the most familiar dimensions of personality, neuroticism (Campbell and Rushton 1978), and with anxiety. Buck (1984) and others have found that accurate senders, i.e. those who are non-verbally more expressive, have a lower level of physiological reactivity to emotional stimuli, and lower GSR and heart-rate. He called them 'externalizers', and contrasted them with 'internalizers', who show strong physiological reactions but little expression. He suggests that internalizers may be those people who are very responsive to punishment (rather than reward), and that this has the effect of inhibiting non-verbal expression, and increasing their physiological reactions.

Dominance, the need to control

This dimension is expressed primarily through speech, not only through the contents of what is said but also by the vocal style – louder, faster, higher pitched, fewer pauses, and more energy. In addition there is a special pattern of gaze – relatively more looking while talking, less smiling, less proximity, more relaxed posture, sometimes pointing or touching. Dominance also correlates with expressiveness (see below). Various measures of dominance have been used, such as Schutz's FIRO (1966) and Jackson's Personality Research Form (1974). Type A personalities are similar, and have additional voice qualities – for instance, a more explosive speech style. The explanation is that these styles of NVC represent attempts to influence the behaviour of others.

Self-monitoring and self-presentation

A lot of bodily behaviour is regularly controlled in order to create certain impressions for others, that is, there is deliberate encoding. The image that is thus presented is often an idealized version of the real self, or one that will be more acceptable to the audience. As Goffman (1956) has pointed out, interactors need information about each other's attributes in order to know how to deal with one another. Direct evidence of, for instance, intelligence or social class is difficult to obtain, so one relies on 'gestures' – that is, on signals which are often associated with such attributes, as accent is with class. It is therefore possible for interactors to use such signals to send information about themselves which is not wholly accurate – to present an improved version of the self. Goffman maintains that interactors work out an agreed consensus, in which their perceptions of one another are agreed; self-presentation takes place by means of quasi-theatrical performances, in which there may be collusion between the members of a team, for example, a family receiving guests, and this occurs in the 'front regions' of premises, e.g. the drawing-room. A person may present several kinds of information about himself – personality traits, intelligence, and so on.

A person may adopt an accent of a certain social class, for example; Labov (1966) found that lower-middle-class people in New York sometimes engaged in 'hyper-correction', i.e. adopted an accent that went beyond upper class usage. Or people may present an image of themselves as deeply devoted husbands, loving parents, etc. One of the main ways of communicating features of the self is via appearance – clothes, hair, use of cosmetics, etc. As we saw in Chapter 15, people go to a lot of trouble to present the appearance that is currently fashionable in their social group, and will alter their appearance depending on whom they are going to meet.

An individual may be particularly keen to present a particular part of his self-image, because it is very important to him, because he thinks that others are mistaken about it, or because it is relevant to a particular group. He may want one group to know that he is a psychologist, another to know that he is not neurotic, another that he comes from Poland, and so on. This is all part of the very important business of sustaining a certain self-image which is sufficiently prestigeful, coherent, and accurate, and it requires some degree of confirmation from others.

The personal attributes which may be communicated are: (1) abilities, intellectual or otherwise; (2) beliefs, values; (3) temperamental qualities and traits, like energy or stability; (4) past history; (5) roles like occupation and social class. Styles of behaviour towards other people function rather differently. An individual may communicate his preferred relationships, such as warm and dominant, and preferred tempo, for example fast and cheerful. However, he has to accommodate to the others present, and may end up by behaving in a quite different way. He may also indicate 'role-distance', indicating that the performer is a special kind of waiter or psychologist, that there is more to him than this role. If he is a spy or criminal he will create the illusion of 'normal appearance' by acting in accordance with his cover identity, and not creating a disturbance.

Everyone has his own favourite or salient dimensions, in terms of which others are classified. If 'class' or 'intelligence' are salient to someone, he will focus first on the cues relevant to this dimension; he will categorize the other early in an encounter, and then adopt an interaction style adapted to the other's class or intelligence. People differ in the number of categories used on a dimension, e.g. two social classes or six. An alternative strategy is to allocate others to social types rather than to points on dimensions; just as males and schizophrenics are types rather than points on dimensions, so are 'public school men' and 'skinheads'. Perceivers vary in the complexity of their classification systems; where some people use eight or more independent dimensions, others use very few. Whether or not self-presentation is perceived correctly depends on the degree of match between the sender's and the receiver's category systems.

Some individuals work harder at self-presentation than others. Snyder (1979) developed the concept of high $v.$ low self-monitoring. High self-monitors carefully watch their own behaviour and its effects on others, and try to modify it to what is most acceptable or successful in each situation. The 25-item self-monitoring scale (SMS) has been factor analysed by Briggs, Cheek, and Buss (1980) with 1,116 subjects, producing three factors. This was later investigated by Riggio and Friedman (1982):

(1) *Extroversion*, associated with spontaneous expressiveness.
(2) *Acting*, the ability to pose expressions.
(3) *Other-directed*, anxious concern with the reactions of others.

These subscales have quite different correlations with other personality traits: *extroversion* with other measures of extroversion, sociability, self-esteem, exhibitionism, and dominance; *acting* with dominance and exhibitionism; *other-directedness* with anxiety and neuroticism (Riggio and Friedman 1982).

Lippa (1976) found that high SMs could role-play introverted or extroverted teachers better than low SMs. Lippa (1978) found that the role-played teaching performance of high SMs was rated as more extroverted and less anxious than that of low SMs, and that for highs the higher their neuroticism, the *less* anxious was their rated performance.

Individual differences in encoding skill

These can be measured from spontaneous or posed expression, and from self-report inventories. The usual way of measuring spontaneous expressiveness is to show subjects a series of slides or videotapes, filming their expressions as they watch, and finding how accurately others can judge which slide was shown or which emotion aroused. A variant is to ask them to talk about the slide or film to the experimenter, and to film them as they speak. Buck (1984) used four slides as described above, with subjects describing the slides. Zuckerman *et al.* (1976) used four videotapes, and filmed subjects both while watching alone and while talking about them.

Posed expressions have been used in a number of studies. Noller (1984) asked husbands and wives to communicate verbally ambiguous utterances in three NV styles (p.19). Zuckerman *et al.* (1976) asked subjects to pose the same emotions which had been aroused spontaneously.

Finally there are a number of self-report tests for expressiveness. Friedman *et al.*'s (1980) Affective Communication Test (ACT) consists of thirteen items, like 'I can send a seductive glance if I want to'. Despite its relative lack of face validity, this scale correlates with ratings by friends for expressiveness (0·39), and scores are higher for people with experience of acting or of 'social' occupations like teaching and sales. This kind of measure correlates better with spontaneous than with posed sending ability (Riggio, Widaman, and Friedman 1985).

Although posed and spontaneous expressiveness are partly independent, it has been found that they are also correlated. Zuckerman *et al.* (1976) found a correlation of 0·46, Cunningham (1977) 0·75, face only 0·62, voice only 0·67, body only 0·10. Furthermore, the questionnaire measures correlate with behavioural measures of expressive ability.

What are the personality correlates of expressive accuracy? All these different measures correlate quite well with extroversion, self-esteem, dominance, social skills, and negatively with neuroticism and anxiety on a variety of different tests (e.g. Cunningham 1977; Friedman *et al.* 1980), and in females with field independence (Buck 1984). One of the origins of encoding ability has been found: good encoders report that their families were very expressive (Halberstadt 1983).

We described the subscales of the self-monitoring scale above; two of them are related to expressiveness:

(1) *Extroversion*, which correlates with the ACT, and with spontaneous expressiveness.
(2) *Acting*, correlated with the ability to pose expressions.

This suggests that there are two correlated aspects of expressiveness: spontaneous, correlating with extroversion and self-confidence, which has been called 'charisma'; and posed, related to acting ability, dominance, and the desire to entertain and put on a performance (Riggio and Friedman 1982).

Are there personality factors in the ability to be deceptive? Machiavellians and high SMs have only a rather small advantage (Zuckerman, DePaulo, and Rosenthal 1981). However, those who are good at sending in general are also good at deceiving, but for males only (Riggio and Friedman 1983).

Individual differences in sensitivity

A number of tests of decoding accuracy have been devised. Ekman and Friesen (1978) produced their Brief Affect Recognition Test (BART), which consists of seventy slides of six emotions in the face, shown for 1/60 second each. It has good samples of emotional expressions, high internal reliability, and produces a good spread of scores. There is some evidence of validity, in that scores are improved by training, and are lower for mental patients.

Rosenthal and his colleagues (1979) produced the Profile of Non-verbal Sensitivity (PONS), which contains 220 two-second segments of videotape, of different combinations of face, body, and content-free sound, made by random splicing. There are eleven samples of twenty emotions, all produced by a single performer, a young woman. This list has been extensively used, and data on 7,000 subjects are reported. There is evidence of validity – it correlates with teaching skill (0·38) and with age (0·34), rated sensitivity (0·20), and popularity (0·15 to 0·25); patients do badly, actors do well. High scorers also have higher scores for dominance, social acceptance, social presence, and achievement on the California Personality Inventory, report better same-sex relationships, being able to make friends more rapidly, but having fewer friends (these may be closer). People who do well on PONS at short exposure times (1/24–1/5 seconds), on the other hand, report *less* satisfactory relationships with others (they see what others do not want them to see).

However, both of these tests used posed emotional expressions, which we have seen are not quite the same as real ones. Buck (1984) devised the Communication of Affect Recognition Ability Test (CARAT) which has thirty-two videotapes of subjects as they watched and talked about four kinds of slide – unusual, unpleasant, sexual, and scenic. It was found that there is high reliability, and that arts students do better than science students. Buck argues that no validity evidence is necessary.

Unfortunately these different tests do not correlate very well together. In a number of studies rather small positive correlations between CARAT and PONS were found (Buck 1984). The correlations between success at these tests and other personality variables are a little different. Women do better at the posed tests, but not at CARAT; and the same applies to socially skilled people. Good decoders (of posed expressions) report that their families were *not* very expressive – presumably they learnt to work hard to decode their families' expressions (Halberstadt 1983).

A further aspect of sensitivity is the ability to detect deception. Early studies suggested that Machiavellian personalities could do this better, but a meta-analysis of six studies found a very small effect here. High self-monitors similarly are only slightly better. So far no consistent personality factors have been found in the detection of perception (Zuckerman, DePaulo, and Rosenthal 1981).

Are individuals with good encoding skills also good at decoding others? A wide range of results has been reported on this issue, and an analysis of seventeen studies found a median correlation of + 0·16, so that it must be concluded that the two skills are fairly independent (DePaulo and Rosenthal 1978).

There are also individual differences in the attention paid to NV cues, as opposed to verbal ones. We shall see that schizophrenics are *less* responsive to NV signals, women *more* responsive. Adults are also more responsive to NV cues and children less (Burgoon and Saine 1978). Little (1976) presented triads of speech stimuli, where two were similar in emotional tone and two in content. It was found that some subjects classified the stimuli primarily by the emotional tone of speech; these were people who classified persons mainly in terms of psychological constructs, i.e. in terms of personality attributes (e.g. introvert), as opposed to physical ones (e.g. tall) or roles (e.g. engineer), and who were presumed to be person-oriented as opposed to thing-oriented.

NVC in mental patients

Mental patients in general, regardless of diagnosis, have a common pattern of NVC. They usually have:

    less facial expression, especially less smiling
    less gaze
    less proximity
    fewer other-directed, more self-directed gestures
    shorter utterances, less talk

From the previous section this will be recognized as a general pattern of withdrawal rather than approach. In addition mental patients suffer from negative emotions, such as depression and anxiety, and display the corresponding NV signals. Specific forms of mental disorder have further peculiarities of NVC, some of which are of theoretical interest since they may help to explain the nature of the disorder. We shall consider three main groups of patients: schizophrenics, depressives, and neurotics.

Schizophrenia

Facial expression tends to be blank, with some grimaces. EMG recording shows that there is more left–right asymmetry (Winkelmayer *et al.* 1978), suggesting a higher degree of inhibition, i.e. by the left-hemisphere (p.125).

Gaze. Early studies found evidence for gaze aversion, when patients talked to psychologists or to strangers (e.g. Williams 1974). However, Rutter (1977b) found that if engaged in conversation about the risky shift choice dilemmas (deciding the level of risk to be taken for various problems), or about TV, or other shared interests with a female nurse from their own hospital, there was no less gaze than in non-psychiatric patients. For autistic children, though, gaze aversion (or possibly face aversion) is a central part of the syndrome – indeed one of its defining cues – though these children may approach an adult backwards, in order to sit on her lap (Argyle and Cook 1976).

Spatial. Schizophrenics need more personal space (see Figure 11.5) than normals, especially in the acute stage, and usually choose seats which are more distant and may orient away from other people, though sometimes they sit too close (Sommer 1969).

Gestures are more directed to the patient's own body, and there may be continuous repetitive self-stimulation, e.g. rubbing finger and hand (Grand *et al.* 1975). They may fail to synchronize with speech, or one part of the body may move at a different speed or rhythm, or the eyes may move independently. Condon and Brosin (1969) found this in eighteen out of forty-eight schizophrenic patients.

Posture. Schizophrenics may be immobile, or adopt symbolic postures, e.g. of being crucified.

Vocal. Schizophrenic speech differs from that of normals in a number of ways – more monotonous, lower pitch and loudness, poor articulation, breathy, poor rhythm and stress. It is not known which is most characteristic (Darby 1981). Rutter (1977a) compared acute schizophrenics with non-psychiatric patients and found that they made shorter utterances, asked more questions but with less acknowledgement or other back-channel feedback, and there was more mutual silence.

Appearance. Schizophrenics can often be recognized from their untidy appearance. They do not wear their clothes well, for example doing up the wrong buttons.

Judgement accuracy. Schizophrenics are considerably worse than controls at judging emotions from posed photographs or videotapes

(Muzekari and Bates 1977). When shown conflicting verbal and vocal cues for friendliness they pay much more attention to the verbal ones, whereas normals attend more to tone of voice (Newman 1977). Schizophrenics do not group photographs of faces on the pleasant–unpleasant dimension, but they do use the arousal dimension – fear, anger, and disgust *v.* sad, happy, and surprise (Mandal 1986). Other studies show that they have difficulty decoding faces (Rosenthal *et al.* 1979). Thought-disordered schizophrenics do particularly badly on Bannister and Fransella's Grid test (1966); subjects rate eight photos of faces on eight scales (kind, stupid, etc.) twice; schizophrenics do this less consistently over time, and with less correlation between the scales than other people (Bannister, Fransella, and Agnew 1971). It looks as if they have particular difficulty in interpreting faces.

Encoding skills. Schizophrenics are the least effective group at expressing emotions in a way that can be decoded by others.

Depression

Facial expression. Depressives, of course, have more depressed faces much of the time. Schwartz *et al.* (1976), using EMG recording, found that depressives produced weaker smiles than controls when asked to think about happy events, but nearly as strong when asked to feel happy. Rubenstein (1969) found that after ECT patients produced more extensive smiles.

Gaze. Depressives look less than other people (Rutter and Stephenson 1972), though so far there has not been a study like Rutter's with schizophrenics to see if discussing impersonal topics with acquaintances makes a difference. They also tend to look downwards, and this whole gaze pattern is used by others to identify them.

Spatial. Reduced proximity (Horowitz, Duff, and Stratton 1969).

Gestures. It has often been found that depressed patients use fewer illustrators and more self-touching, e.g. picking and scratching, than other patients, and than normals (Kiritz 1974). As they recover, depressed patients make more complex movements, involving more parts of the body, which start and stop together (Fisch, Frey, and Hirsbrunner 1983).

Posture. The characteristic depressive posture is head down and drooping.

Vocal. This is the channel which is most affected by depression – lower pitch, loudness and speed, falling pitch contour, and a voice quality which is dull, dead, listless, and lacking in vitality (Darby 1981). Depressed patients speak slowly, mainly because there are a lot of long pauses, probably due to the intrusion of depressed thoughts (Siegman 1985).

Appearance. Depressive patients wear dull, drab, and sombre clothes. Designing, making, and modelling more attractive clothes has been used as a form of therapy with depressed females (Miller 1965), as has the better use of cosmetics for women.

Judgement accuracy. They are if anything *more* accurate at detecting positive responses from others, compared with normals, who tend to be too optimistic.

Encoding skills. No evidence.

Neurosis

Facial expression. The more neurotic, anxious, or disturbed people are, the less facially expressive they are, and the less they smile. The same is also true of those who are socially unskilled (Trower 1980).

Gaze. Some neurotic patients, but by no means all, have gaze aversion.

Spatial. The more anxious or disturbed people are, the greater the distance they keep from others (Hayduk 1983).

Gestures. Again, patients engage in fewer illustrators, more self-touching. Psychoanalysts report the use of symbolic gestures.

Posture. No evidence.

Vocal. When people are anxious they produce more speech disturbances (of the non-ah kind), but Cook (1969) found no difference between patients and normals tested under the same conditions. Very anxious people often talk fast, indistinctly, and in short utterances.

Appearance. Hysterical and manic individuals wear striking, over-dramatic, and colourful clothes, not always suitable for the occasion.

Judgement accuracy. There is some evidence that neuroticism is positively correlated with accuracy (Cunningham 1977). Paranoids are better at decoding spontaneous expressions, worse at simulated ones, where the target person was either going to receive an electric shock or posing this anticipation (LaRusso 1978). We saw earlier that individuals good at the brief exposure version of PONS had less satisfactory relationships (p.275). On the other hand, neurotics have been found to exaggerate the amount of social rejection occurring, both of themselves and others (Young 1980). When are patients better, and when are they worse? Patients do better with spontaneous and subtle cues, especially of rejection; normals do better with posed cues.

Encoding skill. Neurotics are poorer at encoding emotions (Cunningham 1977).

Explanation of NVC in mental patients

There is a common theme running through these findings: most mental patients avoid rather than approach other people, there is less gaze, less smiling, less proximity, less talk, less other-directed gestures. Is this a result of the disorder, or a cause of it? The theory that such failure in communication is primary is supported by the success of social skills training, which often includes training of NVC. The theory that other disturbances are primary is supported by the findign that LSD leads to deterioration of decoding, ECT to improvement. Probably both directions operate, and failure of NVC is an essential component in maintaining the disorder.

Schizophrenics are strong in withdrawal or avoidance, though they are able to communicate fairly successfully with nurses. They are still very unrewarding and have been described as 'socially bankrupt'. In addition, they appear to be very defective in both sending and receiving NV signals, compared with verbal; the reason for this is not yet known.

The dominant feature of depression is, of course, the depressed mood, with corresponding face, voice, and posture. It is often precipitated by loss of a social attachment, is characterized by a feeling of helplessness and inability to control events, but also by social skill failure, and a low level of rewardingness, making it difficult to form other attachments (Lewinsohn 1975).

The dominant feature of most neurosis is anxiety, often including social anxiety, leading to inhibition of facial expression and other-directed gestures, reduced proximity, and short utterances. Neurotics are also very self-conscious and thus concerned with their appearance, and direct gestures to themselves. Their avoidance of others is due to fear of punishment rather than lack of affiliative motivation. In addition, many neurotics are deficient in social skills, including the effective use of NV signals, and can be helped by social skills training (Argyle 1984).

Gender differences

Men and women behave rather differently in the sphere of bodily communication. There have been so many investigations that meta-analysis has been carried out on a hundred or more, and some of the findings of Hall's analysis are given in Table 17.3. There are several ways of combining the results of different studies; we shall cite the overall biserial correlations with male/female, as shown in this table. It can be seen that these are quite large, over 0·50 in some cases, i.e. gender accounted for 25 per cent of the variance.

Table 17.3   *Meta-analysis of correlations between gender and NVC (positive means females score higher)*

Variable		r	Number of studies
Face	smiling	0·30	15
	expressiveness	0·45	5
Voice	filled pauses	−0·51	6
	speech errors	−0·32	7
	interruptions	−0·48	9 (2 quantitative only)
	pitch	0·93	12
	loudness	−0·29	12
Spatial	approaching other (naturalistic studies)	−0·27	17
	approached by others	−0·43	9
Gaze		0·32	30
Body movement	expansiveness	−0·46	6
	restlessness	−0·34	6
	expressiveness	0·28	7
	self-consciousness	0·22	5
	involvement	0·16	7
Expressiveness (face)		0·45	5
Judgement accuracy (face)		0·26	125

Source: Hall 1984

There are other ways of expressing this, for example, gender differences in judgement accuracy on the PONS test, for 133 studies, can be given as:

overall biserial r	0·20
percentage of variance accounted for	4·0
percentage of studies where females do better	80·0
size of difference: proportion of σ	0·47
scores on PONS, female/male	172/166

The size of some of the other gender differences can be illustrated from the data obtained by Frances (1979), who observed forty-four males and forty-four females in two five-minute conversations with strangers of the same and opposite sex (Table 17.4).

Table 17.4   *Some gender differences in NVC*

	Males	Females
smiling (seconds, in 5 minutes)	28·40	42·20
number of laughs	2·80	4·74
gaze (seconds in 5 minutes)	207·20	228·90
number of seat position shifts	0·83	0·46
number of leg position shifts	1·52	0·94
length of utterances (seconds)	14·70	11·20
number of filled pauses	12·10	4·60

Source: Frances 1979

Hall's meta-analysis produced a lot of additional findings, so that different explanations can be tested. For example, some gender differences are found in infants and do not increase with age, while others do and can be traced to the effects of socialization.

We shall discuss other gender differences, based on smaller numbers of studies; there is an extensive review by Vrugt and Kerkstra (1984), and others on particular topics, e.g. Hayduk (1983) on spatial behaviour. Finally we will try to explain the results, using theories at different levels, from physiology to sociology.

Facial expression

It is consistently found that women smile and laugh more, even when alone, but especially with other people, and especially with other women, and are more likely to return the smiles of others (Mackey 1976). Women also frown more, and this is very noticeable because of their normally more smiling face. Female infants do not smile more than males, and the difference in smiling increases with age (r = 0·45). Not all female smiling is affiliative: women smile a lot when they are nervous, and shy women smile a great deal, while nervous men fidget a lot (Frances 1979). The largest gender differences have been found in laboratory settings with strangers. Nevertheless smiling, and being positively expressive, does seem to be an important female trait, in addition to which others smile more at them (Rosenhan and Messick 1966).

Voice

Men have louder (r = 0·29) and lower-pitched (r = 0·93) voices. This is not entirely due to anatomical differences; a further reason for differences in voice quality is that women tend to smile while they speak, which produces a higher-pitched sound. Women make more use of intonation, and of particular intonation patterns, such as a downward glide with surprise, the bright, cheerful, polite pattern often used with children (Brend 1975), and utterances ending with a rising note, as if asking a hesitant question (Lakoff 1973). It is often thought that women speak faster, but there is little difference, and if anything men speak faster; men also interrupt more, and when women do so they ask questions – encouraging the other to elaborate (LaFrance and Mayo 1978). But male interruptions are no more successful than those of women, and may reflect greater ease and spontaneity rather than dominance. Women laugh more, especially when feeling uncomfortable (Frances 1979); and they make more back-channel responses (r = 0·61). Men are less fluent, making more filled pauses (r = 0·51), especially when uncomfortable, and more speech errors in general (r = 0·32) (e.g. Lalljee and Cook 1973). Women's voices are judged to be more positive, pleasant, and anxious, men's voices as more dominant and confident. People talk differently to men and to women: they talk more loudly and in a more businesslike way to men.

Spatial behaviour

Women approach closer than men, especially in naturalistic studies (r = 0·27), though the actual difference is small. The closest pairs are F–F, followed by F–M, with M–M most distant (Hayduk 1983). People approach women more closely than men (r = 0·43), a stronger effect. In other words, when women choose the distance, they choose less proximity than when others choose it. People keep a greater distance from men, especially strange men, and have stronger negative reactions to invaders of territory if they are male. While men dislike those who invade head-on, women dislike those who invade from the side (p.183).

Gaze

Women look more than men (r = 0·32), but only in friendly situations. This is found also in infants, and there is no age effect. There are larger gender differences with same-sex targets (r = 0·45), and people look more at women than at men (r = 0·32). Women do not look more at a distance of 10 ft, probably because they do not regard this as an appropriate distance for friendly interaction (Aiello 1972). Women are more ill at ease if they cannot see, and the other person can (Argyle, Lalljee, and Cook 1968), and they feel more 'observed', i.e. the object of attention for another, if both can see (Argyle and Williams 1969). The pattern of gaze is a little different; women do relatively more looking while listening (the submissive style).

Gesture and bodily movements

Gender differences have been examined for many aspects of bodily movement, and several large differences have been found. The greatest difference is that males are more expansive (r = 0·46), (e.g. legs open rather than crossed, elbows out) and more restless (r = 0·34) (e.g. fidgeting, leg and foot movements, change of bodily position). Females are more expressive (r = 0·28) (e.g. more gestures), more self-conscious (r = 0·22) (e.g. more self-touching, nervous gestures), and more involved (r = 0·16) (e.g. more head-nods, forwards lean). Male restlessness decreases during interaction and probably reflects discomfort (Frances 1979). Detailed research, using Laban analysis, has found that during conversation women make finer movements, with hands, feet, or head, while men make larger movements, with whole body parts, which are wider and stronger, and with more periods of stillness (Davis and Weitz 1978).

The gender of people can be identified from their bodily movements, but not from static photographs, and so can their masculinity and femininity (Bull 1983). Mehrabian (1972) found that females adopted more positive postures than men, i.e. more open, had higher scores on his 'immediacy factor'. Women were also less relaxed, which he interpreted as greater submissiveness. We saw that women use the open-arm position to those they like, and that they make greater use of movement mirroring. In Mehrabian's experiments males adopted a tense, vigilant posture towards men they disliked most – direct orientation, unrelaxed, no sideways lean. Females, on the other hand, orientated away from those they disliked, and were very relaxed.

Birdwhistell (1970) thought that one of the key differences was that women keep their arms closer to the body, and that men move their arms more independently of the body. The first part of this was confirmed by Wex (1979) who analysed over 2,000 photographs of men and women, mainly from newspapers and magazines, mostly German. She found that men take up more space, for example sitting with their legs apart, or stretched out, legs crossed broadly, leaning back with hands on hips or thighs and elbows out. Women, on the other hand, keep their knees and legs close together, toes turned inwards, or legs crossed at bottom; they sit straight, with arms at sides, or arms folded, or hands in lap, taking up much less space, and are more controlled, less relaxed.

Klein (1984) observed 1,200 people on Prague trains and subways, and found that 90 per cent of men had knees and ankles apart while only 16 per cent of women did; 84 per cent of women had knees together or slightly apart, compared with 10 per cent of men. Twenty per cent of women had knees and ankles close together while no men did this. Women used these closed postures a lot more when sitting in facing rows of seats, where they were more visible, while seating did not affect male posture. Women's postures were the same when they wore trousers or skirts.

Men and women also walk differently. Women keep their legs closer together and their arms by their sides; men take up more space and are more relaxed (Eakins and Eakins 1978).

Touch

Henley (1977) thought that men touch women more than vice versa outdoors, and that this is due to a status difference between the sexes. However, most studies have found that women touch men more, though the difference is a small one. There is no gender difference in frequency of being touched, there is more same-sex than opposite-sex touching, at least in the fairly public situations which have been observed, and while women do it a little more than men, they embrace more vigorously (Greenbaum and Rosenfeld 1980). Women react more positively to touch than men do, if it is from someone they know, and it is to an appropriate part of the body. They interpret it as friendly, while men may see it as an aggressive or dominant invasion (Stier and Hall 1984; Vrugt and Kerkstra 1984).

Appearance

No work is needed to show that women spend more time, effort, and money on their appearance than do men, though in fact there is some research to prove it. And they are not wasting their time, since the effect of physical attractiveness on desirability for dating is much greater for women (p.253), and also on their persuasiveness as speakers (Mills and Aronson 1965).

Expressiveness

Experiments on how accurately posed or spontaneous emotional states can be decoded by others find that women are more expressive ($r = 0.31$). The effect is greater for face ($r = 0.45$) than overall visual cues ($r = 0.34$), and there is no difference for voice. This sex difference increases with age ($r = 0.38$). However, women are not better at deception, and tend to leak what they are trying to suppress (Zuckerman *et al.* 1981). Buck (1984) found that women tend to be 'externalizers', that is they show more emotional expression but a weaker physiological response to the same stimuli, compared with men.

Judgement accuracy, sensitivity

In a meta-analysis of 133 PONS studies, Hall (1984) found that women did better, with a median r of 0.20; in an analysis of 125 studies, using various other measures, the overall r was 0.26 (p.281). The effect is found in children, and does not increase with age. The effect is greater for face (0.26) than voice (0.09); Rosenthal and DePaulo (1979) compared five channels and found that the female advantage declined with leakiness of channel. The female advantage is less or disappears when others are being deceptive, with spontaneous rather than posed expressions, and with friends rather than strangers (Buck 1984; Noller 1986).

Women do particularly well with faces; this may be because they look at faces more, and indeed this explains some of the gender differences (Rosenthal *et al.* 1979). Women pay more attention to NVC in general, for example they weight NV cues relatively more than men do (Argyle *et al.* 1970), and this may explain their judgement accuracy.

Why are women less successful at decoding leaky or deceptive messages? It may simply be because they are better at the posed or intended messages. It may be because women are 'accommodating', i.e. attend to positive messages, because the female subculture is simply less deceptive (p.288). It may be because women attend to faces, which convey the intended rather than the leaked message (Hall 1984).

The explanation of gender differences in NVC

The explanation of this complex set of differences requires several levels of analysis, from physiology to sociology. This section anticipates the fuller discussion in Chapter 18.

Physiological and innate factors

Women smile more, use less space, look more, and have greater sensitivity as infants, though differences in smiling and gazing also increase with age. It seems possible that there is an innate interest by females in faces, so that they look at them more, perhaps come closer to do so, and weight them more when judging emotional expression. Safer (1981) found that when pictures of faces were presented to the left hemisphere, women could decode them much better than men; men evidently process faces mainly in the right hemisphere, whereas women use both equally. This could be because the thicker corpus callosum in women produces better L–R transfer of information, and hence links between verbal and non-verbal processes.

Socialization

Gender differences in expressiveness, smiling, and gaze all increase with age; smiling differences correlate 0·45 with age. This is partly because mothers *dis*courage such emotional expression in boys, by being unresponsive to them (p.127). We shall see below that there are male and female subcultural norms, and these are passed on by socialization. Females are more fluent, and this is found as early as two years, perhaps because mothers talk to them more (Eakins and Eakins 1978).

Personality differences

Some of the gender differences in NVC can be seen as part of more global personality differences between the sexes. We shall use the dimensions of behaviour which were described earlier.

Affiliative tendency. Women smile and look more; use closer proximity and softer voices. This is part of a general factor of affiliative, friendly behaviour, though it is not known how it originates.

Social anxiety. Women use more nervous smiles, nervous gestures, self-touching, are more concerned about their appearance; men have more relaxed posture. On the other hand it may be that men and women simply express social anxiety differently – men by speech disturbances and restless bodily movements. The female style could be described as greater involvement, shown by forward lean and head nods.

Dominance. Men have louder voices, interrupt more, and look relatively more when speaking. Women have a submissive, questioning intonation pattern. Women interpret touch as friendly, men as intrusive; both are more disturbed by male invasion of space. It has been suggested by DePaulo *et al.* (1978) that women are concerned with faces because faces express like–dislike so clearly, while men are relatively more concerned with voices because voices convey power and dominance better. One explanation of this gender difference lies in subcultural norms, to which we turn shortly.

Femininity   is another way of describing differences in personality, and includes the three dimensions already mentioned. Questionnaire measures of femininity correlate with expression accuracy (Zuckerman *et al.* 1982). and with smiling, gazing, fewer interruptions, and fewer filled pauses (LaFrance and Carmen 1980).

Sociology

Some of the gender differences in NVC could be accounted for at the sociological level, though this in turn may be reducible to psychological processes like socialization.

Subcultural gender norms. The typical female style of NVC is shown most clearly in the company of other women, and the same applies to men. Gender differences are greatest for M–M *v.* F–F in the cases of gaze, proximity, and loudness of voice. Other studies have found that women are most co-operative when with other women, that they are less dominant, condescending, and businesslike on TV shows towards other women (Hall 1984). The whole style of female behaviour with other women has a special quality – affiliative, open, rewarding, pleasant, trusting, and non-deceptive. Among men, on the other hand, there is greater concern with dominance and competition, behaviour is more deceptive, and they attend to voices since they are leakier channels, likely to reveal what is being concealed. The decoding style of women has been described as 'accommodating', or 'polite', in that they see what others want them to see (i.e. facial expressions) and not what is being concealed, i.e. where there is deception, and via leaky channels (Rosenthal and DePaulo 1979).

Such sex-norms could be passed on by parents, and while interacting with same-sex children, but also during the course of education, games, and other activities for which boys and girls are segregated.

Female low status and oppression. It has been suggested that some aspects of female NVC are due to oppression. For example, women may be more sensitive to compensate for their low power. However, this has not been confirmed. Other low power groups are not high in sensitivity, and women with more liberal views on women's role (i.e. who are less oppressed) are better decoders, as are those with more education (Hall 1984).

Shortage of women   has been offered as an explanation of the greater female concern with social acceptance and physical appearance, and there is some evidence that this concern is greater during periods when the number of available males is small (Guttentag and Secord 1983).

18

The explanation of
bodily communication

Finding the facts is not enough. The true goal of science is arriving at a full explanation and understanding of phenomena, preferably by testable theories. Theories have the great heuristic advantage of being able to generate research. It is sometimes said that theory is weak in the case of non-verbal communication, perhaps because the most popular theories in social psychology do not have much application here. I hope to show how NVC can be explained.

First we will explore the theory that bodily communication is really a kind of language – the 'linguistic model'.

Is NVC a kind of language?

The linguistic model has inspired a lot of research and thinking about NVC. We saw earlier how the origins of this approach were in anthropological linguistics, and the development of methods for discovering which of the sounds made in a strange language were used in a systematic way and contributed to the meaning of utterances. This was then applied by Birdwhistell to the study of gesture, and by Kendon to the analysis of greetings.

There are some obvious and important similarities between language and bodily communication. Both are modes of communication: in each case signals are usually sent with the intention of influencing another person or animal; and the two are difficult to separate since verbal communication is so closely linked with gesture, gaze, vocal qualities, etc.

The question is, to what extent does NVC have the properties of a language? To answer this question we will list some of the key features of languages, and consider how far NVC shares them.

Vocabulary

Languages have a (large) vocabulary of words with generally agreed meanings. NV signals have a much smaller vocabulary – about ten facial expressions, for example. The most extensive vocabulary is in the area of gestures, but many of these are direct translations of verbal phrases (p.191). Verbal vocabulary consists of discrete symbols while many non-verbal signals are continuous, e.g. proximity, gaze, and loudness of voice. Most words have arbitrary meanings, whereas most NV signals are iconic, i.e. similar to what they represent. The NV signs which most resemble language in this way are discrete, arbitrary signs, as in Italian emblematic gestures.

Duality of patterning

In all languages there are two levels of organization – sounds (morphemes) and words. Sounds are mostly meaningless, but can be combined in certain ways to make words. Words have meanings and can be combined in a quite different way to make sentences (Lyons 1972). There is a parallel to this in bird-song, in which notes are combined to form songs. However, human bodily communication does not appear to have this feature. More typically a number of signals with similar meaning are used together, e.g. proximity, gaze, smile.

Syntax

Languages have rules of grammar, whereby words are placed in certain combinations and sequences to convey a message. The clearest example of this in human NVC are the sequences of verbal and non-verbal behaviour found in greetings and other rituals (p.222). There is a certain 'logic' about these sequences, e.g. approaching before engaging in close interaction. There may be more universal principles involved, such as those found in rites of passage. On the other hand there is no generative grammar, by which a variety of new combinations can be put together.

Non-verbal signals can, however, be combined in a number of ways, to produce communications with more complex meanings:

(1) Animals combine facial and postural expressions with direction of gaze and spatial position, indicating who is the intended recipient. An alarm call may contain information about the identity of the caller, and the predator, the degree of danger, and the caller's position (p.39).

(2) Emotions and interpersonal attitudes are usually expressed by a harmonious set of signals via facial expression, tone of voice,

and so on. If an inconsistent pattern is presented, this total signal is regarded as odd or funny, particular attention is paid to the negative elements, and a state of conflict may be inferred.

(3) Self-presentation usually involves a complex message – a combination of roles and traits, with emphasis on particular components, as in the case of a Scottish, upper-class, but intellectual, left-wing, and religious dentist.

Highly structured social events, like greetings and other rituals, have rules of sequence. Some of the rules appear to be basic, like the three-phase structure of rituals; others follow cultural conventions, like the behaviour expected at meals and interviews. However, there is a difference between these rules and verbal grammars, in that the NV rules are of a statistical character, rather than definite and all-or-none.

Chomsky showed that language cannot be generated by 'finite-state' grammars, i.e. where rules specify which word shall follow the words before it: more of a language can be generated by 'phrase-structure' grammars, where links between non-adjacent words are recognized, and where bracketing operations must be carried out first in interpreting a sentence. Two sentences may have the same sequence of words, but a different phrase structure – as in the phrase 'old men and women' (Lyons 1972). Do similar principles apply to NVC? There is no close similarity but there are certainly rules relating to non-adjacent moves. For example, the nature of a farewell is related to the nature of the greeting at the same encounter. There is also the phenomenon of 'embedding' – the actual period of greeting itself has a minor greeting and farewell. More generally, periods of an encounter may be bracketed by NV signals, and interrupt the rest of the encounter, which is resumed later. The NV signals accompanying speech follow phrase-structure which is closely related to that of the words, and indeed may indicate the phrase-structure of the words.

Clarke (1983) points out that non-verbal acts may substitute for verbal acts in such sequences. For example 'yes' and a head-nod are equivalent, so are 'look over there' and pointing, and compliance with a command may take the form of doing or saying something. Thus the rule-governed sequence of utterances can be partly replaced by NV signals.

Meaning

Language is not just a complicated kind of vocal behaviour, it has *meaning*, i.e. it conveys information to another person, it shows that a choice has been made. It is true that utterances have an 'illocutionary' side, i.e. they are intended to influence another's behaviour in some way. However, they can only do so by virtue of the meaning which they convey.

Most NVC does not have meaning in this sense. Facial expressions and tones of voice, for example, have quite direct meanings in terms of emotions or interpersonal attitudes. However, there are ways in which NV signals can have propositional meaning, as in advertisements or propaganda, suggesting that there is some connection between coffee and relaxed gaiety, for example, or between Conservative government and prosperity. NV signals can have complex meanings as part of larger social systems, like games. Psychologists analyse the meaning of signals in terms of the words and images evoked by them. Students of semiotics, however, point out that signs have two kinds of meanings – denotation and connotation. They denote a class of objects or events; they connote the abstract set of ideas which defines this class; connotation depends on the linkage of this sign with other signs in the communication system. Thus a gesture illustrating a large fish both represents the class of large fish and connotes this particular kind of beast. Connotation involves linkages with other concepts – small fish, large animals, etc., both between verbalized concepts and between images of these classes. Connotation often deals in terms of opposition (large *v.* small) and of hierarchies of class (fish as part of the animal kingdom). Some bodily signals have meanings as parts of elaborate sign systems. Pike (1967) has made the point that one could not understand what is going on at a religious service, a baseball game, a fishing expedition, or a scientific experiment unless one understood the ideas and plans in the minds of the participants, together with the whole set of concepts and rules connected with the religious service or baseball game.

Structuralists in linguistics emphasize that the meaning of a word depends on the other words in the language. For example, in English there are 'mat', 'rug', and 'carpet', while in French there are 'tapis', 'paillasson', and 'carpette', and none of the French words corresponds to the English ones (Lyons 1973). Similarly, in the non-verbal sphere, the meaning of a signal depends on the range of alternative signals commonly used by a particular person, or in a particular situation or culture. However, as Lyons points out, there is a common core of meaning, corresponding to the grouping of objects in the outside world. Similarly there are certain universals in the non-verbal sphere – the basic facial expressions, for example.

In bodily communication there is the principle of antithesis, whereby a sign has its meaning by being the opposite of another one – appeasement signals and threats, for example (p.47). The gestures for 'yes' and 'no' are similarly opposed, as are the signals for dominance and submission.

Meaning depends on context

The meaning of words often depends on the context: not only 'he', 'this', and 'here', but 'large', 'difficult', etc. Whole sentences may be ambiguous, if it is not clear whether they are intended to be serious, a joke, a threat: 'What are you laughing at?', for example. And the meaning of an utterance in a conversation depends very much on what has been said before, as 'John's, if he gets here in time', which depends for its meaning on the previous utterance 'Whose car are you going in?' (Lyons 1972).

To make the meaning of an ambiguous sentence clear the deep structure needs to be specified; to make the meaning of an ambiguous non-verbal signal clear the sequence of events and the structure of the situation needs to be shown. A person raises his finger – the meaning of this signal depends on whether he is an umpire at a cricket match, a bidder at an auction sale, or in some other situation, and on the place of this act in the sequence. A sequence of overt behaviour may or may not be an instance of ingratiation or of hustling (i.e. pretending to be very bad at a game before playing for money). There can be more than one deep structure here.

Parts of speech

Gesture languages have clear similarities with verbal languages. Nouns, standing for objects or persons, can be communicated by pointing or by illustrative gestures. Verbs standing for actions, can be communicated by the actions themselves, or reduced versions of them like intention movements. Adverbs are represented by the way the actions are performed, prepositions (in, under, etc.) by gestures. These parts of speech can then be put together in sequence, representing sentences. It is interesting that the main parts of speech can be represented so easily.

However, for other kinds of NVC there are no obvious equivalents. First, there are the different bodily areas involved – face, hands, and so on. Each area has special properties as a communicative system, as described in earlier chapters. Second, there are NV signals, within each area, communicating different kinds of information – illustrating speech, governing synchronization, expressing emotions. However, there is nothing like verbal grammar ruling how the different kinds of units are to be combined.

However, NVC is dependent on language in certain ways. A great many human bodily signals have direct verbal meanings. Emblematic gestures are really translations of words into hand movements. The decoding of NV acts is done better when they can be labelled. It has been found that colours which are most consistently given the same name are recognized more efficiently. Similar results have been found in one of the main areas of NVC: a large number of photographs of an actress were used, representing different emotional states. Consistent verbal codability was found to be related to accuracy of recognition (Frijda and Van der Geer 1961). The encoding of behaviour may also be influenced by verbal labels, and in each culture there are words which label NV acts or styles of behaviour, which may be unique to that culture. Examples are 'machismo' (Mexico) meaning flamboyant bravery; 'chutzpah' (Yiddish), which means outrageous cheek; 'honour' in Spain and elsewhere. Subcultures have such terms too – 'cool', 'weird', 'way-out', in the hippy vocabulary, for example. It seems likely that the existence of the word helps both in the production of the behaviour, and also in its correct recognition. Similar labelling takes place in games: in cricket different balls may be labelled as 'full toss', 'googly', 'leg-break', while the shot played may be labelled as 'cover-drive', 'cut', 'playing back', etc.

Social behaviour in general, including NVC, is partly under the control of verbalized plans, in the form of self-talk. For example, when people try to apply principles from social skills training they think in terms such as: 'should initiate more', 'should look at ends of utterances more', and so on. The cognitive processes behind behaviour are mainly couched in verbal terms (Ginsburg, personal communication).

Bodily communication is dependent on language in a second way, too. It is closely linked with language in the conduct of conversation.

To conclude, NVC does have a lot in common with language. Gestures are like words, some rituals are like sentences, meaning depends on context and on what has gone before, NV signals can be combined together, they can have meanings as part of wider meaning systems, and there is some evidence of the structuralist principle of opposition and contrast. Non-verbal signals are often verbally coded, both by senders and receivers, and NV signals are closely integrated with speech in conversation. On the other hand, the NV vocabulary is small, often not discrete or arbitrary, there are no parts of speech, there is no equivalent of syntax, or of phonemes and morphemes following different rules, and NV signals do not usually convey information through propositional meaning.

Levels of explanation of NVC

Some writers on this subject have tried to explain non-verbal phenomena by processes entirely within the domain of social psychology (e.g. Patterson 1983). I believe that this is a mistake. Take, for
example, the well-established finding that women are better than
men at decoding NV signals. Is this because of an innate difference
between the sexes due to evolutionary processes? Is it due to socialization differences? To a difference in brain physiology? In personality? Or is it the result of sociological factors like the suppression of
women? The evidence for these and other theories was discussed in
Chapter 17. If the correct level of explanation can be decided, the
next step is to decide between the various different theories at this
level.

Evolution: The 'naked ape' approach

The study of bodily communication was born of a union between
social psychologists and primate ethologists. The 'naked ape'
approach drew attention to the many similarities between human
and monkey NVC. Some of the clearest similarities are:

    facial expressions for emotion
    gaze as a social signal
    touch as a greeting signal
    gestures such as pointing, beckoning
    postures for dominance and submission

Most striking of all, perhaps, is the finding that the expression of
emotion and the negotiation of interpersonal relationships in man is
done almost entirely non-verbally – as in apes and monkeys.

We now know that some of these signals are innate in man – they
appear in all cultures, in blind children, as well as in monkeys. And
they are produced by physiological equipment, like the facial muscles
and nerves, which are clearly innate.

While the evolutionary origins are an important part of the explanation of NVC, this takes us right outside social psychology, and
outside familiar methods of verification. As we have seen, evolutionary theories in this area are distinctly speculative, and there is
some doubt, for example, over the origins of smiling (p.37).

There are three main ways in which the bodily communication of
men and monkeys are fundamentally different – and in which the
naked ape approach is misleading:

(1) Human NVC is partly spontaneous, partly under cognitive

control. We do not express the emotions we are feeling in an automatic or reflex way, but depend on judgement of which expression will yield the best results. Even young children make use of restraint and deception, and of strategic communication (p.127). Such processes are much weaker in primates.

(2) Human NVC is modified much more by socialization experiences, and this is how cultural differences are passed on to children. They learn the local styles, such as the right level of distance and gaze, when touch is permissible, and the display rules of the culture.

(3) Human social behaviour nearly always involves speech, and a whole range of NV signals are used to support it, especially patterns of gaze, gesture, and vocalization. These are very closely integrated with speech and are learnt at the same time, during interaction with parents.

Explanation in terms of physiology has more potential for clear-cut verification. We have seen, for example, that the facial nerve is controlled both by the hypothalamus (for spontaneous emotion) and the motor cortex (for learned and intentional expressions) (p.124). It is via this cortical channel that cognition, socialization, and culture can influence facial expression – the non-evolutionary factors.

Other physiological theories of NVC wait to be tested, for example Waynbaum's explanation of facial expressions in terms of controlling the blood supply to different parts of the brain (p.75).

Socialization

Several aspects of NVC can be explained in terms of socialization experiences in the home. Different kinds of research have been used to explore the effects of socialization. One way is to study the early development of NVC. Research on early mother–infant interaction has shown how close co-ordination of gaze, vocalization, and facial expression is established; by the age of twelve months mothers appear to have taught their baby a kind of primitive turn-taking, even before they can speak. It is assumed, though it has not been proved, that this shows learning rather than maturation. A second method is to show the effects of different kinds of child-rearing. Why do women smile more than men? In infancy male babies are more expressive (Malatesta 1985), but this is discouraged by mothers in boys and reinforced in girls. The sex difference correlates with age (r = 0·45). The explanation for female superiority at decoding is quite different, because the sex difference does not change with age. Female infants seem to be more interested in faces, and this may be innate.

Little is known as yet about the social learning processes involved. Parents do give a certain amount of direct instruction on NVC, of the kind 'look at me when you speak to me', 'stop sulking'. It is often noticed that children have very similar facial expressions or gestures to their parents, suggesting that modelling is involved.

Some aspects of NVC are more affected by socialization than others. Facial expressions are very similar in all cultures, and are little affected by socialization, apart from the display rules governing when they can be shown. Gestures, on the other hand, are very different in each culture, and this is the area most obviously influenced by learning.

Individual differences in bodily communication are mainly caused by socialization, though inherited dispositions to extroversion and neuroticism no doubt have some effect as well. The general expressiveness factor is partly a product of extroversion, partly of parental style of socialization.

Cognitive processes

The second neural channel to the facial nerve links facial expression to the motor cortex, and hence to the cognitive control of facial expression. All bodily communication is partly spontaneous, partly under cognitive control in this way. Deception is a common feature of NVC, though it is only partly successful since the voice and body are more difficult to control than the face, and there is some leakage.

The testing of cognitive theories about the encoding of NVC can be done in experiments in which behaviour in public and in private are compared – such as Friesen's experiment on Japanese and Americans watching a disgusting film (p.127). Another method is to compare behaviour with different audiences, or audiences which are thought to have different perceptions of the actor (Tedeschi 1981).

There are cognitive processes on the decoding side, too, in the perception and interpretation of the bodily communication of others. We have seen how people make an active cognitive effort to integrate discrepant cues from face and situation (p.135), and from verbal and non-verbal signals (p.93). Testing of decoding theories is familiar in the study of attributions and person perception.

Social interaction

So far we have dealt with theories which are based on individual behaviour. Theories of social interaction deal with the behaviour of two or more individuals. The author's social skills model is an example.

The social skills model. This model emphasizes the role of gaze in collecting feedback, and the back-channel signals (face, gaze, head-nods, etc.), of which this consists. The model was partly based on early studies by Kendon (Argyle and Kendon 1967), showing that gaze is co-ordinated with speech, and that people look mainly at faces. The model gave NVC a central role in social interaction. It also emphasized the close co-ordination between interactors. This was confirmed, for example by Goodwin (1981), in his finding that speakers look up at crucial points to elicit back-channel signals from listeners.

The social skills model has been very useful in drawing attention to the different ways in which social performers can fail, and in suggesting ways in which they can be trained. On the other hand, it is not a source of very specific testable hypotheses. And as a general description of social interaction it needs to be supplemented, for example by cognitive planning, and the rules of sequence of social behaviour (Argyle 1983).

Goffman's theatrical model. This model has a lot in common with the social skills model. However, it is directed towards a different set of phenomena – the creation of impressions of the self formed by others. Goffman (1956) proposed that individuals and groups put on 'performances' in order to manipulate the impressions formed by 'audiences'. These impressions are often misleading, but the deception can be in the audience's interest, as in the case of doctors and undertakers. Social life is like theatre in these respects, and the performances take place in the 'front regions', of houses, for example, where visitors are received. The illusions and definitions of the situation created on the stage are matched by those generated in real life. A related idea is that of 'body-gloss': people often give gestures in public so that an observer could make sense of what might otherwise be incomprehensible behaviour (1971). Symbolic interactionists similarly describe manipulation of physical settings to create some definition of the situation, for example to make abortion clinics look more 'medical' (Stone 1970).

Bodily communication is of central importance according to this model, since self-presentation is largely done by clothes and other aspects of appearance – to indicate wealth or social class, for example, or by style of behaviour, to indicate personality qualities, like 'hardness' among criminals. There is good experimental evidence that self-presentation and 'face-work' are often done; such behaviour is performed more in public than in private, and after some loss of self-esteem, or if the audience is believed to hold an unfavourable view of the performer (Tedeschi 1981).

While there has been confirmation of some of the key ideas of this theory, and while it has generated a lot of research indirectly, on self-presentation, the specific contents of the theory have been very difficult to test empirically. A rare example is the theory of embarrassment in terms of invasion of back regions (Goffman 1956). There are also doubts about some of the key components of the theory. Is it really the case that people send misleading information much of the time? There are some obvious differences between everyday life and the stage. In real life people are playing their own parts, and the action is only partly scripted beforehand. On the stage life is simplified and dramatized, problems are resolved, and clear, exaggerated, messages are sent.

Culture, sociology, and history

We have seen that there is a basic similarity between cultures in the use of NVC, though there are striking differences in gestures, and in the amount of touch, proximity, and gaze. These differences are mediated by display rules and socialization, but they require further explanation. The first stage of explanation is perhaps to identify broad cultural themes, such as the Italian emphasis on expressiveness, and the Black American emphasis on bodily movement and display, and the use of rhythm. Sometimes the historical roots of a cultural style or element can be traced, such as linking the Japanese inhibition of facial expression to the Samurai tradition, and specific gestures to their original meanings (p.193). The differing uses of gestures accompanying speech may be due to differences in language (p.54). The only application of Marxist thinking to NVC that the author is aware of has been the theory that female superiority in decoding skill is due to the oppression of women, but this has not been confirmed empirically (p.289).

There are two theories of historical processes which are particularly relevant to NVC – those of Huizinger and Harré.

Huizinger   (1949) emphasized the importance of play in society. By play he meant voluntary activities undertaken for fun – that is, set apart from real life (though they can be very serious) – which are disinterested and not aimed to satisfy basic wants, and which take place in a special and limited time and place. They often take the form of a contest, and inside the game special rules operate. Huizinger maintained that play is responsible for most aspects of cultural growth, and that play principles operate in ritual, philosophy, art, and elsewhere. He further suggested that there has been a great decline in play since earlier historical periods. In antiquity there was a great deal of religious ritual; in classical times there were games, circuses, and conspicuous, irrational consumption of all kinds; in the Middle Ages there were chivalry, tournaments, courtly love, heraldry, and a great deal of jesting and buffoonery; in the Renaissance the arts and architecture made great use of mythical, allegorical, and symbolic figures; the Baroque and Rococo periods developed highly fanciful forms of decoration, clothes, and wigs. It was in the nineteenth century that 'all Europe donned the boiler suit', and in many spheres of life the playful, irrational, symbolic aspects of life were replaced by technology, realism, and serious games.

This interpretation of certain historical trends has several implications for NVC:

(1) We have already noted the changes which have taken place in men's clothes. In earlier times clothes were far more flamboyant, part of the tradition of boasting and braggadocio; men also wore symbolic devices like coats of arms. Although clothes still communicate, they do so in a much milder and subtler manner.

(2) There has been a decline in the amount of game and ritual activity which is set apart from life, and has a special symbolic character.

(3) There has been a decline in the extent of fancifully elaborated social relationships such as courtly love and chivalry. Social behaviour has become simpler and less symbolic.

Harré (1979) and Harré, Clarke, and De Carlo (1985) have developed the Goffman model in several ways. The biological, innate side of man is incomplete and has to be supplemented by a socially constructed social order, which can take a variety of forms. There is an instrumental order which deals with the material side of life, and an expressive order which is concerned with the universal quest for respect and reputation. The expressive order is a collective symbolic system, part of society rather than of individuals, consisting of a repertoire of meaningful symbolic acts and rules for using them. The system is maintained by public conversation, which becomes internalized as the private thoughts of individuals. The whole system is, however, partly non-verbal, since many of the social acts are non-verbal in character, with symbolic meanings.

There are several research examples of the use of this model:

(1) *Football hooligans.* What appear to be violent encounters between rival groups of supporters turn out to be symbolic threats, combined with striving for esteem as 'hardness'. There are rules which prevent actual violence among all but the deranged 'nutters'. Non-verbal signals here include the various expressions of threatening behaviour, and the regalia signifying status in the hooligan hierarchy (Marsh, Rosser, and Harré 1978).

(2) *Reputation in primitive societies.* While people seek esteem and reputation, they do so in very different ways, and express it with very different symbols. The Trobriand Islanders achieve reputation by giving away yams, the Sudanese by the virtue of their women, Maoris by giving extravagant feasts, the Pueblo by masculinity, and the Aztecs by humility and control of feelings (Harré 1979).

(3) *Emotions* are seen not only as physiological reactions, but as part of the *shared symbolic order.* For example, pride includes the belief that one has been worthy of victory. This accounts for historical and cultural variation in emotions. We no longer have 'melancholy', an Elizabethan emotion, more positive than depression, and a valued aesthetic state. We do not have the Japanese 'amae', a relation of childish dependence on another adult (Harré, Clarke, and De Carlo 1985).

This is not a verifiable theory in the usual sense. It is a 'structural' rather than a causal theory, in which the goal is to identify the 'templates' in the social order, in the mind, and reflected in language, which generate the observed patterns of behaviour.

The strength of this approach is in encouraging the intensive analysis of symbolic systems, especially in the areas of self-presentation and emotion. The main weakness is the lack of systematic methods for doing so, and the avoidance of explanatory hypotheses.

The meaning of ritual in anthropology

As we have already seen, the meaning of ritual cannot wholly be discovered by interviewing those involved. Field workers have inferred from careful studies of primitive rituals that they seem to acquire meaning in two different ways.

Similarity, metaphor, or analogy. Examples are the cross, and wine for blood. In healing rituals they symbolize parts of the body or physiological processes. Other religious rituals symbolize basic emotional experiences relating to birth, love, death, and so on.

Contiguity, association, or other arbitrary associations. Examples are Catholic relics, and animals or flags representing social groups. In rituals which are concerned with social relationships they symbolize social groups, or relations between people. As we have seen there is no objective means of deciding on the meaning of these rituals. It seems most probable that a ritual can have a number of different meanings at the same time – the same act or object can have a large number of metaphorical links. Turner (1966) suggests that symbols can 'condense' several meanings simultaneously, both analogical bodily meanings and arbitrary reference to social groups. In this way group values become charged with emotion, while basic emotions become ennobled through being linked with social values. Ritual is often closely connected with myth, and the myth provides an interpretation for the ritual. The NV signals used in ritual are quite different from verbal communications. They arouse images and feelings metaphorically, and this is what gives them their power.

Ritual signals often stand for social relationships, and as Leach (1968) has pointed out there are a number of common ways of symbolizing these. Social status is represented by a person being on a higher level, for example. More abstract ideas and feelings about life are expressed metaphorically in terms of everyday social behaviour: washing represents purification or removal of guilt, eating an animal suggests the acquisition of its properties, changes of status suggest death and rebirth, which in turn may be linked with the sun, moon, and the seasons.

Why is so much use made of NVC in religious rituals? In the first place, language is not well adapted to describing subjective emotional experiences and the niceties of social relations, especially for primitive people. Language is designed to communicate about events in the external world, rather than those of the inner world. Second, verbal expression does not evoke powerful emotional feelings, produce bodily or psychological healing, or effect changes in social relationships. What we have called 'ritual work' can be accomplished by NVC, but not by language alone. The power of NV signals here is derived from the emotive associations which they have. Some NV signals are probably used simply to increase the impact of other signals, or to communicate social influence – bodily contact, mutual gaze, and the impressive costume of the priest, for example. Third, some personal and interpersonal problems can evidently be handled better if they do not come fully into consciousness, where their contradictions and difficulties would be disturbing or embarrassing. As Fortes (1966) puts it:

It is not surprising that there is some ritual in most human societies aimed at grasping, binding, and incorporating, into the overt
custom and practices of life, the ambivalences of love and hate,
dependence and self-assertion which underlie the relations of
parents and children, but cannot be understood in causal terms
and dare not be admitted as motives of action.

However, words are used in ritual, and rituals derive meanings
partly through verbalized sets of ideas, such as Christian theology.
Rituals can be described in words and initiated in words, but as Firth
(1970) said, gestures 'have a significance, a propriety, a restorative
effect, a kind of creative force which words alone cannot give'.
Words add to the meanings of NV signals, and religious ritual thus
consists typically of a combination of verbal and non-verbal, where
the two kinds of meaning are combined. This adds the precision of
words to the emotive power of bodily signals.

19

Beyond language

In this final chapter we shall discuss two central issues. The first is the question of why we human beings bother about NVC at all. We can communicate far better than animals about many matters by means of language. Why do we not use language for all communication purposes? Our explorations so far suggest a number of reasons.

Why is bodily communication used by humans?

Lack of verbal coding in some areas

There are relatively few words for shapes, apart from a few very simple ones. Probably language failed to develop in this sphere since shapes can easily be described by drawing or hand movements – non-verbally – so that words are not necessary. Certainly shapes can be communicated more effectively if hand movements are allowed.

Similar considerations apply to the entire interpersonal area. This is handled perfectly well by means of our primitive non-verbal equipment, so that words are not necessary, are not normally used, and are awkward and embarrassing when they are.

Non-verbal signals are more powerful

We have seen that NV signals for interpersonal attitudes are far more powerful than initially similar verbal ones. We can speculate on the reasons for this. Animals have a largely innate NV system for inter-personal signals; we have inherited this system in part. It operates directly, and evokes bodily responses which prepare the receiver for immediate action. Verbal signals, on the other hand, normally convey information about the outside world; the information is considered carefully, and possible implications explored; there is some modification of the recipient's cognitive field, but these do not lead to action unless they are linked through learning to some drive state.

Verbal signals *can* lead to immediate action, as when commands are given to well-trained men, but usually the impact of words is weaker and less direct than the impact of non-verbal signals.

Non-verbal signals are less well controlled and therefore more likely to be genuine

It is a familiar experience that words do not always convey the truth. It is difficult to obtain internal evidence from the words themselves, to indicate whether the speaker is telling the truth or not. In fact, people depend on NV cues like hesitant speech and raised pitch for evidence.

Non-verbal signals, on the other hand, are less easily controlled and are commonly assumed to be genuine. The main exception to this is facial expression, especially in cultures like Britain and Japan where there are strong conventions about looking pleasant. Tone of voice is controlled, and known to be controlled, by most educated people. But the other NV signals are much less commonly controlled – except by actors and those who have studied social psychology. Other signals, like pupil dilation and perspiration, can only be controlled by modifying the emotional state itself, which is more difficult than just modifying bodily signals.

It seems likely that more widespread knowledge about NVC will lead to more people manipulating their own behaviour, and possibly distrusting that of other people, thus destroying part of the value of the NV system. On the other hand, greater awareness should have the effect of increasing social skill and sensitivity.

It would be disturbing to focus attention on some signals or to make them too explicit

When people are negotiating or sustaining interpersonal relationships, it would be very disturbing for one to state openly, for example, that he did not like the other very much, or that he thought he was more important than the other; disturbing, too, if they disagreed about their relationship. Perhaps for this reason the negotiation of social relationships is conducted non-verbally, at the fringe of consciousness, while conversation or task occupy the verbal channel and the focus of consciousness – even though the social task may be far more important.

Similarly it is very convenient for these matters not to be too explicit: people can make up their minds slowly about others and change their minds without being committed to definite relationships.

It is very useful to be able to use a second channel in addition to language

We have just seen that this second channel carries interpersonal information. In addition, the second channel carries a great deal of information which supports language, but which it would be inefficient and confusing to put into words. Synchronizing signals could be put into words by adding 'full stop', or 'end of message', but this would take time; it is much faster for synchronization to be handled non-verbally. Feedback from the listener could not be put into words without constant interruption and double-talking, so that this information is virtually forced into the visual non-verbal channel. NV signals by the speaker which add to or comment on the verbal message add enormously to the complexity of the messages that can be sent.

Expressing the inexpressible

Wittgenstein (1922) is famous for the concluding paragraph of his *Tractatus*: 'Whereof one cannot speak, thereof one should be silent.' However Langer (1942) has suggested that there are two kinds of communication, one based on logic and language, the second designed to express and articulate feeings by means of non-verbal symbolism. Similar dichotomies of two kinds of thinking, or communication, have been put forward by Polanyi (1958) and others.

Music and the other arts, and religion, make much use of NVC. Music, for example, uses properties of sound similar to tones of voice by means of different pitch, speed, etc., and can convey emotions in the same way. Music has extra properties – rhythm, repeated melody, and the elaborate structure of musical composition. As well as conveying emotion, music is perceived as beautiful, and as conveying deeper messages – as triumphant, tragic, dignified, yearning, for example. Langer (1953: 40) suggested that 'art is the creation of forms symbolic of human feeling', and that music is especially capable of representing the inner emotional life of energy, conflict, tension and its reduction, growth, and spontaneity.

The present state of NVC research

The growth of research

There has been a great expansion of research on this topic, and several journals are now wholly or partly devoted to it, such as the *Journal of Nonverbal Behavior*. Several areas have now been quite thoroughly explored, especially facial expression, spatial behaviour, and gaze.

Some findings have been extensively replicated, some are very
subtle and interesting, not at all obvious to common sense. However, in other areas there is still a lot to find out – about tone of voice,
gesture, and appearance, for example. Emotions are coded in voice
quality in complex ways, gestures and bodily movements are very
difficult to describe or measure.

NVC performs several different functions – expressing emotions,
and attitudes towards others, sending information about the self, and
supplementing speech. The encoding process in each case is complicated by display rules, and the combination of spontaneous and
managed messages. Decoding involves the integration of different NV
cues, of verbal and non-verbal, and taking account of the situation.

There has been a great increase in the study of individual differences in NVC, a number of clear dimensions have appeared, and
tests for some of these developed. A number of very striking sex differences have emerged. And there are clear links between bodily
communication, social competence, and mental disorder, some of
them quite unexpected.

Research methods

Rigorous experimental and statistical methods are now generally
accepted as appropriate, and other more qualitative methods used
earlier have been abandoned. There has been a move towards arousal
of real emotions and attitudes, rather than posed ones in encoding
research, and the use of realistic and field settings. While experimental designs have become more sophisticated, this has sometimes led
to elaborate, but artificial procedures, which have not always produced meaningful results.

Theory and explanation

Several different levels of explanation are needed. The facial nerve
goes both to the hypothalamus and to the motor cortex; the first
reflects innate programmes whose origins lie in evolution; the
second reflects social learning and cultural history. In addition there
are the effects of socialization, processes of social interaction, the
sociology of symbolism, and social meaning.

NVC and language

We have seen that NVC is much more powerful than language for
some purposes, like expressing emotions and attitudes to other people,

but it is less powerful for conveying many kinds of information. And while NVC is in some ways like a language, in most respects it is rather different. On the other hand, NVC research has made important contributions to the study of language and conversation. Language in use involves timing, gestures, vocal pitch and emphasis, and patterns of gaze by speakers, and co-ordination with other moves by listeners, the whole making up a tightly integrated system.

Applications

The most important application has been to social skills training – for many kinds of mental patients and for those entering a wide range of occupations. There are common failures of NVC, and more specific ones for different mental disorders. Even presidents and prime ministers have had their NVC problems. A second major application has been to intercultural communication – training people to work abroad, and adding to the understanding and acceptance of those from other ethnic and national groups. Many findings about bodily communication are relevant to problems in everyday life – how to tell when someone is being deceptive, how to communicate friendship (or love, or dominance), and how to be persuasive, for example.

References

Abercrombie, K. (1968) 'Paralangauge', *British Journal of Communication* 3: 55–9.

Adams, J.B. (1957) 'Culture and Conflict in an Egyptian Village', *American Anthropologist* 59: 225–35.

Addington, D.W. (1968) 'The Relationship of Selected Vocal Characteristics to Personality Perception', *Speech Monographs* 35: 492–503.

Aguilera, D.C. (1967) 'Relationship between Physical Contact and Verbal Interaction between Nurses and Patients', *Journal of Psychiatric Nursing and Mental Health Services* 5: 5–21.

Aiello, J.R. (1972) 'A Test of Equilibrium Theory: Visual Interaction in Relation to Orientation, Distance, and Sex of Interactants', *Psychonomic Science* 27: 335–6.

Aiello, J.R. and Aiello, T. de C. (1974) 'The Development of Personal Space: Proxemic Behavior of Children 6 through 16', *Human Ecology* 2: 177–89.

Akkinaso, F.N. and Ajirotutu, C.S. (1982) 'Performance and Ethnic Style in Job Interviews'. In J.J. Gumperz (ed.) *Language and Social Identity*, Cambridge: Cambridge University Press.

Albert, S. and Dabbs, J.M. (1970) 'Physical Distance and Persuasion', *Journal of Personality and Social Psychology* 15: 265–70.

Alexander, I.E. and Babad, E.Y. (1981) 'Returning the Smile of the Stranger: Within-Culture and Cross-Cultural Comparisons of Israeli and American Children', *Genetic Psychology Monographs* 103: 31–77.

Allen, V.L. and Atkinson, M.L. (1981) 'Identification of Spontaneous and Deliberate Behavior', *Journal of Nonverbal Behavior* 5: 224–37.

Allport, G.W. and Vernon, P.E. (1983) *Studies in Expressive Movement*, Boston: Houghton Mifflin.

Altman, I. (1975) *The Environment and Social Behavior*, Monterey, California: Brooks/Cole.

Altman, I. and Haythorn, W.W. (1967) 'The Ecology of Isolated Groups', *Behavioral Science* 12: 169–82.

Altman, I. and Vinsel, A.M. (1977) 'Personal Space: An Analysis of E.T. Hall's Proxemic Framework'. In I. Altman and J. Wohlwill (eds) *Human Behavior and Environment: Advances in Theory and Research*, 2, New York: Plenum.

Andrews, R.J. (1963) 'The Origin and Evolution of the Calls and Facial Expressions of the Primates', *Behaviour* 20: 1–109.

Anisfield, M., Bogo, N., and Lambert, W. (1962) 'Evaluative Reactions to Accented English Speech', *Journal of Abnormal and Social Psychology* 65: 223–31.

Apple, W. and Hecht, K. (1982) 'Speaking Emotionally: the Relation between Verbal and Vocal Communication of Affect', *Journal of Personality and Social Psychology* 42: 864–75.

Apple, W., Streeter, L.A., and Krauss, R.M. (1979) 'Effects of Pitch and Speech Rate on Personal Attributions', *Journal of Personality and Social Psychology* 37: 715–27.

Argyle, M. (1969) *Social Interaction*, London: Methuen.

Argyle, M. (1983) *The Psychology of Interpersonal Behaviour*, 4th edn, Harmondsworth: Penguin.

Argyle, M. (1984) 'Some New Developments in Social Skills Training', *Bulletin of the British Psychological Society* 37: 405–10.

Argyle, M. (1987) *The Psychology of Happiness*, London: Methuen.

Argyle, M. (in press) 'Social Relationships'. In M. Hewstone, W. Stroebe, G. Stephenson, and J.-P. Codol (eds) *Social Psychology: A European Textbook*, Oxford: Blackwell.

Argyle, M., Alkema, F., and Gilmour, R. (1972) 'The Communication of Friendly and Hostile Attitudes by Verbal and Non-Verbal Signals', *European Journal of Social Psychology* 1: 385–402.

Argyle, M. and Cook, M. (1976) *Gaze and Mutual Gaze*, Cambridge: Cambridge University Press.

Argyle, M. and Dean, J. (1965) 'Eye-contact, Distance and Affiliation', *Sociometry* 28: 289–304.

Argyle, M., Furnham, A., and Graham, J.A. (1981) *Social Situations*, Cambridge: Cambridge University Press.

Argyle, M. and Graham, J.A. (1977) 'The Central Europe Experiment – Looking at Persons and Looking at Things', *Journal of Environmental Psychology and Nonverbal Behavior* 1: 6–16.

Argyle, M., Graham, J.A., Campbell, A., and White, P. (1979) 'The Rules of Different Situations', *New Zealand Psychologist* 8: 13–22.

Argyle, M. and Henderson, M. (1985) *The Anatomy of Relationships*, London: Heinemann and Harmondsworth: Penguin.

Argyle, M., Henderson, M., and Furnham, A. (1985) 'The Rules of Social Relationships', *British Journal of Social Psychology* 24: 125–39.

Argyle, M. and Ingham, R. (1972) 'Gaze, Mutual Gaze and Distance', *Semiotica* 1: 32–49.

Argyle, M. and Kendon, A. (1967) 'The Experimental Analysis of Social Performance', *Advances in Experimental Social Psychology* 3: 35–98.

Argyle, M., Lalljee, M., and Cook, M. (1968) 'The Effects of Visibility on Interaction in a Dyad', *Human Relations* 21: 3–17.

Argyle, M., Lalljee, M., and Lydall, M. (unpub.) 'Selling as a Social Skill'.

Argyle, M., Lefebvre, L., and Cook, M. (1974) 'The Meaning of Five Patterns of Gaze', *European Journal of Social Psychology* 4: 385–402.

Argyle, M. and McCallin, M. (unpub.) 'The Rules of Interrupting'.

Argyle, M. and McHenry, R. (1971) 'Do Spectacles Really Affect Judgments of Intelligence', *British Journal of Social and Clinical Psychology* 10: 27–9.

Argyle, M., Salter, V., Nicholson, H., Williams, M., and Burgess, P. (1970) 'The Communication of Inferior and Superior Attitudes by Verbal and Non-Verbal Signals', *British Journal of Social and Clinical Psychology* 9: 221–31.

Argyle, M. and Trower, P. (1979) *Person to Person*, London: Harper.

Argyle, M. and Williams, M. (1969) 'Observer or Observed? A Reversible Perspective in Person Perception', *Sociometry* 32: 396–412.

Arkowitz, H., Lichtenstein, E., McGovern, K., and Hines, P. (1975) 'The Behavioral Assessment of Social Competence in Males', *Behavior Therapy* 6: 3–13.

Ashcraft, N. and Scheflen, A.E. (1976) *People Space*, Garden City, NY: Anchor Books.

Aslin, R.N., Pisoni, D.B., and Jusczyk, P.W. (1983) 'Auditory Development and Speech Perception in Infancy'. In P.H. Mussen (ed.) *Handbook of Child Psychology*, 2, New York: Wiley.

Atkinson, M. (1984) *Our Master's Voices*, London: Methuen.

Bakeman, R. and Brown, J.V. (1977) 'Behavioral Dialogues: An Approach to the Assessment of Mother–Infant Interaction', *Child Development* 48: 195–203.

Bannister, D. and Fransella, F. (1966) 'A Grid Test of Schizophrenic Thought Disorder', *British Journal of Social and Clinical Psychology* 5: 95–202.

Bannister, D., Fransella, F., and Agnew, J. (1971) 'Characteristics and Validity of the Grid Test of Thought Disorder', *British Journal of Social and Clinical Psychology* 10: 144–51.

Barash, D.P. (1973) 'Human Ethology: Personal Space Reiterated', *Environment and Behavior* 5: 67–73.

Barker, R.G. (1966) 'On the Nature of the Environment'. In K.R. Hammond (ed.) *The Psychology of Egon Brunswick*, New York: Holt, Rinehart, & Winston.

Barnlund, D.C. (1975) 'Communication Styles in Two Cultures: Japan and the United States'. In A. Kendon, R.M. Harris, and M.R. Key (eds) *Organization of Behavior in Face-to-Face Interaction*, The Hague: Mouton.

Barroso, F. and Feld, J.K. (1986) 'Self-touching and Attentional Processes: The Role of Task Difficulty, Selection Stage, and Sex Differences', *Journal of Nonverbal Behavior* 10: 51–64.

Barroso, F., Freedman, N., Grand, S., and Van Meel, J. (1978) 'Evocation of Two Types of Hand Movements in Information Processing', *Journal of Experimental Psychology: Human Perception and Performance* 4: 321–9.

Bassili, J.N. (1979) 'Emotion Recognition: The Role of Facial Movement and the Relative Importance of Upper and Lower Areas of the Face', *Journal of Personality and Social Psychology* 37: 2,049–58.

Bates, E., Shore, C., Bretherton, I., and McNew, S. (1983) 'Names, Gestures and Objects: Symbolization in Infancy and Aphasia'. In K.E. Nelson (ed.) *Children's Language*, vol. 4, Hillsdale, NJ: Erlbaum.

Bateson, G. and Mead, M. (1942) *Balinese Character: A Photographic Analysis*, New York: New York Academy of Sciences.

Baum, A. and Singer, J.E. (1982) *Advances in Environmental Psychology, Vol. 4: Environment and Health*, Hillsdale, NJ: Erlbaum.

Baxter, J.C., Winter, E.P., and Hammer, R.E. (1968) 'Gestural Behavior During a Brief Interview as a Function of Cognitive Variables', *Journal of Personality and Social Psychology* 8: 303–7.

Bayes, M.A. (1972) 'Behavioral Cues of Interpersonal Warmth', *Journal of Consulting and Clinical Psychology* 39: 333–9.

Beattie, G.W. (1981) 'A Further Investigation of the Cognitive Interference Hypothesis of Gaze Patterns during Conversation', *British Journal of Social Psychology* 20: 243–8.

Beattie, G.W. (1983) *Talk: An Analysis of Speech and Non-Verbal Behaviour in Conversation*, Milton Keynes: Open University Press.

Beattie, G.W. and Barnard, P.J. (1979) 'The Temporal Structure of Natural Telehone Conversations (Directory Enquiry Calls)', *Linguistics* 17: 213–30.

Beattie, G.W. and Bradbury, R.J. (1979) 'An Experimental Investigation of the Modifiability of the Temporal Structure of Spontaneous Speech', *Journal of Psycholinguistic Research* 8: 225–48.

Beekman, S.J. (unpub.) (1975) 'Sex Differences in Nonverbal Behavior' (cited by Harper, Wiens, and Matarazzo 1978).

Beier, E.G. and Sternberg, D.P. (1977) 'Marital Communication', *Journal of Communication* 27: 92–7.

Bennett, D. and Bennett, J. (1970) 'Making the Scene'. In G. Stone and H. Farberman (eds) *Social Psychology through Symbolic Interaction*, Lexington, Mass.: Ginn-Blaisdell.

Berger, J., Rosenholtz, S.J., and Zelditch, M. (1980) 'Status Organizing Processes', *Annual Review of Sociology* 6: 479–508.

Bernstein, B. (1959) 'A Public Language: Some Sociological Implications of a Linguistic Form', *British Journal of Sociology* 10: 311–26.

Berry, D.S. and McArthur, L.Z. (1985) 'Some Components and Consequences of a Babyface', *Journal of Personality and Social Psychology* 48: 312–23.

Berry, D.S. and McArthur, L.Z. (1986) 'Perceiving Character in Faces: The Impact of Age-Related Craniofacial Changes on Social Perception', *Psychological Bulletin* 100: 3–18.

Berscheid, E., Dion, K., Walster (Hatfield), E., and Walster, G.W. (1971) 'Physical Attractiveness and Dating Choice: A Test of the Matching Hypothesis', *Journal of Experimental Social Psychology* 7: 173–89.

Bickman, L. (1974) 'Social Roles and Uniform: Clothes Make the Person', *Psychology Today* April: 49–51.

Birdwhistell, R.L. (1970) *Kinesics and Context*, Philadelphia: University of Philadelphia Press.

Blurton-Jones, N. and Leach, G.M. (1972) 'Behaviour of Children and their Mothers at Separation and Parting'. In N. Blurton-Jones (ed.) *Ethological Studies of Child Behaviour*, Cambridge: Cambridge University Press.

Boderman, A., Freed, D.W., and Kinnucan, M.T. (1972) 'Touch Me, Like Me: Testing an Encounter Group Assumption', *Journal of Applied Behavioral Science* 8: 527–33.

Boomer, D.S. (1978) 'The Phonemic Clause: Speech Unit in Human Conversation'. In A.W. Siegman and S. Feldstein (eds) *Nonverbal Behavior and Communication*, Hillsdale, NJ: Erlbaum.

Boucher, J.D. and Ekman, P. (1975) 'Facial Areas of Emotional Information', *Journal of Communication* 25: 21–9.

Bowlby, J. (1958) 'The Nature of the Child's Tie to his Mother', *International Journal of Psychoanalysis* 39: 350–73.

Breed, G. and Ricci, J.S. (1973) ' "Touch Me, Like Me": Artifact?', *Proceedings of the American Psychological Association* 8: 153–4.

Brend, R. (1975) 'Male–female Intonation Patterns in American English'. In B. Thorne and N. Henley (eds) *Language and Sex: Difference and Dominance*, Rowley, Mass.: Newbury House.

Briggs, S.R., Cheek, J.M., and Buss, A.H. (1980) 'An Analysis of the Self-monitoring Scale', *Journal of Personality and Social Psychology* 38: 679–86.

Brockman, J., Pressman, B., Cabitt, J., and Moran, P. (1982) 'Nonverbal Intimacy, Sex and Compliance', *Journal of Nonverbal Behavior* 6: 253–8.

Brun, T. (1969) *The International Dictionary of Sign Language*, London: Wolfe.

Bruner, J.S. (1977) 'The Ontogenesis of Speech Acts'. In P. Collett (ed.) *Social Rules and Social Behaviour*, Oxford: Blackwell.

Brunner, L.J. (1979) 'Smiles can be Back Channels', *Journal of Personality and Social Psychology* 37: 728–34.

Buck, R. (1984) *The Communication of Emotion*, New York: Guilford.

Buck, R., Miller, R.E., and Caul, W.F. (1974) 'Sex, Personality and Physiological Variables in the Communication of Emotion via Facial Expression', *Journal of Personality and Social Psychology* 30: 587–96.

Buck, R., Savin, V., Miller, R.E., and Caul, W.F. (1972) 'Nonverbal Communication of Affect in Humans', *Journal of Personality and Social Psychology* 23: 362–71.

Bugental, D.E. (1974) 'Interpretations of Naturally Occurring Discrepancies between Words and Intonation', *Journal of Personality and Social Psychology* 30: 125–33.

Bugental, D.B. (1986) 'Unmasking the "Polite Smile": Situational and Personal Determinants of Managed Affect in Adult–Child Interaction', *Personality and Social Psychology Bulletin* 12: 7–16.

Bugental, D.B., Henker, B., and Whalen, C.K. (1976) 'Attributional Antecedents of Verbal and Vocal Assertiveness', *Journal of Personality and Social Psychology* 34: 405–11.

Bugental, D.B., Kaswan, J.W., and Love, L.R. (1970) 'Perception of Contradictory Meanings Conveyed by Verbal and Nonverbal Channels', *Journal of Personality and Social Psychology* 16: 647–55.

Bugental, D.B., Love, L.R., and Gianetto, R.M. (1971) 'Perfidious Feminine Faces', *Journal of Personality and Social Psychology* 17: 314–18.

Bugental, D.B., Love, L.R., Kaswan, J.W., and April C. (1971) 'Verbal-nonverbal Conflict in Parental Messages to Normal and Disturbed Children', *Journal of Abnormal Psychology* 77: 6–10.

Bull, R. (1979) 'The Psychological Significance of Facial Deformity'. In M. Cook and G. Wilson (eds) *Love and Attraction*, Oxford: Pergamon.

Bull, P. (1983) *Body Movement and Interpersonal Communication*, Chichester: Wiley.

Bull, P. (1987) *Posture and Gesture*, Oxford: Pergamon.

Bull, P. and Connelly, G. (1985) 'Body Movement and Emphasis in Speech', *Journal of Nonverbal Behavior* 9: 169–87.

Burgess, J.W. (1983) 'Developmental Trends in Proxemic Spacing between Surrounding Companions and Strangers in Casual Groups', *Journal of Nonverbal Behavior* 7: 158–69.

Burgoon, J.K. (1984) 'Nonverbal and Relational Communication Associated with Reticence', *Human Communication Research* 10: 601–26.

Burgoon, J.K., Buller, D.B., Hale, J.L., and deTurek, M.A. (1984) 'Relational Messages Associated with Nonverbal Behavior', *Human Communication Research* 10: 351–78.

Burgoon, J.K., Manusov, V., Mineo, P., and Hale, J.L. (1985) 'Effects of Gaze on Hiring, Credibility, Attraction and Relational Message Interpretation', *Journal of Nonverbal Behavior* 9: 133–46.

Burgoon, J. and Saine, T. (1978) *The Unspoken Dialogue*, Boston: Houghton Mifflin.

Burns, T. (1954) 'The Directions of Activity and Communication in a Departmental Executive Group: A Quantitative Study in a British Engineering Factory with a Self-Recording Technique', *Human Relations* 7: 73–97.

Burroughs, W., Schulz, W., and Aubrey, S. (1973) 'Quality of Argument, Leadership Roles and Eye Contact in Three-Person Leaderless Groups', *Journal of Social Psychology* 90: 89–93.

Butler, D.E. (1960) *The British General Election of 1959*, London: Macmillan.

Butterworth, B.L. and Beattie, G.W. (1978) 'Gesture and Silence as Indicators of Planning of Speech'. In R.N. Campbell and P.T. Smith (eds) *Recent Advances in the Psychology of Language: Formal and Experimental Approaches*, New York: Plenum.

Calhoun, J.B. (1962) 'Population Density and Social Pathology', *Scientific American* 207: 139–46.

Campbell, A. and Rushton, J.P. (1978) 'Bodily Communication and Personality', *British Journal of Social and Clinical Psychology* 17: 31–6.

Canter, D. (1977) *The Psychology of Place*, London: Academic Press.

Canter, D., Stringer, P., Griffiths, I., Boyce, P., Walters, D., and Kenny, C. (1975) *Environmental Interaction: Psychological Approaches to our Physical Surroundings*, New York: International University Press.

Capella, J.N. (1981) 'Mutual Influence in Expressive Behavior: Adult–Adult and Infant–Adult Dyadic Interaction', *Psychological Bulletin* 89: 101–32.

Cary, M.S. (1978) 'The Role of Gaze in the Initiation of Conversation', *Social Psychology* 41: 269–71.

Cash, T.F. (1985) 'The Impact of Grooming Style on the Evaluation of Women in Management'. In M.R. Solomon (ed.) *The Psychology of Fashion*, Lexington: Heath.

Cash, T.F. and Cash, D.W. (1982) 'Women's Use of Cosmetics: Psychosocial Correlates and Consequences', *International Journal of Cosmetic Science* 4: 1–14.

Central Policy Review Staff (1978) *Vandalism*, London: HMSO.

Chance, M.R.A. (1967) 'Attention Structure as a Basis of Primate Rank Orders', *Man* 2: 503–18.

Cherulnik, P.D., Neely, W.T., Flanagan, M., and Zachau, M. (1978) 'Social Skill and Visual Interaction', *Journal of Social Psychology* 104: 263–70.

Chevalier-Skolnikoff, S. (1973) 'Facial Expression of Emotion in Non-human Primates'. In P. Ekman (ed.) *Darwin and Facial Expression*, New York and London: Academic Press.

Cialdini, R.B. and Richardson, K.D. (1980) 'Two Indirect Tactics of Image Management: Basking and Blasting', *Journal of Personality and Social Psychology* 39: 406–15.

Ciolek, M.T. (1977) 'Location of Static Gatherings in Pedestrian Areas: An Exploratory Study', *Man–Environment Systems* 7: 41–54.

Clarke, D.D. (1983) *Language and Action*, Oxford: Pergamon.

Cohen, A.A. and Harrison, R.P. (1973) 'Intentionality in the Use of Hand Illustrators in Face-to-face Communication Situations', *Journal of Personality and Social Psychology* 28: 276–9.

Cole, P.M. (1985) 'Display Rules and the Socialization of Affective Displays'. In G. Zivin (ed.) *The Development of Expressive Behavior*, Orlando: Academic Press.

Collett, P. (1971) 'On Training Englishmen in the Non-Verbal Behaviour of Arabs: An Experiment in Intercultural Communication', *International Journal of Psychology* 6: 209–15.

Collett, P. (1972) 'Structure and Content in Cross-Cultural Studies of Self-esteem', *International Journal of Psychology* 7: 169–79.

Collett, P. (1982) 'Meetings and Misunderstandings'. In S. Bochner (ed.) *Cultures in Contact*, Oxford: Pergamon.

Collett, P. (1983) 'Mossi Salutations', *Semiotica* 45: 191–248.

Collett, P. (1984) 'History and Study of Expressive Action'. In K. Gergen and M. Gergen (eds) *Historical Social Psychology*, Hillsdale, NJ: Erlbaum.

Collett, P. and Marsh, P. (1974) 'Patterns of Public Behaviour: Collision Avoidance on a Pedestrian Crossing', *Semiotica* 12: 281–99.

Collier, G. (1984) *Emotional Expression*, Hillsdale, NJ: Erlbaum.

Compton, N. (1962) 'Personal Attributes of Color and Design Preferences in Clothing Fabrics', *Journal of Psychology* 54: 191–5.

Comstock, G., Chaffee, S., Katzman, N., McCombs, M., and Roberts, D. (1978) *Television and Human Behavior*, New York: Columbia University Press.

Condon, W.S. and Brosin, H.W. (1969) 'Micro Linguistic-Kinesic Events in Schizophrenic Behavior'. In D.V. Siva Sankar (ed.) *Schizophrenia: Current Concepts and Research*, Hicksville, NY: PJD Publications.

Condon, W.S. and Ogston, W.D. (1966) 'Sound Film Analysis of Normal and Pathological Behavior Patterns', *Journal of Nervous and Mental Disease* 143: 338–47.

Cook, M. (1969) 'Anxiety, Speech Disturbances, and Speech Rate', *British Journal of Social and Clinical Psychology* 8: 13–21.

Cook, M. (1970) 'Experiments on Orientation and Proxemics', *Human Relations* 23: 61–76.

Cook, M. and Lalljee, M.G. (1972) 'Verbal Substitutes for Visual Signals in Interaction', *Semiotica* 6: 212–21.

Cook, M. and Smith, J.M.C. (1975) 'The Role of Gaze in Impression Formation', *British Journal of Social and Clinical Psychology* 14: 19–25.

Cowen, E.L., Weisberg, R.P., and Lotyczewski, B.S. (1983) 'Physical Contacts in Interaction between Clinicians and Young Children', *Journal of*

Consulting and Clinical Psychology 51: 132–8.

Cox, V.C., Paulus, P.B., and McCairn, G. (1984) 'Prison Crowding Research', *American Psychologist* 39: 1,148–60.

Craig, K.D. and Patrick, C.J. (1985) 'Facial Expression During Induced Pain', *Journal of Personality and Social Psychology* 48: 1,080–91.

Creider, C.A. (1972) 'Systems of Conversational Interaction: A Study of Three East African Tribes', Ph.D. thesis, University of Minnesota (cited by Kendon 1984).

Creider, C.A. (in press) 'Inter-Language Comparisons in the Study of the Interactional Use of Gesture', *Semiotica.*.

Crusco, A.H. and Wetzel, C.G. (1984) 'The Midas Touch: The Effects of Interpersonal Touch on Restaurant Tipping', *Personality and Social Psychology Bulletin* 10: 512–17.

Crystal, D. (1969) *Prosodic Systems and Intonation in English*, Cambridge: Cambridge University Press.

Cunningham, M. (1986) 'Measuring the Physical in Physical Attractiveness: Quasi-experiments on the Sociobiology of Female Facial Beauty', *Journal of Personality and Social Psychology* 50: 925–35.

Cunningham, M.R. (1977) 'Personality and the Structure of the Nonverbal Communication of Emotion', *Journal of Personality* 45: 564–84.

Dabbs, J.M. (1969) 'Similarity of Gestures and Interpersonal Influence', *Proceedings of the Annual Convention of the American Psychological Association* 4: 337–8.

Daly, J.A., Hogg, E., Sacks, D., Smith, M., and Zimring, L. (1983) 'Sex and Relationship Affect Social Self-Grooming', *Journal of Nonverbal Behavior* 7: 183–9.

Darby, J.K. (1981) 'Speech and Voice Studies in Psychiatric Populations'. In J.K. Darby (ed.) *Speech Evaluation in Psychiatry*, New York: Grune & Stratton.

Darwin, C. (1872) *Expression of the Emotions in Man and Animals*, London: Appleton; reprinted University of Chicago Press, 1965.

D'Auguelli, A.R. (1974) 'Nonverbal Behavior of Helpers in Initial Helping Interaction', *Journal of Counseling Psychology* 21: 360–3.

Davis, M. (1979) 'Laban Analysis of Nonverbal Communication'. In S. Weitz (ed.) *Nonverbal Communication*, 2nd edn, New York: Oxford University Press.

Davis, L. and Lennon, S.C. (1985) 'Self-Monitoring, Fashion Opinion Leadership and Attitudes Towards Clothing'. In M.R. Solomon (ed.) *The Psychology of Fashion*, Lexington: Heath.

Davis, M. and Weitz, S. (1978) 'Sex Differences in Nonverbal Communication: A Laban Analysis', cited in S. Weitz (ed.) (1979) *Nonverbal Communication*. New York: Oxford University Press.

Davitz, J.R. (1964) *The Communication of Emotional Meaning*, New York: McGraw Hill.

Dawkins, R. (1976) 'Hierarchical Organization: A Candidate Principle for Zoology'. In P.P.G. Bateson and R.A. Hinde (eds) *Growing Points in Ethology*, Cambridge: Cambridge University Press.

DeJong, W. (1980) 'The Stigma of Obesity: The Consequences of Naive Assumptions Concerning the Causes of Physical Deviance', *Journal of Health and Social Behavior* 21: 75–87.

De Jorio, A. (1832) *La Mimica degli Antichi Investigata nel Gestire Napoletano*, Naples: Associazione Napoletana.

Delgado, J.M.R. (1967) 'Aggression and Defense under Cerebral Radio Control'. In C.D. Clements and D.B. Lindsley (eds) 'Aggression and Defense, Neural Mechanisms and Social Patterns', *Brain Functions* 5: 171–93.

DePaulo, B.M. and Pfeifer, R.L. (1986) 'On-the-Job Experience and Skill at Detecting Deception', *Journal of Applied Social Psychology* 16: 249–67.

DePaulo, B.M., Rosenthal, R., Eisenstat, R., Rogers, P., and Finkelstein, S. (1978) 'Decoding Discrepant Nonverbal Cues', *Journal of Personality and Social Psychology* 36: 313–23.

De Paulo, B.M., and Rosenthal, R. (1979) 'Ambivalence, Discrepancy and Deception in Nonverbal Communication'. In Rosenthal (ed.) (1979) *Skill in Nonverbal Communication*, Cambridge, Mass.: Oelgeschlager, Gunn, & Hain.

Dermer, M. and Thiel, D.L. (1975) 'When Beauty may Fail', *Journal of Personality and Social Psychology* 31: 1,168–76.

Deutsch, F. (1947) 'Analysis of Postural Behavior', *Psychoanalytic Quarterly* 16: 195–213.

Dion, K., Berscheid, E., and Walster, E. (1972) 'What is Beautiful is Good', *Journal of Personality and Social Psychology* 24: 285–90.

Dittman, A.T. (1972) 'The Body Movement–Speech Rhythm Relationship as a Cue to Speech Encoding'. In A.W. Siegman and B. Pope (eds) *Studies in Dyadic Communication*, New York: Pergamon.

Dittman, A.T. and Llewellyn, L.G. (1968) 'The Phonemic Clause as a Unit of Speech Decoding', *Journal of Personality and Social Psychology* 6: 341–9.

Dolgin, K.G. and Azmitia, M. (1985) 'The Development of the Ability to Interpret Emotional Signals – What is and is not Known'. In G. Zivin (ed.) *The Development of Expressive Behavior*, Orlando: Academic Press.

Dosey, M. and Meisels, M. (1969) 'Personal Space and Self-Protection', *Journal of Personality and Social Psychology* 11: 93–7.

Doty, R.L. (1985) 'The Primates. III Humans'. In R.E. Brown and D.W. MacDonald (eds) *Social Odours in Mammals*, Oxford: Clarendon Press.

Duncan, S. (1972) 'Some Signals and Rules for Taking Speaking Turns in Conversations', *Journal of Personality and Social Psychology* 23: 283–92.

Duncan, S. and Fiske, D.W. (1977) *Face-to-Face Interaction: Research Methods and Theory*, Hillsdale, NJ: Erlbaum.

Duncan, S. and Niederehe, G. (1974) 'On Signalling that it's Your Turn to Speak', *Journal of Experimental Social Psychology* 10: 234–47.

Duncan, S.D. and Rosenthal, R. (1968) 'Vocal Emphasis in Experimenter's Instruction Reading as Unintended Determinant of Subjects' Responses', *Language and Speech* 11: 20–6.

Eakins, B.W. and Eakins, R.G. (1978) *Sex Differences in Human Communication*, Boston: Houghton Mifflin.

Edelman, R.J. and Hampson, S.E. (1979) 'Changes in Non-Verbal Behaviour during Embarrassment', *British Journal of Social and Clinical Psychology* 18: 385–90.

Efran, J.S. (1968) 'Looking for Approval: Effect on Visual Behavior of Approbation from Persons Differing in Importance', *Journal of Personality and Social Psychology* 10: 21–5.

Efran, M.G. (1974) 'The Effect of Physical Appearance on the Judgment of

Guilt, Interpersonal Attraction, and Severity of Recommended Punishment in a Simulated Jury Task', *Journal of Research in Personality* 8: 45–54.

Efron, D. (1941) *Gesture and Environment*, New York: King's Crown Press.

Eibl-Eibesfeldt, I. (1972) 'Similarities and Differences between Cultures in Expressive Movements'. In R.A. Hinde (ed.) *Non-verbal Communication*, Cambridge: Royal Society & Cambridge University Press.

Eibl-Eibesfeldt, I. (1975) *Ethology: The Biology of Behavior*, New York: Holt, Rinehart, & Winston.

Ekman, P. (1972) 'Universals and Cultural Differences in Facial Expressions of Emotion'. In J. Cole (ed.) *Nebraska Symposium on Motivation 1971* (vol. 19). Lincoln: University of Nebraska Press.

Ekman, P. (1973) 'Cross-Cultural Studies of Facial Expression'. In P. Ekman (ed.) *Darwin and Facial Expression: A Century of Research in Review*, New York: Academic Press.

Ekman, P. (1979) 'About Brows: Emotional and Conversational Signals'. In M. von Cranach, K. Foppa, W. Lepenies, and D. Ploog (eds) *Human Ethology*, Cambridge: Cambridge University Press.

Ekman, P. (1982) *Emotion in the Human Face*, 2nd edn, Cambridge: Cambridge University Press.

Ekman, P. (1985) *Telling Lies*, New York: Norton.

Ekman, P. and Friesen, W.V. (1976) *Pictures of Facial Affect*, Palo Alto: Consulting Psychologists Press.

Ekman, P. and Friesen, W.V. (1967) 'Head and Body Cues in the Judgment of Emotion: A Reformulation', *Perceptual and Motor Skills* 24: 711–24.

Ekman, P. and Friesen, W.V. (1968) 'Nonverbal Behaviour in Psychotherapy', *Research in Psychotherapy* 3: 179–216.

Ekman, P. and Friesen, W.V. (1969a) 'The Repertoire of Nonverbal Behavior: Categories, Origins, Usage, and Coding', *Semiotica* 1: 49–67.

Ekman, P. and Friesen, W.V. (1969b) 'Nonverbal Leakage and Clues to Deception', *Psychiatry* 32: 88–106.

Ekman, P. and Friesen, W.V. (1971) 'Constants across Cultures in the Face and Emotion', *Journal of Personality and Social Psychology* 17: 124–9.

Ekman, P. and Friesen, W.V. (1975) *Unmasking the Face*, Englewood Cliffs, NJ: Prentice-Hall.

Ekman, P. and Friesen, W.V. (1978) *Facial Affect Coding System (FACS): A Technique for the Measurement of Facial Action*, Palo Alto, Calif.: Psychologists Press.

Ekman, P. and Friesen, W.V. (1982) 'Felt, False, and Miserable Smiles', *Journal of Nonverbal Behavior* 6: 238–52.

Ekman, P., Friesen, W.V., and Ancoli, S. (1980) 'Facial Signs of Emotional Experience', *Journal of Personality and Social Psychology* 39: 1,125–34.

Ekman, P., Friesen, W.V., and Ellsworth, P.B. (1982) 'What are the Relative Contributions of Facial Behavior and Contextual Information to the Judgment of Emotion?'. In P. Ekman (ed.) *Emotion in the Human Face*, Cambridge: Cambridge University Press..

Ekman, P., Friesen, W.V., O'Sullivan, M., and Scherer, K. (1980) 'Relative Importance of Face, Body, and Speech in Judgments of Personality and Affect', *Journal of Personality and Social Psychology* 38: 270–7.

Ekman, P., Friesen, W.V., and Simons, R.C. (1985) 'Is the Startle Reaction an Emotion?', *Journal of Personality and Social Psychology* 49: 1,416–26.

Ekman, P., Friesen, W.V., and Tomkins, S.S. (1971) 'Facial Affect Scoring Technique: A First Validity Study', *Semiotica* 3: 37–58.

Ekman, P., Hager, J.C., and Friesen, W.F. (1981) 'The Symmetry of Emotional and Deliberate Facial Actions', *Psychophysiology* 18: 101–6.

Ekman, P. and Oster, H. (1979) 'Facial Expressions of Emotion', *Annual Review of Psychology* 30: 527–54.

Elliott, M. (1986) 'Children's and Adults' Reactions to Photographs Taken Before and After Facial Surgery, *Journal of Maxillo-facial Surgery* 14: 18–21.

Ellis, D.S. (1967) 'Speech and Social Status in America', *Social Forces* 45: 431–51.

Ellsworth, P.C., Carlsmith, J.M., and Henson, A. (1972) 'The Stare as a Stimulus to Flight in Human Subjects: A Series of Field Experiments', *Journal of Personality and Social Psychology* 21: 302–11.

Ellyson, S.L., Dovidio, J.F., and Corson, R.L. (1981) 'Visual Behavior Differences in Females as a Function of Self-Perceived Expertise', *Journal of Nonverbal Behavior* 5: 164–71.

Ellyson, S.L., Dovidio, J.F., Corson, R.L., and Fehr, B.J. (1981) 'Visual Behavior and Dominance in Women and Men'. In C. Mayo and N.M. Henley (eds) *Gender and Nonverbal Behavior*, New York: Springer-Verlag.

Ellyson, S.L., Dovidio, J.F., Corson, R.L., and Vinicur, D.L. (1980) 'Visual Dominance Behavior in Female Dyads: Situational and Personality Factors', *Social Psychology Quarterly* 43: 328–36.

Erickson, F. (1979) 'Talking Down: Some Cultural Sources of Miscommunication in Interracial Interviews'. In A. Wolfgang (ed.) *Nonverbal Behavior*, New York: Academic Press.

Erickson, M.K. and Sirgy, M.J. (1985) 'Achievement Motivation and Clothing Preference of White-Collar Working Women'. In M.R. Solomon (ed.) *The Psychology of Fashion*, Lexington: Heath.

Exline, R.V. (1963) 'Explorations in the Process of Person Perception: Visual Interaction in Relation to Competition, Sex and Need for Affiliation', *Journal of Personality* 31: 1–20.

Exline, R.V. (1971) 'Visual Interaction: The Glances of Power and Preference', *Nebraska Symposium on Motivation* 19: 163–206.

Exline, R.V. (1985) 'Multichannel Transmission of Nonverbal Behavior and the Perception of Powerful Men: the Presidential Debates of 1976'. In S.L. Ellyson and J.F. Dovidio (eds) *Power, Dominance, and Nonverbal Behavior*, New York: Springer-Verlag.

Exline, R.V., Gottheil, I., Paredes, A., and Winklemeier, D. (1968) 'Gaze Direction as a Factor in Judgment of Non-Verbal Expressions of Affect', *Proceedings of 76th Annual Conference of the APA* 3: 415–16.

Exline, R.V. and Winters, L.C. (1966) 'Affective Relations and Mutual Glances in Dyads'. In S.S. Tomkins and C. Izard (eds) *Affect, Cognition and Personality*, London: Tavistock.

Exline, R.V. and Yellin, A. (1969) 'Eye Contact as a Sign between Man and Monkey', *Proceedings 19th International Congress of Psychology*, London (abstract), published 1971.

Eysenck, H.J. (1976) *The Measurement of Personality*, Lancaster, MTP Press.

Fantz, R.L. (1961) 'The Origin of Form Perception', *Scientific American* 204: 66–72.

Farina, A., Burns, G.L., Austad, C., Bugglin, C., and Fischer, E.H. (1986) 'The Role of Physical Attractiveness in the Readjustment of Discharged Psychiatric Patients', *Journal of Abnormal Psychology* 95: 139–43.

Fast, J. (1970) *Body Language*, New York: M. Evans.

Fehr, B.J. and Exline, R.V. (in press) 'Social Visual Interaction: A Conceptual and Literature Review'. In A.W. Siegman and S. Feldstein (eds) *Nonverbal Communication and Behavior*, 2nd edn, New York: Halsted.

Feinman, S. (1985) 'Emotional Expression, Social Referencing, and Preparedness for Learning in Early Infancy – Mother knows Best, but Sometimes I know Better'. In G. Zivin (ed.) *The Development of Expressive Behavior*, Orlando: Academic Press.

Ferguson, N. (1977) 'Simultaneous Speech Interruptions and Dominance', *British Journal of Social and Clinical Psychology* 16: 295–302.

Fine, G.A., Stitt, J.L., and Finch, M. (1984) 'Couple Tie-Signs and Interpersonal Threat: A Field Experiment', *Social Psychology Quarterly* 47: 282–6.

Firth, R. (1970) 'Postures and Gestures of Respect'. In J. Pouillon and P. Marande (eds) *Echanges et Communications*, The Hague: Mouton.

Fisch, H.-U., Frey, S., and Hirsbrunner, H.-P. (1983) 'Analyzing Nonverbal Behavior in Depression', *Journal of Abnormal Psychology* 92: 307–18.

Fisher, J.D. and Byrne, D. (1975) 'Too Close for Comfort: Sex Differences in Response to Invasions of Personal Space', *Journal of Personality and Social Psychology* 32: 15–21.

Fisher, J.D., Rytting, M., and Heslin, R. (1975) 'Hands Touching Hands: Affective and Evaluative Effects of an Interpersonal Touch', *Sociometry* 39: 416–21.

Flanders, N.A. (1970) *Analyzing Teaching Behavior*, Reading, Mass.: Addison-Wesley.

Florez, C.A. and Goldman, M. (1982) 'Evaluation of Interpersonal Touch by the Sighted and Blind', *Journal of Social Psychology* 116: 229–34.

Foa, U.G. (1961) 'Convergences in the Structure of Interpersonal Behavior', *Psychological Review* 68: 341–53.

Foddy, M. (1978) 'Patterns of Gaze in Co-operative and Competitive Negotiation', *Human Relations* 31: 925–38.

Fonagy, I. (1971) 'Double Coding in Speech', *Semiotica* 3: 189–222.

Forbes, R.J. and Jackson, P.R. (1980) 'Non-verbal Behavior and the Outcome of Selection Interviews', *Journal of Occupational Psychology* 53: 65–72.

Forgas, J.P., O'Connor, K.V., and Morris, S.L. (1983) 'Smile and Punishment: The Effects of Facial Expression on Responsibility Attribution by Groups and Individuals', *Personality and Social Psychology Bulletin* 9: 587–96.

Forsyth, G.A., Kushner, R.I., and Forsyth, P.D. (1981) 'Human Facial Expression Judgment in a Conversational Context', *Journal of Nonverbal Behavior* 6: 115–30.

Forsythe, S.M., Drake, M.F., and Hogan, J.H. (1985) 'Influence of Clothing Attributes on the Perception of Personal Characteristics. In M.R. Solomon (ed.) (1985) *The Psychology of Fashion*, Lexington: Heath.

Fortes, M. (1966) 'Religious Promises and Logical Techniques in Divinatory Ritual'. In J.S. Huxley (ed.) *A Discussion of Ritualization of Behaviour in Animals and Men*, Philosophical Transactions of The Royal Society of London.

Frances, S.J. (1979) 'Sex Differences in Nonverbal Behavior', *Sex Roles* 5: 519–35.

Freedman, D.G. (1969) 'The Survival Value of the Beard', *Psychology Today* October: 36–9.

Freedman, N., Blass, T., Rifkin, A., and Quitkin, F. (1973) 'Body Movements and the Verbal Encoding of Aggressive Affect', *Journal of Personality and Social Psychology* 26: 72–85.

Freedman, N. and Hoffman, S.P. (1967) 'Kinetic Behavior in Altered Clinical States: Approach to Objective Analysis of Motor Behavior during Interviews', *Perceptual and Motor Skills* 24: 527–39.

Freedman, N., O'Hanlon, J., Oltman, P., and Witkin, H.A. (1972) 'The Imprint of Psychological Differentiation on Kinetic Behavior in Varying Communication Contexts', *Journal of Abnormal Psychology* 79: 239–58.

Freud, S. (1905) 'Fragments of an Analysis of a Case of Hysteria'. Reprinted in J. Strachey (ed.) (1953) *The Standard Edition of the Complete Psychological Works of Sigmund Freud*, vol. 7, London: Hogarth Press.

Frick, R.W. (1985) 'Communicating Emotion: The Role of Prosodic Features', *Psychological Bulletin* 97: 412–29.

Friedman, H.S. (1978) 'The Relative Strength of Verbal versus Non-Verbal Cues', *Personality and Social Psychology Bulletin* 4: 157–50.

Friedman, H.S. (1979) 'The Interactive Effects of Facial Expressions of Emotion and Verbal Messages on Perceptions of Affective Meaning', *Journal of Experimental Social Psychology* 15: 453–69.

Friedman, H.S. and DiMatteo, M.R. (1980) 'A Study of the Relationship between Individual Differences in Nonverbal Expressiveness and Factors of Personality and Social Interaction', *Journal of Research in Personality* 14: 351–64.

Friedman, H.S., Prince, L.M., Riggio, R.E., and DiMatteo, M.R. (1980) 'Understanding and Assessing Nonverbal Expressiveness: The Affective Communication Test', *Journal of Personality and Social Psychology* 39: 333–51.

Friesen, W.V. (1972) 'Cultural Differences in Facial Expression: An Experimental Test of the Concept of Display Rules', Ph. D. thesis, University of California, San Francisco.

Frijda, N.H. (1969) 'Recognition of Emotion', *Advances in Experimental Social Psychology* 4: 167–223.

Frijda, N.H. and Van der Geer, J.P. (1961) 'Codability and Recognition: An Experiment with Facial Expression', *Acta Psychologica* 18: 360–8.

Gale, A., Kingsley, E., Brookes, S., and Smith, D. (1978) 'Cortical Arousal and Social Intimacy in the Human Female under Different Conditions of Eye Contact', *Behavioural Processes* 3: 271–5.

Gardner, R.A. and Gardner, B.T. (1978) 'Comparative Psychology and Language Acquisition', *Annals of the New York Academy of Science* 309: 37–76.

Garratt, G.A., Baxter, J.C., and Rozelle, R.M. (1981) 'Training University Police in Black-American Nonverbal Behavior', *Journal of Social Psychology* 113: 217–29.

Gergen, K.J., Gergen, M.M., and Barton, W.H. (1973) 'Deviance in the Dark', *Psychology Today* May: 129–30.

Gibbins, K. (1969) 'Communication Aspects of Women's Clothing and their Relation to Fashionability', *British Journal of Social and Clinical Psychology*, 8: 301–12.

Gibbins, K. and Gwynn, T.K. (1975) 'A New Theory of Fashion Change: A Test of some Predictions', *British Journal of Social and Clinical Psychology* 14: 1–9.

Giles, H. and Powesland, P.F. (1975) *Speech Style and Social Evaluation*, London: Academic Press.

Gillis, J.S. and Avis, W.E. (1980) 'The Male-Taller Norm in Mate Selection', *Personality and Social Psychology Bulletin* 6: 396–401.

Ginsburg, H.J., Pollmen, V.A., and Wauson, M.S. (1977) 'An Ethological Analysis of Nonverbal Inhibitors of Aggressive Behaviour in Male Elementary School Children', *Developmental Psychology* 13: 417–18.

Gittin, S.R. (1970) 'A Dimensional Analysis of Manual Expression', *Journal of Personality and Social Psychology* 15: 271–7.

Goffman, E. (1956) *The Presentation of Self in Everyday Life*, Edinburgh: Edinburgh University Press.

Goffman, E. (1961) *Asylums*, Garden City, NY: Anchor Books.

Goffman, E. (1963) *Behaviour in Public Places*, Glencoe: The Free Press.

Goffman, E. (1971) *Relations in Public*, London: Allen Lane/Penguin Press.

Goldberg, S. and Lewis, M. (1969) 'Play Behavior in the Year-old Infant', *Child Development* 40: 21–31.

Goldberg, S. and Rosenthal, R. (1986) 'Self-Touching Behavior in the Job Interview: Antecedents and Consequences', *Journal of Nonverbal Behavior* 10: 65–80.

Goldman-Eisler, F. (1968) *Psycholinguistics: Experiments in Spontaneous Speech*, London: Academic Press.

Goodall, J. van Lawick (1968) 'The Behaviour of Free-Living Chimpanzees in the Gombe Stream Reserve', *Animal Behaviour Monographs* 1: 161–311.

Goodwin, C. (1981) *Conversational Organization: Interactions between Speaker and Hearers*, New York: Academic Press.

Gottman, J. (1979) *Marital Interaction*, New York: Academic Press.

Graham, J.A. and Argyle, M. (1975) 'A Cross-Cultural Study of the Communication of Extra-Verbal Meaning by Gestures', *International Journal of Psychology* 10: 56–67.

Graham, J.A. and Furnham, A. (1981) 'Sexual Differences in Attractiveness Ratings of Day/Night Cosmetic Use', *Cosmetic Technology* 3: 36–42.

Graham, J.A. and Heywood, S. (1976) 'The Effects of the Elimination of Hand Gestures and of Verbal Codability on Speech Performance', *European Journal of Social Psychology* 5: 189–95.

Graham, J.A. and Jouhar, A.J. (1980) 'Cosmetics Considered in the Context of Physical Attractiveness: A Review', *International Journal of Cosmetic Science* 2: 77–101.

Graham, J.A., Ricci Bitti, P., and Argyle, M. (1975) 'A Cross-Cultural Study of the Communication of Emotion by Facial and Gestural Cues', *Journal of Human Movement Studies* 1: 178–82.

Grand, S., Freedman, N., Steingart, I., and Buckwald, C. (1975) 'Communicative Behavior in Schizophrenia', *Journal of Nervous and Mental Disease* 161: 293–306.

Green, S. and Marler, P. (1979) 'The Analysis of Animal Communication'.

In P. Marler and J.G. Vandenbergh (eds) *Handbook of Behavioral Neurobiology*, vol. 3, New York and London: Plenum.

Green, W.P. and Giles, H. (1973) 'Reactions to a Stranger as a Function of Dress Style: The Tie', *Perceptual and Motor Skills* 37: 676.

Greenbaum, P.F. and Rosenfeld, H.M. (1980) 'Varieties of Touching in Greeting: Sequential Structure and Sex-Related Differences', *Journal of Nonverbal Behavior* 5: 13–25.

Griffit, W., May, J., and Veitch, R. (1974) 'Sexual Stimulation and Interpersonal Behavior: Heterosexual Evaluative Responses, Visual Behavior, and Physical Proximity', *Journal of Personality and Social Psychology* 30: 367–77.

Gumperz, J.J. (1978) 'The Conversational Analysis of Interethnic Communication'. In E.L. Ross (ed.) *Interethnic Communication*, Atlanta, Georgia: Proceedings of Southern Anthropological Society.

Guttentag, M. and Secord, P.F. (1983) *Too Many Women? The Sex Ratio Question*, Beverly Hills: Sage.

Guy, R.F., Rankin, B.A., and Norwell, M.J. (1980) 'The Relation of Sex Type Stereotyping to Body Image', *Journal of Psychology* 105: 167–73.

Hadar, U., Steiner, T.J., and Rose, F.C. (1985) 'Head Movement during Listening Turns in Conversation', *Journal of Nonverbal Behavior* 9: 214–28.

Hager, J.C. (1982) 'Asymmetries in Facial Expression'. In P. Ekman, *Emotion in the Human Face*, Cambridge: Cambridge University Press.

Hager, J.C. and Ekman, P. (1979) 'Long-Distance Transmission of Facial Affect Signals', *Ethology and Sociobiology* 1: 77–82.

Haggard, E.A. and Isaacs, F.S. (1966) 'Micromomentary Facial Expressions as Indicators of Ego Mechanisms in Psychotherapy'. In L.A. Gottschalk and A.A. Auerbach (eds) *Methods of Research in Psychotherapy*, New York: Appleton-Century-Crofts.

Haines, D.B. and Eachus, H.T. (1965) 'A Preliminary Study of Acquiring Cross-Cultural Interaction Skills Through Self-Confrontation', Aerospace Medical Research Laboratories, Wright-Patterson Air Force Base, Ohio.

Halberstadt, A.G. (1983) 'Family Expressiveness Styles and Nonverbal Communication Skills', *Journal of Nonverbal Behavior* 8: 14–26.

Halberstadt, A.G. (1985) 'Differences between Blacks and Whites in Nonverbal Communication'. In A.W. Siegman and S. Feldstein (eds) *Multichannel Integrations of Nonverbal Behavior*, New York: Erlbaum.

Hall, E.T. (1959) *The Silent Language*, Garden City, NY: Doubleday.

Hall, E.T. (1966) *The Hidden Dimension*, New York: Doubleday.

Hall, J.A. (1980) 'Voice Tone and Persuasion', *Journal of Personality and Social Psychology* 38: 924–34.

Hall, J.A. (1984) *Nonverbal Sex Differences*, Baltimore: Johns Hopkins University Press.

Hall, J.A. and Braunwald, K.G. (1981) 'Gender Cues in Conversations', *Journal of Personality and Social Psychology* 40: 99–110.

Hall, K.R.L. (1962) 'The Sexual, Agonistic and Derived Social Behaviour Patterns of the Wild Chacma Baboon, *Papio Ursinus*', *Proceedings of the Zoological Society of London* 139 (II): 283–327.

Hall, K.R.L. and DeVore, I. (1965) 'Baboon Social Behavior'. In I. DeVore (ed.) *Primate Behavior*, New York: Holt, Rinehart, & Winston.

Hallpike, C.R. (1969) 'Social Hair', *Man* 4: 256–64.

Hamid, P.N. (1968) 'Style of Dress as a Perceptual Cue in Impression Formation', *Perceptual and Motor Skills* 26: 904–6.

Hamid, P.N. (1969) 'Change in Person Perception as a Function of Dress', *Perceptual and Motor Skills* 29: 191–4.

Hamid, P.N. (1972) 'Some Effects of Dress Cues on Observational Accuracy: A Perceptual Estimate, and Impression Formation', *Journal of Social Psychology* 86: 279–89.

Hanna, J.L. (1984) 'Black/White Nonverbal Differences, Dance and Dissonance'. In A. Wolfgang (ed.) *Nonverbal Behavior*, Lewiston, NY: C.J. Hofgrefe.

Harlow, H.F. and Harlow, M.K. (1965) 'The Affectional Systems'. In A.M.Schrier, H.F. Harlow, and F. Stollnitz (eds) *Behavior of Nonhuman Primates*, New York and London: Academic Press.

Harms, L.S. (1961) 'Listener Judgments of Status Cues in Speech', *Quarterly Journal of Speech* 47: 164–8.

Harp, S.S., Stretch, S.M., and Harp, D.A. (1985) 'The Influence of Apparel on Responses to Television News Anchorwomen'. In M.R.Solomon (ed.) (1985) *The Psychology of Fashion*, Lexington: Heath.

Harper, R.G., Wiens, A.N., and Matarazzo, J.D. (1978) *Nonverbal Communication*, New York: Wiley.

Harré, R. (1979) *Social Being*, Oxford: Blackwell.

Harré, R., Clarke, D.D., and De Carlo, N. (1985) *Motives and Mechanisms*, London: Methuen.

Harrigan, J.A., Oxman, T.E., and Rosenthal, R. (1985) 'Rapport Expressed through Nonverbal Behavior', *Journal of Nonverbal Behavior* 9: 95–110.

Harrigan, J.A. and Steffen, J.J. (1983) 'Gaze as a Turn-Exchange Signal in Group Conversations', *British Journal of Social Psychology* 22: 167–8.

Harris, C.S., Thackray, R.I., and Schoenberger, R.W. (1966) 'Blink Rate as a Function of Induced Muscular Tension and Manifest Anxiety', *Perceptual and Motor Skills* 22: 155–60.

Harris, P.L., Olthof, T., and Terwogt, M.M. (1981) 'Children's Knowledge of Emotion', *Journal of Child Psychology and Psychiatry* 22: 247–61.

Hartnett, J.J., Bailey, K.G., and Gibson, F.W. (1970) 'Personal Space as Influenced by Sex and Type of Movement, *Journal of Psychology* 76: 139–44.

Hatfield, E. and Sprecher, S. (1986) *Mirror, Mirror, On the Wall*, Albany: State University of New York Press.

Hayduk, L.A. (1983) 'The Permeability of Personal Space', *Canadian Journal of Behavioural Science* 13: 274–87.

Hayduk, L.A. (1983) 'Personal Space: Where We Stand Now', *Psychological Bulletin* 94: 293–335.

Heeschen, V., Schiefenhovel, W., and Eibl-Eibesfeldt, I. (1980) 'Requesting, Giving, and Taking: The Relationship between Verbal and Nonverbal Behavior in the Speech Community of the Eipo, Irian Java (West New Guinea)'. In M.R. Key (ed.) *The Relationship of Verbal and Nonverbal Communication*, The Hague: Mouton.

Henley, M. (1973) 'Status and Sex: Some Touching Observations', *Bulletin Psychonomic Society* 2: 91–3.

Henley, N.M. (1977) *Body Politics*, Englewood Cliffs, NJ: Prentice-Hall.

Heritage, J. and Greatbatch, D. (1986) 'Generating Applause: A Study of Rhetoric and Response at Party Political Conferences', *American Journal of Sociology* 92: 110–57.

Heslin, R. and Alper, T. (1983) 'Touch: A Bonding Gesture'. In J.M. Wiemann and R.P. Harrison (eds) *Nonverbal Interaction*, Beverly Hills: Sage.

Heslin, R. and Boss, D. (1980) 'Nonverbal Intimacy in Airport Arrival and Departure', *Personality and Social Psychology Bulletin* 6: 248–52.

Hess, E.H. (1965) 'Attitude and Pupil Size', *Scientific American* 212 (4): 46–54.

Hess, E.H. (1972) 'Pupilometrics'. In N. Greenfield and R. Sternbach (eds) *Handbook of Psychophysiology*, New York: Holt, Rinehart, & Winston.

Hess, E.H. and Polt, J.M. (1960) 'Pupil Size as Related to Interest Value of Visual Stimuli', *Science* 132: 349–50.

Hewes, G. (1957) 'The Anthropology of Posture', *Scientific American* 196: 123–32.

Hewes, G. (1973) 'Primate Communication and the Gestural Origin of Language', *Current Anthropology* 14: 5–32.

Ho, R. and Mitchell, S. (1982) 'Students' Nonverbal Reactions to Tutors' Warm/Cold Nonverbal Behavior', *Journal of Social Psychology* 118: 121–30.

Hochschild, A.R. (1979) 'Emotion Work, Feeling Rules, and Social Structure', *American Journal of Sociology* 85: 551–75.

Hochschild, A.R. (1983) *The Managed Heart*, Berkeley, Calif.: University of California Press.

Horowitz, M.J., Duff, D.F., and Stratton, L.O. (1969) 'Body-Buffer Zones', *Archives of General Psychiatry* 11: 651–6.

Hoult, T.F. (1954) 'Experimental Measurement of Clothing as a Factor in some Social Ratings of Selected American Men', *American Sociological Review* 19: 324–8.

Huizinger, J. (1949) *Homo Ludens*, London: Paladin.

Hurlock, E.B. (1929) 'Motivation in Fashion', *Archives of Psychology* III.

Iliffe, A.H. (1960) 'A Study of Preferences in Feminine Beauty', *British Journal of Psychology* 51: 267–73.

Ingham, R.J. (1973) 'Cross-Cultural Differences in Social Behaviour', D. Phil. thesis, University of Oxford.

Ittelson, W., Proshansky, H.M., and Rivlin, L.G. (1970) 'The Environmental Psychology of the Psychiatric Ward'. In H.M. Proshansky, W.H. Ittelson, and L.G. Rivlin (eds) *Environmental Psychology*, New York: Holt, Rinehart, & Winston.

Izard, C.E. (1977) *Human Emotions*, New York: Plenum.

Izard, C.E. (1978) 'On the Development of Emotions and Emotion-Cognition Relationships in Infancy'. In M. Lewis and L.A. Rosenbaum (eds) *The Development of Affect*, New York: Plenum.

Izard, C.E. (1979) 'Facial Expression, Emotion and Motivation'. In A. Wolfgang (ed.) *Nonverbal Behavior*, New York: Academic Press.

Izard, C.E. (unpub.) 'The Biological and Social Functions of Facial Expressions: Darwin's Legacy to the Psychology of Emotions', University of Delaware.

Izard, C.E. and Dougherty, L.M. (1981) 'Two Complementary Systems for Measuring Facial Expressions in Infants and Children'. In C.E. Izard (ed.) *Measuring Emotions in Infants and Children*, Cambridge: Cambridge

University Press.

Izard, C.E., Walker, K.E., Cobb, C.A., and Meier, G.W. (unpub.) 'Prosocial and Agonistic Behavior in Rhesus Monkeys with Surgically Sectioned Facial Nerves', University of Delaware.

Jackson, D.N. (1974) *Personality Research Form Manual*, New York: Research Psychologists Press.

Jacobs, D.R. and Schucker, B. (1981) 'Type A Behavior Pattern, Speech, and Coronary Heart Disease'. In J.K. Darby (ed.) *Speech Evaluation in Medicine*, New York: Grune & Stratton.

James, W. (1884) 'What is an Emotion?', *Mind* 9: 188–205.

Jancovic, M., Devoe, S., and Wiener, M. (1975) 'Age-Related Changes in Hand and Arm Movements as Nonverbal Communication: Some Conceptualization and an Empirical Exploration', *Child Development* 46: 922–8.

Jecker, J.D., Maccoby, N., and Breitrose, H.S. (1965) 'Improving Accuracy in Interpreting Non-Verbal Cues of Comprehension', *Psychology in the Schools* 2: 239–44.

Jellison, J.M. and Ickes, W.J. (1974) 'The Power of the Glance: Desire to See and be Seen in Co-operative and Competitive Situations', *Journal of Experimental Social Psychology* 10: 444–50.

Johnson, H.G., Ekman, P., and Friesen, W.V. (1975) 'Communicative Body Movements: American Emblems', *Semiotica* 15: 335–53.

Joiner, J. (1976) 'Social Ritual and Architectural Space'. In H.M. Proshansky, W.H. Ittelson and L.G. Rivlin (eds) *Environmental Psychology*, 2nd edn, New York: Holt, Rinehart, & Winston.

Jones, E.E. (1969) *Ingratiation: A Social Psychological Analysis*, New York: Appleton-Century-Crofts.

Jones, S.E. and Yarborough, A.E. (1985) 'A Naturalistic Study of Meanings of Touch', *Communication Monographs* 52: 19–56.

Jourard, S.M. (1966) 'An Exploratory Study of Body-Accessibility', *British Journal of Social and Clinical Psychology* 5: 221–31.

Jourard, S.M. and Friedman, R. (1970) 'Experimenter-Subject "Distance" and Self-Disclosure', *Journal of Personality and Social Psychology* 15: 278–82.

Jourard, S.M. and Secord, P.F. (1955) 'Body-Cathexis and Personality', *British Journal of Psychology* 46: 130–8.

Kaiser, S.B. (1985) *The Social Psychology of Clothing and Personal Adornment*, London: Collier Macmillan.

Kaye, K. and Fogel, A. (1980) 'The Temporal Structure of Face-to-Face Communication between Mothers and Infants', *Developmental Psychology* 16: 454–64.

Keating, C.F . (1985) 'Gender and the Physiognomy of Dominance and Attractiveness', *Social Psychology Quarterly* 48: 61–70.

Keating, C.F., Mazur, A., Segall, M.H., Cysneiros, P.G., Divale, W.F., Kilbridge, J.E., Komin, S., Leahy, P., Thurman, B., and Wirsing, R. (1981) 'Culture and the Perception of Social Dominance from Facial Expression', *Journal of Personality and Social Psychology* 40: 615–26.

Keith, L.T., Tornatzky, L.G., and Pettigrew, L.E. (1974) 'An Analysis of Verbal and Nonverbal Classroom Teaching Behaviors', *Journal of Experimental Education* 42: 30–5.

Kemp, N.J. (1981) 'Social Psychological Aspects of Blindness: A Review', *Current Psychological Reviews* 1: 69–89.

Kendon, A. (1967) 'Some Functions of Gaze Direction in Social Interaction', *Acta Psychologica* 26: 22–63.

Kendon, A. (1970) 'Movement Co-ordination in Social Interaction: Some Examples Considered', *Acta Psychologica* 32: 1–25.

Kendon, A. (1972) 'Some Relationships between Body Motion and Speech: An Analysis of an Example'. In A.W. Siegman and B. Pope (eds) *Studies in Dyadic Communication*, New York: Pergamon.

Kendon, A. (1977) *Studies in the Behavior of Social Interaction*, Bloomington: University of Indiana Press.

Kendon, A. (1980) 'Sign Language of the Women of Yuendumu: A Preliminary Report on the Structure of Warlpiri Sign Language', *Sign Language Studies* 27: 101–13.

Kendon, A. (1981) 'A Geography of Gesture', *Semiotica* 37: 129–63.

Kendon, A. (1982) 'The Organization of Behavior in Face-to-Face Interaction: Observations on the Development of a Methodology'. In K.R. Scherer and P. Ekman (eds) *Handbook of Methods in Nonverbal Behavior Research*, Cambridge: Cambridge University Press.

Kendon, A. (1983) 'Gesture and Speech: How they Interact'. In J.M. Wiemann and R.P. Harrison (eds) *Nonverbal Interaction*, Beverly Hills: Sage.

Kendon, A. (1984) 'Did Gesture have the Happiness to Escape the Curse at the Confusion at Babel?'. In A. Wolfgang (ed.) *Nonverbal Behavior*, Lewiston, NY: C.J. Hofgrefe.

Kendon, A. and Cook, M. (1969) 'The Consistency of Gaze Patterns in Social Interaction', *British Journal of Psychology* 69: 481–94.

Kendon, A. and Ferber, A. (1973) 'A Description of some Human Greetings'. In R.P. Michael and J.H. Crook (eds) *Comparative Ethology and Behaviour of Primates*, London: Academic Press.

Kimura, D. (1976) 'The Neural Basis of Language *qua* Gesture'. In H. Whitaker and H.A. Whitaker (eds) *Studies in Neurolinguistics*, vol. 2, New York: Academic Press.

Kinzel, A.F. (1970) 'Body-Buffer Zones in Violent Prisoners', *American Journal of Psychiatry* 127: 59–64.

Kiritz, S.A. (1974) 'Hand Movements and Psychopathology' (cited by Harper, Wiens, and Matarazzo 1978).

Kleck, R. (1968) 'Physical Stigma and Non-verbal Cues Emitted in Face-to-Face Interaction', *Human Relations* 21: 19–28.

Kleck, R. (1969) 'Physical Stigma and Task Oriented Interaction', *Human Relations*, 22: 51-60.

Kleck, R.E. and Nuessle, W. (1968) 'Congruence between the Indicative and Communicative Functions of Eye-Contact in Interpersonal Relations', *British Journal of Social and Clinical Psychology* 7: 241–6.

Kleck, R.E. and Rubinstein, S. (1975) 'Physical Attractiveness, Perceived Attitude Similarity, and Interpersonal Attraction in an Opposite-Sex Encounter', *Journal of Personality and Social Psychology* 31: 107–14.

Klein, Z. (1984) 'Sitting Postures in Males and Females', *Semiotica* 48: 119–31.

Kleinke, C.L. (1977) 'Compliance to Requests made by Gazing and Touching Experimenters in Field Settings', *Journal of Experimental Social Psychology* 13: 218–23.

Kleinke, C.L. (1980) 'Interaction between Gaze and Legitimacy of Request on Compliance in a Field Setting', *Journal of Nonverbal Behavior* 5: 3–12.

Kleinke, C.L. (1986) 'Gaze and Eye contact: A Research Review', *Psychological Bulletin* 100: 78–100.

Kleinke, C.L., Bustos, A.A., Meeker, F.B., and Staneski, R.A. (1973) 'Effects of Self-Attributed Gaze in Interpersonal Evaluations between Males and Females', *Journal of Experimental Social Psychology* 9: 154–63.

Kleinke, C.L. and Staneski R.A. (1980) 'First Impressions of Female Bust Size', *Journal of Social Psychology* 110: 123–34.

Knapp, M.L. (1978) *Nonverbal Communication in Human Interaction*, 2nd edn, New York: Holt, Rinehart, & Winston.

Knapp, M.L., Hart, R.P., Friedrich, G.W., and Schulman, G.M. (1973) 'The Rhetoric of Goodbye: Verbal and Nonverbal Correlates of Human Leave-Taking', *Speech Monographs* 40: 182–98.

Knower, F.H. (1941) 'Analysis of some Experimental Variations of Simulated Vocal Expressions of the Emotions', *Journal of Social Psychology* 14: 369–72.

Knowles, E.S. (1973) 'Boundaries around Group Interaction: The Effect of Group Size and Member Status on Boundary Permeability', *Journal of Personality and Social Psychology* 26: 327–32.

Knowles, E.S. (1980) 'An Affiliative Conflict Theory of Personal and Group Spatial Behavior'. In P.B. Paulus (ed.) *Psychology of Group Influence*, Hillsdale, NJ: Erlbaum.

Krasner, L. (1958) 'Studies of the Conditioning of Verbal Behavior', *Psychological Review* 55: 148–70.

Kraus, S. (1985) 'The Studies and the World Outside'. In S. Kraus and R.M. Perloff (eds) *Mass Media and Political Thought*, Beverly Hills: Sage.

Krauss, R.M., Apple, W., Morency, N., Wenzel, C., and Winton, W. (1981) 'Verbal, Vocal, and Visible Factors in Judgments of Another's Affect', *Journal of Personality and Social Psychology* 40: 312–20.

Kraut, R.E. and Johnston, R.E. (1979) 'Social and Emotional Messages of Smiling: An Ethological Approach', *Journal of Personality and Social Psychology* 37: 1,539–53.

Kraut, R.E. and Poe, D. (1980) 'Behavioral Roots of Person Perception: The Deceptive Judgments of Customs Inspectors and Laymen', *Journal of Personality and Social Psychology* 39: 784–98.

Krebs, J.R. and Dawkins, R. (1979) 'Animal Signals: Mind-Reading and Manipulation'. In J.R. Krebs and N.B. Davies (eds) *Behavioural Ecology and Evolutionary Approaches*, 2nd edn, Oxford: Blackwell, 380–402.

Krout, M.H. (1942) *Introduction to Social Psychology*, New York: Harper & Row.

Krout, M.H. (1954) 'An Experimental Attempt to Produce Unconscious Manual Symbolic Movements', *Journal of General Psychology* 51: 93–152.

Kruger, K. and Huckstedt, B. (1969) 'Die Beurteilung der Blickrichtungen', *Zeitschrift fur Experimentalle Angewandt Psychologie* 16: 452–72.

Kudoh, T. and Matsumoto, D. (1985) 'Cross-Cultural Examination of the Semantic Dimensions of Body Postures', *Journal of Personality and Social Psychology* 48: 1,440–6.

Kummer, H. (1968) *Social Organization of Hamadryas Baboons*, Chicago: University of Chicago Press.

Kurtzberg, R.L., Safar, H., and Cavior, N. (1968) 'Surgical and Social Rehabilitation of Adult Offenders', *Proceedings of the 76th Annual Convention of the American Psychological Association* 3: 649–50.

Laban, R. (1975) *Principles of Dance and Movement Notation*, London: Macdonald & Evans.

Labov, W. (1966) *The Social Stratification of Speech in New York City*, Washington, DC: Center for Applied Linguistics.

Lack, D. (1939) 'The Behaviour of the Robin', *Proceedings of the Zoological Society of London* 109: 169–78.

LaFrance, M. (1979) 'Non-Verbal Synchrony and Rapport: An Analysis by the Cross-Lag Panel Technique', *Social Psychology Quarterly* 42: 66–70.

LaFrance, M. (1985) 'Postural Mirroring and Intergroup Relations', *Personality and Social Psychology Bulletin* 11: 207–17.

LaFrance, M. and Carmen, B. (1980) 'The Nonverbal Display of Psychological Androgeny', *Journal of Personality and Social Psychology* 38: 36–44.

LaFrance, M. and Ickes, W. (1981) 'Posture Mirroring and Interactional Involvement: Sex and Sex Typing Effects', *Journal of Nonverbal Behavior* 5: 139–54.

LaFrance, M. and Mayo, C. (1976) 'Racial Differences in Gaze Behavior during Conversations: Two Systematic Observational Studies', *Journal of Personality and Social Psychology* 33: 547–52.

LaFrance, M. and Mayo, C. (1978) *Moving Bodies: Nonverbal Communication in Social Relationships*, Monterey, Calif.: Brooks/Cole.

Laird, J.D. (1984) 'Facial Response and Emotion', *Journal of Personality and Social Psychology* 47: 909–37.

Lakoff, R. (1973) 'Language and Woman's Place', *Language in Society* 2: 45–80.

Lalljee, M.G. (1971) 'Disfluencies in Normal English Speech', D. Phil. thesis, University of Oxford.

Lalljee, M.G. (1978) 'The Role of Gaze in the Expression of Emotion', *Australian Journal of Psychology* 30: 59–67.

Lalljee, M.G. and Cook, M. (1973) 'Uncertainty in First Encounters', *Journal of Personality and Social Psychology* 26: 137–41.

Lambert, W.E., Hodgson, R.C., Gardner, R.C., and Fillenbaum, S. (1960) 'Evaluational Reactions to Spoken Languages', *Journal of Abnormal and Social Psychology* 60: 44–57.

Langer, S.K. (1942) *Philosophy in a New Key*, Cambridge, Massachusetts: Harvard University Press.

Lanzetta, J.T., Cartwright-Smith, J., and Kleck, R.E. (1976) 'Effects of Nonverbal Dissimulation on Emotional Experience and Autonomic Arousal', *Journal of Personality and Social Psychology* 33: 354–70.

Lanzetta, J.T. and Orr, S.P. (1986) 'Excitatory Strength of Expressive Faces: Effects of Happy and Fear Expressions and Context on the Extinction of a Conditioned Fear Response', *Journal of Personality and Social Psychology* 50: 190–4.

L'Armand, K. (1984) 'Preferences in Patterns of Eye Contact in India', *Journal of Social Psychology* 122: 137–8.

LaRusso, L. (1978) 'Sensitivity of Paranoid Patients to Nonverbal Cues', *Journal of Abnormal Psychology* 87: 463–71.

Lazarus, R.S., Averill, J.R., and Opton, E.M. (1970) 'Towards a Cognitive Theory of Emotion'. In M.B. Arnold (ed.) *Feelings and Emotions*, New York: Academic Press.

Leach, E. (1968) 'Ritual', *International Encyclopaedia of the Social Sciences* 13: 520–6.

Leach, E. (1972) 'The Influence of Cultural Context on Non-Verbal Communication in Man. In R. Hinde (ed.) *Non-verbal Communication*, Cambridge: Royal Society and Cambridge University Press.

Leathers, D.G. (1986) *Successful Nonverbal Communication*, London: Collier Macmillan.

Lee, T.R. (1976) *Psychology and the Environment*, London: Methuen.

Lefebvre, L. (1975) 'Bystanders' Evaluations of Different Sorts of Illicit and Attractive Ingratiation Overtures', *British Journal of Social and Clinical Psychology* 14: 33–42.

Leffler, A., Gillespie, D.L., and Conaty, J.C. (1982) 'The Effects of Status Differentiation on Nonverbal Behavior', *Social Psychology Quarterly* 45: 153–61.

Lefkowitz, M., Blake, R., and Mouton, J. (1955) 'Status Factors in Pedestrian Violation of Traffic Signals', *Journal of Abnormal and Social Psychology* 51: 704–6.

Leipold, W.E. (1963) 'Psychological Distance in a Dyadic Interview', Ph. D. thesis, University of North Dakota.

Leventhal, H. and Tomarken, A.J. (1986) 'Emotion: Today's Problems', *Annual Review of Psychology* 37: 565–610.

Levine, M.H. and Sutton-Smith, B. (1973) 'Effects of Age, Sex, and Task on Visual Behavior during Dyadic Interaction', *Development Psychology* 9: 400–5.

Lewinsohn, P.M. (1975) 'The Behavioral Study and Treatment of Depression'. In M. Herson, R.M. Eisler, and P.M. Miller (eds) *Progress in Behavior Modification* 1: 19–64.

Lieberman, M.A., Yalom, I.D., and Miles, M.B. (1973) *Encounter Groups: First Facts*, New York: Basic Books.

Lieberman, P. and Michaels, S.B. (1962) 'Some Aspects of Fundamental Frequency and Envelope Amplitudes as Related to the Emotional Content of Speech', *Journal of the Acoustical Society of America* 34: 922–7.

Lindenfeld, J. (1971) 'Verbal and Non-Verbal Elements in Discourse', *Semiotica* 3: 223–33.

Lippa, R. (1976) 'Expressive Control and the Leakage of Dispositional Introversion-Extraversion during Role-Played Teaching', *Journal of Personality* 44: 541–9.

Lippa, R. (1978) 'Expressive Control, Expressive Consistency, and the Correspondence between Expressive Behavior and Personality', *Journal of Personality* 46: 438–61.

Little, B.R. (1976) 'Specialization and the Varieties of Environmental Experience'. In S. Wapner (ed.) *Experiencing the Environment*, New York: Plenum.

Lomax, A. (1968) *Folk Song Style and Culture*, Washington, DC: American Association for the Advancement of Science.

Lorenz, K. (1952) *King Solomon's Ring*, London: Methuen.

Lott, D.F. and Sommer, R. (1967) 'Seating Arrangements and Status', *Journal of Personality and Social Psychology* 7: 90–5.

Lyons, J. (1972) 'Human Language'. In R.A. Hinde (ed.) *Non-Verbal Communication*, Cambridge: Cambridge University Press.

Lyons, J. (1973) 'Structuralism and Linguistics'. In D. Robey (ed.) *Structuralism*, London: Oxford University Press.

McAdams, D.P., Jackson R.J., and Kirschmit, C. (1984) 'Looking, Laughing and Smiling in Dyads as a Function of Intimacy, Motivation and Reciprocity', *Journal of Personality* 52: 261–73.

McAndrew, F.T. and Warner, J.E. (1986) 'Arousal Seeking and the Maintenance of Mutual Gaze in Same and Mixed Sex Dyads', *Journal of Abnormal Psychology* 89: 250–3.

Maccoby, E.E. and Martin, J.A. (1983) 'Socialization in the Context of the Family: Parent–Child Interaction'. In P.H. Mussen and E.M. Hetherington (eds) *Handbook of Child Psychology*, vol. 4, *Socialization, Personality and Social Development*, New York: Wiley.

McDowall, J.J. (1978) 'Interactional Synchrony: A Reappraisal', *Journal of Personality and Social Psychology* 36: 963–75.

McGrew, W.C. (1972) *An Ethological Study of Children's Behavior*, New York: Academic Press.

McHugo, G.J. (1985) 'Emotional Reactions to a Political Leader's Expressive Displays', *Journal of Personality and Social Psychology* 49: 1,513–29.

McKeachie, W.J. (1952) 'Lipstick as a Determiner of First Impressions of Personality: An Experiment for the General Psychology Course', *Journal of Social Psychology* 36: 241–4.

Mackey, W.C. (1976) 'Parameters of the Smile as a Social Signal', *Journal of Genetic Psychology* 129: 125–30.

McLeod, P.L. and Rosenthal, R. (1983) 'Micromomentary Movement and the Decoding of Face and Body Cues', *Journal of Nonverbal Behavior* 8: 83–90.

McNeill, D. (1985) 'So You Think Gestures Are Nonverbal?', *Psychological Review* 92: 350–71.

McNeill, D. and Levy, E. (1982) 'Conceptual Representations in Language Activity and Gesture'. In R.J. Jarvella and W. Klein (eds) *Speech, Place, and Action*, Chichester: Wiley.

McTear, M. (1985) *Children's Conversation*, Oxford: Blackwell.

Maguire, P. (1981) 'Doctor–Patient Skills'. In M. Argyle (ed.) *Social Skills and Health*, London: Methuen.

Mahl, G.E. (1968) 'Gestures and Body Movements in Interviews', *Research in Psychotherapy* 3: 295–346.

Major, B., Carrington, P.I., and Carnevale, P.J.D. (1984) 'Physical Attractiveness and Self-Esteem: Attributions for Praise from an Other-Sex Evaluator', *Personality and Social Psychology Bulletin* 10: 43–50.

Major, B. and Heslin, R. (1982) 'Perceptions of Same-Sex and Cross-Sex Touching: It's Better to Give than to Receive', *Journal of Nonverbal Behavior* 6: 148–62.

Malatesta, C.Z. (1981) 'Infant Emotion and the Vocal Affect Lexicon', *Motivation and Emotion* 5: 1–23.

Malatesta, C.Z. (1985) 'Developmental Course of Emotion Expression in the Human Infant'. In G. Zivin (ed.) *The Development of Expressive Behavior*, Orlando: Academic Press.

Mandal, M.K. (1986) 'Judgement of Facial Affect among Depressives and Schizophrenics', *British Journal of Clinical Psychology* 25: 87–92.

Marler, P. (1965) 'Communication in Monkeys and Apes'. In I. DeVore (ed.) *Primate Behavior*, New York: Holt, Rinehart, & Winston.

Marler, P. (1976) 'Social Organization, Communication and Graded Signals: The Chimpanzee and the Gorilla'. In P.P.G. Bateson and R.A. Hinde (eds) *Growing Points in Ethology*, Cambridge: Cambridge University Press.

Marsh, P., Rosser, E., and Harré, R. (1978) *The Rules of Disorder*, London: Routledge & Kegan Paul.

Maslow, A. and Mintz, N. (1956) 'Effects of Esthetic Surroundings I: Initial Effects of Three Esthetic Conditions upon Perceiving "Energy" and "Well Being" in Faces', *Journal of Psychology* 41: 247–54.

Mason, W.A. (1985) 'Experiential Influences on the Development of Expressive Behaviors in Rhesus Monkeys'. In G. Zivin (ed.) *The Development of Expressive Behavior*, Orlando: Academic Press.

Matarazzo, J.D., Wiens, A.-N., Saslow, G., and Allen, B.V. (1964) 'Interviewer Head Nodding and Interviewee Speech Durations', *Psychotherapy, Research, and Practice* 1: 54–63.

Mathes, E.W. and Kahn, A. (1975) 'Physical Attractiveness, Happiness, Neuroticism and Self-Esteem', *Journal of Personality* 90: 27–30.

Mathews, A.M., Bancroft, J.H.J., and Slater, P. (1972) 'The Principal Components of Sexual Preference', *British Journal of Social and Clinical Psychology* 11: 35–43.

Maxwell, G.M. and Cook, M.W. (1985) 'Postural Congruence and Judgements of Liking and Perceived Similarity', *New Zealand Journal of Psychology* 14: 20–6.

Maxwell, G.M., Cook, M.W., and Burr, R. (1985) 'The Encoding and Decoding of Liking from Behavioral Cues in both Auditory and Visual Channels', *Journal of Nonverbal Behavior* 9: 239–63.

Mead, M. (1928) *Coming of Age in Samoa*, New York: Morrow.

Mehrabian, A. (1968a) 'Inference of Attitudes from the Posture, Orientation and Distance of a Communicator', *Journal of Consulting and Clinical Psychology* 32: 296–308.

Mehrabian, A. (1968b) 'Relationship of Attitude to Seated Posture, Orientation and Distance', *Journal of Personality and Social Psychology* 10: 26–30.

Mehrabian, A. (1969) 'Significance of Posture and Position in the Communication of Attitude and Status Relationships', *Psychological Bulletin* 71: 359–72.

Mehrabian, A. (1972) *Nonverbal Communication*, Chicago and New York: Aldine-Atherton.

Mehrabian, A. and Friedman, S.L. (1986) 'An Analysis of Fidgeting and Associated Individual Differences', *Journal of Personality* 54: 406–29.

Mehrabian, A. and Williams, M. (1969) 'Nonverbal Concomitants of Perceived and Intended Persuasiveness', *Journal of Personality and Social Psychology* 13: 37–58.

Meltzer, L., Morris, W.N., and Hayes, D.P. (1971) 'Interruption Outcomes and Vocal Amplitude: Explorations in Social Psychophysics', *Journal of*

Personality and Social Psychology 18: 392–402.

Meltzoff, A.N. and Moore, M.K. (1977) 'Imitation of Facial and Manual Gestures by Human Neonates', *Developmental Psychology* 198: 75–8.

Messing, S.D. (1960) 'The Non-Verbal Language of the Ethiopian Toga', *Anthropos* 55: 558–60.

Milgram, S. (1974) *Obedience to Authority*, London: Tavistock.

Millenson, J.S. (1985) 'Psychosocial Strategies for Fashion Advertising'. In M.R. Solomon (ed.) (1985) *The Psychology of Fashion*, Lexington: Heath.

Miller, G.A., Galanter, E., and Pribram, K.H. (1960) *Plans and the Structure of Behavior*, New York: Holt.

Miller, N., Maruyama, G., Beaber, R.J., and Valone, K. (1976) 'Speed of Speech and Persuasion', *Journal of Personality and Social Psychology* 34: 615–24.

Miller, S. and Nardini, K.M. (1977) 'Individual Differences in the Perception of Crowding', *Journal of Nonverbal Behavior* 2: 3–13.

Mills, J. and Aronson, E. (1965) 'Opinion Change as a Function of the Communicator's Attractiveness and Desire to Influence', *Journal of Personality and Social Psychology* 1: 173–7.

Milmoe, S., Rosenthal, R., Blane, H.T., Chafetz, M.E., and Wolf, I. (1967) 'The Doctor's Voice: Postdictor of Successful Referral of Alcoholic Patients', *Journal of Abnormal Psychology* 72: 78–84.

Modigliani, A. (1971) 'Embarrassment, Face-Work and Eye-Contact: Testing a Theory of Embarrassment', *Journal of Personality and Social Psychology* 17: 15–24.

Molloy, J. (1975) *Dress for Success*, New York: Wyden.

Molloy, J. (1977) *The Woman's Dress for Success Book*, Chicago: Follet.

Montgomery, B.M. (1986) 'Playing at Love: Contents and Contexts of Flirtatious Communication', International Conference on Personal and Social Relationships, Herzlya.

Moos, R.A. (1969) 'Sources of Variance in Responses to Questionnaires and in Behavior', *Journal of Abnormal Psychology* 74: 405–12.

Morley, I.E. and Stephenson, G.M. (1969) 'Interpersonal and Interparty Exchange: A Laboratory Simulation of an Industrial Negotiation at the Plant Level', *British Journal of Psychology* 60: 543–5.

Morris, D. (1967) *The Naked Ape*, London: Cape.

Morris, D. (1971) *Intimate Behaviour*, London: Cape.

Morris, D. (1977) *Manwatching*, London: Cape.

Morris, D., Collett, P., Marsh, P., and O'Shaughnessy, M. (1979) *Gestures: Their Origins and Distribution*, London: Cape.

Morsbach, H. (1973) 'Aspects of Nonverbal Communication in Japan', *Journal of Nervous and Mental Disease* 157: 262–77.

Morse, S.J., Gruzen, J., and Reis, H. (1976) 'The Eye of the Beholder: A Neglected Variable in the Study of Physical Attractiveness?', *Journal of Personality* 44: 209–25.

Mueser, K.T., Grau, B.W., Sussman, S., and Rosen, A.J. (1984) 'You're only as Pretty as You Feel: Facial Expression as a Determinant of Physical Attractiveness', *Journal of Personality and Social Psychology* 46: 469–78.

Mulec, A. (1976) 'Assessment and Application of the Revised Speech Dialect Attitudinal Scale', *Communication Monographs* 43: 238–45.

Mulready, P.M. and Lamb, J.M. (1985) 'Cosmetics Therapy for Female Chemotherapy Patients'. In M.R. Solomon (ed.) (1985) *The Psychology of Fashion*, Lexington: Heath.

Munn, N.L. (1940) 'The Effect of Knowledge of the Situation upon Judgement of Emotion from Facial Expressions', *Journal of Abnormal and Social Psychology* 35: 324–38.

Murstein, B.I. (1972) 'Physical Attractiveness and Marital Choice', *Journal of Personality and Social Psychology* 22: 8–12.

Muzekari, L.H. and Bates, M.E. (1977) 'Judgment of Emotion among Chronic Schizophrenics', *Journal of Clinical Psychology* 33: 662–6.

Napoleon, T., Chassin, N., and Young, R.D. (1980) 'A Replication and Extension of "Physical Attractiveness and Mental Illness"', *Journal of Abnormal Psychology* 89: 250–3.

Newman, E.H. (1977) 'Resolution of Inconsistent Attitude Communications in Normal and Schizophrenic Subjects', *Journal of Abnormal Psychology* 86: 41–6.

Newman, R.C. and Pollack, D. (1973) 'Proxemics in Deviant Adolescents', *Journal of Consulting and Clinical Psychology* 40: 6–8.

Nguyen, M.L., Heslin, R., and Nguyen, T. (1975) 'The Meaning of Touch: Sex Differences', *Journal of Communication* 25: 92–103.

Nguyen, M.L., Heslin, R., and Nguyen, T. (1976) 'The Meaning of Touch: Sex and Marital Status Differences', *Representative Research in Social Psychology* 7: 13–18.

Nitobe, I. (1969) *Bushido: The Soul of Japan*, Tokyo: Tuttle.

Noesjirwan, J. (1978) 'A Rule-Based Analysis of Cultural Differences in Social Behaviour: Indonesia and Australia', *International Journal of Psychology* 13: 305–16.

Noesjirwan, J. (1981) (unpub.) 'The Place of Clothes in Social Life: A Symbolic Interactionist Perspective', Kuring-gai College of Further Education, Sydney.

Noller, P. (1984) *Nonverbal Communication and Marital Interaction*, Oxford: Pergamon.

Noller, P. (1986) 'Sex Differences in Nonverbal Communication: Advantage Lost or Supremacy Regained?', *Australian Journal of Psychology* 38: 23–32.

Nummenmaa, T. (1964) *The Language of the Face*, University of Jyvalskyla, Studies in Education, Psychology and Research, no. 9.

Osgood, C.E. (1966) 'Dimensionality of the Semantic Space for Communication via Facial Expression', *Scandinavian Journal of Psychology* 7: 1–30.

O'Sullivan, M., Ekman, P., Friesen, W., and Scherer, K. (1985) 'What You Say and How You Say It: The Contribution of Speech Content and Voice Quality to Judgements of Others', *Journal of Personality and Social Psychology* 48: 54–62.

Papousek, H. and Papousek, M. (1977) 'Mothering and the Cognitive Head-Start: Psychobiological Considerations'. In H.R. Schaffer (ed.) *Studies in Mother–Infant Interaction*, London: Academic Press.

Parnell, R.W. (1958) *Behaviour and Physique: An Introduction to Practical and Applied Somatometry*, London: Edward Arnold.

Passingham, R.E. (1982) *The Human Primate*, Oxford: W.H. Freeman.

Patrick, C., Craig, K., and Prkachin, K. (1986) 'Observer Judgments of Acute Pain: Facial Action Determinants', *Journal of Personality and Social Psychology* 50: 1,291–8.

Patterson, M.L. (1968) 'Spatial Factors in Social Interaction', *Human Relations* 21: 351–61.

Patterson, M.L. (1973) 'Compensation in Nonverbal Immediacy Behaviors: A Review', *Sociometry* 36: 237–52.

Patterson, M.L. (1976) 'An Arousal Model of Interpersonal Intimacy', *Psychological Review* 83: 235–45.

Patterson, M.L. (1983) *Nonverbal Behavior: A Functional Perspective*, New York: Springer.

Patterson, M.L. (1984) (ed.) 'Non-Verbal Intimacy and Exchange', *Journal of Nonverbal Behavior* 8: No. 4.

Patterson, M.L., Powell, J.L., and Lenihan, M.G. (1986) 'Touch, Compliance and Interpersonal Affect', *Journal of Nonverbal Behavior* 10: 41–50.

Patterson, M.L. and Sechrest, L.B. (1970) 'Interpersonal Distance and Impression Formation', *Journal of Personality* 38: 161–6.

Paulsell, S. and Goldman, M. (1984) 'The Effect of Touching Different Body Areas on Prosocial Behavior', *Journal of Social Psychology* 122: 269–73.

Pearce, W.B. and Conklin, F. (1971) 'Nonverbal Vocalic Communication and Perceptions of a Speaker', *Speech Monographs* 38: 235–41.

Peery, J.C. and Crane, P.M. (1980) 'Personal Space Regulation: Approach–Withdrawal – Approach Proxemic Behavior during Adult–Preschooler Interaction at Close Range', *Journal of Psychology* 106: 63–75.

Pellegrini, J. (1973) 'Impressions of the Male Personality as a Function of Beardedness', *Psychology* 10: 29–33.

Pike, K. (1967) *Language in Relation to a Unified Theory of Human Behavior*, The Hague: Mouton.

Pisano, M.D., Wall, S.M., and Foster, A. (1986) 'Perceptions of Nonreciprocal Touch in Romantic Relationships', *Journal of Nonverbal Behavior* 10: 29–40.

Polanyi, M. (1958) *Personal Knowledge*, London: Routledge & Kegan Paul.

Polhemus, T. (1973) 'Fashion, Anti-Fashion and the Body Image', *New Society* 11 October.

Polhemus, T. (1978) *Social Aspects of the Human Body*, Harmondsworth: Penguin.

Porter, E., Argyle, M., and Salter, V. (1970) 'What is Signalled by Proximity?', *Perceptual and Motor Skills* 30: 39–42.

Poyatos, F. (1983) *New Perspectives in Nonverbal Communication*, Oxford: Pergamon.

Purvis, J.A., Dabbs, J.M., and Hopper, C.H. (1984) 'The "Opener": Skilled User of Facial Expression and Speech Pattern', *Personality and Social Behavior Bulletin* 10: 61–6.

Quinn, R., Tabor, J., and Gordon, L. (1968) *The Decision to Discriminate*, Ann Arbor, Mich.: Survey Research Center.

Ramsey, S. (1984) 'Double Vision: Nonverbal Behavior East and West'. In A. Wolfgang (ed.) *Nonverbal Behavior*, Lewiston, NY: C.J. Hofgrefe.

Redican, W.K. (1982) 'An Evolutionary Perspective on Human Facial

References   337

Displays. In P. Ekman (ed.) *Emotion in the Human Face*, Cambridge, Cambridge University Press.

Rees, D., Williams, L., and Giles, H. (1974) 'Dress Style and Symbolic Meaning', *International Journal of Symbology* 5: 1–8.

Reis, H.T., Wheeler, L., Spiegel, N., Kernis, M.H., Nezlek, K.J., and Perri, M. (1982) 'Physical Attractiveness in Social Interaction: II. Why Does Appearance Affect Social Experience', *Journal of Personality and Social Psychology* 43: 979–96.

Reizenstein, R. (1983) 'The Schachter Theory of Emotion: Two Decades Later', *Psychological Bulletin* 94: 239–64.

Remland, M.S. (1984) 'Leadership Impressions and Nonverbal Communication in a Superior–Subordinate Interaction', *Communication Quarterly* 32: 41–8.

Richardson, E. (1967) *The Environment of Learning*, London: Nelson.

Richardson, J. and Kroeber, A.L. (1940) 'Three Centuries of Women's Dress Fashions: A Quantitative Analysis', *Anthropological Records* 5: 111–53.

Ridgeway, C.L., Berger, J., and Smith, L. (1985) 'Nonverbal Cues and Status: An Expectation States Approach', *American Journal of Sociology* 90: 955–78.

Riggio, R.E. and Friedman, H.S. (1982) 'The Interrelationships of Self-Monitoring Factors, Personality Traits, and Nonverbal Social Skills', *Journal of Nonverbal Behavior* 7: 33–45.

Riggio, R.E. and Friedman, H.S. (1983) 'Individual Differences and Cues to Deception', *Journal of Personality and Social Psychology* 45: 899–915.

Riggio, R.E. and Friedman, H.S. (1986) 'Impression Formation: The Role of Expressive Behavior', *Journal of Personality and Social Psychology* 50: 421–7.

Riggio, R.E., Widaman, K.F., and Friedman, H.S. (1985) 'Actual and Perceived Emotional Sending and Personality Correlates', *Journal of Nonverbal Behavior* 9: 69–83.

Rimé, B., Schiaratura, L., Hupet, M., and Ghysselinckx, A. (1984) 'Effects of Relative Immobilization on the Speaker's Nonverbal Behavior and on the Dialogue Imagery', *Motivation and Emotion* 8: 311–25.

Rinn, W.E. (1984) 'The Neuropsychology of Facial Expression: A Review of the Neurological and Psychological Mechanisms for Producing Facial Expressions', *Psychological Bulletin* 95: 52–77.

Riseborough, M.G. (1981) 'Physiographic Gestures as Decoding Facilitators: Three Experiments Exploring a Neglected Facet of Communication', *Journal of Nonverbal Behavior* 5: 172–83.

Riskind, J.H. and Gotay, C.C. (1982) 'Physical Posture: Could it Have Regulating or Feedback Effects on Motivation and Emotion?', *Motivation and Emotion* 6: 273–98.

Roach, M.E. and Eicher, J.B. (eds) (1965) *Dress, Adornment, and the Social Order*, New York: Wiley.

Robbins, O., Devoe, S., and Wiener, M. (1978) 'Social Patterns of Turn-taking: Nonverbal Regulators', *Journal of Communication* 28: 38–46.

Roberts, K. (1983) *Leisure*, 2nd edn, London: Longman.

Robinson, D.A. (1968) 'The Oculomotor Control System: A Review', *Proceedings of the Institute of Electric & Electronic Engineers* 56: 1,032–49.

Robson, K.S. (1967) 'The Role of Eye-to-Eye Contact in Maternal–Infant Attachment', *Journal of Child Psychology and Psychiatry* 8: 13–25.

Rohwer, S. (1977) 'Status Signalling in Harris's Sparrows: Some Experiments in Deception', *Behaviour*, 61: 107–29.

Rook, D.W. (1985) 'Body Cathexis and Market Segmentation'. In M.R. Solomon (ed.) (1985) *The Psychology of Fashion*, Lexington: Heath.

Rosa, E. and Mazur, A. (1979) 'Incipient Status in Small Groups', *Social Forces* 58: 18–37.

Rosenberg, G.B. and Langer, J. (1965) 'A Study of Postural–Gestural Communication', *Journal of Personality and Social Psychology* 2: 593–7.

Rosenfeld, H.M. (1966) 'Approval-Seeking and Approval-Inducing Functions of Verbal and Nonverbal Responses', *Journal of Personality and Social Psychology* 4: 597–605.

Rosenfeld, H.M. (1967) 'Non-verbal Reciprocation of Approval: An Experimental Analysis', *Journal of Personality and Social Psychology* 3: 102–11.

Rosenfeld, H.M. (1978) 'Conversational Control Functions of Nonverbal Behavior'. In A.W. Siegman and B. Pope (eds) *Nonverbal Behavior and Communication*, Hillsdale, NJ: Erlbaum.

Rosenfeld, H.M. (1982) 'Measurement of Body Motion and Orientation'. In K.R. Scherer and P. Ekman (eds) *Handbook of Methods in Nonverbal Behavior Research*, Cambridge: Cambridge University Press.

Rosenfeld, H.M. and Hancks, M. (1980) 'The Nonverbal Context of Verbal Listener Responses'. In M.R. Key (ed.) *The Relationship of Verbal and Nonverbal Communication*, The Hague: Mouton.

Rosenfeld, L.B. and Plax, T.G. (1977) 'Clothing as Communication', *Journal of Communication* 27: 24–31.

Rosenhan, D. and Messick, S. (1966) 'Affect and Expectation', *Journal of Personality and Social Psychology* 3: 38–44.

Rosenthal, R. (1966) *Experimenter Effects in Behavioral Research*, New York: Appleton-Century-Crofts.

Rosenthal, R. (ed.) (1979) *Skill in Nonverbal Communication: Individual Differences*, Cambridge, Mass.: Oelgeschlager, Gunn, & Hain.

Rosenthal, R. and DePaulo, B. (1979) 'Sex Differences in Eavesdropping on Nonverbal Cues', *Journal of Personality and Social Psychology* 37: 273–85.

Rosenthal, R., Hall, J.A., DiMatteo, M.R., Rogers, P.L., and Archer, D. (1979) *Sensitivity to Nonverbal Communication: The PONS Test*, Baltimore: Johns Hopkins University Press.

Rosenthal, R. and Jacobson, L. (1968) *Pygmalion in the Classroom*, New York: Rinehart & Winston.

Rowell, T. (1972) *The Social Behaviour of Monkeys*, Harmondsworth: Penguin.

Rubenstein, L. (1969) 'Facial Expressions: An Objective Method in the Quantitative Evaluation of Emotional Change', *Behavior Research Methods and Instruments* 1: 305–6.

Rubin, Z. (1970) 'Measurement of Romantic Love', *Journal of Personality and Social Psychology* 16: 265–73.

Rumsey, N., Bull, R., and Gahagan, D. (1982) 'The Effect of Facial Disfigurement on the Proxemic Behavior of the General Public', *Journal of Applied Social Psychology* 12: 137–50.

Russell, J.C., Firestone, L.J., and Baron, R.M. (1980) 'Seating Arrangement and Social Influence: Moderated by Reinforcement Meaning and Internal–External Control', *Social Psychology Quarterly* 43: 103–9.

Rutter, D.R. (1976) 'Visual Interaction in Recently Admitted and Chronic Long-Stay Schizophrenic Patients', *British Journal of Social and Clinical Psychology* 15: 295–303.

Rutter, D.R. (1977a) 'Speech Patterning in Recently Admitted and Chronic Long-Stay Schizophrenic Patients', *British Journal of Social and Clinical Psychology* 16: 47–55.

Rutter, D.R. (1977b) 'Visual Interaction and Speech Patterning in Remitted and Acute Schizophrenic Patients', *British Journal of Social and Clinical Psychology* 16: 357–61.

Rutter, D.R. (in press) *Communicating by Telephone*, Oxford: Pergamon.

Rutter, D.R. and Stephenson, G.M. (1972) 'Visual Interaction in a Group of Schizophrenic and Depressive Patients', *British Journal of Social and Clinical Psychology* 11: 57–65.

Rutter, D.R. and Stephenson, G.M. (1977) 'The Role of Visual Communication in Synchronizing Conversation', *European Journal of Social Psychology* 7: 29–37.

Rutter, D.R. and Stephenson, G.M. (1979) 'The Functions of Looking: Effects of Friendship on Gaze', *British Journal of Social and Clinical Psychology* 11: 57–65.

Rutter, D.R., Stephenson, G.M., Ayling, K., and White, P.A. (1978) 'The Timing of Looks in Dyadic Communication', *British Journal of Social and Clinical Psychology* 17: 17–21.

Saarni, C. (1979) 'Children's Understanding of Display Rules for Expressive Behavior', *Developmental Psychology* 15: 424–9.

Sackett, G.P. (1966) 'Monkeys Reared in Isolation with Pictures as Visual Input: Evidence for an Innate Releasing Mechanism', *Science* 154: 1,468–73.

Sacks, H., Schegloff, E.A., and Jefferson, G. (1974) 'A Simplest Systematics for the Organization of Turn-Taking for Conversation', *Language* 50: 696–735.

Safer, M.A. (1981) 'Sex and Hemisphere Differences in Access to Codes for Processing Emotional Expressions and Faces', *Journal of Experimental Psychology: General* 110: 86–100.

Saigh, P.A. (1981) 'Effects of Nonverbal Examiner Praise on Selected WAIS Subtest Performance of Lebanese Undergraduates', *Journal of Nonverbal Behavior* 6: 84–6.

Saitz, R.L. and Cervenka, E.J. (1972) *Handbook of Gestures: Colombia and the United States*. In T.A. Sebeok (ed.) *Approaches to Semiotics*, The Hague: Mouton.

Sarbin, T.R. and Hardyck, C.D. (1953) (unpub.) 'Contributions to Role-Taking Theory: Role Perception on the Basis of Postural Cues', University of California, Berkeley.

Sargant, W. (1957) *Battle for the Mind*, London: Heinemann.

Scaife, M. (1974) 'The Responses of Animals to Eyes and Eyelike Patterns', D. Phil. thesis, University of Oxford.

Scaife, M. and Bruner, J.A. (1975) 'The Capacity for Joint Visual Attention in the Infant', *Nature* 253: 265–6.

Schachter, S. (1964) 'The Interaction of Cognitive and Physiological Determinants of Emotional State', *Advances in Experimental Social Psychology* 1:
49–80.

Schaffer, H.R. (1971) *The Growth of Sociability*, Harmondsworth: Penguin.

Schaffer, H.R. (1984) *The Child's Entry into a Social World*, London: Academic
Press.

Schaffer, H.R., Collis, G.M., and Parsons, G. (1977) 'Vocal Interchange and
Visual Regard in Verbal and Preverbal Children'. In H.R. Schaffer (ed.)
Studies in Mother–Child Interaction, London: Academic Press.

Schaffer, H.R. and Emerson, P.E. (1964) 'Patterns of Response to Physical
Contact in Early Human Development', *Journal of Child Psychology and
Psychiatry* 5: 1–13.

Scheflen, A.E. (1964) 'The Significance of Posture in Communication Systems', *Psychiatry* 27: 316–31.

Scheflen, A.E. (1965) 'Quasi-Courtship Behavior in Psychotherapy', *Psychiatry* 28: 245–57.

Scheflen, A.E. (1973) *Communicational Structure: Analysis of a Psychotherapy
Transaction*, Bloomington: Indiana University Press.

Scheflen, A.E. and Scheflen, A. (1972) *Body Language and the Social Order*
Englewood Cliffs, NJ: Prentice-Hall.

Scherer, K.R. (1978) 'Inference Rules in Personality Attribution from Voice
Quality: The Loud Voice of Extraversion', *European Journal of Social Psychology* 8: 467–87.

Scherer, K.R. (1979a) 'Personality Markers in Speech'. In K.R. Scherer and
H. Giles (eds) *Social Markers in Speech*, Cambridge: Cambridge University
Press.

Scherer, K.R. (1979b) 'Voice and Speech Correlates of Perceived Social
Influence in Simulated Juries'. In H. Giles and R.N. St Clair (eds) *Language and Social Psychology*, Oxford: Blackwell.

Scherer, K.R. (1981) 'Speech and Emotional States'. In J.K. Darby (ed.)
Speech Evaluation in Psychiatry, New York: Grune & Stratton.

Scherer, K.R. (1982) 'Parameters of Research on Vocal Communication:
Paradigms and Parameters'. In K.R. Scherer and P. Ekman (eds) *Handbook
of Research Methods in Nonverbal Communication Research*, Cambridge:
Cambridge University Press.

Scherer, K.R. (1986) 'Vocal Affect Expression: A Review and Model for
Further Research', *Psychological Bulletin* 99: 143–65.

Scherer, K.R. and Ekman, P. (1982) 'Methodological Issues in Studying
Nonverbal Behavior'. In K.R. Scherer and P. Ekman (eds) *Handbook of
Methods in Nonverbal Behavior Research*, Cambridge: Cambridge Univer-
sity Press.

Scherer, K.R. and Oshinsky, J.S. (1977) 'Cue Utilization in Emotion Attribution from Auditory Stimuli', *Motivation and Emotion* 1: 331–46.

Schiffrin, D. (1974) 'Handwork as Ceremony: The Case of the Handshake',
Semiotica 12: 189–202.

Schleidt, M., Hold, B., and Attili, G. (1981) 'Cross-Cultural Study on the
Attitude Towards Personal Odours', *Journal of Chemical Ecology* 7: 19–31.

Schutz, W.C. (1958) *FIRO: A Three-Dimensional Theory of Interpersonal Behavior*, New York: Holt, Rinehart, & Winston.

Schutz, W.C. (1967) *Joy*, New York: Grove Press.

Schutzenberger, A.A. and Geffroy, Y. (1979) 'The Body and the Group: The New Body Therapies'. In S. Weitz (ed.) *Nonverbal Communication*, 2nd edn, New York: Oxford University Press.

Schwartz, B., Tesser, A., and Powell, E. (1982) 'Dominance Cues in Nonverbal Behavior', *Social Psychology Quarterly* 45: 114–20.

Schwartz, G.E., Fair, P.L., Salt, P., Mandel, M.R., and Kleiman, G.L. (1976) 'Facial Expression and Imagery in Depression: An Electromyographic Study', *Psychosomatic Medicine* 38: 337–47.

Schwartz, L.M., Foa, U.G., and Foa, E.B. (1983) 'Multichannel Nonverbal Communication: Evidence for Combinatory Rules', *Journal of Personality and Social Psychology* 45: 274–81.

Seaford, H.W. (1978) 'Maximizing Replicability in Describing Facial Behavior', *Semiotica* 24: 1–32.

Secord, P.F., Dukes, W.F., and Bevan, W. (1959) 'Personalities in Faces. I: An Experiment in Social Perceiving', *Genetic Psychology Monographs* 49: 231–79.

Secord, P.F. and Muthard, J.E. (1955) 'Personalities in Faces: A Descriptive Analysis of the Perception of Women's Faces and the Identification of some Physiognomic Determinants', *Journal of Psychology* 39: 269–78.

Sereno, K.K. and Hawkins, G.J. (1967) 'The Effect of Variations in Speakers' Nonfluency, upon Audience Ratings of Attitude toward the Speech Topic and Speakers' Credibility', *Speech Monographs* 34: 58–64.

Shaw, W. (1986) 'Effect of Teeth on Attractiveness in Children', paper at Grange-over-Sands Conference on *The Face*.

Shea, M. and Rosenfeld, H.M. (1976) 'Functional Employment of Nonverbal Social Reinforcers in Dyadic Learning', *Journal of Personality and Social Psychology* 34: 228–39.

Sheldon, W.H., Dupertuis, C.V., and McDermott, E. (1954) *Atlas of Men: A Guide for Somatotyping the Adult Male of all Ages*, New York: Harper & Row.

Shimoda, K., Argyle, M., and Ricci Bitti, P. (1978) 'The Intercultural Recognition of Emotional Expression by their National Groups', *European Journal of Social Psychology* 8: 169–79.

Short, J., Williams, E., and Christie, B. (1976) *The Social Psychology of Telecommunications*, London: Wiley.

Shuter, R. (1976) 'Proxemics and Tactility in Latin America', *Journal of Communication* 26: 46–52.

Shuter, R. (1979) 'Gaze Behavior in Interracial and Intraracial Interaction', *International and Intercultural Communication Annual* 5: 48–55.

Sidney, E. and Argyle, M. (1969) *Training in Selection Interviewing*, London: Mantra.

Siegel, J.C. (1980) 'Effects of Objective Evidence of Expertness, Nonverbal Behavior, and Subject Sex on Client-Perceived Expertness', *Journal of Counseling Psychology* 27: 188–92.

Siegman, A.W. (1978) 'The Tell Tale Voice: Nonverbal Messages of Verbal Communication'. In A.W. Siegman and S. Feldstein (eds) *Nonverbal Behavior and Communication*, New York: Erlbaum.

Siegman, A.W. (1985) 'Anxiety and Speech Disfluencies'. In A.W. Siegman and S. Feldstein (eds) *Multichannel Integrations of Nonverbal Behaviour*, New York: Erlbaum.

Siegman, A.W. and Feldstein, S. (1979) *Of Speech and Time*, Hillsdale, NJ: Erlbaum.

Simmel, G. (1904) 'Fashion', *International Quarterly* 1: 130–55.

Simmel, G. (1921) 'Sociology of the Senses: Visual Interaction'. In R.E. Park and E.W. Burgess (eds) *Introduction to the Science of Sociology*, Chicago: University of Chicago Press.

Singer, J.E. (1964) 'The Use of Manipulation Strategies: Machiavellianism and Attractiveness', *Sociometry* 27: 138–50.

Sissons, M. (1971) 'The Psychology of Social Class'. In *Money, Wealth and Class*, Milton Keynes: Open University Press.

Skolnick, P., Frasier, L., and Hadar, I. (1977) 'Do You Speak to Strangers? A Study of Invasions of Personal Space', *European Journal of Social Psychology* 7: 375–81.

Slugoski, B.R. (1985) 'Grice's Theory of Conversation as a Social Psychological Model', D. Phil. thesis, University of Oxford.

Smith, D.E., Gier, J.A., and Willis, F.N. (1982) 'Interpersonal Touch and Compliance with a Marketing Request', *Basic and Applied Social Psychology* 3: 35–8.

Smith, D.E., Willis, F.N., and Gier, J.A. (1980) 'Success and Interpersonal Touch in a Competitive Setting', *Journal of Nonverbal Behavior* 5: 26–34.

Smith, P.M. (1979) 'Sex Markers in Speech'. In K.R. Scherer and H. Giles (eds) *Social Markers in Speech*, Cambridge: Cambridge University Press.

Snow, C.E. (1977) 'The Development of Conversation between Mothers and Babies', *Journal of Child Language* 4: 1–22.

Snyder, C.R. and Fromkin, H.L. (1980) *Uniqueness: The Human Pursuit of Difference*, New York: Plenum.

Snyder, M. (1979) 'Self-Monitoring Processes', *Advances in Experimental Social Psychology* 12: 85–128.

Snyder, M., Grether, J., and Keller, C. (1974) 'Staring and Compliance: A Field Experiment on Hitchhiking', *Journal of Applied Social Psychology* 4: 165–70.

Solomon, M.R. (ed.) (1985) *The Psychology of Fashion*, Lexington: Heath.

Solomon, M.R. and Schopler, J. (1982) 'Self-Consciousness and Clothing', *Personality and Social Psychology Bulletin* 8: 508–14.

Sommer, R. (1969) *Personal Space*, Englewood Cliffs, NJ: Prentice-Hall.

Sommer, R. and Becker, F.D. (1969) 'Territorial Defense and the Good Neighbor', *Journal of Personality and Social Psychology* 11: 85–92.

Sousa-Poza, J.F. and Rohrberg, R. (1977) 'Body Movement in Relation to the Type of Information (Person- and Non-Person-Oriented) and Cognitive Style (Field Dependence)', *Human Communication Research* 4: 19–29.

Sparhawk, C.M. (1978) 'Contrastive-Identification Features of Persian Gesture', *Semiotica* 24: 49–86.

Spiegel, J. and Machotka, P. (1974) *Messages of the Body*, London: Collier Macmillan.

Spignesi, A. and Shor, R.E. (1981) 'The Judgment of Emotion from Facial Expressions, Contexts, and their Combination', *Journal of General*

Psychology 104: 41–58.

Spitz, R.A. and Wolf, K.M. (1946) 'The Smiling Response: A Contribution to the Ontogenesis of Social Relationships', *Genetic Psychology Monographs* 34: 57–125.

Stammers, R.F., Byrd, D.M., and Gabriel, R. (1985) 'The Time It Takes to Identify Facial Expressions: Effects of Age, Gender of Subject, Sex of Sender, and Type of Expression', *Journal of Nonverbal Behavior* 9: 201–13.

Stass, J.W. and Willis, F.N., Jr (1967) 'Eye Contact, Pupil Dilation, and Personal Preferences', *Psychonomic Science* 7: 375–6.

Steckler, N.A. and Rosenthal, R. (1985) 'Sex Differences in Nonverbal and Verbal Communication with Bosses, Peers and Subordinates', *Journal of Applied Psychology* 70: 157–63.

Steinzor, B. (1950) 'The Spatial Factor in Face-to-Face Discussion Groups', *Journal of Abnormal and Social Psychology* 45: 552–5.

Stern, D. (1974) 'Mother and Infant at Play: The Dyadic Interaction Involving Facial, Vocal and Gaze Behaviors'. In M. Lewis and L.A. Rosenblum (eds) *The Origins of Behavior*, vol. 1, *The Effects of the Infant on its Caregiver*, New York: Wiley.

Stern, D. (1977) *The First Relationship*, London: Open Books.

Stier, D.S. and Hall, J.A. (1984) 'Gender Differences in Touch: An Empirical and Theoretical Review', *Journal of Personality and Social Psychology* 47: 440–59.

Stone, G.P. (1970) 'Appearance and the Self'. In G.P. Stone and H.A. Farberman (eds) *Social Psychology through Symbolic Interaction*, Waltham, Mass.: Ginn-Blaisdell.

Straub, R.R. and Roberts, D.M. (1983) 'Effects of Nonverbal Oriented Social Awareness Training Program on Social Interaction Ability of Learning Disabled Children', *Journal of Nonverbal Behavior* 7: 195–201.

Stringer, P. and May, P. (1981) 'Attributional Asymmetries in the Perception of Moving, Static, Chimeric and Hemisected Faces, *Journal of Nonverbal Behavior* 5: 238–52.

Strodtbeck, F.L. and Hook, L.H. (1961) 'The Social Dimension of a Twelve-Man Jury Table', *Sociometry* 24: 397–415.

Strongman, K.T. and Champness, B.G. (1968) 'Dominance Hierarchies and Conflict in Eye Contact', *Acta Psychologica* 28: 376–86.

Strube, M.J., Turner, C.W., Cerro, D., Stevens, J., and Hinchey, F. (1984) 'Interpersonal Aggression and the Type A Coronary-Prone Behaviour Pattern: A Theoretical Distinction and Practical Implications', *Journal of Personality and Social Psychology* 47: 839– 47.

Strube, M.J. and Werner, C. (1984) 'Personal Space Claims as a Function of Interpersonal Threat: The Mediating Role of Need for Control', *Journal of Nonverbal Behavior* 8: 195–209.

Suedfeld, P., Bochner, A., and Matas, C. (1971) 'Petitioner's Attire and Petition Signing by Peace Demonstrators: A Field Experiment on Reference Group Similarity', *Journal of Applied Social Psychology* 1: 278–83.

Sundstrom, E. and Altman, I. (1976) 'Interpersonal Relationships and Personal Space: Research Review and Theoretical Model', *Human Ecology* 4: 47–67.

Sussman, N.M. and Rosenfeld, H.M. (1978) 'Touch, Justification and Sex:

Influences on the Aversiveness of Spatial Violation', *Journal of Social Psychology* 106: 215–25.

Sweat, S.J. and Zentner, M.A. (1985) 'Attributions toward Female Appearance Styles'. In M.R. Solomon (ed.) (1985) *The Psychology of Fashion*, Lexington: Heath.

Tagiuri, R. (1958) 'Social Preference and its Perception'. In R. Tagiuri and L. Petrullo (eds) *Person Reception and Interpersonal Behavior*, Stanford, California: Stanford University Press.

Takeda, R. (1966) 'Development of Vocal Communicaiton in Man-Raised Japanese Monkeys', II, *Primates* 7: 73–116.

Taylor, R.B. and Ferguson, G. (1980) 'Solitude and Intimacy: Linking Territoriality and Private Experience', *Journal of Nonverbal Behavior* 4: 227–39.

Tedeschi, J.T. (ed.) (1981) *Impression Management and Social Psychological Research*, New York: Academic Press.

Tharin, L. (1981) 'Dress Codes, Observed Attire, and Behavior in a Recreational Setting', unpublished ms, University of California, Davis, cited by Kaiser (1985).

Thayer, S. (1969) 'The Effect of Interpersonal Looking Duration on Dominance Judgments', *Journal of Social Psychology* 79: 285–6.

Thayer, S. and Alban, L. (1972) 'A Field Experiment on the Effect of Political and Cultural Factors on the Use of Personal Space', *Journal of Social Psychology* 88: 267–72.

Thomas, L. (1973) 'Clothing and Counterculture: An Empirical Study', *Adolescence* 8: 93–112.

Thomsen, C.E. (1974) 'Eye Contact by Non-Human Primates toward a Human Observer', *Animal Behavior* 22: 144–9.

Thorpe, W.H. (1972) 'Vocal Communication in Birds'. In R. Hinde (ed.) *Non-Verbal Communication*, Cambridge: Cambridge University Press.

Tinbergen, N. (1951) *The Study of Instinct*, London: Oxford University Press.

Tomkins, S.S. (1962–3) *Affect, Imagery and Consciousness*, 2 vols, New York: Springer.

Tomkins, S.S. and McCarter, R. (1964) 'What and Where Are the Primary Affects? Some Evidence for a Theory', *Perceptual and Motor Skills* 18: 119–58.

Trimboli, A. (1984) 'The Communication of Affect: When Words Fail', Ph. D. thesis, University of Sydney.

Tronick, E.Z. (1982) *Social Interchange in Infancy: Affect, Cognition and Communication*, Baltimore: University Park Press.

Tronick, E.Z., Als, H., and Brazelton, T.B. (1980) 'Monadic Phases: A Structural Descriptive Analysis of Infant–Mother Face-to-Face Interaction', *Merrill-Palmer Quarterly* 26: 3–24.

Trout, D.L. and Rosenfeld, H.M. (1980) 'The Effect of Postural Lean and Body Congruence on the Judgment of Psychotherapeutic Rapport', *Journal of Nonverbal Behavior* 4: 176–90.

Trower, P. (1980) 'Situational Analysis of the Components and Processes of Socially Skilled and Unskilled Patients', *Journal of Consulting and Clinical Psychology* 48: 327–39.

Turner, V.W. (1966) 'The Syntax of Symbolism in an African Religion'. In

J.S. Huxley (ed.) *A Discussion of Ritualization of Behaviour in Animals and Men*, Philosophical Transactions of the Royal Society of London.

Turner, V.W. (1967) *The Forest of Symbols*, Ithaca and London: Cornell University Press.

Van Hooff, J.A.R.A.M. (1982) 'Categories and Sequences of Behavior: A Description and Analysis'. In K.R. Scherer and P. Ekman (eds) *Handbook of Methods in Nonverbal Behavior Research*, Cambridge: Cambridge University Press.

Van Lancker, D. (1981) 'Speech Behavior as a Communication Process'. In J.K. Darby (ed.) *Speech Evaluation in Psychiatry*, New York: Grune & Stratton.

Veblen, T. (1899) *The Theory of the Leisure Class*, New York: Viking.

Vermes, G. (1962) *The Dead Sea Scrolls in English*, Harmondsworth: Penguin.

Vine, I. (1973) 'Social Spacing in Animals and Man', *Social Science Information* 12: 7–50.

Von Beyer, C.L. (1981) 'Impression Management in the Job Interview: When the Female Applicant Meets the Male (Chauvinist) Interviewer', *Personality and Social Psychology Bulletin* 7: 45–51.

Von Cranach, M. and Ellgring, J.H. (1973) 'The Perception of Looking Behaviour'. In M. von Cranach and I. Vine (eds) *Social Communication and Movement*, London: Academic Press.

Von Frisch, K. (1967) *The Dance Language and the Orientation of Bees*, Cambridge, Mass.: Harvard University Press.

Vrugt, A. and Kerkstra, A. (1984) 'Sex Differences in Nonverbal Communication', *Semiotica* 50: 1–41.

Wagner, H.L., MacDonald, C.J., and Manstead, A.S.R. (1986) 'Communication of Individual Emotions by Spontaneous Facial Expressions', *Journal of Personality and Social Psychology* 50: 737–43.

Walker, M.B. (1977) 'The Relative Importance of Verbal–Non-Verbal Cues in the Expression of Confidence', *Australian Journal of Psychology* 29: 45–57.

Walker, M.B. (1982) 'Smooth Transitions in Conversational Turn-Taking: Implications for Theory', *Journal of Psychology* 110: 31–7.

Walker, M.B. and Nazmi, M.K. (1979) 'Communicating by Words and Gestures', *Australian Journal of Psychology* 31: 137–43.

Walker, M.B. and Trimboli, C. (1983) 'The Expressive Function of the Eye Flash', *Journal of Nonverbal Behavior* 8: 3–13.

Walster, E., Aronson, V., Abrahams, A., and Rohmann, L. (1966) 'Importance of Physical Attractiveness in Dating Behavior', *Journal of Personality and Social Psychology* 4: 508–16.

Wasserman, T. and Kassinove, H. (1976) 'Effects of Types of Recommendation, Attire and Perceived Expertise on Parental Compliance', *Journal of Social Psychology* 99: 43–50.

Watson, O.M. (1970) *Proxemic Behavior: A Cross-Cultural Study*, The Hague: Mouton.

Waynbaum, I. (1907) *La Physionomie Humaine: Son Méchanisme et Son Role Sociale*, Paris: Alcan.

Waxer, P.H. (1978) *Nonverbal Aspects of Psychotherapy*, New York: Praeger.

Weitz, S. (1972) 'Attitude, Voice and Behavior', *Journal of Personality and*

Social Psychology 24: 14–21.

Wells, W. and Siegel, B. (1961) 'Stereotyped Somatypes', *Psychological Reports* 8: 77–8.

Wex, M. (1979) *Let's Take Back our Space*, Frauen Literaturverlag Hermine Fehr.

Whitcher, S.J. and Fisher, J.D. (1979) 'Multidimensional Reaction to Therapeutic Touch in a Hospital Setting', *Journal of Personality and Social Psychology* 37: 87–96.

Wiener, M., DeVoe, S., Rubinow, S., and Geller, J. (1972) 'Nonverbal Behavior and Nonverbal Communication', *Psychological Review* 79: 185–214.

Wiggers, M. (1982) 'Judgments of Facial Expressions of Emotion Predicted from Facial Behavior', *Journal of Nonverbal Behavior* 7: 101–16.

Wiggins, J.S., Wiggins (Hirschberg), N., and Conger, J.C. (1968) 'Correlates of Heterosexual Somatic Preference', *Journal of Personality and Social Psychology* 10: 82–90.

Williams, C.E. and Stevens, K.N. (1972) 'Emotions and Speech: Some Acoustical Correlates', *Journal of the Acoustical Society of America* 52: 1,238–50.

Williams, C.E. and Stevens, K.N. (1981) 'Vocal Correlates of Emotional States'. In J.K. Darby (ed.) *Speech Evaluation in Psychiatry*, New York: Grune & Stratton.

Williams, E. (1974) 'An Analysis of Gaze in Schizophrenics', *British Journal of Social and Clinical Psychology* 13: 1–8.

Williams, J.L. (1971) 'Personal Space and its Relation to Extraversion–Introversion', *Canadian Journal of Behavioural Science* 3: 156–60.

Willis, F.N. (1966) 'Initial Speaking Distance as a Function of the Speakers' Relationship', *Psychonomic Science* 5: 221–2.

Willis, F.N. and Hamm, H.K. (1980) 'The Use of Interpersonal Touch in Securing Compliance', *Journal of Nonverbal Behavior* 5: 49–55.

Willis, F.N. and Hoffman, G.E. (1975) 'Development of Tactile Patterns in Relation to Age, Sex, and Race', *Developmental Psychology* 11: 866.

Wilson, G. and Nias, D. (1976) *Love's Mysteries: The Psychology of Sexual Attraction*, London: Open Books.

Wilson, P.R. (1968) 'Perceptual Distortion of Height as a Function of Ascribed Academic Status', *Journal of Social Psychology* 74: 97–102.

Winkelmayer, R., Exline, R.V., Gottheil, E., and Paredes, A. (1978) 'The Relative Accuracy of US, British, and Mexican Raters in Judging the Emotional Displays of Schizophrenic and Normal US Women', *Journal of Clinical Psychology* 34: 600–8.

Winton, W.M. (1986) 'The Role of Facial Responses in Self-Reports of Emotion: A Critique of Laird', *Journal of Personality and Social Psychology* 50; 808–12.

Wish, M. (1979) 'Dimensions of Dyadic Communication'. In S. Weitz (ed.) *Nonverbal Communication*, 2nd edn, New York: Oxford University Press.

Wittgenstein, L. (1922) *Tractatus Logico-Philosophicus*, London: Kegan Paul, Trench, & Trubner.

Wolff, C. (1945) *A Psychology of Gesture*, London: Methuen.

Wolff, P.H. (1963) 'Observations on the Early Development of Smiling'. In B.M. Foss (ed.) *Determinants of Infant Behaviour*, vol. II, London: Methuen.

Wolff, P.H. (1969) 'The Natural History of Crying and Other Vocalizations in Early Infancy'. In B.M. Foss (ed.) *Determinants of Infant Behaviour*, vol. IV, London: Methuen.

Woodall, W.G. and Burgoon, J.K. (1981) 'The Effects of Nonverbal Synchrony on Message Comprehension and Persuasiveness', *Journal of Nonverbal Behavior* 5: 207–23.

Woodworth, R.S. (1938) *Experimental Psychology*, New York: Holt.

Yarbus, A.L. (1967) *Eye Movement and Vision*, translated by Basil Haigh, New York: Plenum Press.

Young, G.C.D. (1980) 'Selective Perception in Neurotics', D. Phil thesis, University of Oxford.

Zajonc, R.B. (1985) 'Emotion and Facial Efference: A Theory Reclaimed', *Science* 228: 15–21.

Zuckerman, M., Amidon, M.D., Bishop, S.E., and Pomerantz, S.D. (1982) 'Face and Tone of Voice in the Communication of Deception', *Journal of Personality and Social Psychology* 43: 347–57.

Zuckerman, M., DePaulo, B., and Rosenthal, R. (1981) 'Verbal and Nonverbal Communication of Deception', *Advances in Experimental Social Psychology* 14: 1–59.

Zuckerman, M. and Driver, R.E. (1985) 'Telling Lies: Verbal and Nonverbal Correlates of Deception'. In A.W. Siegman and S. Feldstein (eds) *Multichannel Integrations of Nonverbal Behavior*, Hillsdale, NJ: Erlbaum.

Zuckerman, M., Hall, J.A., DeFrank, R.S., and Rosenthal, R. (1976) 'Encoding and Decoding of Spontaneous and Posed Facial Expressions', *Journal of Personality and Social Psychology* 34: 966–77.

Zuckerman, M., Koestner, R., and Colella, M.J. (1985) 'Learning to Detect Deception from Three Communication Channels', *Journal of Nonverbal Behavior* 9: 188–94.

Zuckerman, M., Larrance, D., Hall, J., DeFrank, R., and Rosenthal, R. (1979) 'Posed and Spontaneous Communication of Emotion via Facial and Vocal Cues', *Journal of Personality* 47: 712–33.

Zuckerman, M., Larrance, D.T., Spiegel, N.H., and Klorman, R. (1981) 'Controlling Nonverbal Displays: Facial Expressions and Tone of Voice', *Journal of Experimental Social Psychology* 17: 506–24.

Zweigenhaft, R. (1976) 'Personal Space in the Faculty Office: Desk Placement and the Student-Faculty Interaction', *Journal of Applied Psychology* 61: 529–32.

Author Index

Subject Index

interspecies signals 29; sexual
signals 28-9
furniture 184-5

gaze 153-67; in animals 41-2, 157;
and attitudes 161-5; cultural
differences 57-8, 158; and
development 157-8; effects of
160-1; and emotions 165-6;
gender differences 281, 284; and
personality 166-7; in public
places 165; research 154-7; and
speech 108-10, 112, 114, 159-60
gender differences and NVC 219,
229, 281-9; appearance 286;
expressiveness 281, 286; face
281-3; gaze 281, 284; gesture
281, 284-5; sensitivity 286-7;
spatial behaviour 281, 283-4;
theory of 287-9; touch 285-6;
voice 150-1, 281, 283
Germany 62, 65
'gestural dance' 16, 118-19
gestures 188-202; in animals 42-3,
189; cultural differences 52-7,
67, 191; and development 190;
emblems 191-4; and emotions
197-200; gender differences 281,
284-5; illustrators 194-7; and
personality 200-2; and
physiology 190-1; research
188-9; speech-linked 54-7, 67;
107-8; 111-12, 116
Greece 53-60 *passim*, 65-9, 158,
193
greetings 17-18, 221-3; in animals
40-1; cultural rituals 61, 68
groups, social 237-8, 263-4

hair 247-9
hand-shaking 61, 222-3, 225
height 246

illustrators 54-7, 194-7
impression management 236; *see
also* self-presentation
Indians 59, 60, 172
individual differences in NVC
19-20; encoding 273-4;

sensitivity 274-5; touching
231-2
infants 22, 105-6; animals 29;
decoding 131-2; facial expression
126-8; gaze 157-8; gesture 190;
spatial behaviour 172; touch
214-15; vocalization 142-3
influence 228-9; *see also* persuasion
information, communication of
34-5, 38-40
interaction: model 299; signals for
178-80, 221-4
intimacy 93-7; courtship 97-100
isolation 184
Italians 51-9, 65, 66, 69, 158, 193,
197

Japan 51-2, 60-2, 64-5, 67-9, 218

kinemes 122-3

laboratory research 23-4
language, NVC as 290-5
Latin America 58-60, 158
leakage 78, 81, 146

marriage 102-3, 162
meaning of NVC 7-8, 226-7,
292-4
men *see* gender differences
mental illness 276-81; depression
278-9; neurosis 279-80;
schizophrenia 19, 177, 276-8,
280; theory 280-1
monkeys 35-45; facial expression
35-7; gaze 41-2; gesture 42-3;
touch 40-1; vocalization 38-40
music 307

neurosis 279-80
non-verbal communication (NVC)
1-10, 305-9; in animals 27-48;
and appearance 233-54; and
attitudes 85-103; and clothes,
physique, *etc.* 233-54; cultural
differences 49-70; emotional
expression 71-84; facial
expression 121-38; gaze 153-67;
gesture 188-202; meaning of 7-8;